December 1976

The
Dallas Junior League
Cookbook

The JUNIOR LEAGUE OF DALLAS is a volunteer organization whose purpose is to train their members for effective participation in the community through a program of education and volunteer service of the highest quality.

Profits resulting from the sale of this cookbook will be returned to our Community Service Trust Fund for projects and programs sponsored by the JUNIOR LEAGUE OF DALLAS, INC.

First Printing 12,000 Copies
September 7, 1976

Second Printing 12,000 Copies
November 7, 1976

TABLE OF CONTENTS

ILLUSTRATIONS
by True Redd

The Junior League of Dallas would like to thank the many members who participated in the creation of THE DALLAS JUNIOR LEAGUE COOKBOOK — the numerous testers, proofreaders, and the heads of all committees. Without the continuous support from our dedicated members, this book could never have been written.

COOKBOOK COMMITTEE

Chairman	Mrs. Searcy M. Ferguson, Jr.
Co-Chairmen	Mrs. Joe E. Funk, Jr. Mrs. Denys Slater, Jr.
Sustaining Co-Chairmen	Mrs. Mark L. Lemmon, Jr. Mrs. Theodore P. Votteler
Editing and Typing	
Chairman	Mrs. M. Weatherby Carr
Co-Chairmen	Mrs. Robert B. Allison Mrs. Frank Joseph Jenull
Proofreading	Mrs. Harold W. Kimmerling
Creative Writing	Mrs. Ralph G. Greenlee, Jr. Mrs. Dale E. Selzer Mrs. Don Rott
Creative Writing Editor	Mrs. Howard V. Tygrett, Jr.
Creative Entertaining	Mrs. John A. Hammack Mrs. Charles P. Storey Mrs. Stephen J. Summers Mrs. Edward W. Rose III
Cover Design	Anne Coke
Photography	True Redd
Art Director	Priscilla Davis Gravely
Food Stylist	Dorothy Berry
Indexing	Peggy Simmons
Wine Consultant	Victor B. Wdowiak

TESTING COMMITTEE

Mrs. Joe B. Abbey
Mrs. John Alexander
Mrs. James W. Aston, Jr.
Mrs. Kenneth Bernecker
Mrs. Robert M. Blakeney
Mrs. John P. Boone
Mrs. George W. Bramblett, Jr.
Mrs. Floyd T. Burke
Mrs. Fred W. Burnett, Jr.
Mrs. W. Lee Carter III
Mrs. John Castleman
Mrs. Ronald R. Cathey
Mrs. Ray A. Edsel
Mrs. Robert W. Enholm
Mrs. Earl Fain III
Mrs. John Ferguson
Mrs. Patrick C. Guillot
Mrs. James Holmes
Mrs. Donald R. Howe
Mrs. Minor L. Huck
Mrs. Mickey Hudnall
Mrs. George W. Jalonick IV
Mrs. E. Patrick Jenevein
Mrs. Harold W. Kimmerling
Mrs. John L. King
Mrs. John T. Kipp
Mrs. James Lambert
Mrs. John Lancaster
Mrs. Robert P. Lancaster
Mrs. John Ridings Lee
Mrs. William B. Madden

Mrs. James Mason
Mrs. Richard K. Marks
Mrs. Justin McCarty, Jr.
Mrs. Don McIlyar
Mrs. Blair Gray Mercer
Mrs. Allen P. Miller
Mrs. Bruce Monning
Mrs. Fulton Murray, Jr.
Mrs. Horace Nash, Jr.
Mrs. Larry M. Nobles
Mrs. Charles Pierce, Jr.
Mrs. Thomas Philip Reilly, Jr.
Mrs. James I. Riddle III
Mrs. Edward W. Rose III
Mrs. Curtis Sanford, Jr.
Mrs. Alan C. Schoellkopf
Mrs. Dale Selzer, Jr.
Mrs. Denys Slater, Jr.
Mrs. Glenn L. Stephenson, Jr.
Mrs. David C. Smith
Mrs. G. Duffield Smith
Mrs. Norman Smith
Mrs. George H. Spencer, Jr.
Mrs. Peter M. Tart
Mrs. Gifford Touchstone
Mrs. Webb L. Wallace
Mrs. George S. Watson
Mrs. Ralph Wood, Jr.
Mrs. Margaret Worsham
Mrs. Arthur C. White

Festive Gatherings

Caviar Pie

Snails in Ramekins

Veal Flambéed with Grapes

Tomatoes Stuffed with Salsify and Carrots

Grated Zucchini in Lemon Butter

Limestone Lettuce, Mushrooms,
and Celery Root Vinaigrette

Cracker Bread

Chocolate Mint Roll

Montrachet and Champagne

NEW YEAR'S EVE SEATED DINNER

New Year's Eve is the time to celebrate! So do just that with the added entertainment of a Prediction Dinner.

Assign guests individual topics for each to make brilliant forays into the future on: politics, weddings, economics are a few suggestions, but add your own imaginative topics. Select a scribe to record predictions for posterity and resurrect these wise words each year to entertain old and new friends.

As a departure from Yuletide greenery, decorate the table with long, festive balloons interspersed with white tapers. Small favors of your choice at each place setting are a must.

New Year's Eve deserves a seated dinner. Serve a Caviar Pie with cocktails, a divine sustainer for the long evening. Then leisurely parade a four course meal.

Guests will appreciate the opportunity to savor the pleasure of Snails in Ramekins accompanied by great rounds of Cracker Bread. The veal dish is dramatic and beautiful as a main course. Tomatoes provide more color, and the unusual combination of salsify and carrots is simple in taste and unique in shape. Don't fail to include Mushrooms and Celery Root Vinaigrette with Limestone Lettuce. Celery root is a wonderful winter vegetable, too little known in this country.

The Chocolate Roll is a perfect way to end a year-long diet or resolve to begin a new one. Have champagne in abundance to toast a perfect evening and to pop open at midnight to ring in the New Year.

**Macadamia Chicken Salad
in Pineapple Ring**

Endive Soufflé

Strawberry and Apple Breads

Beautiful Filled Angel Food Cake

GRANDMOTHER'S BABY SHOWER

Let the jubilant new grandmother take top billing in this new approach to a baby shower.

There is no prouder person than the proverbial photo carrier, praise singer, and toy shopper. She is the perfect candidate for showering with gifts meant for pampering her little one.

Invitations of pastel plaids, prints, or florals could summon guests to meet the tiny new family member. A child's rocking chair, perhaps with the baby's name printed on back, can cradle pots of fresh flowers to decorate the buffet table. Use balloons, lollipops, stuffed animals, and other childlike items to further your theme. Guests can admire the precious newborn nestled in an antique cradle or buggy.

As friends arrive, offer each chilled wine in a large wine glass enhanced with a dainty pink rose bud tied on with white satin ribbon. Macadamia Nut Chicken Salad in Pineapple Rings is refreshing for luncheon. This can be prepared hours ahead, leaving time for making the accompanying Endive Soufflé. Include Strawberry and Apple Bread to be passed each guest.

A tasty and light dessert of Beautiful Filled Angel Food Cake will assure your reputation as a unique and successful party giver.

Cream of Corn Soup

Louisiana Meat Pies

Pickled Shallots

Marinated Cold Vegetable Salad

Lemon Tarts

California Jug Wine (Ruby Cabernet)

FEBRUARY PICNIC BY THE FIRE

Celebrate winter and herald spring with a picnic by the fire. Let your home radiate with colorful spring blossoms arranged in a variety of basket shapes and sizes. A large wicker picnic hamper bursting with flowers will perfectly compliment a blue gingham table cloth on the buffet table.

Vegetable baskets lined with bandanas make unique individual picnic servers. Tuck into each a plastic knife and fork wrapped in colorful paper napkins. Cover the buffet table with these perky individual parcels, each filled to the brim.

Guests will love Louisiana Meat Pies. This is a glorious rendition of the Southern fried pie. These may be made ahead of time and frozen. Pickled Shallots are a delicious surprise. Add marinated cold salad in opened green peppers and, for a sweet treat, pop in tangy Lemon Tarts. A big washtub tied with a gingham bow can be filled with wine, beer, and soft drinks.

Family quilts spread near the glowing fire make a cozy spot to dine. Later, when the fire is soft embers, serve coffee, enjoy fireside chats, and plan for a summer sequel.

Cucumber Dip
with Raw Vegetables

Mushroom Soup

Flank Steak
Béarnaise Sauce

Bibb Lettuce Salad
with Bacon, Sesame Seeds, and Bean Sprouts

Sour Dough Rolls

Café Brûlot

California Zinfandel (Sutter Home)

KITCHEN BUFFET SUPPER
(For Six or Eight)

Last minute gatherings should be a part of every hostess' lifestyle. If you remember to take it easy and make it easy, it can be a memorable event. An individual loaf of French bread with a small invitation attached could be hand delivered. A Sunday — whether lazy or busy — is a wonderful time to round up a few friends for an old-fashioned kitchen buffet supper. Everyone participates, and no one goes away hungry.

Start everyone off with Spritzers (white wine and club soda), or put a touch of cassis in white wine for a delightful concoction called Kir (pronounced *kear*). Now you can slip away for a last minute look at your table. In the center you might have a simple colander or copper pot filled with brown and white eggs, onions, wooden spoons, and wild flowers in vials — whatever you have on hand, just let your own creative imagination go. Perhaps you'll want to use a country checked tablecloth and big checked napkins.

Back to your guests now with something tasty. How about a big, red cabbage spiked in swirls of crudities on toothpicks — cherry tomatoes, green olives, carrot cubes, and baby artichoke hearts? For an extra touch you might scoop out the cabbage center and fill with a creamy Cucumber Dip. The next offering could be a tray of mugs piping with Mushroom Soup. While your guests sip, you set the buffet on the kitchen counter, starting with a large platter of Marinated Flank Steak cut on the diagonal, next to a big basket of individual Sour Dough Rolls, and then a bowl of Béarnaise Sauce. Summon your friends to create their own sandwiches — and remind them not to miss the salad — romaine, Bibb, and leaf lettuce tossed with toasted sesame seeds, bacon, bean sprouts, yellow squash, and a lemon-olive oil-garlic dressing, which sits across the counter.

For dessert let your husband share a little of the glory with his own version of Café Brûlot, a spicy and showy, but very easy finale.

Bloody Marys
with Caraway Cheese Pastries

Avocado Boats
with Crab and Caviar Salad

Slices of Persian Melon and Kiwi Fruit
Garnished with Frosted Grapes

Miniature Bolillos

Cold Coffee Soufflé
with Sand Tarts and Chocolate Mint Squares

Polish Vodka

LUNCH ON A PRIVATE JET

Texans need little reason to plan extravagant entertaining. Perhaps your excuse is that the turbos of the family jet are gathering cobwebs or maybe there's just an uncontrollable urge to rent one of those jazzy stratostreakers.

Make it a party! Here's a Texas-sized idea for a super extra-extravagant jet-away entertaining.

This could be your special fabulous treat for those committee chairmen who helped make this year's Charity Ball a record-breaking success, or maybe you just want to give your Tuesday gin club an extraordinary little treat. Keep your destination a secret, but do give guests tips on what to pack.

At take-off serve Bloody Marys with Caraway Cheese Pastries. Set the mood for luncheon by using spring flowered cotton squares to cover each tray. Tuck a fresh camelia into each napkin for an elegant surprise.

Airborne, you are ready to unfurl the super-fabulous lunch; avocado boats filled with crab and caviar salad and garnished with lemon wedges, and alternating slices of Persian Melon and Kiwi Fruit topped with Frosted Grapes. In addition, pass a tray of Miniature Bolillos. Delight guests with a dessert of Coffee Soufflé with Sand Tarts and Chocolate Mint Squares.

Party on until touch-down with backgammon or gin or guessing games in anticipation of your mini-vacation destination.

Salmon Mousse
Fresh Dill Sauce

Steak au Poivre
Bordelaise Sauce

Tomatoes Stuffed with Mushroom Soufflé

Potato Balls

Watercress and Endive Salad

Whole Wheat Cheese Straws

Orange-poached Pears in Chocolate Sauce

Salmon Mousse — Meursault

Steak au Poivre — Richebourg

BLACK TIE FORTIETH BIRTHDAY PARTY

A cozy party of special friends and a splendid meal; what better way to celebrate a significant birthday?

This intimate dinner is the perfect time to create placecard holders from your favorite collection of glass paperweights, animals, or shells. Use birthdates rather than names to mark the placecards.

Begin with a bare table accented with large snowy damask napkins folded into "Bishop Hats," white roses, and silver candlesticks holding tall tapers. For a spring birthday party use flowering pear or quince blossoms arranged in crystal vases and surrounded by crystal candlesticks.

The classic menu begins with delicate Salmon Mousse passed with Fresh Dill Sauce and Wholewheat Cheese Straws. The entrée of Peppered Steak is distinguished by a superb Bordelaise Sauce. Tomatoes stuffed with an airy Mushroom Soufflé are an exceptional vegetable as are Potato Balls created with a melon cutter.

Climax the meal with the sweet combination of pears and chocolate and complete the festivities with champagne, perfect for an occasion meant to toast the night away.

Borscht

Seneca Leg of Lamb

Red Beans with Plum Sauce

Rice Pilaf

Cucumber and Sour Cream Salad

Paskha

Kulich

St. Emilion (Chateau Figeac)

RUSSIAN EASTER DINNER

None celebrate Easter as do the Russians. Natives of that country have special traditions for celebrating this significant holiday. Perhaps just coming out from under all that snow adds to their feeling of jubilation.

Served in a setting of fresh spring flowers, this Russian Easter Dinner is delicious, unusual, and impressive.

If there are Russian students nearby, or if you have Russian friends, ask for assistance in writing the menu in their native language with an added English translation.

Borscht is a beet soup probably unlike any beet soup you have ever tasted. Accompanied by the traditional sour cream, this rich, meaty soup makes a fabulous beginning to any meal. It is best if prepared ahead of time. Follow with the Stuffed Boned Leg of Lamb. Accompany with Red Beans and Plum Sauce, providing a new taste to most, and the unusual Rice Pilaf, an interesting combination of dried fruits, rice and nuts. Cucumbers, sour cream, dill, dill pickles and pickled mushrooms are frequently included in a Russian meal.

Complete the dinner with traditional Paskha and Kulich. The Paskha is made in a pyramid shaped frame. Its taste is somewhat akin to a splendid cheesecake. Paskha is always served with Kulich, a rather dry, dome-shaped bread. Paskha is traditionally decorated with a single red rose placed atop the pyramid symbolizing the homage to spring which Easter signals.

Sangria and Frozen Margaritas

Ceviche

Chalupas

Guacamole and Fresh Raw Vegetables

Avocado Halves Filled with Caviar

Black Bean Soup

Watermelon Ice

Lace Cookies

CINCO DE MAYO

Initiate summer with a poolside celebration of the day in May when Mexico gained her independence from France. This is a festive and colorful holiday for our neighbors south of the border, and one we can enjoy participating in.

Tie-dye white tablecloths in bright Acapulco colors. For center-pieces use large clam shells filled with ferns. The occasion calls for many colored votive candles, and for a dramatic touch float candles in the pool. A warm, starry May night, pitchers of Sangría or frozen Margaritas, and your back yard becomes the next best thing to being at a Spanish retreat.

Let nature provide serving pieces. Ceviche could be presented in clam shells surrounded with limes, preferably juicy Mexican ones. Fill the center of scooped-out artichokes with Guacamole and surround them with raw vegetables for dipping, or serve them with caviar and sour cream.

Include fresh cilantro garnish in Black Bean Soup. Cilantro is fresh coriander, an absolute necessity in every Mexican kitchen. This herb is easily grown in many areas north of the border.

The Chalupa is a Mexican version of an open-faced sandwich. Treat it as such and let guests create their own.

Finally, soothe the palate with superb Watermelon Ice elegantly served in halved coconut shells, a final touch for your tropical setting.

LUNCH

Grilled Lime Chicken

Whole Wheat Bread and Butter Sandwiches

Fresh Fruit

Lemonade

Gatorade

DINNER

Cold Poached Salmon

Grilled Butterflied Leg of Lamb

Cold Greek Salad

Feta Cheese

Lemon-Pepper Pita Bread

Pepper Jelly

Ambrosia

St. Julien (Chateau Talbot)

OLYMPIC MARATHON PARTY

Celebrate the physical fitness craze with your outdoorsy friends at a large park where a playing field and tennis courts are included.

Serve a "Breakfast of Champions" as an energy booster for a day-long party of planned athletic activities. Include in this nutritious 10 a.m. breakfast Bran Muffins with crocks of Honey Butter, ginseng tea and, "biceps boosters," a liquid bouquet of instant energy.

During breakfast guests may sign up for events on a poster indicating starting times, points, etc. Include as many events as possible such as tennis, chipping, ping-pong, backgammon, frisbee throw, 100 yard dash, broad jump, horseshoes, and a finale of volleyball.

Permit everyone to collapse gratefully at 1 o'clock for an elegant, healthful pick-up of Grilled Lime Chicken, Fresh Fruit, Lemonade and Gatorade.

After time-out in the shade hardy participants may continue games in the afternoon.

A bacchanalian feast at home with a presentation of laurel wreaths to contest winners could highlight evening activities. Suggest togas as the dress, and decorate with grape clusters, fig leaves, and Olympic torches. Lace the feast with plenty of wine as you serve a refreshing dinner of Cold Salmon, Greek Salad, Grilled Lamb, Pita Bread, and, for dessert, a cool Ambrosia, the feast of the gods.

Cold Country Ham

Marinated Vegetables

Blackeyed Pea Chowder

Dilly Okra-Watermelon Pickles

Biscuits and Cornbread

Homemade Preserves

Devils Food Cake

Apple Pie

Homemade Caramel Ice Cream

California Gamay Beaujolais
(Stag's Leap)

HOME-GROWN SUPPER

Transform the fruits of your labor into a Home Grown Supper for friends and neighbors who teased that the sole beneficiaries of your gardening efforts would be the squirrels.

Choose a Sunday afternoon near the close of summer when your vegetables are at their peak.

Print invitations on a recipe card for a clever beginning. At party time display garden fare on a long table set under the trees. Use a red and white check tablecloth or antique quilts centered with baskets of luscious, sun-ripened, home grown vegetables.

Extend the country fair atmosphere and advertise your talents with favors of balloons tied in the trees, each numbered indicating a take-home jar of jam, relish, or carafes of herbed vinegar.

This menu is simple and hearty; Cold Country Ham next to an oversize iron pot of Blackeyed Pea Chowder, marinated sliced tomatoes, peppers, zucchini, red onions, and Dilly Okra should satisfy even the country gentleman in the crowd.

Be sure to have plenty of Biscuits and Cornbread to top with Homemade Preserves and condiments such as pear honey or the Bobbitt family apple preserves.

Children can participate by churning up a cake of butter, a special activity for younger ones providing a tasty treat for all. Have lots of games planned, such as sack races, etc.

Tin tubs filled with beer and crockery coolers of iced tea and cold apple cider provide thirst quenchers. In addition, have a pitcher of buttermilk handy for the die-hard farmers.

The dessert — what else but a sensational Devils Food Cake, Apple Pie, and Homemade Caramel Ice Cream.

**Caviar and Cream Cheese
on Artichoke Rounds**

Smoked Salmon

Chicken Crêpes

**Bibb Lettuce
with Mandarin Oranges and Nasturtium Leaves**

Créme Brûlée

Champagne (Laurent Perrier Grand Siecle)

POST-SYMPHONY SUPPER

A small, delicious supper superbly planned, easily executed, and prepared totally in advance is the perfect way to savor pleasures of a memorable evening of music.

Before leaving for the evening, set the table with your own masterpiece: rolled sheets of music, each enclosing fresh flowers and placed in a large crystal bowl. Or, if the flowers are hardy, tuck individual rolls in the refrigerator and whisk them out at the appointed hour to decorate each place setting.

Leave your favorite symphony recording ready to begin at the push of a stereo button, and sail out the door knowing the supper only awaits your return.

For menu starters try Caviar and Smoked Salmon served with frozen vodka. Use a good Russian vodka; put ½ tablespoon peppercorns and the zest of one small lemon in the vodka bottle. Freeze the bottle encased in a milk carton of water. When the carton is pulled away, the vodka makes a spectacular debut surrounded by ice. Serve in small cut crystal liqueur glasses.

For your entrée, Chicken Crêpes are rich and spicy and need only a Bibb Lettuce Salad enhanced by mandarin oranges and nasturtiums when in season.

To further insure your successful performance, cap the evening with individual Créme Brulées and demitasses of coffee.

Iced Lemon Soup

Chicken Chutney Cream Cheese Sandwiches

Marinated Shrimp and Mushrooms

Artichokes with Curried Mayonnaise

Cold Peach Soufflé

California Pinot Chardonnay
(Freemark Abbey)

TAILGATE PICNIC

Precede the sports contest of your choice or follow a Sunday country drive with the tailgate picnic. This informal meal moves into haute cuisine when you provide a car full of surprises.

Beguile guests by offering each a plexiglas folding chair. Add a dramatic touch by rolling out a favorite small Oriental rug and center it with a red lacquer basket of persimmons and long-stemmed Oriental poppies.

For sophisticated outdoor serving, use pewter plates, giant linen napkins, and throw pillows.

Offer chilled wine from beginning to end. A superb menu starter is found in skewers of Marinated Shrimp and Mushrooms and Cold Lemon Soup, subtle introduction to an exotic entrée of Chicken Chutney Sandwiches. Artichokes with Curried Mayonnaise provide an artful alternative to a green salad. For dessert a Cold Peach Soufflé with candied ginger is unusual and spectacular and a fitting finalé to a first class production.

Grilled Venison Backstrap

Grilled Venison Sausage

Delectable Wild Duck
Barley Pilaf

Quail with Wild Rice
and Wheat Berries

Spinach and Apple Salad

Baked Tomatoes Parmesan

Buttered Sage Biscuits
Whole Wheat Rolls

Persimmon Pudding with Hard Sauce

Rhone Valley wine
(Chateauneuf-du-Pape)

WILD GAME DINNER

While he is out stalking game, prepare for his triumphant return.

Create a forest setting with an arrangement of nuts, dried flowers, weeds, pods, thistles, mushrooms, and pine cones nestled in sphangnum moss and placed on a paisley cloth of browns, oranges, and golds. Add brass, bronze, or pewter candlesticks with brown or buff tapers. Place individual crocks of salted nuts at each place setting. The crocks should be inscribed with each guest's name and also serve as place cards.

For hors-d'oeuvres try Grilled Venison Sausage and Grilled Venison Backstrap thinly sliced and served on buttered Sage Biscuits.

Your friends will want to embrace the life of the noble savage when you serve Delectable Wild Duck or Quail. Try duck with Barley Pilaf. Barley is an often overlooked grain, delicious in soups, and a subtle accompaniment to fowl. Wild Rice with Wheat Berries garnished with parsley and kumquats accompany the quail.

The remaining menu forms a brilliant partnership with whichever bird you choose. The Spinach and Apple Salad is a distinctive combination adding color and texture. Baked Tomatoes Parmesan and Whole Wheat Yeast Rolls are simple and delicious.

For a final jewel in your crown, try Persimmon Pudding with Hard Sauce. Even if you always thought persimmons were meant only to decorate persimmon trees, you will find them equally beautiful in pudding, and their inclusion will insure your reputation as an imaginative cook.

Grilled
Knackwurst — Bratwurst — Brockwurst

Salmon Pâté
Braunschweiger Pâté

Whole Grain Breads
Kaiser Rolls

Cheese
Jarlsberg — Muenster — Crema Danica

Guava Jelly

Fresh Fruit

Carmelized Apple Tart

Dark and Light Beer

OKTOBERFEST

Here's a party plan perfect for beating the malaise that sets in between Labor Day and Christmas. Stage an Oktoberfest in your backyard.

Invitations inscribed on the back of beer coasters set the mood. To reduce costs of decorations, ask a local beer distributor to sell or give you promotional cups, coasters, napkins, and signs.

At seven o'clock your friends will cross the Rhine to enter an authentic German beer garden outlined with strings of tiny white lights. As accordions play, guests will satisfy appetites at a table laden with skewers of Knackwurst, Bratwurst, and Brockwurst, accompanied by hot German mustard and Kaiser Rolls. A smaller table holds baskets of pretzels and Rhine wine. Have several kegs of both dark and light beer on hand.

Tempt guests inside with other German favorites such as a terrine of Salmon or Braunschweiger pâté. Pumpernickel, rye, and whole grain breads bulging from baskets will urge your friends to sample Muenster, Jarlsberg and Crema Danica cheeses accompanied by Guava Jelly.

Weight watchers will appreciate baskets of pears, grapes, and apples but will undoubtedly find it difficult to resist squares of Carmelized Apple Tart and mugs of steaming coffee adorning the dessert table.

Antipasto

Lasagne Verde

Polenta Ring

Sautéed Zucchini

Fresh Tomato Sauce

Marinated Sweet Anise or Fennel

Lemon Ice

Judy's Roll-up Cookies

Chianti Riserva (Villa Antinori)

ITALIAN DINNER

An Italian dinner blends well with cool, crisp days of autumn. A warm, glowing fire in the living room and soft candlelight throughout the house create an atmosphere for enjoying Italian cuisine. Moreover, this unique dinner is distinguished while inexpensive.

Oversized baskets of Italian vegetables such as eggplant, zucchini, and artichokes or twig baskets filled with various Italian pasta and breadsticks and tied with red bows make colorful decorations. Use an assortment of colored napkins for an added festive touch.

For a fresh concept serve antipasto on skewers passed on trays. Let your imagination flourish as many foods qualify as antipasto. Try carrots, artichoke hearts, pepperoni, or mushrooms. Marinate your selection with a spicy vinaigrette sauce flavored with basil and oregano.

Serve Lasagne Verde, green noodles in a béchamel sauce with fresh tomatoes, as a light and delicate entrée. The accompanying Polenta Ring is made from corn meal. Instant Polenta may be found in many grocery stores. This recipe suggests making the ring in a bundt pan. Mozzarella cheese covered with proscuitto serve as the filling. The result resembles a corn cake. It is sliced very thin and served with Sautéed Zucchini and Fresh Tomato Sauce. Marinated Anise or Fennel is an exotic addition to this dish. This crunchy bulb root gives a slight licorice taste and is found in many Italian kitchens.

Gelati Limone with Roll-up Cookies will seal your fame as an Italian cook. This is a version of lemon sherbet served with a most delicious cookie. Expresso adds just the right finalé to this Italian feast.

Roast Turkey with Cornbread Dressing
Sour Cream Gravy

Sweet Potatoes Alexander

Squash Casserole

Green Beans in Lemon Butter

Yeast Rolls
Wine Jelly

Mince Custard Pie

Mincemeat Pie with Hard Sauce

Beaujolais — Brouilly

THANKSGIVING IN THE SOUTH

Southern hospitality expresses its warm generosity in the celebration of family holidays.

This Thanksgiving setting presents colors and flavors in a memorable format and will satisfy each guest's vision of a Southern Thanksgiving dinner.

Greet family and friends in the living room or library with a demitasse of Pumpkin Soup served from a hollowed pumpkin nestled on a bed of autumn leaves and nuts. Enhance the dining table with a paisley cloth of muted autumn colors accented with an antique basket of wheat, pheasant feathers and ecru straw flowers.

Serve traditional Roast Turkey with Cornbread Dressing and Sour Cream Gravy, a simple and delicious departure from the standard giblet version. Surround the bird with crabapples and small orange halves filled with cranberry-orange relish. Sweet potatoes in harmony with apples, peaches, and bananas; a crunchy Squash Casserole, green beans tossed in lemon butter and yeast rolls with wine jelly complete the main course.

For dessert offer Mince Custard Pie for those wishing only a taste of something sweet or the traditional Mincemeat Pie with Hard Sauce for a robust flavor testing the limits of taste.

Baron of Peppered Beef

Chicken Liver Paté
in French Bread Wreath

Lobster Tarts

Scalloped Oysters

Assorted Cheeses

Fresh Coconut Cake

Fudge

Pralines

Grapefruit Peel Candy

<u>Children's Menu</u>

Miniature Hamburgers

Chili Con Queso Dip

Carrot Sticks

Chocolate Turtles

Chablis (Les Clos) and
Chambertin

CHRISTMAS EVE BUFFET

This Christmas party will surely become a family tradition to be shared annually with friends, and what a glorious season to hostess a much-anticipated evening!

If this becomes a yearly event, remember children grow up quickly and soon those toddlers will be teenagers raiding the adult buffet table. That may call for a menu change, but by then you will be an old hand at family parties.

Decorations should be simple, allowing you time to concentrate efforts on preparing the feast and wrapping family Christmas gifts. On the adult table use apple trees accompanied by candlesticks created from red apples, each holding a red candle tied with a red and white checked ribbon. On the children's table display a cookie tree made of painted dowels decorated with Christmas sugar cookies tied on with red yarn.

Music is a necessity, so entertain with holiday favorites. Perhaps you could arrange for the bell choir from your church or invite a group of carollers to sing. For a big splash, engage the Salvation Army Band. It is a nice way to donate to a charity. Or for a quieter mood, ask for the flutist from your local symphony.

A continuous form of entertainment is suggested for the children. A mime movie such as "The Red Balloon" projected on a playroom wall might be the answer.

The buffet table should be laden with specialities. The Baron of Peppered Beef can be prepared beforehand as can the Chicken Liver Pâté. The Wreath of French Bread sounds more difficult than it is and looks so spectacular for a Christmas party that it is worth the effort.

This occasion warrants the queen of cheese, Brie, and oysters and lobsters are certainly proper consorts. Offer a choice of rich eggnog or a dry red wine and be prepared for most guests to enjoy both.

A special feast for the children could include a buffet of Miniature Hamburgers, Chili Con Queso Dip, carrot sticks, cookies and Chocolate Turtles. Hot or cold apple cider is a good drink choice, making their menu festive, but familiar.

Offer an abundance of all your family's favorite treats on the dessert table. Don't hold back!

Gifts of Love

Throughout the year remember all your occasions for gift giving as you make shopping stops in these particular stores:

Gourmet shops	Garden shops and nurseries
Country stores	Fabric shops
Import shops	Greeting card shops
Discount houses	Household accessory shops
Hardware stores	Basket shops
Craft shops	Antique shops

While reading our cookbook, jot down ideas for gifts beside names on your giving list. Visit suggested shops and imaginatively select from a variety of baskets, casseroles, serving dishes, platters, cache pôts, flower pots, cooking utensils, and jars. Ribbons, yarns, cellophane, gift wrapping, and tissue papers, fabrics, etc., are an aid in coordinating your creativity.

The culinary gift doesn't necessarily need to be related to its packaging. The purpose is to make your gift unique for the receiver. Your selection may range from small to grand — let the sky be the limit!

ESPECIALLY FROM YOU

Present delicious chocolate cookies or Chocolate Turtles in a ceramic or earthenware turtle-shaped container.

For New Year's an earthenware or china pitcher of waffle or pancake batter with a jar of fresh berries and one of homemade pear honey is a treat.

Sour dough starter in a sealed plastic container can accompany fresh sour dough bread placed on a wooden bread board. Wrap in plastic or cellophane, tie with natural jute string, and attach the recipe.

Grandmother will love a special blend of tea accompanied by an individual tea pot with matching tea cup and saucer.

Place herbed, minted, garlic, and shrimp butters in small stoneware crocks sealed with corks, and nestle in a basket lined with sphanghum moss. Decorate with a plaid ribbon catching a sprig of fresh herbs.

Line a Mexican straw hat with a print napkin, fill with tostados, and add a corked crock of hot or piquante sauce.

Jalapeño Jelly, Rosy Relish, and a pepper plant take on special airs in a Mexican basket lined with colored tissue and tied with colorful yarn.

Chocolate Leaves shine packaged in a small tin and tied with an embroidered ribbon or placed in a small flower pot wrapped in cellophane and accented with a dainty bow. These leaves are an attractive garnish for a favorite mousse, ice cream, pie, or ice box cake. They store well in the refrigerator for several weeks.

Tall glass carafes make sophisticated containers for coffee and other homemade liqueurs. Cork and tie with elegant ribbon. The recipe follows:

COFFEE LIQUEUR

2 c. boiling water
3 c. granulated sugar
1 2-oz. jar powdered instant coffee
1 fifth vodka or bourbon
1 large vanilla bean, cut in small pieces.

Combine 1 cup boiling water and sugar in heavy saucepan. Cook uncovered over medium heat for about 10 minutes to make a thin syrup. Add 1 cup boiling water to the instant coffee, stirring to dissolve, then add to the syrup. Remove from heat; cool to lukewarm; stir in vodka or bourbon and vanilla bean. Pour into a clean, half-gallon jar, cap tightly, and store for 3 weeks before using.

Pack a picnic basket with homemade spaghetti sauce, pasta, a crock of garlic butter, crusty bread, and salad greens. Add a set of colorful napkins and delight a friend with a change of taste dinner for Christmas night.

Jars of English Boiled Custard and homemade gingerbread make a special Christmas morning treat.

Create the illusion of a pine cone by overlapping pecan halves in rows on a cheese ball. Tie in plastic wrap with Christmas green or plaid ribbon and attach a sprig of fresh pine needles.

Vinegars seasoned with various home grown herbs can be attractively bottled in large wine carafes, sealed with parafin and corked. Attach a label reading: "From the herb garden of . . ."

Homemade chocolate sauce in a glass jar would be a treat for sweet-lovers. Attach an old-fashioned ice cream scoop as that something extra.

Flavored sugars are unusual packed in corked jars or old-fashioned tins. Create vanilla sugar by adding a vanilla bean to granulated sugar. Cinnamon sugar is a combination of two-thirds ground cinnamon to one-third granulated sugar.

Christmas mugs accompanying a stoneware crock of homemade eggnog exhibits a true labor of love.

Crème Brulée shows off its elegance in individual custard cups nesting in a natural basket lined with sphanghum moss. Cover with plastic wrap and tie with a plaid ribbon.

A porcelain au gratin dish of Escargots in Mushroom Caps would capture the attention of a famous gourmet hostess.

Contribute to the Fourth of July picnic with Watermelon Ice. Transport in and serve from the watermelon rind which also serves as an insulator.

Create an unusual pomander by placing cinnamon sticks upright in a small Indian basket. Decorate the basket with bright ribbon woven in and out and add a bow and lots of streamers.

Homemade soup is always a perfect gift. This cook book contains an abundance of soup ideas ranging from delicate to hearty, clear to creamy, and hot and spicy to refreshingly cold. Venison Chili is fabulous in a brown earthenware casserole accompanied by a basket of Jalepeño Corn Bread. A friend hard at work on a huge committee job will think you are really special when you surprise her with a souper supper. Or wouldn't a relative love to receive a Cream of Artichoke Soup in an antique soup tureen?

For a housewarming try Black Bean Soup, tostados, and homemade hot sauce packed in a basket lined with a set of bandana napkins. Fill cork-topped glass cylinders with homemade soup, Cheese straws, and cookies. A complete meal presented in an addition to a new kitchen.

Hors-d'oeuvres packaged for the freezer in a container meant for cooking and serving are a welcome surprise for anyone who enjoys entertaining. This cookbook offers a variety of appetizers to make ahead. Try Whole Wheat Cheese Straws, Aspen Artichoke Appetizer, or Chicken Liver Pâté. Cocktail napkins of bright calico could accompany an hors-d'oeuvre gift.

A man in the family or a hard-to-buy-for bachelor will appreciate a jar of Barbecue Sauce, several ready-to-grill chickens, a barbecue mitt, and matching apron, all packaged on a serving tray.

A quiche or muffin tin is a perfect container for breakfast rolls, coffee cakes, or dinner rolls. Cover with plastic wrap; add a huge red satin bow and a sprig of fresh holly.

Plum Pudding, the traditional Yuletide dessert, is elegant in its own steamer accompanied by a jar of Hard Sauce or Whiskey Sauce and enhanced with a bright red bow.

For a special friend have the butcher cube a beef tenderloin, place cubes in a lucite salad bowl, and surround with crocks of assorted fondue sauces.

For fans of Italian cuisine try a gift of freshly grated Parmesan cheese, packaged green noodles, and the recipe for Lasagne Verde, packaged in a basket tied with green, red and white ribbon.

ESPECIALLY FOR CHILDREN

Delight your godchild, nieces, or nephews with a basket of Corny Dogs, Cowboy Cookies, and a box of sparklers for a real Texas Fourth of July treat.

Tin or enamel lunch pails can be filled to the brim with assorted cookies and cookie cutters for your favorite first grader. Be sure to include the recipe.

A red clay flower pot filled with flower, herb, or vegetable seed packets and a few simple recipes would delight a child of any age. What could be more fun than cooking with your own home growns.

A colorful straw wastebasket piled high with popcorn balls in plastic wrap would make a special gift for a teenager. Tie it all with candy striped ribbon and lots of candy canes.

Going on a car trip? Pack each child a separate basket brimming with snacks of fruit, homemade cookies, candies, granola and seeds, and their favorite surprises from the five and ten.

Children love to be thought of separately at Christmastime, too. Fill toy trucks and sandpails with assorted cookies and candies.

A fun way to remember a child in the hospital or at home is with a cookie tree. A graceful branch could be pressed into floral clay in the bottom of a flower pot sized according to the size of the "tree". Fill the pot with edible seeds or granola to steady the branch. Tie cookies, candy, small decorations, and cookie cutters on with ribbon.

Back packers — the new generation — would delight in a backpack stocked with air-tight containers of beef jerky, granola, and dried fruits.

Things Grandmother Never Told Me

Add zip to store-bought French dressing by putting a clove of garlic in the bottle.

For fluffier mashed potatoes add a pinch of baking soda as well as milk and butter.

To refrigerate egg yolks, place in a dish and cover with cold water.

Dipping citrus fruits in hot water before squeezing will increase the amount of obtainable juice.

Chicken is easily skinned and boned if slightly frozen.

A soufflé will remain light and fluffy if ¼ tsp. cream of tartar is added to egg whites during mixing.

If Hollandaise curdles, gradually beat one well-beaten egg yolk into the mixture.

For a curdled custard slowly blend a beaten egg into the hot liquid.

If two glasses stick together, do not force them apart. Fill the inside one with cold water and set the outer one in warm. They will separate easily.

When separating an egg, if a bit of yolk gets into the white, remove with a piece of shell.

Dust a little flour or cornstarch on your cake before icing; this way the icing won't run off.

It is sometimes possible to hide an excess of salt with a pinch of sugar.

Always store mushrooms in a paper bag; plastic causes a moisture build up. Also be aware that mushrooms are their freshest if the gills are not open.

When making cream of tomato soup, add tomato juice to milk, not vice versa, to insure against curdling.

Roast meat and fowl will carve more easily if first allowed to stand at room temperature for about 15 minutes.

When searing meat, use tongs to turn; piercing will allow the juices to escape.

An egg slicer works well for slicing mushrooms.

Salad greens should never be cut with a knife; this bruises them, making them bitter. Tear them gently into bite size pieces.

Eggs should always be cooked at a low to moderate temperature as high heat tends to toughen them.

When hard boiling eggs, pierce the broad end with a pin first to prevent cracking.

Egg whites will yield more volume if beaten at room temperature.

As soon as a hard boiled egg is done, plunge it into cold water, thus preventing the grayish color from forming around the yolk.

Lemon juice is good to prevent discoloration on cut surfaces of apples, pears, avocados, bananas, and mushrooms.

Try the pizazz of fresh ground nutmeg.

The quickest way to chop parsley is to snip with scissors.

Do not use an aluminum sauce pan to make a white sauce. It tends to absorb the grayish color from the pan.

Brussel sprouts should be washed, trimmed, and cut with an "X" in the stem end to insure uniform, faster cooking.

To make lighter muffins, place greased pans into the oven for a few mements before adding batter.

Removing a cake from the pan is a breeze. Grease or oil bottom and sides of pan, following with a light sprinkling of flour. Tilt pan back and forth until all sides are evenly coated. Invert pan over sink and tap to dislodge all loose flour. Cover the bottom of the pan with a piece of wax paper cut to fit. A Bundt or tube pan presents more of a challenge. Following the greasing, spray with vegetable shortening. Always cool a cake in the pan for the recommended time. The cake should then fall out of the pan with no problem.

Nuggets of beef or chicken fat are invaluable as a base for sauces and for sautéeing or frying.

Never sift a biscuit, pancake, or cake mix.

Become acquainted with the idiosyncracies of your oven, making adjustments in temperature and timing accordingly.

One of the most indispensable convenience foods is frozen chopped onions. One cup of these treasures equals one large onion, chopped.

Home-made bread crumbs are infinitely superior to those bought in a store. Dry bread in a slow oven without browning. Make the crumbs using a blender or meat grinder. A great way to utilize leftover bread.

Parts of ham or roast that do not slice well may be cut in hunks and ground. This makes a good sandwich spread, croquettes, or filling for an omelet.

Prepare everything as far in advance as possible, assembling things in order of use.

An attractive menu should balance in flavor, color, texture, and nutrition.

For mustard in a sauce a Dijon has the best flavor; and the Maille mustard even better.

Correct seasoning means adding salt and pepper to taste, usually done as the final touch.

Igniting the brandy or Cognac takes away the raw taste and sends the calories up in smoke. Also a cheap brandy is all right for flaming dishes.

Paprika will not darken if kept in the refrigerator.

Egg whites may be kept in the refrigerator for several weeks if placed in a closed jar.

While leftover wine is not good to drink, it is still fine for cooking, if refrigerated. Remember a sweet wine will ruin most sauces.

Bacon grease keeps well if refrigerated. It is excellent for seasoning vegetables and greasing sweet or Irish potatoes before baking. A mixture of half butter and half bacon grease is a good addition to green or lima beans, squash, and spinach.

Store-bought mayonnaise cannot touch your own homemade. But if you must resort to it, keep on hand some with no sugar as this often ruins the flavor of salads and sandwiches.

Herbs should be used with a light discerning hand. A tiny pinch can be surprisingly potent.

Preparing noodles for a casserole, reduce their cooking time by one-third. They will finish cooking in the oven.

French wire whips are a great boon to the kitchen. They quickly take the lumps out of sauces and gravies.

Nothing improves saltine crackers like a short visit to a warm, not hot, oven.

When a recipe calls for crumbled bacon, cut the bacon with scissors before cooking. Fry slowly, remove with a slotted spoon, and drain well.

Shortening is easily measured in cold water. If half a cup is needed, fill a cup half full of water and add shortening until water level reaches one cup. Pour off water and, presto, one half cup shortening that can be depended upon as to volume and does not need to be scraped out of the cup.

Coeur á LaCreme with Caviar

Use cocoa rather than flour to dust pans for chocolate cake.

The size of an egg does affect a recipe, a large egg being the safest size. Extra large eggs may necessitate adding a little more flour; small eggs, a little less.

Be certain a meringue topping on a pie touches the edge of the crust; otherwise, it may shrink from the sides.

If your muffin batter is full of lumps, it is perfect.

Self-rising flour contains 1½ teaspoons baking powder and ½ teaspoon salt per one cup. One must remember this when converting a recipe to either add or delete accordingly.

Always preheat oven for at least 10 minutes unless otherwise stated in the recipe.

Solidified grease is easily pried off the top of gravy or stock. This nugget of beef or chicken fat is invaluable as a base to sauté, fry, or make a sauce. It may be frozen and used as needed.

Brown rice has more food value, roughage, and taste than white. It takes longer to cook but is worth the trouble.

Sending cookies to the children? Pack them in popcorn. It keeps the cookies from breaking and is good to eat, too.

Fresh pineapples are of the best quality when they are heavy and have a fruity smell.

Cream is easiest to whip when chilled. Also chill bowl and beaters.

One half pound cheese yields about two cups shredded cheese.

For soup with a rich, brown taste, brown the bones first. That is right! Place beef bones plus carrots and onions under the broiler long enough to get good and brown. Transfer to soup kettle and add other ingredients. The soup will have that beautiful brown taste and color.

To divide an egg, beat first then measure.

One tablespoon butter in water will keep macaroni from boiling over.

To blanch almonds, cover shelled nuts with boiling water, cool, and slip off skins.

A little sugar in pancake or waffle batter will make them brown more quickly.

Serving fresh coconut? First drain milk and place coconut in oven until hot to touch. Remove and tap all over with a hammer, giving one hard knock at the end to crack open. Lift shell off, peel brown skin, and cool before grating or grinding.

When melting chocolate, first grease pot in which it is to be melted.

One teaspoon of salt or vinegar in water will keep egg white from escaping a cracked shell while boiling.

Pie pastry may be rolled between two sheets of wax paper. Peel off the top paper and flip the bottom into pie pan, removing paper. So easy! And no mess.

When using glass ovenware, lower the temperature by 25 degrees.

To scald milk without scorching, rinse pan in hot water before using.

If honey turns to sugar, stand jar in hot water until it liquefies.

To measure molasses, grease cup in which it is measured.

Add curry or chili powder to a recipe during the browning not to the sauce directly as this will remove the bitter taste.

White pepper is stronger than black; use only about half as much.

Restaurants

This chapter contains the recipes of some of Dallas' finest restaurants.

LES FILETS DE SOLE AUX RAISINS SAUCE CURRY

12 pieces filet of sole or
  flounder
Fish bones
1 onion, chopped
1 carrot, chopped
1 stalk celery, chopped
1 c. white wine
2 bay leaves
A touch of thyme
2 c. water
Salt and whole black pepper
½ onion, chopped fine
½ c. white wine
1½ c. heavy cream
2 t. Madras curry powder
2 T. butter
3 T. flour
¼ c. seedless, peeled white
  grapes
Salt and pepper to taste

Bring to a boil the following ingredients and simmer for 20 minutes: fish bones, onion, carrot, celery, white wine, bay leaves, thyme, water, salt, and whole black pepper. Strain the stock. Place ½ chopped onion in a buttered pan. Fold the filets of sole and place them in the pan side by side. Pour the white wine over the fish. Cover and bring to a boil. Put the pan in a 350° oven for approximately 12-15 minutes or until fish is done. Reduce the heavy cream with curry powder to about a third of its original volume. Add strained fish stock and thicken with the butter-flour mixture. Boil on low heat for approximately 10 minutes. Remove the filets carefully from the pan and place on a serving dish. Add the seedless grapes to the sauce and pour over the filets. Serve with rice pilaf or steamed rice.
Serves 6.

The Fairmont Hotel, Pyramid Room

RACK OF LAMB PROVENÇALE

3 pieces rack of lamb (each
  approx. 16-20 oz.)
Dijon mustard
3 T. butter
3 T. olive oil
3 cloves garlic, chopped
9 cloves shallots, chopped
1 oz. dry bread crumbs
½ oz. chopped parsley
Salt and pepper to taste

Roast rack of lamb for 30 minutes at 375°, so that it stays medium rare. Cover the rack with Dijon mustard and put it under the broiler for a few minutes. Prepare your Provençale. Sauté the shallots and garlic in butter until lightly brown. Add bread crumbs, parsley, salt, and pepper. Place this mixture on top of the rack and finish it under the broiler until golden brown. Serve with broiled tomatoes and fresh green beans.
Serves 6.

The Fairmont Hotel, Pyramid Room

MATEUS SHERBET

½ qt. water
8 oz. sugar
12 oz. Mateus wine

Boil water and sugar until dissolved. Add wine. Pour into a deep pan, cool, and freeze. Just before serving, scrape the ice with a scoop or a strong spoon and serve in a glass with sugared rim or in a frozen glass.
Serves 8.

The Fairmont Hotel, Pyramid Room

CREPES ROMANOFF

CREPE BATTER:
2 c. milk
1 egg
1 egg yolk
3 T. flour
Grated peel from 1 orange
Pinch salt
1 t. sugar
ORANGE SAUCE:
12 oz. fresh orange juice
Grated skin from 3 oranges
Juice from 1 lemon
10 oz. sugar
6 oz. butter
3 eggs
FILLING:
Strawberries
Powdered sugar
Grand Marnier liqueur
Vanilla ice cream (optional)

Mix crêpe batter and prepare 12 crêpes. Mix all sauce ingredients together and under constant stirring, bring to the edge of boiling. DO NOT BOIL. Have the sauce in a crêpe pan and soak the pancakes in it for a few minutes. Into each pancake wrap approximately 6-8 strawberries, depending on the size, which have been marinated in powdered sugar and Grand Marnier liqueur. Serve 2 pancakes to each person on a warm dessert plate with the remaining sauce on top. Serve with vanilla ice cream (optional.)
Serves 6.

The Fairmont Hotel, Pyramid Room

POTAGE CRESSON
(Watercress soup)

Cresson has a special taste of its own, slightly bitter and piquant, recalling that of mustard. We use it raw, to garnish grilled and roast meats, or in salads. Our English friends combine it with fresh sweet butter to make delicate tea sandwiches. Rarely you will find a recipe that calls for it cooked, although it provides excellent dishes. When eaten raw, cresson should be carefully picked over, yellow leaves removed as well as the thicker stems. Wash it quickly in running water and *never* leave it to soak. This lovely soup is quick and simple to prepare and your guests will love it.

1 onion, minced
2 T. butter
2 medium potatoes, diced
2 bunches watercress
4 c. water
½ t. sugar
1 pinch white pepper
2 pinches salt
½ c. heavy cream

Wash watercress and set aside ½ cup leaves for garnish. In a saucepan melt butter and sauté onions until transparent. Add watercress, potatoes, salt, pepper, and water. Cook for 25 minutes. Purée in the blender. Stir in heavy cream and watercress leaves. Season to taste. Serves 6.

Oz Restaurant

SELLE D'AGNEAU ROTIE AUX HERBES
(Saddle of Lamb with Herbs)

Saddle of lamb, 4-5 lbs.
STUFFING:
2 egg yolks
1 lb. freshly cooked spinach, drained and chopped
1 T. fresh chervil, chopped
1 T. fresh parsley, chopped
1 dash dried thyme, chopped
1 dash dried rosemary, chopped
1 t. fresh garlic, chopped
1 dash white pepper
GRAVY:
1 c. white wine
1 c. water

Preheat oven to 450°. Bone saddle of lamb and remove all fat. Salt and pepper the inside of the saddle then add the stuffing. Roll up and tie the saddle. Cook for 45 minutes. Remove saddle from pan and set aside for 10 minutes. Skim all fat from the drippings in the pan. Add water and white wine to drippings, strain, and serve with the saddle. Serves 6.

Oz Restaurant

STRIPED BASS
(Braisé au Fénouil)

3 whole striped bass
  about 2½ lbs. each
2 pts. heavy cream
½ bottle of Chablis
2 bunches fresh fennel
3 oz. Pernod
1 lb. butter
3 pinches thyme
9 bay leaves, sliced
  lengthwise
2 oz. chopped shallots
9 slices lemon
Juice of ½ lemon
Salt and pepper

Preheat oven to 400°. Thoroughly clean and scrape bass and wash well. Salt and pepper moderately. Pour a small amount of Pernod inside fish and add fennel, pulling some through fish's mouth. Make 6 — 2″ incisions lengthwise on each fish. Alternate slices of bay leaves and lemon in each slit. Marinate fish in white wine, Pernod, and shallots for 4 hours. Place fish in a large, deep pan and bake for 1 hour, basting occasionally with marinade. Reserve stock when done. To serve, place fish on a hot platter and garnish with lemon, parsley, and a bouquet of fresh vegetables for decoration. To make Fish Sauce Elysienne, strain remaining fish stock and simmer until reduced. Add cream and simmer until slightly thickened. Remove from stove and add butter, whipping slowly. Add lemon juice and season to taste. This magnificent fish dish can be served as an appetizer or as a main course with pommes anglaise.
Serves 6.   *Oz Restaurant*

TARTE AUX POIRES

12 beautiful pears
1 lb. sugar
5 pts. water
1 vanilla stick
CREME D'AMANDE:
½ lb. almond powder
6 oz. granulated sugar
4 eggs
2 oz. softened butter
1 drop almond extract
MERINGUE:
4 egg whites
8 oz. sugar
1 drop vanilla

Follow directions for short dough (pâte sucrée) under Tarte aux Pommes. Remove skins from 12 beautiful pears and cut in half lengthwise. Prepare a syrup by mixing and heating sugar, water, and vanilla stick. Cook pears in syrup until done. Strain pears and let dry. For crème combine all ingredients. Roll short dough and place in a special tart mold. Add crème d'amande. Arrange pear halves in a circular pattern around the mold toward the middle. Cook for 35 minutes at 350°. Beat all meringue ingredients together until stiff. Place in a pastry bag and squeeze on top of each pear in tart mold. Cook for 4 minutes at 450°. Serve at once.
Serves 12.   *Oz Restaurant*

SHRIMP AND SCALLOPS ARTHUR'S

12 medium-sized shrimp,
  peeled and deveined
½ lb. cape scallops
1 c. white wine
1 c. water
1 c. heavy cream
½ t. oregano
⅛ lb. butter
½ c. bread crumbs
1 T. parsley, chopped

Poach shrimp and scallops in white wine and water. Remove and set aside when cooked (approximately 8-10 minutes.) Add oregano, cream, and butter. Simmer for approximately 15 minutes or until reduced by one-half. Salt and pepper to taste. Place shrimp and scallops in casserole. Top with bread crumbs mixed with parsley. Brown in oven at 375°.
Serves 4.

Arthur's Restaurant

CREVETTES PROVENCALE

24 shrimp, peeled and deveined
¼ lb. butter
2 shallots, finely sliced
Juice of 2 lemons
2 pods garlic, minced
1½ oz. Pernod

Dust shrimp lightly in flour and sauté in butter until almost done. Remove and set aside. Add garlic and shallots. Simmer until shallots are clear (do not overcook!). Return shrimp; add Pernod and lemon juice. Simmer for 3 minutes. Salt and pepper to taste.
Serves 4.

Old Warsaw Restaurant

SCAMPI LIVORNESE

12 2-oz. Danish lobster tails,
  peeled and deveined
4 shallots, sliced
½ c. light olive oil
3 pods garlic, minced
⅛ lb. butter
Juice of 2 lemons

Dust lobster tails lightly in flour. Sauté in olive oil until almost done and set aside. Drain all but about 1 tablespoon of olive oil. Add butter; simmer garlic and shallots until clear (do not overcook.) Return lobster tails and add lemon juice. Salt and pepper to taste.
Serves 4.

Mario's Restaurant

VEAL WITH ARTICHOKE HEARTS AND MUSHROOMS

12 veal scallops, thinly sliced
12 artichoke hearts (fresh or canned)
8 medium mushrooms, sliced
½ c. white wine
½ lb. butter
Juice of 2 lemons
1 c. chicken stock

Parboil fresh artichoke hearts. Dust scallops lightly with flour. Sauté in butter until done. Set aside. Add mushrooms and cook until done. Add artichoke hearts, white wine, lemon juice, and chicken stock. Cook until reduced by a third. Return veal and cook for 2-3 minutes until hot.
Serves 4.

Mario's Restaurant

TOURNEDOS DE CHEVREUIL GRAND VENEUR

8 3-oz. slices of sirloin of venison, marinated
¼ lb. butter
2 oz. Cognac
½ c. heavy cream
2 T. cranberry sauce
MARINADE:
2 c. vegetable oil
1 pt. red wine
1 onion, quartered
2 cloves garlic, crushed
2 carrots, diced
2 stalks celery, diced
1 T. cracked pepper
6 bay leaves
½ t. thyme
½ c. red wine vinegar

Combine marinade ingredients and let venison marinate for one week. Sauté venison in butter until cooked to desired doneness. Add cognac and flame. Remove meat and set aside. Add to the skillet 2 cups of marinade and simmer until reduced by a third. Add cranberry sauce and cream; simmer for 3 minutes. Salt and pepper to taste. Place 2 tournedos on each plate. Top with sauce. Accompany with chestnut purée, wild rice, and currant jelly.
Serves 4.

Old Warsaw Restaurant

FRENCH BREAD
(Straight dough)

6½ c. hard wheat flour
2 c. water, room temperature
1 T. salt
2 oz. sugar
1 cake compressed yeast

Put flour, salt, sugar, and 1½ cups water in a bowl. Dissolve yeast in ½ cup of lukewarm water and add to bowl. Mix 10-12 minutes until smooth. Let dough rise 1 hour, covered to avoid draft. Punch it down and let it rise again for 30 minutes. Shape it as desired and let rise to double its size. Bake in a 350° oven for 30-35 minutes. Remove from pan and cool on a wire rack.

Makes 1 large loaf, or can be braided and shaped into a wreath for Christmas, fill the center with Chicken Liver Paté.

Arthur's Restaurant

ARTHUR'S SPECIAL STUFFED FILET MIGNON

4 8-oz. filet mignons
½ lb. fresh lump crabmeat
3 shallots, sliced
1 T. Chives, chopped
⅛ lb. butter
8 medium-sized mushrooms, sliced and sautéed
Butter for sautéeing mushrooms
2 c. beef stock
1 c. Madeira wine

In 2 tablespoons of butter sauté shallots and add crabmeat and chives. Set aside. Take filets and butterfly, flattening slightly. To one side add crabmeat filling and close. Sauté in an extra-hot skillet until brown on both sides. Place in oven at 450° until desired doneness. To skillet add beef stock, cooked mushrooms, and wine. Salt and pepper to taste. Allow to reduce by one-half (may be thickened with basic roux.) Place filet on plate and top with mushroom sauce. Wild rice is an excellent accompaniment.

Serves 4.

Arthur's Restaurant

APPETIZERS

ALMOND BUTTER STICKS

1 stick butter at room
  temperature
⅓ c. blanched almonds, finely
  chopped
8 slices bread
Parmesan cheese, freshly
  grated

Mix butter and almonds together. Remove crust from bread slices. Cut each piece into 3 strips. Toast the bread under the broiler of the oven until lightly browned. Turn over and spread untoasted side with the butter mixture. Sprinkle with cheese and toast until lightly browned. Makes 24 sticks. This is a marvelous substitute for crackers when serving a salad plate or bowl of soup.
Serves 12.

Mrs. Peter M. Tart

APPETIZER CRESCENT ROLLS

1 pkg. (8-oz.) refrigerated
  crescent rolls
½ c. sour cream
½ t. onion salt
½ lb. bacon, cooked crisp,
  drained, and crumbled

Unroll rolls, spread with sour cream, and sprinkle with onion salt. Top with bacon. Cut each roll into three equal wedges lengthwise. Roll up each one, starting at the point of the wedge. Place "roll-ups" on greased baking sheets and bake at 375° for 12-15 minutes or until golden brown. Serve warm. Yields 24 appetizers. Can be frozen.

Mrs. James G. Aldridge

MEXICAN PIZZA CANAPES

1 15-oz. can tomato sauce
1 large onion, chopped
¼ c. Romano cheese, grated
1 4-oz. pkg. hard salami
1 pkg. small round tostados
Cheddar cheese

Put tomato sauce and onion in a deep pan and boil until it becomes a thick paste, stirring constantly to keep from sticking. Add Romano cheese and remove from heat. Cut salami into small bits with scissors and add to paste. (This much can be done the day before and refrigerated. If done this way, reheat in the top of a double boiler.) Slice Cheddar cheese into small squares that fit the top of the tostados. Put a heaping tablespoon of the tomato mixture on top of the cheese. Place on cookie sheets and heat at 350° until the cheese melts.

Makes approximately 50 canapés.

Mrs. L. G. Pondrom

CHILI CON QUESO

1 c. chopped onions
1 clove garlic, chopped
1 T. butter
1½ c. tomatoes, chopped and
　well-drained
1 4 oz. can green chiles,
　chopped
1 t. salt
½ t. pepper
1 lb. Velveeta cheese, grated

Sauté onions and garlic in shortening; add tomatoes, chiles, salt, pepper, and cheese. Cook in double boiler 50-60 minutes. If mixture gets too thick, add tomato sauce or juice from chiles.

Serves 24 for hor-d'oeuvres.

Mrs. Ralph Greenlee, Jr.

ACAPULCO CANAPES

FILLING:
1 or 2 hot peppers to taste
3 or more tomatoes, peeled and diced
1 or 2 bunches green onions, sliced
Salt
PASTRY:
2 c. Quaker Masa Harina
1⅓ c. warm water

For filling, season to taste with salt and minced hot peppers. Cook and simmer until it looks like relish. Make a pastry of the two ingredients. Form pieces of dough into the size of a silver dollar with a little ridge around each to hold the mixture. Cook in deep fat until golden. Fill with mixture and grate white Mexican cheese on top.
Makes about 5 doz. canapés.

Mrs. Jack Vaughn

CHUTNEY PIE
(Hors-d'oeuvre)

1 8 oz. pkg. cream cheese, softened
1 8-oz. pkg. sharp cheddar cheese, softened
1 t. curry powder
2 T. sherry
⅔ small jar chutney
Green onions, sliced

Mix cheeses, curry, and sherry. Grease and fill pie tin with mixture. Chill until 1 hour before serving. Turn out onto platter. Top with chutney and green onions. Serve at room temperature with wheat crackers.
Serves 16 as appetizer.

Mrs. Floyd T. Burke

CHEESE BALL

8 oz. cream cheese
8 oz. Velveeta cheese
1 c. nuts, ground very fine
1 clove garlic, mashed
Dash of salt
Chili powder

Let cheese stand at room temperature to soften. Combine all but chili powder in electric mixer. Put in refrigerator 30 minutes to firm up for handling. Roll in ball and roll in chili powder. Freezes well. Left-over ball may be reshaped and frozen again.
Makes enough for 16.

Mrs. Joe M. Bashara, Jr.

CHEESE BALLS

2 c. flour
1 lb. mild cheese, grated
1½ t. salt
¼-½ t. cayenne pepper
½ lb. butter, softened
Sesame seeds

Mix all ingredients and chill. Form into one-inch balls and roll in sesame seeds. Freeze. Bake at 375° for 10 to 12 minutes. (We like ours to be crusty.)
Makes 6 dozen.

Mrs. William W. Lynch, Jr.

PINE-CHEESE BALL

2 pkg. 8 oz. cream cheese
1 8½ oz. can crushed pineapple, well drained
1½ c. pecans, chopped
¼ c. green pepper, finely chopped
2 T. green onion, finely chopped
1 t. seasoned salt

Beat cream cheese with fork until smooth. Gradually stir in pineapple, 1 c. of pecans; gradually add green pepper, onion, and salt. Shape into a ball and roll in remaining nuts. May be frozen.
Serves 20 as a spread.

Mrs. Larry K. Casey

LIPTAUER CHEESE . . . Hungary

8 heaping T. cottage cheese
3 oz. cream cheese
½ medium onion, grated
1½ t. capers, drained
¾ t. caraway seeds
1 heaping t. anchovy paste
½ t. dry mustard
½ t. paprika
1 T. Parmesan cheese
1 T. white wine

Sieve and blend cottage cheese with cream cheese. Beat in onion and all other ingredients, folding in capers. Chill at least 2 hours before serving with thin crunchy wafers.
Serves 8 as a spread.

Cook Book Committee

CHEESE OLIVES

1 c. cheese, grated
3 T. butter, softened
½ c. flour
¼ t. salt
½ t. paprika
Dash cayenne
Olives

Blend cheese and butter; and stir in flour, salt, paprika, and cayenne. Drain olives on a paper towel. Roll 1 t. cheese dough around each olive, covering completely. Freeze. When ready to serve, place on cookie sheet and bake 15 minutes at 400°.
Makes about 4 doz.

Mrs. John F. Hickman

CHEESE AND OLIVE SPREAD

1 c. ripe olives, chopped
½ c. green onion, minced
1½ c. sharp Cheddar cheese, grated
½ c. mayonnaise
½ t. salt
½ t. curry powder or chili powder
Biscuits or English muffins

Combine ingredients. Use refrigerated biscuits, English muffins, or split bake-and-serve rolls prepared as directed. Spread the cheese and olive mixture on split rolls and broil until cheese has melted. It is great for Sunday supper with soup or salad. It is also good on split hamburger buns that have been buttered and lightly browned and then spread with cheese. Also can be a hot appetizer. Keeps two weeks.
Serves 15 as a spread.

Mrs. John H. Childers

CHEESE AND CHILI LOAF

2 8-oz. pkg. cream cheese
3 heaping t. mayonnaise
2 c. ground pecans
2½ T. dill pickle juice
2½ T. Worcestershire sauce
Salt to taste
Chili powder

Form in loaf after mixing all ingredients except chili powder. Usually makes two loaves. Chill in refrigerator. Roll in chili powder when ready to use. Serve with Ritz crackers.
Will serve 16.

Mrs. Craig Canon

WHOLE WHEAT CHEESE STRAWS

1 lb. N.Y. State Black Rind Cheese, grated
1 c. whole wheat flour
1 c. unbleached flour
2 t. salt
¾-1 t. cayenne pepper
1½ sticks butter, softened

Combine all ingredients, and chill. Roll out and cut into rectangles about ½" by 3". Bake at 350° for about 15 minutes. Delicious hot or cold and with soup.
Makes 5 dozen.

Mrs. Charles M. Best II

TEXAS CHEESE STRAWS

½ lb. sharp cheese, grated
1 t. red pepper
1 t. salt
½ lemon, juiced
1 t. onion juice
1 stick butter, softened
2 c. flour
1 t. Worcestershire

Work all ingredients together and squeeze out of cookie decorator. Easier to squeeze if you keep warm. Bake at 400° for 10-15 minutes or until golden. Makes 3 dozen.

Mrs. Charles P. Storey

CARAWAY CHEESE PASTRIES

2 c. all-purpose flour, sifted
½ t. salt
1 t. caraway seeds
⅔ c. shortening
½ c. American cheese, shredded
¼ c. cold milk

Combine flour, salt, and caraway seeds. Cut in shortening until particles are smooth. Toss with cheese. Add milk slowly to make a stiff dough. Turn on a lightly floured board and roll to ⅛" thickness. Cut in desired shapes and place on an ungreased cookie sheet. Bake at 425° for 10 minutes until golden brown. Remove to a rack to cool. Store in an airtight container to keep crisp. Use with any kind of dip.
Makes about 4 dozen.

Mrs. Mark Lemmon, Jr.

GRUYERE CHEESE CANAPES

4 T. onion, grated
3 T. butter
3 T. flour
1½ t. salt
¼ t. pepper, freshly ground
½ t. dry mustard
1 c. milk
2 c. Gruyère cheese, grated
(½ lb. in wedges)
¼ c. beer
1 egg yolk, beaten
Toasted bread rounds

Sauté the onion in butter for about 3 minutes. Blend in the flour, salt, pepper, and mustard; and stir until slightly browned. Gradually add the milk, stirring constantly until it reaches the boiling point. Cook over low heat for 5 minutes. Mix in the cheese and beer until cheese is melted. Gradually add a little of the hot mixture to the beaten egg yolk, mixing steadily to prevent curdling, then return the egg yolk mixture to the cheese mixture. Allow to cool. Spread on toasted bread rounds, not quite to the edge. Arrange on baking sheet and place under broiler until browned. Keeps several weeks in the refrigerator.
Makes about 3 dozen canapés.

Mrs. John W. McDonough

JUDY'S CHEESE

½ stick butter
1 lb. jar sharp Cheddar cheese
spread
¼ t.•cracked pepper
½ heaping t. onion salt or 1
small onion, grated
¼ t. garlic powder or 1 clove
garlic, crushed
¾ t. Worcestershire sauce

Cream butter, cheese, pepper, onion salt, and garlic until soft. Add Worcestershire and store in refrigerator. Spread thickly on split English muffins and bake at 300° for 7 minutes, cut into quarters, and serve hot. Also, serve cold as a spread.
Serves about 20.

Mrs. John Bagwell

HOT CHEESE SQUARES

Sharp cheese, grated
Worcestershire sauce
Onion, grated
Tabasco
¼-½ c. mayonnaise
4 T. Dijon mustard
Seasoning salt
Lemon-pepper marinade

Mix all ingredients together using amount to your own taste. Take one loaf of Pepperidge Farm Cracked Wheat Bread, lightly buttered and bake at 400° until crisp. Cool. When ready to serve, cut bread into bite-size pieces and top with cheese mixture. Run under broiler and serve hot. Can sprinkle crushed pecans over top of cheese before broiling. This mixture can also be spread on an English muffin and served with a hot soup for a winter lunch or supper.
Serves 24.

Mrs. B. Thomas McElroy

ARTICHOKE DIP

2 cans artichoke hearts (each
  8½-oz. dr. wt.)
1 c. mayonnaise
1 T. chopped onion
3 T. Spice Islands' imitation
  bacon seasoning with chives
1 t. salt
1 t. pepper
1 t. cayenne pepper

Chop artichoke hearts finely. Add mayonnaise, seasonings, and mix well. Use as a dip with Melba rounds or serve in hollowed tomato shells as a salad.
Serves 8.

Mrs. John Alexander

CHEESE-CRAB DIP

½ bottle blue cheese salad
  dressing
½ bottle thousand island salad
  dressing
1 3-oz pkg. cream cheese,
  softened
2 T. mayonnaise
1 small clove garlic, pressed
1 t. lemon juice
1 c. crabmeat

Combine all ingredients, chill, and serve. Can be made the day before.
Serves about 8.

Mrs. Norman Smith

DUTCHIE'S CHILI DIP

1 lb. ground chuck
1 onion, chopped
1 pkg. Frito Chili-O mix
1 8-oz. can tomato sauce with bits
1 can Ro-tel tomatoes with green chiles
1 lb. Longhorn cheese, cut into small pieces

Brown chuck with onion. Mix Chili-O mix with it and cook 10-15 minutes. Add tomatoes. Melt cheese and stir into meat mixture very well. Serve hot with tostados.
Serves 8.

Mrs. Patrick C. Guillot

A FRIEND'S GREEN CHILI DIP

2 cans (4-oz. each) green chiles, chopped
2 cans (4½-oz. each) black olives, chopped
2 tomatoes, chopped
4 green onions, chopped
2 T. wine vinegar
1 T. olive oil

Mix all ingredients together and chill. Serve with tostados. This is not really hot or too spicy.
Serves about 12.

Mrs. John P. Castleman, Jr.

CUCUMBER DIP

8-oz. pkg. cream cheese, softened
Mayonnaise
11 shakes Tabasco sauce
7 shakes Beau Monde
Salt to taste
1 cucumber

Mash cream cheese with a fork and add mayonnaise to make an easy consistency. Add spices. Remove peeling and seeds from cucumber and chop fine. Add to cheese mixture. Good for a spread on sandwiches or stuffed in cherry tomatoes.
Makes about 12 sandwiches or 36 cherry tomatoes.

Mrs. Allen L. Oliver, Jr.

HERB-CURRY DIP

1 c. mayonnaise
½ c. sour cream
1 t. crushed mixed herbs
¼ t. salt
⅛ t. curry powder
1 T. fresh parsley, snipped or 1 t. dried parsley flakes
1 T. onion, grated
1½ t. lemon juice
½ t. capers, drained
½ t. Worcestershire sauce

Blend all ingredients, preferably the day before serving or the morning to be used. Chill well and serve in a small bowl surrounded by a variety of cold, raw vegetables: e.g. celery, cauliflower, carrots, red or white radishes, cucumbers, summer or zucchini squash, cherry tomatoes, etc. Makes approximately 1½ cups of sauce.

Mrs. Frederick J. Coyle, Jr.

SEARCY'S GUACAMOLE

2 avocados
1 c. real mayonnaise
½ onion, chopped fine
1 medium tomato, chopped
Salt
Pepper
Lemon juice
Hot sauce

Purée avocado. Add rest of ingredients and check seasonings. Place avocado seed in center and chill until ready to serve. (Seed will keep guacamole from turning brown.)
Serves 12.

Mrs. Searcy Ferguson, Jr.

JALAPEÑO BEAN DIP

2 cans Ranch Style Beans, drained (save juice)
1 stick butter
½ lb. Cheddar cheese, grated
½ large onion, minced
1 clove garlic, pressed
2 Jalapeño peppers, chopped

Grind or mash beans. Melt butter in the top of a double boiler. Add cheese. After cheese has melted, add remaining ingredients. Add juice from beans if mixture is too thick.
Serves 12.

Mrs. Larry M. Nobles

OYSTER CHIP DIP

1 large can smoked oysters, undrained and chopped
2 t. lemon juice
1 t. Worcestershire
3 oz. cottage cheese
3 oz. cream cheese
¼ c. potato chips, crushed
Salt and pepper to taste

Cream cottage cheese and cream cheese with lemon juice and Worcestershire. Fold in remaining ingredients and refrigerate.
Serves 6-8.

Mrs. Peter M. Tart

1 can Ro-tel tomatoes
16 oz. cream cheese
½ c. green olives with
    pimientoes chopped
Dash of Worcestershire Sauce
Lawry's Seasoning Salt and
    Pepper to taste
½ t. lemon juice

OLIVE-TOMATO DIP

Mix all ingredients thoroughly and chill. Serve with crackers or raw vegetables. Serves 8-10.

Mrs. Robert S. Addison

1 can tomato soup
3 3-oz. pkgs. cream cheese
1 envelope unflavored gelatin
3 7½-oz. cans shrimp, drained
    and chopped
1 small onion, chopped or
    grated
½ c. celery, finely chopped
1 c. mayonnaise
1 t. lemon juice
¼ c. cold water
Salt, pepper, and garlic salt

SHRIMP MOLD DIP

Heat soup and dissolve cream cheese in it. Mix well using an electric mixer. Dissolve gelatin in cold water and add to hot mixture, mixing well. Cool for 30 minutes. Add remaining ingredients. Grease a mold lightly with oil and pour in mixture. May have to dip in hot water to release when ready to serve.
Serves 40 as spread.

Mrs. James G. Aldridge

Flank steak
Medium ground pepper
Salt

BEEF JERKY

Slice meat thinly with the grain into strips. This is easier if the meat is slightly frozen. Place strips on a rack with a pan underneath. Salt lightly and pepper heavily both sides of meat. Cook at a low temperature (approximately 200°) for 6 hours. Excellent with beer.
Serves 12.

Mrs. Rene Kendzior

1 lb. hot suasage (bulk)
3 c. Bisquick
12 oz. sharp Cheddar cheese,
    grated

HOT SAUSAGE BALLS

Mix sausage, Bisquick, and cheese, and roll into small balls. Bake on cookie sheet at 350° for about 15 minutes or until brown. These can be made ahead and frozen.
Makes about 6 dozen.

Mrs. John Shelley

HUNGARIAN HAM APPETIZERS

¼ c. butter
¼ c. cracker crumbs
1 c. sour cream
¼ c. Swiss cheese, grated
1½ c. cooked ham, minced
2 t. caraway seeds
6 eggs

Beat eggs until light and thick. Combine all and pour onto a greased cookie sheet with sides. Bake at 375° until nicely browned, about 15 minutes. Cut into squares and serve hot.
Makes 24.

Mrs. Mark Lemmon, Jr.

CAMPAIGN SPECIAL

4½ pounds chicken wings
Paprika — enough to sprinkle
    both sides of chicken
1 c. lemon juice
1 c. white wine vinegar
2 c. oil
Soy sauce — enough to cut
    tartness
1 T. Tarragon
3 or 4 bay leaves
Pepper to taste
2 T. salt
1 t. oregano
2 T. parsley, chopped

Wash chicken wings and cut off the tips. Sprinkle with paprika, front and back. Place in pans. Mix all ingredients together (can be done in blender) and pour over chicken. Marinate for 4-5 hours, turning chicken from time to time. Cook on hooded barbecue slowly for 1 hour or until chicken is tender. Baste frequently with sauce during cooking. Recipe can be easily doubled, tripled, etc., but not frozen.
Serves 24 for appetizers.

Mrs. Ben Munson IV

CHICKEN "PICK-UPS"

5 lbs. chicken wings
1½ t. Accent
1 c. Italian salad dressing
3 t. seasoned salt
3 c. flour, sifted
½ c. sesame seeds
Pepper to taste
2 t. paprika
1½ c. butter, melted
1 T. Worcestershire sauce

Wash and clean wings (singe if necessary) cut off tip ends and discard. Cut in two at joints. Drain and dry thoroughly on paper towel, placing in a large bowl. Sprinkle with Accent, salad dressing, and 1 t. salt. Cover and let marinate several hours or overnight. In one large pan mix flour, seeds, remaining 2 t. salt, pepper, and paprika. In another large pan melt butter and Worcestershire. Dip each piece of wing in butter mixture, shake off excess, then dip in flour mixture. Place about 1 inch apart on greased cookie sheet or broiler pan and bake in 350° oven for 1 hour. Slip under broiler for 2 or 3 minutes to brown on both sides.
Serves 25.

Mrs. Robert H. Holmes

SMOKED WILD GOOSE

1 wild goose
1½ c. vegetable oil
1½ c. dry vermouth
Salt and cayenne pepper

Thaw goose; marinate in oil and vermouth for several hours. Drain and generously salt and pepper inside and out. Place on smoker (preferably the type with water pan — follow mfg. instructions) for about 6 hours. Refrigerate until thoroughly chilled. To serve, remove skin and discard. Slice breast and legs very thinly. Serve as hors-d'oeuvres with crackers and German mustard. May be refrozen after smoking.
Serves 8-12.

Mrs. Charles Clymer

BRAUNSCHWEIGER PATE

1 can Campbell's beef
   consommé
1 T. unflavored gelatin
1 8-oz. cream cheese with
   chives
8-oz. Braunschweiger, best
   quality (goose liver)
Lemon juice
Tabasco sauce
½ t. dill weed
Salt

Dissolve gelatin in little water. Heat soup and add gelatin mixture. Mix cheese and goose liver; season with lemon juice, tabasco sauce, dill weed, and salt. Pour ½ gelatin-consommé mixture in bottom of small glass mixing bowl (buttered.) Then put cheese-goose liver mixture on congealed consommé gelatin mixture. After that is pressed on carefully and firm, put second half gelatin-consommé mixture on top. Reheat if necessary to soften. Chill until firm. Turn out and decorate pâté mold. Serve with Melba toast rounds.

Mrs. Mark Lemmon

CHICKEN LIVER AND ONION PATE

¼ c. butter
2 yellow onions, sliced
1 clove garlic, grated fine
1 lb. chicken livers, cut up
2 t. Port
Ground pepper

Sauté onions and garlic in butter for 10 minutes. Add chicken livers and cook until done about 5 to 10 minutes. Put all this through a meat grinder on fine (or place in blender until finely chopped). Add Port (more if wanted) and pepper to taste.
Serves 12.

Mrs. Denys Slater, Jr.

KATIE STAPLETON'S OUT-OF-SIGHT PATE

About 5 oz. beef marrow
1 c. rich, gelatinous stock or
   beef bouillon
3 oz. stale bread, crusts
   removed and crumbled
1 small clove garlic
1 lb. chicken livers
Salt, pepper, and cayenne to
   taste
Large pinch herbs (thyme,
   savory, oregano, marjoram)
3 eggs
½ c. heavy cream
2 T. Cognac
Butter for mold

Beef marrow can often be obtained free from your butcher. Have him saw it into sections. Place in ice-cold water to degorge it. Then poach the marrow by putting it into boiling water and taking it away from the heat for about 3 minutes. Then it is easy to extricate. Combine stock and bread crumbs. Reduce, stirring with a wooden spoon, until it is the consistency of a firm paste. Pound the garlic to a paste in a mortar and mix with the bread-stock mixture (panade). Put livers, marrow, and panade into the blender. Blend, season, and blend again. Discard any stringy tissue. Add eggs, 1 at a time, while blender is still on, then Cognac and cream. Pour into a buttered 1 quart mold. Poach, ¾ immersed in hot, never boiling water, in a 350° oven for 1 hour, or until center is firm to the touch. Loaf shrinks slightly while cooling. Unmold it when only tepid, pressing a plastic wrap around it to protect it from the air contact. Serve well chilled. It may, once chilled, be simply decorated with a chicken or veal jelly, or a crust, making it a pâté en croûte. Except for its beige exterior, it should be uniform and delicate rose throughout. Chilling gives it body.
Serves 24.

Mrs. Dan Burney

MUSHROOM AND CHICKEN LIVER PATE

2 lbs. chicken livers
1½ c. fresh mushrooms, sliced
4 sticks butter, softened
1 bunch parsley, chopped
½ of an 8-oz. jar French
   mustard
1 c. white wine
2 garlic cloves
Salt and pepper
1 bunch of green onions and
   tops, chopped

Drain chicken livers and sauté in ½ stick butter. Cook until done. Sauté mushrooms and onions in ½ stick butter. Combine with livers; add garlic, salt, pepper, parsley, and wine. Cook on low heat for 20 minutes. Put in blender while hot and blend until smooth. When completely cooled, add 3 more sticks of butter, and mustard; correct seasoning. Pack into crocks. Freezes well.
Serves 20.

Mrs. Searcy Ferguson, Jr.

QUICK LIVER PATE

1 8-oz. pkg. cream cheese
½ lb. liver sausage
¼ c. green onion, finely
   chopped
6 slices bacon, fried crisp and
   crumbled
2 T. parsley, minced
2 t. Worcestershire sauce

Bring cream cheese and sausage to room temperature. Cream together and add onion, bacon, parsley, and Worcestershire sauce. Shape into one large ball or two medium balls and roll either in parsley or chopped pecans. For the holidays make an icing of softened cream cheese with a little milk and ice the ball, adding piece of holly for decoration.
Serves 12.

Mrs. Larry Casey

SALMON PATE

½ lb. cooked fresh or canned
   salmon
½ lb. unsalted butter, softened
3 small shallots, finely minced
Salt and freshly ground white
   pepper
½ t. nutmeg, freshly grated
Cayenne pepper
1 t. white wine vinegar

Gently sauté shallots in a little butter. Remove any skin or bones from salmon. Put through the fine blade of a food mill or purée in an electric blender. Beat in butter, shallots, and seasonings. Pack in crocks and cover with clarified butter ⅛" thick. Makes about 2 cups.

Mrs. Stephen Summers

CAVIAR PIE

8 oz. cream cheese
¼ c. mayonnaise
2-3 t. onion, grated
1-2 t. Worchestershire sauce
1-2 t. lemon juice
Caviar (inexpensive)
Parsley, chopped
Hard-cooked egg, grated
Onion, finely chopped
Melba toast rounds

Soften and blend the cream cheese with mayonnaise. Season cheese with grated onion, Worcestershire sauce, and lemon juice. Spread in center of plate or tray in a circle about 1 inch thick. Cover the top with caviar and the sides with parsley. Sprinkle hard-cooked egg and onion on top. Chill and serve with Melba toast rounds.
Serves 8-12.

Mrs. John Lancaster III

COEUR A LA CREME WITH CAVIAR

8 oz. cream cheese
8 oz. cottage cheese
¾ c. whipping cream
1 t. lemon juice
¾ t. onion, grated
Caviar

Put cream cheese and cottage cheese through a sieve. Beat whipping cream into cheese gradually. Add grated onion and lemon juice, beating until mixed. Line a coeur à la Crème basket with cheesecloth and fill it with cheese mixture. Put basket on a plate and let stand overnight in refrigerator to drain and set. Unmold and surround with caviar.
Serves 24.

Mrs. Denys Slater, Jr.

CEVICHE

1 lb. white fish, chopped
Juice of 7 limes
1 small white onion, chopped
1 small can Jalapeño peppers,
   chopped (can omit if hot is
   not to your liking)
5-oz. jar Spanish olives,
   drained and chopped
2 T. red wine vinegar
1 T. olive oil
Pinch of oregano and cumin
2 cans Ro-tel tomatoes

Mix all ingredients and marinate. Serve with tostados.
Serves 25-30 as a dip.

Mrs. Jack Shook, Jr.

CRABMEAT CREAM PUFFS

PUFFS:
1 stick butter
1 c. boiling water
1 c. flour
¼ t. salt
4 eggs
CRABMEAT MIXTURE:
1½ c. fresh crabmeat
2 c. sharp Cheddar cheese
2 c. Mayonnaise
2 T. Worcestershire sauce
2 t. Tabasco sauce
½ T. onion, minced
½ c. celery, diced

Melt butter in boiling water. Add flour and salt. Stir vigorously until mixture is smooth and forms soft ball that does not separate. Cool mixture slightly. Add eggs one at a time. Beat vigorously after each egg. Drop mixture by teaspoon onto greased cookie sheet. Put in 450° oven for 5 minutes; then cook at 350° for 15 minutes. Allow to cool. Crabmeat mixture: Mix thoroughly crabmeat with all other ingredients. If time allows, chill mixture before filling puffs. Put into bite sized cream puffs. Heat til cheese begins to melt.
Makes 3 dozen small puffs.

Mrs. John J. Kendrick, Jr.

CRAB-SWISS BITES

½ lb. fresh crabmeat
1 T. green onion, sliced
4 oz. Swiss cheese, grated
½ c. Mayonnaise
1 t. lemon juice
¼ t. curry powder
1 pkg. flaky-style rolls
Salt to taste

Combine crabmeat, green onion, Swiss cheese, mayonnaise, lemon juice, and curry powder. Mix well. Separate rolls each into 3 layers. Place on ungreased baking sheet. Spoon on crabmeat mixture. Bake at 400° 9-12 minutes or til golden brown.
The crab mixture may be made 2-3 hours in advance. One hour before serving, the rolls may be spread with the mixture and refrigerated until baking time.
Makes 36.

Mrs. Joe E. Funk, Jr.

CRABMEAT MOLD

½ lb. lump crab meat
2 hardboiled eggs, grated
5 T. green olives, chopped
1 small jar chopped pimiento
¼ c. water
1 envelope unflavored gelatin
8 oz. mayonnaise
4 oz. hot, sweet mustard
1 T. onion salt
1 t. Accent

Mix the first 4 ingredients together. Put remaining ingredients in a double boiler and cook only until well mixed. Mix into the crab mixture. Pour into greased 4-cup mold and chill until firm. Serve with crackers.
Serves 8.

Mrs. J. Frank Holt III

FRED'S CRABMEAT CAVIAR FANTASTIC

1 lb. lump crabmeat
½ c. mayonnaise
½ c. chili sauce
1 avocado, sliced thin
8 oz. caviar
Lemon juice
Salt and pepper

Remove cartilage from crabmeat. Toss all ingredients and serve on toast or fill in half an avocado and serve as salad. Serves 12 as appetizer or 4 for salad.

Cookbook Committee

NANTUCKET CRABMEAT

1 lb. crabmeat, shells removed
1 bottle chili sauce
1 8-oz. cream cheese
½ c. mayonnaise
¼ c. parsley, chopped

Soften cheese with mayonnaise. Spread in the bottom of a pie pan. Cover with chili sauce, then crab, then parsley. Serve with Melba rounds. Serves 10.

Cookbook Committee

SKRUMPIES

1 pkg. cherry tomatoes
1 7½-oz. can crab meat
½ c. mayonnaise
1 t. green onion, chopped
1 t. green onion stems, chopped
½ t. Worcestershire sauce

Wash, drain, and core cherry tomatoes. Mix the crab, mayonnaise, green onions, stems and Worcestershire sauce. Stuff the tomatoes with the crab mixture. Refrigerate. Can be made ahead. Serves 8.

Mrs. Joe B. Abbey

ESCARGOTS IN RAMEKINS

½ c. celery, finely chopped
½ c. onions, finely chopped
1 lb. mushrooms, sliced
4 T. butter
36-48 large snails, cut in half
1 clove garlic, minced
2 T. parsley, minced
1 egg, beaten
1 c. heavy cream
¼ c. sherry
Salt and pepper

Sauté onion, celery, garlic in butter about 5 min. Add mushrooms and cook 10-15 min. Remove from heat and add snails, cream, eggs, parsley, sherry, salt and pepper. Put into ramekins, bake at 350° 15-20 min. Serves 10

Mrs. Denys Slater, Jr.

ESCARGOT IN MUSHROOMS

½ garlic clove, minced
2 T. fresh parsley, chopped
1 large can of snails, halved
1 stick of butter, softened
24 large mushroom caps
2 shallots, minced

Combine butter with last three ingredients. Remove stems from mushrooms and place one snail on each; top with butter mixture. Bake in a 350° oven for 10 minutes or until bubbly. Shrimp may be used if escargot are not available. You may also stuff in cooked pasta shells. Serves 8-10

Mrs. Searcy Ferguson, Jr.

OYSTERS IN MUSHROOM CAPS

24 large mushrooms
¼ c. green onions, minced
⅔ c. butter, melted
24 oysters, well-drained
Salt and pepper to taste
½ c. parsley, chopped

Remove stems from clean mushrooms. Sauté mushrooms and onions in ⅓ cup butter until barely tender. Place mushrooms cut side up in a greased shallow pan, just large enough to hold them. Place an oyster in each one and season. Pour a little melted butter on top and bake at 425° just until oysters curl — about 5 minutes. Top with parsley and serve.
Serves 6.

Mrs. H. W. Kimmerling

LOBSTER CANAPE

4 T. butter
4 T. flour
¼ t. salt
1 c. half and half cream
½ lb. cooked lobster (crab or
   tuna may be substituted)
½ lb. mushrooms, sautéed in 2
   T. butter
1 T. green pepper, chopped
   finely
1 T. pimiento, chopped
½ t. salt or to taste
¼ t. paprika
¼ t. curry powder or 1 t.
   Worcestershire sauce or 2 T.
   sherry
1 T. chives, chopped (optional)
Toast rounds
Parmesan or Swiss cheese,
   grated
Butter

Melt butter; whisk in flour and salt. Add half and half and stir until thick and bubbly. Combine 1 cup of cream sauce, lobster, mushrooms, green pepper, pimiento, salt, paprika, curry powder or Worcestershire sauce or Sherry and chives, if desired. Heap on rounds of toast. Sprinkle with cheese and dot with butter. Just before serving, heat under the broiler until cheese melts.
Serves 6.

Mrs. B. Thomas McElroy

CAROLE'S SALMON BALL

1 lb. can salmon or any leftover
   cooked salmon
1 8-oz. cream cheese
1 T. lemon juice
2 t. onion, grated
1 T. horseradish
¼ t. salt
¼ t. liquid smoke
½ c. pecans, chopped
3 T. parsley, chopped

Drain and flake salmon. Combine everything except parsley and pecans. Chill. Roll ball in a combination of parsley and pecans. Can be made and frozen immediately or made one or two days ahead and kept in refrigerator.
As an hors-d'oeuvres, will feed 12 people easily. but should be doubled for 20 or more.

Mrs. Arthur C. White

SALMON-STUFFED CUCUMBERS

2 cucumbers
6 oz. cream cheese
3 T. onion, minced
12 black olives, chopped
7 ¾ oz. can salmon, drained and
   flaked
Salt and pepper to taste
4 T. mayonnaise

Score cucumbers and cut into pieces about 1" thick. Scoop out centers, discard seeds, and chop flesh. Mix chopped cucumber with remaining ingredients. Fill cucumber cups and chill well before serving. A super appetizer on a summer evening.
Serves 8.

Mrs. Curtis Sanford, Jr.

SALMON LOG

1 1-lb. can salmon, drained and flaked, skin and bones removed
1 8-oz. pkg. cream cheese, softened
1 T. lemon juice
2 T. grated onion
1 t. prepared horseradish
¼ t. salt
1 t. liquid smoke seasoning
½ c. walnuts, chopped
3 T. parsley, finely chopped

Combine salmon with next 6 ingredients and mix well. Chill for several hours. Combine walnuts and parsley. Shape the salmon mixture into an 8" x 2" log and roll in nut mixture. Chill well. Serve with crackers as an hors-d'oeuvre.
Serves 8-12.

Mrs. Michael N. Robertson

SMOKED SALMON ROLLS WITH HORSERADISH CREAM

1 c. cream cheese
1 c. sour cream
1 c. horseradish, freshly grated
Salt
12 slices Nova Scotia smoked salmon, cut thin and long
Capers
Chopped parsley
Lemon wedges

Beat the cream cheese and sour cream to a smooth paste and add the horseradish, reserving a little for garnish. Add salt to taste. Spread the slices of salmon with the mixture and roll them loosely. To serve, arrange rolls on individual serving plates and garnish with capers, parsley, lemon wedges, and reserved horseradish. Pass thin rye bread and butter sandwiches cut in tiny fingers.
Serves 6.

Mrs. Mark Lemmon, Jr.

SHRIMP MOLD APPETIZER

11 oz. cream cheese, softened
3 T. mayonnaise
1 pkg. plain gelatin
2 T. cold water
1½ T. lemon juice
1 lb. or more cooked shrimp, finely chopped
½ c. celery, finely diced
½ onion, grated or diced
1 green pepper, diced
2 hard boiled eggs, diced
¼ t. Tabasco
Salt and pepper to taste

Combine cream cheese and mayonnaise. Soften gelatin in water. Heat this; then cool it and add to cream cheese mixture. Then add all remaining ingredients. Chill and serve with crackers. Also good to stuff tomatoes.
Serves 10-12.

Mrs. R. C. Bibby

SHRIMP ARNAUD

1½ lb. cooked, peeled, and
  deveined shrimp
SAUCE:
¼ c. celery, minced
¼ c. green onions, minced
¼ c. parsley, chopped
½ c. prepared mustard (prefer
  Dijon)
½ c. olive oil
½ c. white-wine vinegar
1 T. crushed red pepper
1 t. salt

Mix all sauce ingredients well. Mix
shrimp in sauce. Refrigerate 3-4 hours.
Serves 4-6.

Mrs. John P. Boone

SHRIMP BALLS

1¼ lbs. cooked shrimp
1 c. water chestnuts, minced
1 t. salt
1 clove of garlic, pressed
Cornstarch
1 egg
¼ c. green onions, minced
Wesson oil

Grind shrimp in a food grinder; mix in
water chestnuts, salt, 2 t. cornstarch, egg,
and onion. Chill. Roll into bite-size balls,
roll in cornstarch and sauté in oil until
brown. Serve with your favorite sweet
and sour sauce.
Makes 60 small balls.

Mrs. Frederick W. Burnett, Jr.

SHRIMP BUTTER

1 stick butter
1 8-oz. pkg. cream cheese
Juice of one lemon
4 T. mayonnaise
Salt, pepper and garlic to taste
4 oz. shrimp

Mix all ingredients together and chill.
May be kept in the refrigerator three
days. Serve with crackers or Doritos.
Serves 12.

Mrs. Frank W. Perry

Avocado with Ripe Olives, Green Peppers and Scallions Vinaigrette

SPINACH HORS-D'OEUVRE

1 pkg. frozen chopped spinach, defrosted
½ c. parsley, chopped
2-3 green onions, finely chopped tops and all
1 t. salt
1 t. pepper
Mayonnaise

Spinach must be drained very well in a sieve, using a fork to press water out. Don't skimp on the pepper and use mayonnaise somewhat sparingly (let it change the color of the spinach some.) Mix all ingredients together well and refrigerate several hours before using. Best served with rye or pumpernickel bread rounds but also good with vegetables or mild crackers.
Serves 6-8 as hors-d'oeuvres.

Mrs. J. Robert Ransone

MUSHROOM ROLLS

12-14 thin slices white bread
Softened butter
½ lb. fresh mushrooms, finely chopped
2 T. melted butter
½ t. curry powder
1 T. lemon juice
½ t. salt
Dash freshly ground black pepper
Dash cayenne pepper

Remove crusts from bread slices and roll slices to ⅛" thickness. Spread surface of bread thinly with softened butter and set aside. Sauté mushrooms until tender in melted butter with curry powder and lemon juice. Add salt, pepper, and cayenne. Spread 1 T. mushroom mixture over each slice of buttered bread. Roll like jelly roll and fasten ends with food picks. Place on baking sheets. Brush lightly with additional melted butter and bake in preheated over at 425° until lightly brown or about 15 minutes. May be sliced in half and frozen before baking. If so, bake frozen and allow additional baking time.
Serves 24.

Mrs. Larry K. Casey

MUSHROOMS STUFFED WITH SHRIMP

24 medium mushrooms,
   remove stems
½ stick butter
Salt and pepper to taste
1 c. Italian dressing
24 medium shrimp, cooked
Dill weed

Marinate shrimp in Italian dressing for 6 hours. Sauté mushrooms in butter for about 5 minutes. Remove and drain. Drain shrimp and place on mushrooms, securing with toothpicks. Sprinkle with dill. chill, and serve.
Makes 24.

Mrs. Searcy Ferguson, Jr.

SHRIMP REMOULADE

2 lbs. shrimp
¾ c. olive oil
½ c. wine vinegar
2 T. chili sauce
¼ c. Creole mustard
½ c. celery, minced
½ c. green onions, minced
1 bay leaf
1 t. salt
½ t. cayenne pepper
1 T. paprika

Mix all ingredients together and marinate shrimp in mixture for at least several hours and preferably overnight. Serve in a bowl with toothpicks for hors-d'oeuvres or several on shredded lettuce and sliced tomatoes as a salad. Garnish with cucumbers or avocados.
Serves 12.

Mrs. B. Thomas McElroy

SHRIMP TOAST

1 lb. raw shrimp
1 5-oz. can water chestnuts
¼ c. chives or green onions,
   sliced thinly
2 t. salt
1 t. sugar
1 beaten egg
15 slices extra thin bread
Fine dry bread crumbs

Grind shrimp, water chestnuts, and chives in meat grinder. Add salt, sugar, and egg: mix well. Spread on the bread and sprinkle with crumbs. Slice into four triangles. Fry shrimp side down first in 1″ oil heated to 400°. Drain and freeze. Place frozen shrimp toast in 400° oven for 5-7 minutes.
Makes 60.

Mrs. Larry Casey

ARTICHOKES
(Carciofe Alla Guida)

Choose fresh and very green artichokes. Pull off bottom row of tough leaves; cut off top to leave 3" of artichokes, at least. With a small sharp knife, working from bottom toward the top, turning artichokes slowly, taper it. The thorns and tops of tough outer leaves are tapered off, leaving the edible parts. The artichoke now resembles a flower. Cut off stems; rinse in cold water to which lemon juice has been added. Drain and dry. Holding artichoke at bottom, top head down on table to spread the leaves a little, sprinkle salt and pepper inside. Place artichokes in a deep saucepan, heads down and not too close together. Cover with olive oil and fry slowly over medium heat. Then turn on sides turning often to fry and brown evenly. When they are soft to pressure of a spoon, arrange in former position, heads down. Gently and slowly press bottoms firmly towards bottom of pan, raising heat a little so they will be crisp. When done Carciofe Alla Guida should resemble a chrysanthemum rather flat with widely spread leaves. To give them fried crispness (crócante) traditional to this dish, wet the hand with cold water and shake lightly over boiling oil, spraying it. Drain and serve hot.

Mrs. Mark Lemmon, Jr.

ASPEN ARTICHOKE APPETIZER

2 6-oz. jars marinated artichokes, finely chopped
1 small yellow onion, finely chopped
1 clove garlic, pressed
4 eggs
¼ c. bread or cracker crumbs, finely crushed
¼ t. black pepper
¼ t. oregano
¼ t. Tabasco
½ lb. sharp Cheddar cheese, shredded
2 T. parsley

Retain marinade from artichoke jars and sauté finely chopped onion in it. Add the garlic. After the onion and garlic are transparent and cooked, put a couple of thicknesses of paper towels over the skillet and soak up the excess oil. Beat the eggs; add the crumbs and seasonings. Add the cheese, onions, what is left of the marinade, and the chopped artichokes. Pour into a well-buttered 7" x 11" pan. Bake at 350° for approximately 30 minutes, or until you press it with your finger and it feels softly set. Cool in the pan before cutting into 1½" squares. It may be served warm, but cool it to cut into squares before warming it again. Freezes well.
Serves 24.

Mrs. Hubert M. Cook

ANTIPASTO

⅔ c. white vinegar
⅔ c. olive oil (or half Crisco)
¼ c. minced dry onion
2½ t. Italian seasoning
1 t. each salt, seasoning salt,
    garlic salt, onion salt, Accent
    and sugar
½ t. pepper
1 8-oz. can sliced mushrooms,
    drained
1 14-oz. can artichoke hearts,
    drained and chopped
1 small jar Spanish olives,
    drained and sliced
1 small can ripe olives
¼ c. bell pepper, chopped
½ c. celery, chopped

Combine and bring to a boil vinegar, oil, dry onion, Italian seasoning, salts, sugar, and pepper. Pour over vegetables and chill. May be served with crackers (Triscuits are good) as hors d'oeuvres or on a bed of lettuce as an appetizer.
Serves 36.

Mrs. John J. Kendrick, Jr.

ANTIPASTO

2 carrots, cut in rounds
1 green pepper, squared
1 4-oz. can button mushrooms
1 small jar cocktail onions
1 can artichoke hearts (8½-oz.
    dr. wt.), drained
1 7¾-oz. can pitted ripe olives,
    drained
MARINADE:
½ c. red wine vinegar
⅔ c. salad oil
1 t. garlic powder
1 6-oz. can tomato paste
3 t. Worcestershire
1 t. oregano
¼ t. basil
½ t. salt
¼ t. sugar
GARNISH:
Thin salami slices
Anchovies
Sardines
Provolone cheese
Crackers

Mix marinade ingredients together and pour over vegetables. Refrigerate at least overnight. Serve with a choice of garnish.
Serves 8

Mrs. J. Brevard Haynes

STUFFED BRUSSELS SPROUTS

½ lb. blue cheese, softened
¼ lb. cottage or ricotta cheese,
  drained if necessary
2 T. whipped butter
Cayenne pepper
Salt and pepper to taste
2½ lb. fresh Brussels sprouts
Dry vermouth
Lemon juice

Combine the cheeses, whipped butter, cayenne pepper, salt, and pepper. Sieve the mixture into another bowl; then chill until firm but still of spreading consistency. In a large kettle cook Brussels sprouts, which have been trimmed and rinsed, in boiling salted water for 10 minutes, or until they are just barely blanched and tender. Drain the sprouts and refresh them under cold running water. Marinate for at least 4-5 hours in equal parts of dry vermouth and lemon juice. At the end of marinating time pat the sprouts dry with paper towels and remove the centers with a small melon ball cutter. Fill the cavities with the cheese mixture and refrigerate.

Yield: Approximately 70 hors-d'oeuvres

Mrs. Hubert M. Cook

EASY HORS-D'OEUVRES

2 cans artichoke hearts,
  drained and quartered
2 cans hearts of palm, drained
  and sliced
2 cans button mushrooms,
  drained
1 pkg. Good Seasons Cheese-
  Garlic Dressing Mix

Put artichokes and palms in large container and cover with mixed Cheese-Garlic Dressing. Refrigerate and let marinate at least all day before serving. Add mushrooms at least ½ hour before serving. Drain vegetables from marinade before serving. Can be done a day ahead. Serves 10-12.

Mrs. G. Mark Cullum

KOHLRABI

6 kohlrabi
6 chili petines
Kosher salt
2 T. melted butter
2 T. mild vinegar
¼ t. prepared mustard
¼ c. mayonnaise
Dash Angostura Bitters
2 T. olive oil
1 T. buttermilk
1 t. celery seed

Trim off outside leaves and stems of kohlrabi. Boil in water with chili petines and heavy salt until fork can pierce kohlrabi but they are still firm. Blanch immediately to stop cooking and slice crossgrain in thin slices as soon as they can be handled. Douse in the butter while still warm. Pour on vinegar. In a bowl mix salt and mustard. Blend in the mayonnaise, bitters, olive oil, buttermilk, and celery seed; toss the kohlrabi lightly around till they are coated. Chill. Serve on shredded lettuce as an appetizer. To dress up each plate, add an artichoke heart, slice of pimiento stuffed green olive, bit of fresh parsley, squeeze of lemon.
Serves 8.

CRISP POTATO SKINS

Hollow out baked potato skins, using inside for creamed or sautéed potatoes, then cut the skins into long strips. Butter thoroughly. Sprinkle with salt and pepper (ground) and place in a 375-400° oven until crisp. These may be served with sour cream and chive dip or by themselves and are delicious with cocktails.

Mrs. Julian A. Wells

SWEET POTATO CHIPS

Peel and slice crosswise into very thin slices as many potatoes as desired. Soak in cold water overnight or in ice water a few hours. Drain and dry. Fry in hot deep fat (375°) until crisp. Drain and sprinkle with salt or a little powdered sugar. Excellent with salads.

Mrs. Julian A. Wells

MUSHROOM SQUARES ANN MARIE

1 4-oz. can mushrooms, stems and pieces, drained and chopped
2 slices bacon, crumbled
2 T. Swiss cheese (or any white cheese), shredded
2 T. mayonnaise or salad dressing
1 T. dried parsley flakes
⅛ t. crumbled dried rosemary leaves
Few grains of salt
6 slices white bread
Soft butter

Mix first 7 ingredients. Heat oven to 400°. Trim crusts from bread, butter lightly, and cut each into four squares. Place squares buttered-side down on cookie sheet. Spoon a small amount of mushroom onto each square. Bake for 5 minutes and serve hot.

Makes 24 canapes.

Mrs. John Bagwell

MUSHROOM TURNOVERS

PASTRY:
8 oz. cream cheese, softened
½ lb. butter, softened
Dash salt
2 c. sifted flour
FILLING:
½ lb. mushrooms
1 onion, minced
3 T. butter
2 t. flour
½ t. salt
Pepper to taste
½ c. sour cream
1 t. dried dill
1 egg yolk
2 t. milk or cream

Combine cheese, butter, and salt at room temperature; work into flour with fork or fingers until smooth dough is formed. Refrigerate several hours or overnight. Trim, wash, and mince mushrooms. Sauté with onion in butter until tender. Stir in flour, salt, and pepper. Cook 1-2 minutes. Remove from heat. Add sour cream and dill. Cool. Roll pastry about ⅛" thick on floured surface. Cut into 2" circles. Place a teaspoon of filling just off center on each circle. Fold and crimp edges with floured fork tines to seal. Brush tops with egg yolk beaten with milk or cream. Freeze. Bake frozen at 375° for 15-20 minutes, until light gold in color.

Serves 24

Mrs. John D. Williamson, Jr.

MARINATED MUSHROOMS

1 lb. can imported mushrooms, drained
2 T. fresh lemon juice
⅔ c. salad oil
1 clove garlic, minced
½ c. celery, sliced
2 T. stuffed green olives, sliced
2 T. ripe olives, sliced
1 T. parsley, chopped
1 T. capers
1 T. wine vinegar
Salt to taste

Mix ingredients together. Refrigerate at least 24 hours for flavors to blend. Drain before serving. Serve chilled.
Note: Can use Green Giant frozen mushrooms and cook according to package directions.
Serves 12.

Mrs. John P. Boone

STUFFED MUSHROOMS

1 lb. large fresh mushrooms
3 T. Parmesan cheese, grated
1 small onion, finely chopped
1 c. bread crumbs
1 T. parsley, chopped
2 T. melted butter
Salt and pepper to taste
Cooking oil

Remove stems from mushrooms after they have been washed. Chop stems and add remaining ingredients. Mix well and stuff inside mushroom caps — be generous! Place in pan which has been spread with 2 T. cooking oil or butter. Melt 2 more T. butter and pour over mushrooms. Bake 20 minutes at 350°.
Serves 8-10.

Mrs. James B. Hudnall III

BEVERAGES

AEROBICS BICEPS BOOSTER

6 oz. apple juice
½ banana
2 t. protein powder
1 t. lecithin powder
1 egg yolk
3 ice cubes

Blend all ingredients at least 3 minutes.
Serves 1.

Cookbook Committee

BLOODY MARYS FOR A CROWD

1 46-oz. can tomato juice
23 oz. vodka (½ of tomato juice can)
1 oz. lemon juice
1 oz. Worcestershire
12 to 20 drops Tabasco
1½ t. celery salt
1½ t. salt
6 pinches garlic powder
Black pepper to taste

Mix all ingredients well, and pour into pitchers.
Serves 12.

Mrs. Larry M. Nobles

CRANBERRY TEA

1 qt. cranberries
2 qts. water
1 c. sugar
1 c. orange juice
½ c. lemon juice
1 cinnamon stick

Boil berries in water until berries pop; strain. Add remaining ingredients and boil until it makes a syrup. Serve hot or cold.
Serves 10.

DOMENICA RUM PUNCH

3 oz. añjeo rum
3 T. lime juice
3 T. simple syrup
Nutmeg, freshly grated

Mix first 3 ingredients and pour over ice. Grate nutmeg over top.
Serves 1.

Dr. Harold Kimmerling

FRAPPE
(Fruit Punch)

1 qt. orange juice
1 pt. grape juice
1 pt. lemon juice
1 pt. grenadine (pomegranite juice)
3 32-oz. bottles ginger ale
1 gal. pineapple sherbet

Mix all ingredients together.
Serves 40.

Mrs. Walter F. Sosnowski

GREEN LIZARD

1 6-oz. can frozen limeade
1 can vodka
Fresh mint

Fill blender with ice, limeade, vodka, and a handful of fresh mint. Blend until slushy and serve.
Serves 2-4

Mrs. John Bagwell

HOT BUTTERED RUM AND CIDER

2" strip orange peel
1 t. brown sugar
½ jigger warmed rum
1 jigger rum
1 generous t. unsalted butter
Small piece of cinnamon stick
3 pinches ground cloves
3 pinches allspice
Hot cider

Put the first 3 ingredients into a flame-proof silver or pewter cup. Ignite the rum and let it burn out. Add remaining ingredients, fill the cup with scalding hot cider, and stir vigorously. Fabulous on a cold night.
Serves 1.

Cookbook Committee

HOT CRANBERRY PUNCH

2 t. whole allspice
⅓ c. brown sugar
2 sticks cinnamon
2 t. whole cloves
1 pt. cranberry juice
2½ c. pineapple juice
½ c. water

This is made in an electric percolator and barely serves 6 because everyone will want "seconds" . . . so, be ready to make a second pot. Put the spices into the basket and liquid in the pot. Let percolate until hot. Especially good around Christmas.

Mrs. James H. Holmes III

KENTUCKY TEA

1 gal. apple cider
Cloves
Stick cinnamon
Brown sugar
Allspice
Lemon juice
1 qt. gin

To apple cider add to taste, cloves, stick cinnamon, brown sugar, allspice, lemon juice, then add gin.
Serves 24.

Geneva Ashby Jones

MAI-TAI

2 oz. pineapple juice
2 oz. lime juice
1 oz. orange juice
2 oz. orgeat syrup
½ oz. grenadine
4 oz. Curaçao
4 oz. light rum
4 oz. dark rum

Mix all ingredients and pour into 4 old fashion glasses filled with finely crushed ice. Garnish with a pineapple strip. Serves 4.

Mrs. Peter Tart

MEXICAN COFFEE

½ c. instant powdered
   chocolate mix
½ c. instant coffee
¼ c. sugar or more
1 c. hot water
4 c. milk
1 T. cinnamon
1 t. vanilla
½ c. heavy cream, beaten stiffly
6 3″ pieces cinnamon sticks
   (optional)

Dissolve powdered chocolate mix, instant coffee, and sugar in hot water. In a large saucepan heat milk, cinnamon, and vanilla just to simmering. Using a rotary or electric beater, whisk in heavy cream.
Serves 6.

Mrs. Mark Lemmon, Jr.

GEORGE'S BRANDY MILK PUNCH

6½ c. brandy
8 pts. light cream
5 t. vanilla
6½ oz. powdered sugar
3 pts. vanilla ice cream
Nutmeg

Combine brandy, cream, and vanilla, mixing thoroughly. Add powdered sugar, stirring constantly until well dissolved. Cover and refrigerate for a minimum of 6 hours, or until very well chilled. (This may be done overnight.) Two hours before serving, add ice cream. Mix well until all ice cream is dissolved. Return to refrigerator until ready to serve. Sprinkle nutmeg to taste on individual servings.

This recipe will yield approximately 1¾ gallons of milk punch, enough for about 20 people.

Mrs. George W. Jalonick IV

MULLED WINE

2 c. sugar
10 whole cloves
8 cinnamon sticks
3 lemons, thinly sliced
⅓ c. brandy
½ gallon red wine (Burgundy)

In a 5-qt. kettle combine sugar, cloves, cinnamon sticks, and 4 cups of water. Bring to a boil, stirring; boil, uncovered, for 5 minutes. Remove from heat. Add lemons and let stand, covered, for 10 minutes. With a slotted spoon, lift out cloves and cinnamon sticks. Add brandy and wine. To serve, simmer, uncovered, just until hot. Serve in mugs. Makes 3 quarts.
Serves 24.

Cookbook Committee

ORANGE FLIP

1 6-oz. can frozen orange juice
2 cans ice cold water
1 c. crushed ice
2 eggs
2 t. sugar (or more to taste)

Put all ingredients in blender, and blend for about 1 minute, or until of the consistency of soft sherbet. Serve in 2 large glasses to youngsters in too big a hurry for breakfast or in small old-fashioned glasses to 6.

Mrs. John McDonough

SANGRIA

½ lb. strawberries, washed and halved
2 ripe peaches, peeled and cut into small pieces
2 bananas, peeled and sliced
Juice and rind of 1 lemon
1½ T. sugar
¾ t. cinnamon
2 bottles ordinary red wine

In a large pitcher put strawberries, peaches, bananas, lemon juice and rind, sugar, and cinnamon. Add wine and stir the mixture thoroughly, mashing the fruit slightly. Let the Sangria stand at room temperature for at least 1 hour. Just before serving, add 20 ice cubes and stir the mixture briskly until it is ice cold. Substitute pineapple, oranges, etc. if above fruit is not available.

Cookbook Committee

OGLESBY'S SANGRIA

½ c. sugar
1 c. cold water
1 lemon
1 lime, thinly sliced
1 orange, thinly sliced
12-16 ice cubes
1 bottle red wine
Add brandy or Cointreau, (optional)

Combine sugar and water. Place over moderate heat. Stir constantly until sugar dissolves. When just boiling, remove and add lemon, lime and orange. Marinate at least four hours. Place contents of ice tray in pitcher and add 6 slices of marinated fruit and ½ c. syrup. Fill pitcher with bottle of red wine. Place 1 slice of orange and lime in each glass. (If you can get peaches, put that in it.) Makes 1 quart.

Mrs. Enslie O. Oglesby, Jr.

MINT ICED TEA

3 c. boiling water
12 sprigs fresh mint
4 regular tea bags
1 c. orange juice
Juice of 2 lemons
1 c. sugar
6 c. cold water

Combine first three ingredients and steep for 8 minutes. Remove tea bags and mint and let cool. Combine juices with sugar and water, stirring to dissolve sugar. Strain mint-tea mixture and add to juices. Serve over ice garnished with a sprig of mint.
Serves 6.

Mrs. Horace R. Nash, Jr.

SPICED TEA MIX

2 c. sugar
2 c. Tang
1 small jar lemon-flavored tea
   (1-oz.)
1 heaping t. cinnamon
1 level t. ground cloves

Put all ingredients in a large bowl, and mix well. Store in a jar. For 1 cup of hot spiced tea, put 2 t. of mixture in a cup, fill with boiling water and stir.

Mrs. Peter M. Tart

THE FAMOUS VELVET HAMMER

1 qt. vanilla ice cream
4 jiggers brandy
2 jiggers Cointreau
2 jiggers crème de cacao

Put all ingredients into blender and mix. Serve at once in chilled stemmed glasses. Great dessert with rolled cookies or as an after-dinner drink.
Serves 4.

Mrs. Larry M. Nobles

SALADS

ARTICHOKE SALAD

2 cans water-packed artichoke
hearts (8½-oz. dr. wt. each)
1 6½-oz. can water chestnuts
8 good-sized white mushroom
caps
6 green onions
Oil and vinegar
Salt and pepper
1 T. mayonnaise
Bibb or romaine lettuce

Wash artichoke hearts, drain, and put them in a salad bowl. Slice water chestnuts as thinly as you can and add to bowl. Also, slice mushroom caps thinly and the same with the green onions, using some of the green tops. Put on bed of lettuce. Make a dressing of oil and vinegar, salt, pepper, and add mayonnaise. Beat well and pour over salad. Serves 4-6.

Mrs. John Bagwell

ARTICHOKES WITH NINON SAUCE

2 fresh artichokes
2 lemon slices
Water
1 T. salt
NINON SAUCE:
5 T. peanut oil
2 T. white wine vinegar
1 shallot or green onion, finely
chopped
1 hard-cooked egg, seived
1 T. Dijon mustard
1 T. mixed parsley and chives
(or green onion tops)
Salt and pepper to taste

Remove discolored leaves from well-washed artichokes. Trim off about ½ inch of the top of each leaf. Trim the base even with the leaves. Place lemon slices in a large saucepan and put the artichokes on top of them. Add about 1½ inches of water and 1 T. of salt. Boil until tender, covered (about 50 minutes). Serve either warm or cold with Ninon Sauce.

Sauce: Mix oil and vinegar well then add other ingredients, mixing well. Serve in a bowl for dipping artichoke leaves. Serves 2.

Mrs. Harold W. Kimmerling

MARINATED ASPARAGUS-ARTICHOKE SALAD

⅔ c. olive oil
⅓ c. tarragon vinegar
2 T. sweet pickle relish
1 T. chives, minced
1 hard-boiled egg, diced
¾ t. salt
1 small jar pimiento, chopped
Pepper
2 T. parsley, chopped
2 large cans white asparagus
1 large can artichoke hearts

Make vinagrette dressing by slowly adding vinegar to oil, stirring constantly. Add rest of ingredients. Pour over vegetables and refrigerate. Pretty and good with beef.
Serves 6.

Mrs. Charles J. Pierce, Jr.

ANNE BARTON'S SALAD

3 cans (8½-oz. dr. wt. each)
  artichoke hearts, quartered
3 lbs. asparagus, cooked until
  barely tender and cut on the
  slant
1 can (8 oz. dr. wt.) hearts of
  palm, cut in slices
½ onion, minced
⅔ c. oil (⅓ c. olive and ⅓ c.
  salad oil)
½ c. lemon juice
1½ t. salt
1 t. Dijon mustard
Seasoned pepper

Combine all ingredients and marinate overnight.
Serves 12.

Mrs. Harold W. Kimmerling

AVOCADO LIME SALAD

½ c. water
½ c. pineapple juice
1 3-oz. pkg. lime Jello
½ c. whipping cream
½ c. mayonnaise
1 8-oz. can crushed pineapple,
  drained
1 avocado, diced
3 T. lemon juice
Pinch of salt

Bring water and pineapple juice to a boil, add Jello, and let cool until slightly firm. Whip cream; blend in mayonnaise, pineapple, avocado, lemon juice and salt. Fold into cooled Jello. Pour into a mold or individual molds until set.
Serves 8.

Mrs. George W. Jalonick III

AVOCADO-MUSHROOM PIQUANT

2 barely ripe avocados, peeled
  and sliced
3 cups (8 oz.) fresh mushrooms,
  sliced
½ c. salad oil
3 T. tarragon vinegar
2 T. lemon juice
2 T. water
1 T. parsley, snipped
1 clove garlic, minced
¾ t. salt
Dash of pepper

Mix well all ingredients except avocados and mushrooms and pour over the vegetables. Chill several hours and drain before serving. Wonderful summer dish. Serves 8.

Mrs. Larry K. Casey

GRAPEFRUIT AND AVOCADO SALAD

Pink grapefruit slices
Avocado slices
Candied ginger
½ c. hot ketchup
½ c. salad oil
½ c. white vinegar
¾ c. sugar
¼ t. celery seed
1 T. chives
1 clove garlic, peeled and cut in
  half
Salt and pepper to taste

For the dressing, mix all except the first three ingredients together in a blender (omitting garlic) and blend. Add garlic, pour into a jar, and store in the refrigerator overnight or for several days. Remove garlic before pouring over salad. For salad, arrange grapefruit and avocado slices on lettuce leaves and sprinkle with chopped, candied ginger. Pour dressing over all.
Serves 8.

Mrs. E. Don Rott

THREE BEAN SALAD

1 1-lb. can cut green beans
1 1-lb. can cut wax beans
1 1-lb. can kidney beans
1 4-oz. jar pimientos, chopped
1 large onion, sliced thin

MARINADE:
⅓ c. wine vinegar
⅓ c. salad oil
⅓ c. sugar
1 t. salt
½ t. pepper
½ t. celery seed
¼ t. basil

Drain beans well and add onion and pimiento.

Add beans and onion mixture to marinade and place in covered bowl in refrigerator. Leave several hours before serving and toss several times. This will keep well for a week or more.
Serves 12.

Mrs. David Grafe

CALIFORNIA SALAD BOWL

1 head lettuce
1 bunch watercress
1 avocado
1 lemon
1 lb. boned chicken breast,
   cooked and cubed
12 slices crisp-cooked bacon,
   crumbeld
3 medium tomatoes, chopped
   or 18 cherry tomatoes
⅓ c. blue cheese, crumbled
1 c. pimiento-stuffed olives,
   sliced
DRESSING:
¼ c. red wine vinegar
2 t. dried tarragon
½ t. salt
Freshly-ground pepper
½ c. salad oil
1 T. Dijon mustard

Wash lettuce and watercress, draining well. Dry greens with a paper towel and chop lettuce and watercress in a large salad bowl. Peel and slice avocado into thin wedges, then sprinkle with lemon juice. Arrange attractively avocado, chicken, crumbled bacon, tomatoes, blue cheese, and olives on top of the greens. Refrigerate and make a dressing by mixing vinegar, tarragon, salt, and pepper to taste in a jar. Let stand at least 30 minutes. Beat in oil and mustard. Toss on salad or serve to the side.
Serves 6.

Mrs. Arthur C. White

CHICKEN SALAD

1 2½-lb. chicken
Chopped celery, to taste
1 t. salt
½ t. pepper
1¼ c. mayonnaise
Toasted almonds
Green grapes

Parboil chicken in covered pan with a small amount of water, salt, and pepper. When cooked, reduce broth in which chicken was cooked until ¾ cup left. Add broth to mayonnaise, chopped chicken, and chopped celery and garnish with almonds and/or green grapes.
Serves 6.

Mrs. Arnold Schoellkopf

COLD CURRIED CHICKEN SALAD

2 c. uncooked rice
1 c. raw cauliflower buds,
chopped in ¼" pieces
8 oz. creamy French dressing,
bottled
1 c. mayonnaise
1 T. curry powder, or more
1 T. salt
1½ t. pepper
½ c. milk
6-7 c. cooked chicken, diced
1 c. green pepper, chopped
1 c. celery, chopped
1 c. red onion, chopped

Cook rice, wash, and chill. Toss chilled rice, cauliflower, and French dressing. Chill in refrigerator. Mix mayonnaise, curry powder, salt, and pepper. Slowly mix in milk, then chicken. Refrigerate. Next day combine rice and chicken mixtures with green pepper, celery, and onion.

Serves 12-14.

Mrs. George W. Bramblett, Jr.

MACADAMIA CHICKEN SALAD

2 c. white chicken meat, cooked
1 T. tarragon, freshly chopped
(or 1 t. dried tarragon soaked
in 2 T. white wine for 45
minutes)
1 c. mayonnaise
½ c. sour cream
⅔ c. macadamia nuts
4 hard-boiled eggs, quartered
Salt and pepper to taste
¼ c. capers (optional)

Combine chicken with tarragon. Add mayonnaise to sour cream and beat well. Salt and pepper to taste. Combine chicken, sour cream, mayonnaise, and macadamia nuts. Serve on a lettuce leaf; garnish with mayonnaise, capers, and hard-boiled eggs.

Serves 4-6.

Mrs. Wade C. Smith

HOT CHICKEN-ALMOND SALAD

2 c. cooked chicken, diced
1½ c. celery, diced
¼ c. almonds, chopped
5 t. onion, chopped
1 T. lemon juice
⅛ t. pepper
1 c. mayonnaise
Salt to taste
½ c. stuffed olives, chopped
1½ c. cheddar cheese, shredded
(reserve ½ c. for top)
2 T. chicken stock,
approximately

Mix all ingredients together and place in lightly greased casserole. Top with reserve cheese. Bake 375° for 25 minutes or until cheese on top is bubbling. Can be made in the morning and baked later.

Serves 4.

Mrs. Jerry D. Oden

CHUTNEY TURKEY SALAD

2 c. cooked turkey breast (or chicken), diced
1 c. drained pineapple tidbits (13¼-oz. can)
1 c. celery, sliced
¼ c. salted peanuts
½ c. green onions, sliced
¾ c. apple (unpeeled), cubed
DRESSING:
1 c. mayonnaise
3 T. chutney, chopped
½ t. lime rind, grated
2 T. lime juice
2 t. preserved ginger, minced
½ t. curry powder
¼ t. salt

Toss salad ingredients and add dressing. Mix well, chill, and serve on lettuce. Serves 6-8.

Miss Byrd Fuertes

CREAM COLESLAW

½ medium head cabbage, shredded
½ c. sour cream
2 T. sugar
2 T. vinegar
½ t. salt
Dash of pepper
Red onion, sliced thin
Paprika

Toss cabbage with all ingredients except onion and paprika. Spread sliced onion on top and sprinkle with paprika. Serves 4-6.

Mrs. W. Plack Carr, Jr.

CRAB AND RICE SALAD

1½ lbs. fresh white crabmeat
2 c. raw rice (not instant)
12 hard-boiled eggs, chopped
4 c. celery, chopped
1 pt. mayonnaise
1 pt. sour cream
1 c. olive oil
Frozen chives
Dried parsley flakes
Lemon-pepper Marinade
Lemon juice
Onion salt
1 c. ripe olives, chopped

Cook rice in salted water, drain and wash in cold water. Let stand in colander until it has dripped dry. Pick through crab for pieces of shell. Put crab in a large bowl; add cooked rice, eggs, celery, olives, chives, and parsley. Mix in mayonnaise, sour cream, and olive oil. Then add onion salt, lemon-pepper marinade, and lemon juice to taste. Chill well. It is wise to make this the day it is to be used. Serve on a large tray with lettuce leaves around it and a variety of fresh salad vegetables, all marinated. Serve with ham, hot rolls, and a dessert. Serves 12-16.

Mrs. L. G. Pondrom

CUCUMBER AND SOUR CREAM SALAD

4 cucumbers, peeled, halved,
  seeded, and cut into slices
2 T. salt
2 T. white vinegar
DRESSING:
2 hard-boiled eggs
½ t. salt
1 t. Dijon mustard
¾ c. sour cream
1 T. white wine vinegar
½ t. sugar
1 t. olive oil
White pepper to taste
1 t. fresh dill leaves, minced or
  ½ t. dried dill leaves
Few drops of lemon juice to
  taste

Combine cucumber slices, salt, and vinegar and toss. Marinate at room temperature for 30 minutes; then drain and pat dry with paper towels. For dressing separate yolks from the whites of the eggs. Cut whites into strips and add to cucumber. Mash egg yolks with a fork. Slowly beat in mustard, sour cream, white wine vinegar, sugar, and pepper. Add lemon juice to taste and the dill leaves. Pour over cucumbers and toss gently. Refrigerate until ready to serve.
Serves 4-6.

Mrs. Edward W. Rose III

EGG SALAD

6 hard-boiled eggs
3 heaping T. mayonnaise
½ t. mustard
3 dashes Worcestershire sauce
8 pieces bacon, fried crisp
Lawry's Seasoned Salt to taste
Salt and pepper to taste

Put eggs through an egg slicer, then chop the slices up thoroughly. Mix the chopped egg with the mayonnaise, mustard, Worcestershire sauce, Lawry's, and salt and pepper. Crumble the bacon into medium-sized bits and mix with other ingredients. Refrigerate and allow to sit for about 4 hours for flavors to blend well.
Serves 4.

Mrs. George W. Jalonick III

GRANDMOTHER'S SALAD

4 unpeeled apples, chopped
5 bananas, sliced
½ c. nuts, chopped
½ c. sugar
2 T. flour
¼ t. salt
1 c. milk
½ stick butter

Mix and cook the last 5 ingredients over medium heat until thickened. Cool several hours or overnight before adding to apples and bananas. Must be served immediately.
Serves 12-14.
Always on Thanksgiving and Christmas.

Mrs. Carey G. King, Jr.

GREEK SALAD

1 medium eggplant
2-3 zucchini, chopped
1 clove garlic, minced
1 medium onion, minced
2 tomatoes or
    12 cherry tomatoes
½ c. pine nuts, lightly roasted
½ c. parsley, chopped
Salt and pepper
¼-½ c. oil (olive, or half salad
    and half olive)
Lemon wedges

Chop unpeeled eggplant and zucchini, sauté with onion, and garlic in oil until just tender. Cool. Add peeled, seeded, and chopped tomatoes (or halved cherry tomatoes), pine nuts, and parsley. Season well with salt, pepper, and lemon juice. Chill before serving, and garnish with lemon wedges. Serves 6-8.

Mrs. Edward W. Rose III

DAY-AHEAD GREEN SALAD

Iceberg lettuce in bite-size
    pieces
Fresh spinach in bite-size
    pieces
Pkg. frozen peas, uncooked
2 bunches green onions, sliced
8 pieces crisp bacon, crumbled
5 hard-boiled eggs, sliced
DRESSING:
1 c. sour cream
½ c. mayonnaise
1 pkg. Good Season's Italian
    Salad Dressing

In a long pyrex dish, layer lettuce, spinach, peas, onions, eggs, and bacon. Mix dressing ingredients together and spread over top. Seal and let sit in refrigerator for 24 hours. Sprinkle with croutons before serving.
Serves 8-10.

Mrs. Wade C. Smith

HERB GARDEN SALAD

6 ripe tomatoes, peeled and
   chopped
2 small or 1 large cucumber,
   chopped
1 t. salt
¼ t. coarse black pepper
1 t. sugar
½ t. thyme
1 t. dill, snipped
¼ c. parsley, chopped
¼ c. chives, chopped
⅔ c. salad oil
¼ c. tarragon vinegar
1 red onion, sliced paper thin

Place vegetables in a bowl and sprinkle with seasonings and herbs. Combine oil and vinegar and pour over all. Chill several hours or overnight, spooning dressing over vegetables occasionally. Drain off dressing to serve.
Serves 6.

Mrs. Stephen Summers

ITALIAN SALAD

SALAD:
⅓ part romaine lettuce
⅔ part iceberg lettuce
Feta cheese, crumbled
Green onions, sliced
Ripe olives
DRESSING:
1 pt. olive oil
6 oz. white wine vinegar
1 T. oregano
Salt and pepper to taste
1 lemon, squeezed and dropped
   in
Fresh garlic, minced

Let salad sit, mixed, for 5 to 10 minutes.
Serves 6-8.

Mrs. Oscar J. Lalla III

POTATO SALAD

3 lbs. new potatoes
1½ t. vinegar
2 T. oil
1½ t. salt, pepper and garlic salt
¾ t. dill
1 c. celery, sliced
⅓ c. green onions, chopped
1 8-oz. carton yoghurt
2 t. prepared mustard
1 t. honey

Cook potatoes until done, peel and add to other ingredients. Chill.
Serves 6-8.

Mrs. Mark Lemmon, Jr.

HOT POTATO SALAD

3 lbs. potatoes, medium-sized
1 c. green onions, chopped
½ t. celery seed
2 t. salt
⅛ t. pepper
6 slices bacon, diced
½ c. apple cider or wine vinegar
2 T. sugar (or less)
3 T. water
1 egg, room temperature,
   beaten
2 T. parsley, minced

Cook potatoes until tender and cool. Peel and slice into a large bowl. Add onion and next 3 ingredients. Mix and keep warm. Cook bacon until crisp and drain, saving drippings. Mix vinegar, sugar, and water with cool bacon drippings. Heat to simmering, add slowly to egg, beating constantly. Pour over potatoes, add ½ of bacon and parsley. Mix and serve warm decorating top with remaining bacon and parsley.
Makes 8 servings.

Mrs. Walter N. Kuntz III

SALADE NIÇOISE

1 pkg. frozen green beans, any
   cut
1 7½-oz. can best-grade white
   tuna, chilled
½ c. olive oil
¼ c. tarragon vinegar
Pinch of salad herbs
1 T. onion salt
Dash Tabasco
2 large fresh tomatoes, peeled
   and quartered
4 hard-boiled eggs, quartered
Greek black olives
8 anchovy filets
Lettuce

Cook beans until just barely tender in salted water. Drain immediately and put in a bowl. Add olive oil, vinegar, salad herbs, onion salt, and Tabasco. Stir well. Cover and refrigerate at least 24 hours. Stir once a day if left for several days. Just before time to serve quarter the eggs and peel and quarter the tomatoes. Tear enough lettuce for 4 servings and put in a bowl with beans and toss. (There should be some extra dressing in the bowl which can be poured off for use in a moment; if not, make a little more in a small bowl from the ingredients used in the first dressing.) Arrange the beans and lettuce on 4 plates, making a hole in the middle. Divide the tuna into 4 parts and put into the center of each plate. Put 2 tomato quarters and 4 egg quarters on each plate. Spoon excess dressing over. Cross 2 anchovy filets on top of each helping of tuna. Halve some black olives and distribute around. Serve with crisp crackers or hot cheese bread. Can substitute chicken or shrimp for tuna.
Serves 4.

Mrs. L. G. Pondrom

SAUERKRAUT SALAD RUISSE

1 lb. jar sauerkraut
1 medium onion, chopped
1 medium green pepper, diced
1 16-oz. can whole-berry
  cranberry sauce
½ c. sugar
½ c. vinegar
2 c. celery, chopped
1 2-oz. jar pimientos, chopped

Drain sauerkraut, keeping juice. Mix sugar, juice, and vinegar and heat. Pour over kraut and add remaining ingredients. Refrigerate. Much better the second day.
Serves 8.

Mrs. Arnold Schoellkopf

RUSSIAN SALAD

3 or 4 tomatoes, peeled
8 cold new potatoes, boiled,
  unpeeled
2 cucumbers
½ bunch radishes
1 c. fresh or frozen peas,
  steamed until tender and
  chilled
2 or 3 carrots, peeled
Lots of fresh dill, minced
4 cooked and chilled chicken
  breasts (may substitute tuna,
  crab, or shrimp)
DRESSING:
1 c. sour cream
1 c. mayonnaise
3-4 T. good oil and vinegar-
  based French dressing
  (optional)

Dice and combine all ingredients. Salt and pepper to taste. Mix dressing and combine with vegetables. Serve very cold on lettuce leaves with bread sticks, homemake Melba toast, or a warm crusty French bread. A very healthy lunch all in one dish — great to keep on hand on the weekend.
Serves 12.

Mrs. Edward W. Rose III

SALMON SALAD

1 c. canned or fresh cooked
  salmon
⅔ c. hot cooked rice (not
  instant)
¼ c. bottled French dressing
¾ c. mayonnaise
½ t. celery salt
1 hard-boiled egg, grated
½ t. salt
½ t. pepper
1 T. onion, minced
1 t. fresh horseradish
½ c. celery, chopped

Add French dressing to hot rice. Cool a bit then add remaining ingredients. Allow to marinate in refrigerator at least 5 hours though better overnight.
Serves 4.

Mrs. Theodore P. Votteler

SHRIMP REMOULADE

1 lb. cooked shrimp
½ lb. king crab legs, cooked and
  cut into chunks
Lettuce
SAUCE:
2 c. mayonnaise
2 T. finely chopped cucumber
  pickle or relish
2 T. drained capers, chopped
2 T. prepared mustard
2 T. parsley, finely chopped
¼ c. tarragon, crushed
½ t. chervil, crushed
1½ t. anchovy paste
Dash of Tabasco
2 T. fresh lemon juice
Hard cooked eggs
Cucumber
Tomatoes
Ripe olives
Radishes
Green pepper, sliced

Mix all of the sauce ingredients together. To serve, line center of individual plates with lettuce leaves. Place some shredded lettuce in the center of each plate. Mound shrimp and crab on lettuce. On the rim of your plate put a quartered egg, quartered cucumber, quartered tomato, ripe olive, radishes, and slices of green pepper. Spoon sauce generously over the shrimp and crab. Pass additional sauce. Serves 4-6.

Mrs. William Henry Marsh III

CURRIED SHRIMP SALAD

1 lb. shelled and cooked
  shrimp, chilled
½ c. green pepper, chopped
1 c. celery, chopped
4 whole green onions, chopped
½ c. mayonnaise
½ c. sour cream
Juice of 1 lemon
1½ t. curry powder
½ t. salt
Coarse ground pepper to taste

Cut shrimp into bite-size chunks; add green pepper, celery, and green onions. Mix remaining ingredients together to make a sauce. Stir sauce into shrimp mixture until all shrimp are well coated. Refrigerate for at least 4 hours before serving. Flavors will blend better during that period and salt and lemon flavors will subside some. Lump crabmeat may be substituted for the shrimp. Serves 4.

Mrs. George W. Jalonick IV

SPINACH AND APPLE SALAD

4 bunches fresh spinach,
washed, dried, and stems
removed
1 c. red onion rings, thinly
sliced
1 c. walnuts, coarsely chopped
1 red delicious apple, cored and
thinly sliced
DRESSING:
3 T. lemon juice
½ c. salad oil
2 T. sugar
1 small clove garlic, crushed
1 t. salt

Mix dressing ingredients together and
pour over salad ingredients. Toss.
Serves 8.

Mrs. Edward W. Rose III

SPINACH SALAD

Garlic pod
5-6 strips bacon, cooked, and
bacon grease reserved
1 can mandarin oranges
1 T. tarragon vinegar
1 pkg. fresh spinach, washed
and drained
Beau Monde, salt, and pepper
to taste

Rub wooden bowl with garlic pod. Drain
juice from oranges and boil until thick.
To make dressing combine 2 T. bacon
grease, mandarin orange juice, and tarragon vinegar. Warm. Pour over spinach.
Spinach should wilt slightly. Toss with
mandarin oranges and bacon, crumbled.
Season with Beau Monde, salt, and pepper. Top with croutons and sliced red
onions.
Serves 4-6.

Mrs. W. Plack Carr, Jr.

ANNE'S SPINACH SALAD WITH LEMON DRESSING

1 lb. fresh spinach
1 clove garlic
1 t. sugar
1 lemon rind, grated
½ t. salt
¼ t. pepper
¼ t. paprika
3 T. lemon juice
3 T. sour cream
½ c. oil

Blend all ingredients except spinach for
15 seconds. Toss with spinach and serve.
Serves 4.

Mrs. John Bagwell

FRESH SPINACH SALAD

DRESSING:
3 stalks celery, chopped
1 large onion sliced and divided
   into rings
1 garlic clove, minced
2 T. sugar
1 T. Worcestershire
2½ T. dry mustard
½ c. vinegar
⅔ c. oil
½ c. chili sauce
Paprika
SALAD INGREDIENTS:
1 pkg. fresh spinach, washed
   and drained
10 large fresh mushrooms,
   sliced
2-3 hard-boiled eggs, sliced
6 slices crisp bacon, crumbled

Marinate the dressing at least 8 hours, the longer the better. Toss over salad ingredients.
Serves 4.

Mrs. Walker Harman

STEAK AND MUSHROOM SALAD

12 small fresh mushrooms
1-1½ lb. leftover roast or steak,
   thinly sliced
12 cherry tomatoes, halved
1 can artichoke hearts, drained
   or 1 large avocado
1 head lettuce
2 T. parsley, chopped
3 T. blue cheese, crumbled
DRESSING:
½ c. olive oil
¼ c. red wine vinegar
2 t. Dijon mustard
1 garlic clove, crushed
1 t. salt
Freshly ground pepper
½ t. sugar

Combine dressing ingredients in a jar and shake well. Wash and rinse mushrooms. Slice and combine in a bowl with beef and tomatoes. Cut artichokes in half or fourths and add to beef. Marinate several hours or overnight. Line salad bowl with chilled shredded lettuce and arrange beef on it. Sprinkle with parsley and cheese. Great for lunch with wine and French bread.
Serves 4-5.

Mrs. Don McIlyar

TABOLLI

1 c. fine cracked wheat
1-2 tomatoes, chopped
4 green onions, chopped
3 sprigs fresh mint, chopped
4 sprigs fresh parsley, chopped
Juice of 2-3 large lemons
4 T. olive oil
1-2 t. salt
½ t. pepper, freshly ground

Soak the wheat for 15 minutes until soft. Squeeze water from wheat with hands very thoroughly. Then add the tomatoes, green onions, mint, and parsley. Mix the lemon juice, olive oil, salt, and pepper and add to wheat mixture. Mix all ingredients well. This is best made several hours ahead.
Serves 6.

Mrs. Oscar J. Lalla III

TACO SALAD

SALAD BOWL:
Chopped lettuce
Tomatoes
SKILLET:
2 lbs. ground meat
1 onion, chopped
1 green pepper, chopped
1 c. celery, chopped
1 T. cumin
¼ t. chili powder
Garlic salt to taste
DOUBLE BOILER:
1 lb. Velveeta cheese
½ can Ro-tel tomatoes
Corn chips

Brown meat with onion, green pepper, and celery. Add remaining skillet ingredients. Pour meat mixture over salad mixture. Pour cheese mixture over all. Crunch corn chips over top.
Serves 8.

Mrs. Don McIlyar

TOMATO SALAD

2 tomatoes, medium to large
½ c. oil
3 T. vinegar
1 t. Worcestershire sauce
¾ t. salt
⅛ t. pepper
1 T. sugar
½ clove garlic, minced
1 t. sweet basil
Pinch of thyme
2 T. green onion, chopped

Slice tomatoes and place in medium sized bowl. Combine remaining ingredients and pour over tomatoes. Refrigerate 1 hour. Drain tomatoes and serve on a bed of crisp greens.
Serves 4.

Mrs. George E. Seay, Jr.

MARINATED TOMATOES

6 fresh garden tomatoes,
  peeled, or good, whole
  canned tomatoes
⅔ c. salad oil
¼ c. fresh parsley, snipped
¼ c. green onions, sliced
¼ t. pepper
1 clove garlic, minced
¼ c. red wine vinegar
1 t. salt
½ t. thyme
½ t. marjoram

Marinate tomatoes in the remaining ingredients for 24 hours. Drain and serve as a salad on lettuce leaves.

Mrs. E. Don Rott

MARINATED VEGETABLE SALAD I

1 cauliflower
1 cucumber
1 green pepper
3 carrots
2 celery stalks
3 green onions, tops included
¾ c. vinegar
¼ c. oil
½ t. salt
¼ t. pepper
½ t. celery salt
¼ t. lemon-pepper marinade
¼ t. celery seed
¼ t. Lawry's seasoning salt

Cut all vegetables into bite-sized pieces. Mix remaining ingredients and pour over vegetables. Chill in refrigerator.
Serves 12.

Mrs. John R. Hill, Jr.

MARINATED VEGETABLE SALAD II

1½ c. fresh mushrooms, sliced
2 pkg. frozen asparagus,
  cooked and cut up
½ c. ripe olives, sliced
½ c. pimiento-stuffed olives,
  sliced
1 pkg. frozen artichoke hearts
  (may use canned or 2 jars
  marinated)
1 small onion, thinly sliced
MARINADE:
1½ c. corn oil
½ c. red wine vinegar
2 T. corn syrup
2 t. seasoned salt
1 T. basil
½ t. seasoned pepper

Mix marinade and pour over vegetables. Marinate for at least 2 hours in the refrigerator. Drain and reserve liquid. Mix vegetables with 2 heads torn lettuce. Drizzle dressing over top.
Serves 8-10.

Mrs. Robert G. Mebus

MIXED VEGETABLE SALAD

24-oz. pkg. frozen vegetables,
  chopped
1 c. mayonnaise
1 T. sugar
1 T. vinegar
2 T. dill weed (or more to taste)
3 small green onions, chopped
  with tops

Cook frozen vegetables about half the time suggested on the package, drain well, and let cool. Add remaining ingredients and chill overnight.
Serves 8.

Mrs. Joe Abbey

WATERCRESS SALAD

2 bunches watercress
1 cucumber
1 c. celery, chopped
½ c. lemon juice
½ c. olive oil
Cracked pepper
Salt
4-oz. pkg. blue cheese

Wash watercress. Slice cucumber (leave rind on cucumber for color) and celery. Toss together. Mix lemon juice, olive oil, pepper, and salt together. Pour over salad greens and toss. Top with crumbled cheese. Can be made in the morning if dressing is applied just before serving. Serves 8.

Mrs. Fulton Murray, Jr.

ASPARAGUS SALAD MOLD

1 pkg. lime Jello
1 c. boiling liquid (asparagus
  juice and enough water to
  make 1 cup)
¼ t. salt

1 c. mayonnaise
½ c. milk
1 3-oz. pkg. cream cheese
1 T. grated onion
1 T. vinegar
Dash of red pepper

Mix together salt, liquid, and Jello.

Blend these ingredients together. Combine both mixtures and add 14½-oz. can asparagus cut up. Pour into 8 individual molds, scooping asparagus into each one and chill.
Serves 8. Excellent with hot tuna and mushroom sandwich for lunch.

Mrs. M. Weatherby Carr

AVOCADO-CRANBERRY SALAD

1 3-oz. pkg. lemon jello
3 T. sugar
2 c. boiling water
1½ c. cold water
1 c. fresh cranberries, ground
1½ t. prepared horseradish
  (optional)
1 3-oz. pkg. lime jello
½ t. salt
1 T. lemon juice
1 ripe avocado, peeled and
  mashed
3 T. sour cream

Dissolve lemon jello and sugar in 1 c. boiling water. Add ¾ c. cold water. Chill until thickened. Fold in cranberries and horseradish; pour into 1½ quart mold. Chill until set but not firm. Dissolve lime jello and salt in 1 c. boiling water. Add ¾ c. cold water. Blend in avocado, lemon juice, and sour cream. Chill until slightly thickened; spoon over cranberry layer in mold. Chill until firm.
Makes 8-10 servings.

Mrs. Frank B. Houseman

AVOCADO MOLDED SALAD

2 envelopes unflavored gelatin
½ c. cold water
1 can consommé, heated
¼ c. cold water
½ small onion, grated
⅛ t. pepper
1 t. Worcestershire
¼ c. vinegar
2 t. lemon juice
3 t. sugar
2 avocados, coarsely chopped
½ c. celery, chopped fine
½ c. pimientos, chopped fine
Dash of Tabasco

Dissolve gelatin in ½ c. cold water and then put in hot consommé. Then add the next 7 ingredients. Fold in avocados, celery, and pimiento. Add Tabasco. Pour in individual molds and chill. Can be made the day before.
Serves 6-8.

Mrs. Denys Slater, Jr.

AVOCADO SALAD MOLD

1 6-oz. pkg. lemon jello
1 c. boiling water
1 c. mayonnaise
2 ripe avocados, mashed
  smooth
1 c. sour cream
¼ onion, finely grated

Pour boiling water over jello; stir and let cool. Add sour cream, mayonnaise, avocados, and onion. Pour in a wet mold and chill. Serve with watercress and mayonnaise.
Serves 8.

Mrs. John Ridings Lee

CONDIMENTS: Jalapeño Jelly, Rosy Relish

CHICKEN MOUSSE WITH PISTACHIOS

2 whole chicken breasts
½ c. chicken broth
1 pkg. unflavored gelatin
½ c. white wine
1 medium onion, diced
½ c. mayonnaise
Salt, pepper, nutmeg
1 c. heavy cream
⅓ c. pistachios, shelled and
  peeled

Boil chicken until tender, skin and bone and dice fine. Boil chicken broth, remove from flame and add gelatin, presoftened in wine, stir well. Cool to room temperature. Put in blender with onion, mayonnaise and blend at high speed while adding chicken bit by bit until puréed. Season with salt, pepper and nutmeg to taste and chill in shallow bowl until starts to set, 30-40 minutes. Beat cream, fold with pistachios into mixture, put in 6-cup ring mold (rinsed in cold water) and refrigerate.
Serves 6-8.

Cookbook Committee

CHILI SAUCE ASPIC

1 large bottle of chili sauce
½ green pepper, minced
½ onion, chopped
Few drops Tabasco
Salt
1 c. water
1 T. gelatin softened in ¼ c.
  water

Simmer for 20 minutes all of the ingredients except gelatin. Add gelatin mixture to hot sauce and stir. Pour into individual molds and chill. Finely chopped water chestnuts, minced lobster, or crabmeat may be added to the aspic.
Serves 6.

Mrs. Searcy Ferguson, Jr.

JELLIED CRANBERRY SALAD

3 envelopes gelatin
½ c. cold water
1 orange
1 lb. fresh cranberries
1 8½-oz. can crushed pineapple
3 c. sugar
1 c. boiling water
1 c. pecans, chopped
Pinch of salt
DRESSING:
1½ c. mayonnaise
½ c. sour cream
Sugar
2 T. frozen concentrated orange
   juice
Poppy seeds

Put gelatin in a large bowl and pour water over it. Stir well. Wash cranberries and orange and drain. Cut orange into quarters and grind with the cranberries in a meat grinder, catching the juice. Add 1 cup boiling water to the softened gelatin. Stir well to dissolve all the gelatin. Add sugar, salt, pineapple, the ground cranberries and orange plus the juice, and the pecans. Mix well and ladle into a mold or individual molds. For the dressing, mix mayonnaise, sour cream and orange juice, stirring to thaw the juice. Add sugar to taste and some poppy seeds. Serve salad on lettuce with dressing on top.
Serves 12-16.

Mrs. L. G. Pondrom

RAW CRANBERRY SALAD

1 qt. raw cranberries
2 oranges
1½ c. sugar
1 T. unflavored gelatin
¼ c. cold water
2 pkgs. raspberry gelatin
2¾ c. water
1 c. nuts, chopped

One day ahead: Put cranberries and both oranges (use peeling from one) through meat grinder or blender, add sugar and let stand overnight. Soften gelatin in cold water; make raspberry gelatin using 1 cup boiling water and 1¾ cups cold water. Add unflavored gelatin to hot mixture. Add cranberry mixture and nuts. Pour into a 12″ × 16″ glass pan. Chill until firm, usually overnight.
Serves 15.

Mrs. Justin S. McCarty, Jr.

CUCUMBER RING

¼ c. distilled white pickling vinegar
1 T. tarragon vinegar
¾ c. water
3 T. sugar
1 t. salt
A few grains red pepper
1 t. Worcestershire (more, if desired)
½ c. onion, chopped
2 cloves garlic, crushed
3 T. Knox gelatin
3 medium-size cucumbers, shredded
½ c. celery, chopped
½ c. mayonnaise
½ c. heavy cream, whipped
3 or 4 drops green coloring

Mix the vinegars with water. (White vinegar gives a lighter color but cider vinegar or even malt vinegar would do, and white wine vinegar would be delicious.) Add the sugar, salt, red pepper, Worcestershire, onion and crushed garlic cloves. Heat one cupful of this vinegar-water mixture and in it dissolve the gelatin. Add to the rest of the vinegar-water mixture and allow to cool 10-15 minutes. Meanwhile, shred cucumbers. (The Saladmaster is perfect for this job. If the cucumbers are young and tender they need not be peeled.) Add cucumbers and celery to the cooled vinegar-water mixture. Place in the refrigerator until partially congealed. Fold in mayonnaise and whipped cream. Add just enough green coloring to give a delicate pastel hue. Pour into a 1-qt. ring mold which has been rinsed in cold water. Allow to stand in the refrigerator at least 3-4 hours to set.
Serves 8-10.

Mrs. Mark Lemmon, Jr.

HAM MOUSSE

1 T. gelatin soaked in ¼ c. cold
  water
3 c. ham, cooked and ground
¼ c. celery, chopped
1 T. onion, grated
½ c. homemade mayonnaise (or
  commercial)
Worcestershire to taste
Salt and pepper to taste
Hard-cooked eggs

Combine gelatin mixture with ham, celery, onion, and mayonnaise. Add seasonings to taste. Moisten a mold with cold water. Decorate sides and bottom with eggs. Add other ingredients. Chill until firm. Unmold on bed of lettuce and garnish with tomato wedges and cold asparagus. Serve with extra mayonnaise. Serves 6-8.

Mrs. Winfield Oldham, Jr.

MRS. GARRETT O. MOORE'S MOLDED EGG SALAD

12 eggs
Salt and pepper
½ c. melted butter
2 T. catsup
1 t. Worcestershire sauce
Tabasco to taste
Thick tomato slices, marinated
  in oil and vinegar
Lettuce
SAUCE:
1 c. mayonnaise
Dash of Angostura bitters
1 T. Worcestershire sauce
1 T. lemon juice
½ bottle catsup
Dash red pepper

Boil eggs hard. Mix melted butter, catsup, Worcestershire sauce, and Tabasco. Peel eggs while hot. (The trick to this is to roll them on the table until the shell breaks at the rounded end of the egg, where the air sac is.) Salt and pepper each egg, pour over the liquid mixture, and press through a colander. Mix well and pack into muffin tins. Chill. Place tomato slices on bed of lettuce, top with molded egg. Pour over sauce.

Sauce: Blend all sauce ingredients. Chill. Serves 6-8. An ice cream scoop can be used instead of muffin tins.

Note: Could also use egg mixture to stuff cherry tomatoes. Can use sauce as a salad dressing.

Mrs. L. L. May, Jr.

LIME AND SOUR CREAM SALAD

1 small package lime Jello
½ c. hot water
½ pint (1 c.) sour cream
Small can crushed pineapple,
   drained

Stir Jello into hot water until dissolved and let stand 5 minutes. Add sour cream. Mix well, then add pineapple. Mold to cut in squares, little fancy cups, or in a ring mold with strawberries in center. Serves 6.

Mrs. Howell D. Harralson

MANGO SALAD

3 pkg. lemon Jello
3 c. water, boiling
large can mango juice
1 large can mangos
8 oz. cream cheese
DRESSING:
Honey
Brown sugar
Sour cream

Dissolve Jello in boiling water and add mango juice when Jello is cooled, about 30 minutes. Blend in blender mangos and cream cheese. Add blended mixture to cool jello mixture and refrigerate until congealed.

Dressing: Add honey and brown sugar to sour cream until sweet and according to taste. Sprinkle brown sugar on top. Serves 12.

Mrs. Craig O. Canon

SALMON MOUSSE

1 T. unflavored gelatin,
   softened in ¼ c. cold water
1 c. sour cream, heated (do not
   boil)
1 lb. can of salmon or 2 c.
   cooked salmon or other fish
¼ c. mayonnaise
1 T. onion, grated
¼ c. celery, finely chopped
1 c. heavy cream, whipped
Salt and white pepper to taste

Add softened gelatin to hot sour cream. Cool. Add the salmon, mayonnaise, onion, and celery. When mixture begins to congeal, fold in the whipped cream, correct seasonings and pour into greased 1 quart mold or 8 individual molds (½ c. each). Chill. Decorate with slices of pimiento and black olives. Serves 8.

Mrs. Ernest F. Kennedy, Jr.

SALMON SALAD MOLD

1 envelope gelatin
¼ c. cold water
1 c. mayonnaise
1 c. sour cream
1 T. onion, grated
2 T. lemon juice
¾ t. salt
1 lb. can red salmon, drained
   and flaked
2 hard cooked eggs, chopped
½ c. ripe olives, chopped
½ c. slivered almonds

Soak gelatin in water over hot water until dissolved. Stir in mayonnaise, sour cream, onion, lemon juice, and salt. Fold in salmon, eggs, olives, and almonds. Mold and chill until firm.
Serves 8.

Mrs. Peter R. Thompson

SHRIMP MOLD

1 can condensed tomato soup
2 8-oz. pkgs. Philadelphia
   cream cheese
2 T. unflavored gelatin
1 c. mayonnaise
1½ c. celery, chopped
1½ c. onion, chopped
2 c. cooked shrimp
CUCUMBER DRESSING:
1 cucumber, chopped
1 small onion, minced
1 8-oz. carton sour cream
1 T. mayonnaise
1 t. vinegar
1 t. salt

Heat soup, add cheese and melt. Dissolve gelatin in ½ c. cold water, add to soup mixture and cool. Add mayonnaise, onion, celery, and shrimp. Place in refrigerator overnight — either in loaf pan for easy slicing or a mold (covered). Serve with cucumber dressing. For dressing, mix all ingredients together and pour over individual servings. Garnish with tomato wedges and paprika.
Makes 10 2″ × 3″ squares.

Mrs. Sarah I. Roby

SWEET ANISE SALAD

1 head Bibb lettuce
1 bulb sweet anise
1 c. oil and vinegar dressing

Slice sweet anise in ¼″ slices. Use bulb and some of the spears. Marinate in the dressing for at least 3 hours. Serve on a bed of lettuce. The sweet anise can be used alone as a condiment with meat. It has a light licorice flavor.
Serves 6.

Mrs. Searcy Ferguson, Jr.

TOMATO-ARTICHOKE ASPIC

1 envelope unflavored gelatin
½ c. tomato juice, chilled
1 c. tomato juice, heated
¼ c. chili sauce
1 t. onion, grated
1 jar artichoke hearts, drained
 and chopped
½ c. green olives, chopped
½ c. celery, chopped
1 T. lemon juice
Salt and pepper to taste

Soak gelatin in chilled tomato juice for 5 minutes. Add heated tomato juice to gelatin and stir until gelatin is dissolved. Stir in remaining ingredients and chill. Serves 6-8.

Mrs. Robert S. Addison

TUNA MOUSSE

1 env. unflavored gelatin
2 T. lemon juice
½ c. boiling chicken broth
½ c. mayonnaise
¼ c. milk
2 T. chopped parsley
1 T. minced green onion
1 t. prepared mustard
1 t. dried dill weed
¼ t. pepper
1 7-oz. can tuna, drained and
 flaked
½ c. shredded cucumber

Soften gelatin in lemon juice in a large mixing bowl. Add broth. Stir to dissolve gelatin. Add next 7 ingredients. Beat until well mixed. Chill for 30 minutes or until slightly thickened. Beat until frothy. Fold in tuna and cucumbers. Turn into a 2-cup mold and chill 3 hours or until firm.
Serves 4.

Mrs. Robert G. Hallam

FRUIT SALAD DRESSING I

1 egg, well-beaten
1 c. sugar
Juice and grated rind of 1
 lemon, 1 lime, and 1 orange

Combine all ingredients in a saucepan. Cook over medium heat, stirring constantly, until boiling. Boil one minute. Remove and cool. Store in a covered jar in refrigerator. Will keep about two weeks. This is for fresh fruit.
Makes about 2 cups.

Mrs. George Searcy Watson

CREAMY FRUIT SALAD DRESSING

1 c. dates, sliced
½ c. Sauterne
1 T. fresh lemon juice
¼ t. salt
¼ t. grated orange rind
Few drops almond flavor
1 c. commercial sour cream
Maraschino cherry juice or grenadine
1-2 drops red food coloring
½ c. whipping cream, whipped

Mix dates, Sauterne, lemon juice, salt, orange rind, and almond flavor together and refrigerate for 2 hours or more. Blend sour cream, cherry juice, and food coloring. Stir into date mixture. Fold in whipped cream. Use over fresh fruits — watermelon, cantaloupe, honeydew, blueberries, pineapple, etc. Be sure to drain fruits and add dressing at the last minute.
Makes about 3 cups.

Mrs. J. Reynolds VanCleve

FRUIT SALAD DRESSING II

1 t. salt
1 t. celery seed
½ t. paprika
½ c. sugar
1 t. dry mustard
¼ c. vinegar
1 T. mayonnaise
1 t. onion juice or clove of garlic, crushed
1 c. salad oil

Put dry ingredients in bowl and mix. Add vinegar, mayonnaise, and onion juice or garlic and mix. Slowly add oil while beating with a wire whisk. Continue beating until it makes an emulsion. Remove garlic pieces before serving. Refrigerate. Stir before serving. Excellent on fruit salads.
Makes 2 c.

Mrs. J. Michael Brown

HONEY LIME DRESSING

1 c. sugar
½ c. honey
2 T. dry mustard
1 T. dry ginger
1 t. salt
⅓ c. lime juice
½ c. water
2 c. salad oil

Mix sugar, honey, mustard, ginger, and salt in a blender on low speed. Add lime juice and water. Add oil very slowly with blender on high. Delicious on fruit salad.
Makes about 1 quart.

Mrs. E. Don Rott

MINT DRESSING

¾ c. sugar
1 t. dry mustard
1 t. salt
⅓ c. vinegar
2 T. onion
3 T. fresh mint leaves
1 c. salad oil

Mix sugar, mustard, salt, and vinegar in blender. Add onion and mint and blend on high speed. Add oil very slowly and blend until thick. Store in refrigerator and serve on fresh fruit salad.
Makes approx. 2 cups.

Mrs. Patrick C. Guillot

BETTY NEALE'S SALAD DRESSING

3 whole eggs
1 qt. buttermilk
1 qt. salad oil
1½ t. garlic
½ T. Accent
½ t. dry mustard
1 T. salt
1½ t. Worcestershire sauce
¼ c. lemon juice
1 t. onion salt
Anchovies, optional

Beat eggs well. Add dry ingredients. Slowly add oil (like when making mayonnaise.) When ⅔ of the oil has been added, add lemon juice and Worcestershire. Add remaining oil, then buttermilk. Add anchovies if desired.
Makes about 2½ quarts.

Mrs. William F. Neale, Jr.

BLUE CHEESE SALAD DRESSING

4 oz. blue cheese, softened
¾ c. mayonnaise
½ c. sour cream
¼ t. cayenne or less
Salt
Tarragon vinegar
2 T. dried minced onions
Light cream

Put cheese in a pint jar and mash it against the sides of the jar with a fork, getting out as many lumps as possible. The smoother the cheese is the better the dressing will be. Add mayonnaise, sour cream, and cayenne and stir to mix well. Add salt and vinegar to taste. Add dried onions last. Fill jar to the top with light cream and chill. This will keep an indefinite period in the refrigerator.
Makes 1 pt.

Mrs. L. G. Pondrom

DUTCHIE'S BLUE CHEESE DRESSING

4 oz. blue cheese
½ c. mayonnaise
½ c. sour cream
3 T. milk
2 T. lemon juice
Salt to taste

Mix all ingredients and put on tossed salad.
Makes approx. 1½ cups.

Mrs. Patrick C. Guillot

CALAVO DRESSING

2 ripe calavos (avocados)
½ c. celery, chopped
2 T. onion, finely chopped
1 clove garlic, crushed
3 c. heavy French dressing

Mash avocados with a fork. Add along with celery, onion and garlic, to the dressing. This makes 4-5 cups of dressing. (If you want a thicker dressing, use only 2 cups of the French dressing.) Keeps well in the refrigerator in a tightly-covered jar.

Mrs. Mark Lemmon, Jr.

CUCUMBER SAUCE OR DRESSING

1 c. mayonnaise
1 c. cucumber, chopped
2 t. chives, chopped
1 t. parsley, chopped
½ t. salt
½ t. dill weed

Combine ingredients and chill.
Makes 1 pt.

Mrs. Joe E. Funk, Jr.

FRENCH DRESSING

1 c. salad oil
⅓ c. vinegar
2 T. sugar
2 t. ketchup
2 t. chili sauce
2 t. prepared mustard
1 t. salt
1 small onion, grated

Mix all ingredients well and shake before serving.
Makes 1½ c.

Mrs. W. Weatherby Carr

BLENDER FRENCH DRESSING

2 egg yolks
1 pt. salad oil
½ c. sugar
Dash red pepper
1 t. salt (scant)
1 T. sweet Hungarian paprika
½ c. vinegar (⅔ white, ⅓ tarragon)
1 clove garlic, minced very fine or crushed

Beat raw eggs until creamy. Add oil and beat and beat again. Add all dry ingredients. Then add vinegar, beating constantly. Add garlic. This is a very heavy dressing and can be made very well and quickly in the blender.

Mrs. Mark Lemmon, Jr.

GREEN GODDESS DRESSING

1 2-oz. can anchovies
1 large avocado, peeled and seeded
1 clove garlic, grated
⅓ c. tarragon vinegar
⅓ c. mayonnaise

Drain anchovies, reserving oil. Put anchovies and avocado through ricer. Add garlic. Combine anchovy oil, vinegar, and mayonnaise. Add to avocado mixture. Serve at once on shredded lettuce.
Makes about 1¼ c. dressing.

Mrs. L. K. Lancaster, 1948 Junior League Cookbook

GORGONZOLA SALAD DRESSING

2 oz. Gorgonzola cheese
1 garlic clove, minced
½ t. dried tarragon
½ t. oregano
½ t. basil
⅓ c. olive oil
1 T. red wine vinegar

In a blender mix all ingredients except olive oil. Add oil slowly. Salt and pepper to taste.
Makes about ¾ of a cup.

Mrs. John D. Worley

ROQUEFORT DRESSING

1 pint mayonnaise
½ pt. sour cream
2 T. lemon juice
Dash of salt
Dash of garlic salt
2 t. grated onion
4 to 7 oz. Roquefort cheese or
   blue cheese

Mix all ingredients well and store in the refrigerator indefinitely.
Makes about 4 cups.

Mrs. Larry K. Casey

RUSSIAN DRESSING

Homemade mayonnaise or
   Hellman's
Caviar
Capers
Anchovies, minced
Chives, chopped
Chili sauce

Add all ingredients to mayonnaise to taste. Serve over crisp salad greens.

Geneva Ashby Jones

COOKED SALAD DRESSING

½ c. mild vinegar
¼ c. sugar
¼ t. salt
½ t. celery seed
½ t. dry mustard
¼ t. white pepper
Dash of cayenne
¼ c. butter
½ T. flour
2 egg yolks, beaten
Whipped cream

Mix vinegar and spices in a cup and set aside. Melt butter, add flour, and stir until smooth. Then add vinegar mixture. Stir until thick. Slowly pour over well beaten egg yolks, stirring constantly. Add whipped cream when ready to serve to desired consistency and taste. Makes about 1½ c.

Mrs. R. W. Thompson, Jr.

PARMESAN SALAD DRESSING

1 T. salt
1 T. dry mustard
1 t. sugar
5 T. vinegar
1 c. olive oil
¼ c. Parmesan cheese, grated
5 T. mayonnaise
1 clove garlic, crushed

Combine salt, mustard, sugar, and vinegar. Gradually add oil, cheese, and mayonnaise, beating constantly. Pour into a jar with garlic. Chill. Shake well before using.

Makes 1 pint.

Mrs. Lewis Grinnan, Jr., 1948 Junior League
Cookbook

SHRIMP DRESSING FOR VEGETABLE SALADS

1 c. shrimp, cooked and cut
  very fine
1 can anchovy filets, well
  drained
½ c. olive oil
2 hard-boiled eggs, chopped
3 T. tarragon vinegar
¼ t. onion salt
½ t. Lemon-pepper Marinade
1 t. dried parsley flakes

Mix all ingredients in a large jar and chill. This dressing must be made the day it is to be used — cannot be kept. (only half the anchovies can be used if desired.) This dressing can be tossed with any combination of vegetables or spooned over asparagus spears.

Makes enough for 4.

Mrs. L. G. Pondrom

DIJON SALAD DRESSING

1 T. Dijon mustard
1 T. good red wine vinegar
½ clove garlic, crushed
2 T. olive oil
Boston lettuce
Onions, thinly sliced

Blend well, the mustard, vinegar, and garlic. Add olive oil. Dress salad of Boston lettuce and onions adding salt and pepper to taste. Dressing may be doubled, tripled, etc. successfully. Serves 4-5.

Mrs. Bedford Shelmire, Jr.

SWISS SALAD DRESSING

½ t. Knorr AROMAT seasoning
¾ t. sugar
1 t. mayonnaise
1 t. prepared mustard
2 t. cider vinegar
3½ T. Wesson oil
Salt and pepper to taste
Onion flavoring if desired

Mix all ingredients together, blending with a fork. May vary amounts of sugar and Aromat according to taste. Makes approximately ½ cup.

Mrs. G. L. Street

SAUCES AND CONDIMENTS

ROUX

A roux is a cooked mixture of flour and butter used as thickening agent for sauces and gravies. Flour and butter or fat are blended in varying proportions and heated slowly in a double boiler over extremely low heat. The darker the roux, the darker the sauce in which it is used. For example, the roux for a brown sauce is cooked slowly until it turns nut brown. A white sauce is made from a white roux plus milk or white stock. The roux may be made in quantity and refrigerated until ready to use then reheated in a double boiler.

BASIC BROWN ROUX

4 Tbs. flour
6 Tbs. clarified butter or cooking oil or rendered fresh pork fat

Blend flour and oil in a double boiler over low heat until flour slowly turns nut brown. It is most important that the flour not burn as this will prevent the sauce from thickening and impart an unpleasant taste.

BASIC WHITE ROUX
(WHITE SAUCE)

2 Tbs. butter
3 Tbs. flour

Blend melted butter with flour over low heat in a double boiler. Stir constantly until butter and flour froth together without coloring. This is now a white roux ready for the addition of hot liquid and spices to create the sauce of your choice.

The thickness of a sauce is in direct proportion to the amounts of flour used per cup of liquid.

Thin sauce or soup	1	Tbs. flour per 1 cup liquid
Medium, all-purpose sauce	1½	Tbs. flour per 1 cup liquid
Thick sauce	2	Tbs. flour per 1 cup liquid
Soufflé base	3	Tbs. flour per 1 cup liquid

VINAIGRETTE SAUCE

¾ cup oil
¼ cup lemon juice
Salt and pepper to taste
½ t. dry mustard
1 T. capers, chopped
1 t. pickles (dill or sour),
   finely chopped
½ t. parsley flakes
½ t. chervil, chopped
½ t. chives, chopped

Combine all ingredients and chill. This is an excellent marinade for asparagus. It is also good served over seafood or served lukewarm over hot boiled beef.
Makes approximately 1¼ cups.

BLENDER HOLLANDAISE SAUCE

3 egg yolks
3 T. lemon juice
1⅓ stick melted butter
¼ cup boiling water

Place first three ingredients in a blender; then slowly add boiling water. Blend two minutes. Place mixture in double boiler over low heat. Stir until thick. This can be refrigerated and reheated.
Makes about 1¼ cups.

BLENDER MAYONNAISE

2 eggs
5 T. lemon juice
1 t. salt
¼ t. dry mustard
½ t. garlic salt
½ t. celery salt
1 T. parsley flakes
2 cups salad oil

Place first 7 ingredients in blender. Add ⅓ cup oil. Turn on blender for 10 seconds; then slowly start adding remainder of oil. When a total of one cup of oil has been added, turn off blender and stir with a spoon. Turn blender on again adding the rest of the oil slowly. Stir once more before removing from blender.
Makes 1 pint.

HERB BUTTER

2 sticks unsalted butter
3 green onions, tops
   included, finely chopped
½ t. summer savory
½ t. thyme
½ t. oregano
Juice of ½ lemon

Cream butter and add remaining ingredients. Mix well and let sit overnight in the refrigerator for the most flavor. Delightful on homemade bread and roast beef sandwiches, baked potatoes, and broiled tomatoes.

Mrs. J. Thomas Hedrick

BASIL SAUCE FOR SPAGHETTI

1 clove garlic
2 parsley sprigs, chopped
1 large branch basil (or 1 t. dried)
¼ stick butter
⅓ of a 3-oz. pkg. cream cheese
1 oz. blue cheese
¼ c. olive oil
2 t. grated Parmesan cheese
Salt and pepper to taste

Mince garlic and add it to the chopped parsley and basil. Mash together with a fork the butter, cream cheese and blue cheese. Add to it the olive oil, Parmesan cheese and salt and pepper. Mix with the garlic mixture and pour into a screw-top jar. Pour over hot pasta.

Serves 2 generously. Can be doubled or tripled to serve more. This is fabulous to take on trips — wherever you will have a stove to boil the water for the spaghetti. Serve with a green salad and white wine.

Mrs. Edward James Henry III

BEST-EVER BARBEQUE SAUCE

¼ c. wine vinegar
½ c. water
2 T. sugar
1 T. mustard
¼ t. pepper
1½ t. salt
2 dashes cayenne pepper
1 thick slice lemon
1 onion, sliced
¼ c. butter
½ c. catsup
2½ t. Worcestershire
1½ t. Liquid Smoke

In a saucepan, combine all ingredients except last three. Simmer uncovered 15-20 minutes. Add remaining ingredients and bring to a boil. Excellent on ribs, chicken, etc.

Mrs. Don McIlyar

BEARNAISE SAUCE

3 egg yolks
¼ t. salt
1 T. tarragon vinegar
Dash of cayenne
2 T. heavy whipping cream
4 oz. butter, sliced very thin
  and frozen
1 shallot, chopped very fine
1 T. parsley, finely chopped
½ t. tarragon dried (crush it)
Tiny speck of tomato paste
Tiny speck of meat glaze

Put egg yolks in a small porcelain bowl, beat in salt, vinegar, cayenne and whipping cream. Stand the bowl in a shallow pan of hot water (not boiling); stir, do not beat, with a wire whisk until it begins to thicken. When thick, stir in butter one piece at a time, allowing each piece to thoroughly melt before adding the next. Add the shallot, parsley, tarragon, tomato paste and meat glaze. You can cover the bowl with a plastic wrap and leave it in the warm water until ready to serve.
Serves 4.

Mrs. Justin McCarty, Jr.

BORDELAISE SAUCE

¼ c. butter
2 shallots, finely chopped
2 cloves garlic
2 slices onion
2 slices carrot
2 sprigs parsley
10 whole peppercorns
2 whole cloves
2 bay leaves
3 T. flour
½ t. meat extract
1 can condensed beef bouillon
1 c. Cooking Wine for
  bordelaise sauce (can use 1
  cup burgundy)
Salt and pepper to taste
2 T. finely chopped parsley

Melt butter in a skillet and sauté onions, shallots, garlic, carrots, parsley, peppercorns, cloves and bay leaves until golden brown. REMOVE FROM HEAT. Add flour and mix. Cook over low heat 5 minutes, stirring constantly. Remove from heat, add meat extract mixed with a little flour to make a paste. Stir in bouillon and ¾ cup wine. Over medium heat, bring to a boil, stirring constantly. Reduce heat and simmer, uncovered for 10 minutes, stirring constantly. Strain, discarding vegetables and spices. Return sauce to skillet and add remaining ¼ cup wine, salt, pepper and parsley. Add more meat extract paste if too thin or water if too thick. Excellent with beef tenderloin.

Mrs. Julian Wells

CHILI SAUCE

1 1¼-oz. box of pickle spices,
   tied in cheesecloth
1 peck (approx. 15-20) tomatoes
6 medium onions, chopped
3 large green peppers, chopped
2 large red peppers, chopped
1 hot red pepper, chopped
1 stick of cinnamon
2 c. brown sugar
Salt to taste
2 c. vinegar

Peel tomatoes and cook until tender. Add all other ingredients and cook over low heat until very well done. Better while still hot.

Mrs. Denys Slater, Jr.

CURRY SAUCE

1 c. butter
½ c. celery, chopped
½ c. onion, chopped
2 T. cumin
2 T. turmeric
2 T. coriander
½ t. cayenne
1 t. salt
¾ c. flour
3 c. chicken broth
2 c. milk
1 c. heavy cream
1 T. lemon juice

Sauté onion and celery in butter until onions are yellow. Add next five ingredients and cook, stirring over low heat for 4 minutes. Add flour and stir over low heat for 5 minutes. Add chicken broth and bring to a boil, stirring with a wire whisk. Boil stirring for 2 minutes. Turn off heat and add milk. Simmer for 10 minutes stirring occasionally. Add cream and lemon juice and cook 2 minutes more. Add 6 cups of chicken or lamb and simmer about 15 minutes and serve. The sauce may be made the day before. It will thicken and thin out when heated. This will serve 12.

Mrs. Denys Slater, Jr.

AUSTRIAN SAUCES FOR FONDUE BOURGUIGNON

MAYONNAISE SAUCE
2 c. olive oil
2-3 eggs
1 t. salt
¼ t. pepper
½ t. Dijon mustard
Juice of ½ lemon
ANDALUSIA SAUCE
Mayonnaise
1½ T. catsup
1 t. Worcestershire sauce
⅛ t. marjoram
Dash of salt and pepper
¼ t. lemon juice
¼ t. Dijon mustard
1 T. fresh parsley, minced
1 t. sherry
CURRY SAUCE
Mayonnaise
½ t. curry powder
¾ t. hot mustard
½ t. lemon juice
Dash of salt and pepper
¾ t. Cognac
SAUCE TARTAR
Mayonnaise
2 T. dill pickles, minced
1 T. fresh parsley, minced
¼ t. dillweed
¼ t. marjoram
¼ t. tarragon
1 T. finely minced green onion
   (include a little of the green
   top)
1 hard-boiled egg, chopped
   finely
½ t. lemon juice
Pinch of salt
¼ t. pepper
¼ t. Dijon mustard

For mayonnaise sauce, place eggs, salt, pepper, and mustard in bowl and blend. Slowly beating, add ¼ c. oil drop by drop for about 3 minutes. Then add the remaining oil 1 T. at a time. Add lemon juice and blend. Divide mayonnaise into 4 bowls. Keep one plain and make other 3 sauces with remainders.
Serves 6-8.

Mrs. James Lambert

MOCK DEVONSHIRE CREAM

1 3-oz. pkg. cream cheese
¼ t. grated lemon rind
⅓ c. cream
1 T. lemon juice
1½ t. sugar

Mash the cream cheese with a fork. Blend in the remaining ingredients. It should be the consistency of very heavy cream. If a thinner sauce is desired, add a little canned fruit syrup. Serve over apricots, peaches, or any other fruit. Serves 4.

Mrs. Dan C. Williams, Jr. — 1948 Junior
League Cookbook

EASY HOT SAUCE

3 1-lb. cans tomatoes
1 T. vinegar
2 T. salad oil
1 t. salt
4 or 5 garlic buds (chipped or put through a garlic press)
1 or 2 t. small dried Japanese red peppers, chipped fine

Pour all liquid from tomatoes and mash them. The most satisfactory way is to do it with your hands. Do not use a blender as it purées them and they are to be coarse. Add remaining ingredients. Make several days ahead so that flavors blend well.

Suggestion: use only one teaspoon of red pepper the first time.
Makes about 1½-2 pts.

Mrs. Ben C. Doherty III

HAM SAUCE

1 T. flour
1 T. dry mustard
1 c. brown sugar (loose)
1 c. light cream
3 T. vinegar mixed with 1 T. water

Mix first 4 ingredients in a double boiler and cook 45 minutes. Add vinegar mixture and cook 5 more minutes. Stores well in refrigerator. Reheat to use.
Makes about 1½ c.

Mrs. Clint M. Josey, Jr.

HOLLANDAISE SAUCE

4 egg yolks
2 T. lemon juice
Dash red pepper
2 sticks butter

Put first three ingredients in mixer on high and beat until very thick. Melt butter and pour very slowly into the egg mixture. Be sure it goes in very slowly as this is the way the egg yolks are cooked. This can be done about two hours ahead and just put a top on it until ready to use. This may be stored in a glass jar and reheated in a pan of warm water gradually. Never return to heat. Good on left-over vegetables.
Serves 8.

Mrs. Minor L. Huck

NEVER-FAIL HOLLANDAISE

2 egg yolks, ice cold
1 stick of butter, ice cold
Juice of ½ lemon, ice cold
Salt
Cayenne

In a saucepan over low to medium heat put all ingredients and stir. If it separates, drop in 1 ice cube and stir. The secret is to have ingredients *ice cold* at the very beginning.
Serves 4-6.

Mrs. John Majors

FANNIE NELL'S HOT SAUCE

1 10-oz. can Rotel tomatoes
1 16-oz. can stewed tomatoes
1½ T. white vinegar
2 T. salad oil
½ t. garlic powder
1 t. salt
1 t. red pepper, crushed

Put all ingredients in blender, turn on for a couple of seconds then turn off and let settle. Turn on again for same time, then off.
Makes 2 pints.

Mrs. Walter T. Henderson

JEZEBEL SAUCE

1 10-oz. jar apple jelly
1 10-oz. jar pineapple preserves
1 5-oz. jar pure horseradish

Mix all ingredients and refrigerate. Divine with all meats, on sandwiches, and as a side relish dish.

Mrs. M. Weatherby Carr

SAUCE MOUTARDE

3 T. Dijon-style mustard
3 T. vinegar
1 t. salt
¼ t. white pepper
6 T. salad oil
¼ c. sour cream

Combine mustard, vinegar, salt, and pepper in a small bowl. With a rotary beater or wire whisk gradually beat in the oil, then blend in the sour cream. Serve at room temperature over hot asparagus, broccoli, or green beans.
Makes ¾ cup of sauce.
This sauce is one of this cook's best friends. Keep it on hand in the refrigerator and a little can be added to melted butter for a different approach to green vegetables. Or, add a little to mayonnaise to use as a dressing for a tomato salad. The sour cream can be omitted and the sauce used with ham, beef, or lamb.

Mrs. John W. McDonough

SOUR CREAM GRAVY

1 c. left-over gravy
½ c. sour cream

Heat gravy slightly and beat in sour cream with a wire whisk. Heat just to boiling point but do not boil. Salt and pepper to taste. If gravy is thin, melt 2 T. meat fat or butter, blend in 2 T. flour and add a cup of the thin gravy. When it is thick enough, add sour cream.

Mrs. L. G. Pondrom

HOT MUSTARD

1⅛ oz. can dry mustard
1 c. white vinegar
1 egg, beaten
1 c. sugar

Mix mustard and vinegar in saucepan and set aside. Mix egg and sugar. Combine two mixtures in the saucepan and heat, stirring often. The mixture will thicken slightly but not to a really thick consistency. Great with ham and perks up most meat sandwiches. Keeps well in the refrigerator.

Mrs. James H. Holmes III

FLORENCE'S HOT MUSTARD

3 eggs beaten
1½ cans Coleman's Mustard
   dissolved in ¼ c. water
3 T. flour
½ c. consomme
1 c. cider vinegar
1 c. light brown sugar

Cook the ingredients in the top of a double boiler till thick — stir often.
Makes 2½ cups.

Mrs. Don McIlyar

MUSTARD SAUCE FOR HAM

½ c. tomato soup, undiluted
½ c. prepared mustard
½ c. sugar
½ c. butter or margarine
3 egg yolks
½ c. vinegar

Combine all ingredients except the vinegar. Then add the vinegar. Cook slowly, stirring all the time, in a double boiler, until thick. Good hot or cold. Keeps well in the refrigerator.
Makes 2½-3 cups.

Mrs. Dan C. Williams

REMOULADE SAUCE

1 c. mayonnaise
Dash of Angostura bitters
Twist of lemon peel (zest)
1 T. ground mustard seed
1 T. prepared horseradish
2 t. ketchup or tomato paste
¼ t. filé
¼ t. seasoning salt (Lawry's)
½ t. paprika
Tabasco to taste

Blend all ingredients and serve with cooked shrimp.
Makes 1½ cups.

Mrs. Robert W. Enholm

LUCILLE'S STEAK SAUCE

1 stick butter
5 T. Worcestershire
5 T. Dijon mustard

Combine ingredients, place over low heat and stir until butter is melted. Do not let boil.
Makes 1½ cups.

Geneva Ashby Jones

CORN RELISH

12 ears yellow corn
1 qt. yellow onions
1 qt. ripe tomatoes
1 qt. cucumbers
3 green peppers
3 sweet red peppers
6 small hot red peppers
1 bunch celery
2 T. turmeric
2 qts. vinegar
2 T. mustard seed
1 scant c. sugar
⅓ c. salt

Cut corn from cob. Peel onions, tomatoes, and cucumbers and chop. Remove veins and seeds from peppers and chop fine. Discard all but heart and tender parts of the celery and mince. Dissolve tumeric in a little of the vinegar. Add mustard seed. Dissolve sugar and salt in the remaining vinegar. Combine all ingredients and boil for 1 hour. Pour into hot sterilized jars and seal.
Makes 6 half pints.

Mrs. Nelson Waggener — 1948 Junior League Cookbook

HOT CUCUMBER RELISH

12 large cucumbers
4 green peppers
4 large onions
½ c. salt
1 c. horseradish
1 c. sugar
1 T. mustard seed
1 T. celery seed
White vinegar

Peel cucumbers, quarter, and remove seeds. Put all vegetables through a food grinder. Add salt, mix well and let stand overnight. In the morning drain and add horseradish and other seasonings. Pack tightly in sterile jars, add hot vinegar to cover, and seal.
Makes 5 pints.

Mrs. Leo F. Corrigan, Jr.

ROSY RELISH

1 c. cider vinegar
2 c. sugar
1 T. salt
1 3" cinnamon stick
2 T. mustard seed
8 whole cloves
2 c. ripe peeled tomatoes, chopped
4-5 c. tart apples, peeled and chopped
1 c. onion, chopped
1 c. celery, chopped
1 c. red bell pepper, seeded and chopped
2 T. hot red pepper, chopped

Combine all ingredients and bring to a rapid boil. Simmer until mixture is thick and clear (about 30-45 minutes). Pour into hot sterilized jars and seal. (Red food coloring may be added if more color is desired.) Process in hot water bath for 10 minutes.

Makes approximately 4-5 pints. Chill before serving. An excellent condiment for pork roast or chops. Good with all game.

Mrs. James Lambert

BREAD AND BUTTER PICKLES

25 medium cucumbers, sliced
12 onions, sliced
8 green peppers, cut in strips
½ c. salt
Ice water
PICKLING MIXTURE:
1 qt. vinegar
2 c. sugar
2 t. mustard seed
2 t. turmeric
2 t. celery seed
1 stick cinnamon

Soak cucumbers, onions, and peppers in ice water with salt for 3 hours. Heat pickling mixture to boiling; add cucumbers, onions, and peppers and heat for 2 minutes. Do not let boil. Fill sterile jars and seal. It may be necessary to double pickling mixture if cucumbers are large. Serve ice cold.

Makes 5 quarts.

Mrs. Leo Corrigan, Jr

DILLY OKRA

Garlic (1 clove per pint)
Hot pepper (1 pod per pint)
Okra (4 lbs. approx.)
Dill seed (1 t. per pint)
5 c. cider vinegar (4% acidity)
½ c. salt (non-iodized)
5 c. water
Mustard seed (½ t. per pint)

Wash okra after having cut off the stems but not the tops of the okra pods. In hot sterilized jars place garlic, dill seed, mustard seed, and hot pepper pod. Bring the water-vinegar-salt solution to a boil and pour over okra in jar which has been packed, but not crushed, in the jars. Fill jars to ½" of top. Adjust lids and process jars in a hot water bath for 10 minutes. Chill before serving. Good as an appetizer or as a pickle with outdoor meals.

Yield: approx. 6-7 pints.

Mrs. James Lamber

SUNSHINE DILL PICKLES

In each jar, put:
2 grape leaves
Cucumbers to fill
1 bunch dill
1 clove garlic
Chopped onion
Pickling spices
(1 hot fresh chili — optional)
BRINE:
1½ c. Kosher salt
10 c. water
¾ c. cider vinegar

Scrub medium cucumbers well. Sterilize quart jars in the dishwasher. Put ingredients listed into each jar. Boil brine until salt is dissolved. Take 1 cup of the solution and add ¾ c. cider vinegar to it. Pour over packed jars, seal, and set in direct sunlight for 8 days.

Mrs. Leo F. Corrigan, Jr.

MRS. GANNON'S WATERMELON PICKLES

Use only the best Black Diamond Watermelons from East Texas. Ripe only in August, around the first week usually. Cut all the green peel off; also leave none of the soft pink part. Very important in pickle making as they should be hard and crisp when finished. After cut, as uniformly as possible, put in crocks. Soak in lime water overnight using a good rounded T. of lime to a gallon of water. Be certain the rinds are covered. Next day remove rinds from lime water and rinse 3 times in alum water using 1 t. powdered alum for each quart of water. Rinse thoroughly through two clear waters. Next boil in clear water until rinds are tender and can be pierced with ice pick. Make syrup 1½ times as many lbs. of sugar as pounds of rind. Weigh your cooking pot before adding rinds to cook, then subtract weight of pot from total and you have the amount of sugar 1½ times to add. Add whole cloves tied in cheese cloth. Cook for 4 hours or until done. Could be less time. To each jar add a whole stick of cinnamon and seal tightly.

Mrs. Mark Lemmon, Jr.

THE BOBBITT FAMILY APPLE PRESERVES

24 firm apples — Jonathan or
   Winesap, peeled, cored and
   quartered
8 c. sugar
4 c. water
4 c. white Karo syrup

In a very large pan boil together sugar, water and syrup. When this begins to thicken, add apples slowly so that boiling does not stop. Turn heat to medium low and cook until apples are translucent and the syrup is thick. (This takes at least one hour). Remove from heat and, using a large spoon, put preserves in sterilized jelly jar. Seal with parafin. Or use half pint fruit jars and seal with rubber lids. Apples will be pink when cool.
Makes 12-15 jelly jars or half pints.

Mrs. Rhodes R. Bobbitt

SPICY PRESERVED ORANGE SLICES

8 oranges, sliced ¼ inch thick;
   seeded, unpeeled (about 8 c.)
4 c. sugar
1 c. white vinegar
½ c. water
10 whole cloves
2 cinnamon sticks

Discard the end pieces of orange so that the slices are fairly uniform. Cover orange slices with water and simmer, covered for 45 minutes to 1 hour — or until tender. Drain carefully. Boil sugar, vinegar, water, and spices for 5 minutes. Carefully add the orange slices and simmer about 45 minutes, or until orange slices are well glazed (uncovered). Transfer the slices carefully into jars, trying to stack them evenly. Pour over the hot syrup, distributing the spices if desired, seal. Serve with poultry, duck, goose, venison. Best if refrigerated before serving.
Makes about 3½ pints.

Mrs. John W. McDonough

DORIS' PEACH CONSERVE

1 lemon, thinly sliced
1 orange, thinly sliced
½ c. sugar
½ c. water
5 c. tree ripened peaches
¼ c. lemon juice
7 c. sugar
1 c. pecans, broken
1 t. cinnamon
1 t. cloves
1 t. allspice
1 bottle pectin (Certo)

In small pan boil lemon and orange slices in ½ c. sugar and water until tender. In another pan, put remaining ingredients except pectin in to boil together. Bring to rolling boil. Mash fruit with potato masher and keep skimming top. Add cooked lemon and orange. Add pectin. Cook 5 minutes. Pour into jars or glasses which have been boiled.

Mrs. Spencer Carver

PEACH CONSERVE

18 ripe peaches
3¼ lbs. sugar
6 oranges, ground
¼ lb. almonds, chopped

Let all ingredients stand in a bowl for 2½ hours, then cook over low heat 1½ hours. Stir from the bottom. Pour into jars.

Mrs. Charles P. Storey

THE BOBBITT FAMILY PEACH PRESERVES

1 c. peaches
1 c. sugar
    This is the proportion: e.g., 8
    c. peaches, 8 c. sugar

Peel peaches and slice. Remove seeds, but don't throw them away. Add sugar to peaches and seeds and let it set overnight in the refrigerator. Put into pan and bring to a boil. Simmer 1 hour or more. Remove seeds. Let cool completely. Put into sterilized jelly jars and seal with parafin or into half-pint fruit jars and seal with rubber lids.

Mrs. Rhodes R. Bobbitt

NECTARINE-APPLE RELISH

½ c. water
3 T. basil vinegar *or* 3 T. white vinegar and ½ t. basil
2 T. sugar
½ t. salt
3 dashes of liquid red pepper seasoning
2-3 fresh nectarines
1 green apple
⅔ c. red onion rings

Combine water, vinegar, sugar, salt, and liquid red pepper seasoning in saucepan; bring to boil. Cool. Cut nectarines into slices to make 1 cup. Cut remainder into chunks to make about 1 cup. Cut apple into thin slices. Arrange nectarines, apple, and onion in layers in shallow dish. Pour dressing over; cover and refrigerate about 2 hours. Serve with meat or poultry.
Makes about 3 cups.

Mrs. Mark L. Lemmon, Jr.

PEAR RELISH

15 large hard pears, peeled and cored
12 large white onions, peeled
12 bell peppers, seeds removed (include a few red peppers)
6-12 hot peppers, some red, some green (seeds add hotness)
2 T. celery seed
2 c. white vinegar
2 c. Louisiana creole mustard (conventional prepared mustard will do)
2 c. sugar
1 T. salt

Put first 4 ingredients through the coarse blade of the food chopper. Mix the remaining ingredients, add the first 4 and bring to a boil, cooking slowly, stirring occasionally for 30 minutes. Pour into sterilized jars and seal. Refrigerate before serving.

PICKLED SHALLOTS OR PEARL ONIONS

1 gal. shallots or pearl onions
1 pt. uniodized salt to 1 gallon
  water
Red peppers
Green peppers
1 pt. water
1 qt. white vinegar
1 c. sugar
1 t. celery seed
1 t. mustard seed

Pour boiling water over onions to cover and let stand for 2 hours. Peel. Mix salt with water and put over onions, leave overnight. Everyday pour off brine and replace it with a new batch. Repeat two days. Last time, rinse in water several times. Put one red and one green pepper into each sterilized jar. Bring last 5 ingredients to a boil and pour over onions. Seal.

Makes up to 8 pts.

Mrs. Clint M. Josey, Jr.

NECTARINE-TOMATO CHUTNEY

2-2¼ lbs. fresh nectarines (6-7
  large)
1 lb. fresh tomatoes (2 large)
1 c. granulated sugar
½ c. brown sugar
¾-1 c. vinegar
1 T. Worcestershire sauce
Few dashes of liquid red
  pepper seasoning
1 t. garlic, minced
½ t. salt
½ t. ground ginger
½ t. ground cloves
½ t. basil
½ c. green pepper, diced
1 3½-oz. jar small cocktail
  onions, drained *or* ½ c.
  onions, chopped

Blanch nectarines in boiling water about 1 minute, rinse in cold water. Peel and chop to measure 5 to 5½ cups. Blanch, rinse, peel, and chop tomatoes to measure 2 cups. Combine nectarines and tomatoes in large kettle with all remaining ingredients except green pepper and onions. Bring to boil quickly, stirring frequently; reduce heat and boil gently with occasional stirring for 30 minutes. Add green pepper and onions. Boil 10 minutes, stirring frequently to keep mixture from sticking to bottom of kettle. Remove from heat; cool and store in covered container in refrigerator. Or if you wish, ladle immediately into jars, seal for future use, and store in a cool dry place.

Makes 1 quart.

Mrs. Mark L. Lemmon, Jr.

PEAR CHUTNEY

10 lbs. (8 qts.) hard pears,
   peeled, cored, and cut into
   small pieces
2 qts. water
1 T. ginger
10 lb. sugar
1½ pts. (3 c.) vinegar
3 large onions, chopped
¼ t. ground bay leaf
1 lb. raisins
1 T. ground cloves
1 T. ground ginger
1 T. ground cinnamon
1 T. curry powder
1 T. turmeric
8 oz. crystalized ginger or jar
   ginger marmalade (or: 8 oz.
   ginger root cooked with
   pears)

Cover pears with water and 1 T. ginger and boil 5 minutes. Straining is optional. Cover with sugar and let stand overnight. Next day: Cook pears without adding water until syrup is thick and fruit is done — 1 to 3 hours, stirring. Syrup will becone clear and brownish. Then add vinegar, onions, raisins, and spices. Blend well. Then add ginger if not cooked with pears. Put in sterile jars. Makes 10 pints.

Mrs. Frank N. Graves

PEAR HONEY

8-10 c. chopped underripe
   pears
¾ c. sugar for each cup of pears
1 lemon, seeded and ground
   through grinder
1 whole orange, seeded and put
   through a grinder

Combine all ingredients. Allow to stand, stirring occasionally, until sugar is dissolved. Then cook slowly until thick and syrupy — the consistency of honey. Pour into sterilized jars or jelly glasses and seal. Superb with waffles, French toast, biscuits, English muffins, etc.

Mrs. John W. McDonough

Cioppino Seafood Stew

PEPPER JELLY

¾ c. bell peppers, ground
(about 3 peppers)
1½ c. cider vinegar
6½ c. sugar
¼ c. hot peppers, ground
1 bottle Certo
Green or red food coloring

Use green bell peppers if you wish to have green jelly and red bell peppers if you wish to have red pepper jelly. Remove seeds from bell peppers and grind, saving the pulp and juice. (This may be done in a blender, but be careful not to grind the peppers too finely.) Mix the peppers, hot peppers, cider vinegar, and sugar in a large saucepan (at least 4- to 6-quart pan) and bring to a rolling boil. Add Certo and bring to a full, rolling boil again, stirring constantly for 1 minute. Remove from burner and let stand for a minute or two and then skim off foam. Add food coloring to achieve desired coloring. Pour into hot sterilized jelly jars and seal. This jelly is very good when served over cream cheese with crackers as an appetizer or when served as a condiment for game. It is especially good with barbecued doves wrapped in bacon and charcoal grilled. Chill before serving.

Yield: approx. 6 half-pints.

Mrs. James Lambert

WINE JELLY

2 c. red or white wine
3 c. sugar
½ bottle Certo

Mix wine and sugar in top of double boiler and place over boiling water, stirring until sugar is dissolved. Remove from heat and stir in Certo at once. Pour into jelly glasses and either seal or cover with ⅛" hot parafin. Good with roasts and game.

Mrs. James Lambert

HOT FRUIT

3 c. peach halves
3 c. pear halves
3 c. sliced pineapple or chunks
⅓ c. butter
¾ c. brown sugar
1 t. ginger

Mix butter, sugar and ginger. Stir over low heat until butter has melted. Pour over fruit that has been drained well and placed in a casserole. Bake at 325° for 30 minutes or until hot and bubbly. Maraschino cherries can be added for color. Excellent with wild game.

Mrs. M. Weatherby Carr

SOUPS

ALMOND AND GRAPE SOUP

1½ c. milk
½ c. whole blanched almonds
3 T. butter
1 small onion, finely sliced
2½ T. flour
4 c. well-flavored chicken stock
Salt and pepper
2 stalks celery, sliced
2 egg yolks
2-3 T. heavy cream
1½ c. (⅓ lb.) seedless green
  grapes
1 T. parsley (for garnish)

Scald the milk, add almonds, cover pan and leave to infuse for 15 minutes. In a large pan melt butter, add onion, and cook until soft. Stir in the flour; add chicken stock; season; and stir until boiling. Add celery and simmer gently for 15 minutes. Emulsify the almond and milk mixture in a blender or work it through a fine nylon sieve. Strain chicken stock and add liquid to the almond milk. Reheat the soup; adjust the seasoning; and add a little to the liaison of egg yolks and cream. Return this mixture to remaining soup off the heat; reheat until the soup thickens, but do not boil. Cover the soup and chill. Serve sprinkled with parsley and add a few grapes to each bowl.

Mrs. Mark Lemmon, Jr.

ARTICHOKE SOUP

4 large or 6 medium artichokes
6 T. butter
½ c. onions, finely chopped
½ c. celery, finely chopped
6 T. flour
6 c. clear chicken broth
¼ c. lemon juice
1 bay leaf
1 t. salt
¼ t. pepper
¼ t. thyme
2 egg yolks, beaten
2 c. light cream
Lemon slices
Parsley

Boil artichokes for 1 hour. Scrape leaves and finely chop bottoms. In saucepan sauté onion and celery in butter until soft, not brown. Add flour and cook 1 minute, stirring constantly. Add stock and lemon juice and stir until blended. Add bay leaf, salt, pepper, thyme, artichoke scrapings, and bottoms. Cover and simmer 20 minutes or until slightly thickened. When ready to serve heat to boiling point and remove from heat. Add cream and egg yolks which have been beaten together. Keep heated over hot water. Serve garnished with lemon slices and parsley.
Serves 12.

Mrs. Mark Lemmon, Jr.

MINTED ARTICHOKE SOUP

6 fresh artichokes
1 T. cider vinegar or juice of 1
lemon
4-5 c. well-seasoned chicken
stock
½-¾ c. heavy cream
1 egg yolk, lightly beaten
Freshly ground black pepper
Salt to taste
Finely chopped fresh mint

Drop artichokes in boiling water seasoned with vinegar or lemon juice for about 45 minutes, covered. When artichokes are cooked, remove the leaves. (Reserve leaves to serve on another occasion with a dip. Or, if you prefer, you may scrape each leaf and add the meat to the purée for the soup. Or, you may enjoy eating them while you are cooking the soup!) Clean the hearts and purée them in the blender. Put the artichoke purée in a pan and gradually add the stock until the desired consistency is reached. Heat together gently for 10 minutes, stirring occasionally. Remove pan from heat and stir in cream. Thicken with an egg yolk, if necessary. Garnish with mint. Serve immediately. Once the egg yolk has been added, DO NOT BOIL. To reheat, put mixture in the top of a double boiler.

Mrs. Margaret C. Worsham

SHERRIED AVOCADO CREAM SOUP

2 large ripe avocados
1 clove garlic, crushed
1 c. light cream
2 juiced lemons
2 c. clear chicken broth
1 bunch scallions, coarsely
chopped
Dry sherry

Put cut avocado into blender, reserving a few neat balls cut with a melon scoop for garnish. Add crushed garlic plus ½ c. cream. Add 1 T. lemon juice, 1½ c. chicken broth, and scallions. Blend at high speed 30 seconds. Transfer soup to a mixing bowl and add chicken broth, lemon juice, and cream to achieve the desired taste. Add salt and pepper to taste. The final consistency should be that of thin cream. Chill several hours. Add about 2 T. dry sherry per serving. Garnish and serve 4 in large bowls.
Serves 8-10 in demitasse cups, omitting garnish and adding only 1 T. sherry per cup.

Mrs. Harold W. Kimmerling

BARLEY AND MUSHROOM SOUP

1 onion, thinly sliced
Butter, for sautéing onion
½ c. barley, rinsed in water
2 qt. beef stock or bouillon
2 T. butter
½ lb. fresh mushrooms, sliced
Salt and pepper to taste
Sour cream
Parsley

Sauté onion in butter until light yellow, then add barley, beef stock, and cook for 1 hour or until the barley is soft. In a skillet melt 2 T. butter; add sliced mushrooms and fry at high heat for about 1-2 minutes. Add to the soup; simmer for 10 more minutes. Serve hot with dab of sour cream and chopped parsley on top. Serves 8.

Mrs. Ralph G. Greenlee, Jr.

CUBAN BLACK BEAN SOUP

1 lb. black beans
2 onions, finely chopped
1 green pepper, finely chopped
2 cloves garlic, minced
4 T. olive oil
3 T. vinegar
3 qt. water
Salt, pepper, and oregano to taste
Cooked rice
Chopped chives

Wash beans and soak overnight. Simmer in the same water until almost tender. Sauté onions, pepper, and garlic in olive oil until tender; add to the beans together with seasonings and vinegar. Cook slowly and cautiously in a heavy pot to prevent burning. Mash beans occasionally so they will be thick. Much better if made the day before and reheated. Serve over fluffy dry rice and sprinkle chives on top.
Serves 10.

Mrs. William H. Marsh III

FLAMING BEAN SOUP

2 celery stalks, chopped
1 large onion, chopped
1 T. vegetable oil
1 16-oz. can beans in tomato sauce
3 c. light stock or water
½ t. salt
Ham bone (or ham)
2 bay leaves
4 cloves
¼ t. celery seed
¼ t. dry mustard
Salt and pepper
3 T. bourbon
2 hard-boiled eggs, sliced
1 lemon, thinly sliced

Sauté celery and onion in oil until just golden. Add beans, stock, salt, ham bone, bay leaves, cloves, celery seed, and mustard. Simmer 1 hour. Discard bone, bay leaves, and cloves. Season to taste. At the table heat soup. Warm bourbon in a soup ladle, ignite, and pour into soup. Pass egg and lemon slices.
Serves 6.

Mrs. W. W. Overton, Jr.

BORSCHT

3 lbs. beef (chuck or brisket)
3 qts. cold water
1 large onion, coarsely chopped
1 bay leaf
1 T. chopped parsley
2 t. salt
3 medium-size red beets, raw
½ c. tomato sauce
1 T. vinegar
2 carrots, large
1 head cabbage, small,
   shredded
2 potatoes, peeled and cubed
Salt and pepper to taste
2 apples
Sour cream and parsley for
   topping

Cover meat with cold water. Add ½ chopped onion, bay leaf, parsley and salt. Bring to a boil, reduce heat, and simmer 2 hours or more until meat is tender. Remove meat, skim off grease, and strain soup stock. Peel beets, cut them in shoestring strips, and cook them in stock, covered, on low heat with tomato sauce and vinegar. Add shoestring-cut carrots. Cook 10 minutes or until beets are getting soft. Add peeled and cut up potatoes, remaining ½ onion, chopped, and continue cooking. When potatoes are almost done, add chopped apples with peelings and shredded cabbage. Cook until all are tender, adding more water if needed. Add salt and pepper to taste. If desired, add 1 T. additional vinegar and 1 t. sugar. Before serving, let the soup cook for 15 minutes over very low heat. Serve with a bowl of sour cream and chopped parsley. The cooked meat should be chopped and added to the soup just before serving.
Serves 8.

Mrs. Ralph G. Greenlee, Jr.

CREAM OF BROCCOLI SOUP

3 T. butter
3-4 T. onion, minced
3 T. flour
3 c. milk
1 c. vegetable water or bouillon
2 t. salt, speck of pepper
2 c. cooked broccoli, finely
   chopped
½ t. A-1 sauce
Paprika

Melt butter in a double boiler. Add onion and cook over direct heat until tender. Add flour, stir until smooth; add milk and vegetable water and cook over boiling water until smooth and thick. Add seasonings, broccoli, and A-1. Heat and serve sprinkled with paprika. (Soup may be put through a blender before reheating if finer broccoli is preferred.)
Serves 4-6.

Mrs. Curtis Sanford, Jr.

CANADIAN CHEESE SOUP

½ c. butter
¾ c. finely diced onion
½ c. finely diced carrots
½ c. finely diced celery
½ c. flour
2 T. cornstarch
1 qt. chicken stock
1 qt. milk
⅛ t. soda
1 c. Cheddar cheese, grated
Salt and pepper to taste
2 T. parsley, finely chopped

Melt butter in large pot. Add onions, carrots, and celery and sauté until soft. Add flour and cornstarch and stir well. Add chicken stock and milk. Cook, stirring constantly, until mixture has smooth velvet texture and thickens. Add soda and cheese and stir until blended. Season with salt and pepper. Add parsley a few minutes before serving time.
Serves 10 to 12.

Mrs. James B. Hudnall III

CARROT SOUP

1 c. onion, thinly sliced
4 c. carrots, thinly sliced
6 T. butter
1 t. salt
⅛ t. pepper
¼ t. thyme
3 cans (10½-oz. each)
   condensed chicken broth,
   undiluted
4 c. water
½ c. rice
Sour cream

In a large saucepan cook onions and carrots in 4 T. of butter for 1 minute. Cover and steam for 10 minutes. Add salt, pepper, thyme, broth, and water. Heat to boiling and sprinkle in rice. Reduce heat, cover, and simmer 40 minutes. Let partially cool and purée mixture in blender. Return to saucepan and heat. Stir in remaining 2 T. butter until melted. Serve topped with a dollop of sour cream.
Serves 8-12.

Mrs. John P. Boone

CREAM OF CELERY ROOT SOUP

2 celery roots, peeled and diced
1 large potato, peeled and diced
2 carrots, peeled and diced
1 onion, peeled and diced
Pinch of cayenne
White pepper to taste
Celery salt to taste
1½ qts. water
1 c. whipped cream

Sauté diced vegetables in butter until tender. Add water and let simmer gently until vegetables are well cooked. Cool and put mixture through a blender. Return to pan and add whipped cream while simmering gently until soup is just slightly thickened and creamy. Serve with chopped parsley.
Serves 4-6.

Cook Book Committee

CHICKEN AND MUSHROOM SOUP

1 pint chicken stock
½ lb. fresh mushrooms
½ stick butter or ¼ c. chicken fat
¼ c. flour
1 pint light cream
¼ c. sour cream
Salt and pepper to taste
Dried parsley flakes or freshly chopped parsley

The chicken stock must be greaseless and strong in flavor. If canned stock is used, start with 2 pints and reduce by cooking to 1 pint. Peel the mushrooms, chop them very fine and let them stand in salted water. Melt butter or chicken fat in a heavy pan. Blend in the flour. Add chicken stock and all but ½ cup light cream. Cook slowly, stirring often. When it begins to thicken, add the mushrooms which have been drained and mashed through your hands to relieve them of as much moisture as possible. Continue slow cooking and frequent stirring. Mix the remaining light cream with the sour cream, beating with a wire whisk. When soup is the desired thickness, add sour cream mixture and let simmer 5 more minutes. Add salt and pepper. Garnish with parsley. Mushrooms can be omitted, and bits of chopped chicken and cooked rice can be added.
Makes 4 large servings.

Mrs. L. G. Pondrom

ROLLING ROCK CLUB CHIPPEWA SOUP

2 lbs. split peas, soaked in water at least 6 hours and cooked
½ gallon beef stock
24 oz. can tomato paste
4-6 T. curry
3 carrots, diced
3 stalks celery, diced
2 medium onions, diced
1 c. heavy cream

Brown carrots, celery, and onions in oil in a heavy soup pot. Add curry and cook 5-10 minutes longer. Then add peas, tomatoes, and stock and cook slowly for one hour. Strain; then add cream and correct seasoning. Serve hot or cold. Freezes well.
Serves 12.

Mrs. Fred Schoellkopf, Jr.

CREAM OF CORN SOUP

6 ears corn
½ small onion, finely chopped
3 T. butter
2 T. flour
1½ c. chicken stock
1½ c. milk
½ c. cream
Salt and white pepper to taste

Cut corn from cob, scraping each ear well and getting out all the milk. Sauté onion in butter until just tender; then add corn and cook another 2 minutes. Sprinkle on flour and cook 1 more minute while stirring. Blend in stock and milk, and cook 5 minutes. Add cream and season with salt and pepper. Heat and serve with chopped chives or parsley sprinkled on top. This can be changed by adding ½ c. of lump crabmeat and curry to taste.
Serves 6.

Mrs. Edward W. Rose III

CRAB BISQUE

1 c. fresh Alaskan King Crab
1 T. onion, finely chopped
3 T. butter
3 T. flour
3 c. milk
1 t. salt
Dash of paprika
1 c. light cream
2 T. chives, chopped
3-5 T. dry sherry
Tabasco or cayenne to taste

In a large saucepan or double boiler sauté onion in butter until soft. Add crabmeat and flour. Mix well; add milk, salt, paprika, and cream. Cook over low heat, stirring constantly, until thickened. DO NOT BOIL. Add chives and sherry. Let stand over hot water until ready to serve.
Serves 6.

Mrs. Jack B. Shook, Jr.

COLD CREAM OF CUCUMBER SOUP

5 cucumbers
½ c. minced shallots
½ c. minced onions
6 T. butter
1 t. salt
1 t. pepper
10 c. chicken stock
1 T. white wine vinegar
1½ t. dill weed
6 T. quick cooking farina
(cream of wheat)
1½ c. sour cream
½ c. sour cream (for garnish)

Peel cucumbers and cut into half-inch chunks. Cook shallots and onions in butter until yellow in a sauce pan. Add cucumber chunks, chicken broth, vinegar, and herbs. Bring to a boil and stir in farina. Simmer partially covered 30 minutes. Cool and purée in electric blender. Return soup to pan, thinning out with more liquid if necessary. Stir in sour cream. Let cool uncovered. Then cover and chill overnight. When serving put 1 t. sour cream on top of each bowl of soup. Serves 12.

Mrs. Denys Slater, Jr.

GAZPACHO I

2 cans consommé
1 18-oz. can tomato juice
1 clove garlic, chopped
1 small onion, chopped
1 cucumber, peeled and grated
1 large tomato, peeled and
    chopped
1 small green pepper, chopped
3 T. olive oil
1 T. fresh lime juice
2 large soda crackers, rolled
1 T. sugar
Salt and pepper
Tabasco to taste

Mix consommé, tomato juice, garlic, and onion together and let stand in the refrigerator for 3 hours. Strain, and add all other ingredients, seasoning highly with salt and Tabasco. Chill well and beat thoroughly until the olive oil is completely incorporated in the soup. Serve in chilled soup plates.
Serves 6.

Mrs. Paul B. Horton

GAZPACHO II

3 medium tomatoes, peeled and
  quartered or 2½ c. very best
  grade canned tomatoes
1 medium onion, quartered
1 medium green pepper, seeded
  and cut up
1 medium cucumber, peeled
  and cut up
1 T. parsley, chopped
¼ c. olive oil
6 T. bread crumbs
2 c. tomato juice
2 c. chicken stock
Juice of 1 lemon
Dash of Tabasco sauce
Salt and pepper to taste

Combine all vegetables, olive oil, and bread crumbs in blender and mix well. Stir in tomato juice, stock, lemon juice, and Tabasco. Season to taste. Chill thoroughly before serving. Garnish with thin slice of lemon and chopped parsley. Serves 6 to 8.

Mrs. Joseph Irion Worsham

GAZPACHO WITHOUT OIL

3 cans (10-oz. each) Snappy
  Tom
1 can (46-oz.) tomato juice
⅓-½ c. fresh lemon juice
2 cucumbers, peeled and
  chopped
1 green pepper, chopped
1 medium onion, chopped
2 small tomatoes, peeled and
  chopped
2 t. Sweet 'n Low
Salt and pepper
MSG
Worcestershire
Tabasco

Put vegetables and lemon juice into blender and blend. Add juices and seasonings and blend again. Refrigerate. A good low-calorie cold soup. Serves 10-12.

Mrs. Earl Fain III

GUMBO

½ c. cooking oil
⅓ c. flour
1 c. celery, chopped
1½ c. onions, chopped
½ c. green peppers, chopped
4 cloves garlic, minced
2 1-lb. cans plum tomatoes
  (reserve liquid)
3 qts. liquid (use oyster water,
  reserved tomato liquid, and
  water)
3 bay leaves
½ t. thyme
¼ bunch parsley, chopped
3 pkgs. frozen okra, cut up
1½ lbs. shrimp, peeled and
  deveined (raw)
1 pt. oysters
1 lb. crab claws
Cayenne pepper
Black pepper
Salt

Make a roux of the oil and flour (should be the color of a paper bag). Add celery, onions, peppers, and garlic and brown. Add tomatoes and simmer 10 minutes. Add 3 qts. liquid, bay leaves, thyme, and parsley and simmer 30 minutes. Add okra and simmer 5 minutes. Add shrimp and cook 5 minutes; the oysters and cook 3 minutes; and the crab claws and cook until warm. After seasonings are added you may begin to salt and pepper (cayenne and black). Be careful with salt. Put chopped parsley and green onions on top of gumbo in tureen. Serve over steamed rice. Will freeze well.
Serves 12.

Mrs. Harold Kimmerling

HOLLANDAISE SOUP

5 c. well-flavored chicken stock
¼ c. butter
¼ c. flour
6 T. light cream
2 egg yolks
Salt and pepper
GARNISH:
3 T. green peas
2 T. carrot "peas" (scooped
  from the carrot with a small
  vegetable ball cutter)
2 T. turnip "peas"

Melt butter in a large pan, stir in the flour, and cook a few seconds. Pour on the stock, blend and stir until boiling. Simmer 10 minutes and skim if necessary. Meanwhile, prepare the garnish and cook in boiling salted water for 8 minutes or until vegetables are tender. Drain. Combine cream and egg yolks. Stir in a little hot soup and stir this mixture into the remaining soup, off the heat. Add the garnish, season, and reheat the soup until it thickens slightly; do not boil. May be served hot or cold.
Serves 6.

Mrs. Mark Lemmon, Jr.

ICED LEMON SOUP

1 can cream of chicken soup
1 c. light cream
1 c. chicken stock
3 T. mint leaves, chopped
Juice of 2 lemons

Strain soup; add cream and chicken stock; chop mint leaves finely and add with lemon juice. Soup must be served ice-cold.
Serves 4.

Cookbook Committee

HEARTY MEATBALL SOUP

1½ lbs. ground chuck
3 T. butter
1 can (1 lb. 2 oz.) tomatoes
2 cans consommé
1 can or pkg. dry onion soup
  mix
4 carrots, pared
¼ c. celery tops, chopped
¼ c. parsley, chopped
1 bay leaf
¼ t. oregano leaves
¼ t. basil
½ t. salt
10 peppercorns
1 c. cut okra
1 c. water

With hands, lightly shape chuck into 1-inch balls. In hot butter in a 6-qt. pan, sauté meatballs, turning until browned all over. Drain off fat. Add remaining ingredients and bring just to boiling. Reduce heat, and simmer covered 45 minutes, stirring occasionally to break up tomatoes. Serve very hot. Is better the second day.
Serves 6.

Mrs. George E. Wilkin, Jr.

MUSHROOM SOUP

1 lb. fresh mushrooms, sliced
½ medium yellow onion, sliced
Salt and pepper to taste
¾ stick butter
2 c. well-seasoned chicken or
  beef broth or mixture of both
1 pt. heavy cream

Melt butter and sauté onions and mushrooms. Lightly season with salt and pepper. Add stock and simmer for 5 minutes. Add cream. Once the cream has been added, do not let the soup boil. Check the seasoning.
Serves 4.

Mrs. Margaret C. Worsham

CLEAR MUSHROOM SOUP

1 lb. fresh mushrooms (closed),
    washed and drained
⅓ oz. dried Italian mushrooms
½ c. lukewarm water
3 T. best grade olive oil
¼ c. butter
2 garlic cloves, mashed
¼ c. diced yellow onion
Black pepper
Cayenne pepper
Salt
5 c. boiling beef broth
½ c. red wine
½ c. heavy cream

Remove mushroom stems and chop fine. Slice caps thinly and chop coarsely. Soak dried mushrooms in lukewarm water. Drain and save water. Chop the mushrooms. Place olive oil and butter in medium-size sauce pan. Heat and add garlic, stirring well to extract flavor. Discard pieces of garlic. Add onion and sauté until medium brown. Add diced mushrooms and chopped stems and sauté for 15 minutes. Add peppers to taste, also salt, broth, and wine. Bring to a rapid boil, remove from heat, and stir in cream.
Serves 4-5.

Mrs. Steven Summers

CREAM OF MUSHROOM SOUP

4 shallots, chopped
3 T. butter
1 lb. fresh mushrooms
4 c. chicken broth
1 c. cream
Dash of salt and white pepper
¼ c. sherry, optional

Sauté shallots in melted butter in a pan and add the mushrooms. Continue to sauté for 5 minutes, then add the chicken broth. Bring soup to a boil and simmer for about ½ hour. Pour into a blender gradually and mix until smooth. Return soup to the pan; add cream, salt, pepper, and sherry. Serve very hot.
Yields 6-8 cups.

Mrs. Van Alen Hollomon

ONION SOUP

½ lb. onions
2 T. butter
1 qt. strong beef or chicken
    stock
4 slices buttered dried bread
4 heaping T. Parmesan cheese
1 T. olive oil

Heat the stock in the top of a double boiler. While stock is heating, sauté the onions which have been sliced into half moons. When almost transparent, put them in with the stock and cook until very tender. Season and ladle the onions into individual casseroles, pouring in as much stock as possible. On top of each place a slice of bread and a heaping tablespoon of Parmesan cheese. Place under the broiler until cheese is brown.
Serves 4.

Mrs. Maurice E. Purnell, 1948 Junior League
Cookbook

OYSTER BISQUE FLORENTINE

1 pt. small oysters
1 pt. greaseless chicken stock
½ pkg. frozen chopped spinach
½ stick butter
2 T. flour
2 t. lemon juice
Salt
Cayenne pepper
¾ c. light cream
½ c. sour cream

Cut the oysters up, saving the juice. Cook the spinach in a deep pan of boiling water. Dig at it with a large kitchen fork to separate it, and do not cook it after it all falls apart. Drain and put in the blender with ½ cup light cream and blend. Melt butter in a heavy pan and blend in flour. Add oyster juice, stock, and spinach. Cook slowly, stirring constantly, until it begins to thicken ever so slightly. Add chopped oysters and lemon juice. Beat the remaining ¼ cup of light cream with the sour cream and add to soup. Add salt and pepper to taste. Allow the bisque to heat, but do not let it boil. Serve hot with crisp crackers.
Serves 4.

Mrs. L. G. Pondrom

OYSTER STEW

½ bunch parsley
½ bunch green onions
½ stalk celery
1½ pts. oysters
1 qt. half-and-half
1 pt. milk
¼ lb. butter
Salt and pepper

Put parsley, onions, and celery through a food chopper. Melt butter in a skillet. Add vegetables and simmer until tender but not brown. Add oysters and juice, and cook until the edges curl. Add cream, milk, salt, and pepper. Bring to the boiling point, but do not boil. Serve at once.
Serves 8.

Mrs. M. Weatherby Carr

BLACKEYED PEA CHOWDER

½ lb. smoked bacon, diced
2 c. celery, chopped
2 c. green pepper, chopped
2 c. onion, chopped
1 can beef consommé
2 cans (1 lb. each) tomatoes
2 cans (1 lb. each) blackeyed
  peas

Sauté bacon with celery, green pepper, and onion. Add tomatoes, peas, and consomme; simmer 30-40 minutes. Serve in soup bowls. Accompany with jalapeño cornbread.
Serves 6 to 8.

Mrs. Bess Sullivan

GREEN PEA AND CURRY SOUP

¼ c. plus 2 T. vegetable oil
1 yellow onion, finely sliced
2 t. curry powder
1 t. salt
1½ t. sugar
Dash cayenne pepper
2 pkg. frozen green peas or 4 c. fresh shelled peas
1½ c. water
2 T. rice flour or 1 T. all-purpose flour
2 c. chicken stock
⅛ t. nutmeg, freshly grated
⅛ t. mace
1 t. sugar
½ c. light cream
½ c. heavy cream
1 T. fresh chives, finely chopped
3 oz. cooked turkey or chicken, diced

Heat ¼ cup vegetable oil in large, heavy pan. Add the onion and sauté until golden brown; add the curry powder, salt, 1½ t. sugar, and cayenne pepper. Cook over very low heat for 5 minutes. Add 2 T. vegetable oil to the pan; add the peas and ½ cup water. Cover and cook over very low heat until the peas are just soft. Remove from heat and stir in the flour, 1 cup water, and chicken stock. Put the pan over moderate heat, and stir until the mixture comes to a rolling boil. Add the nutmeg, mace, a little more cayenne pepper, and 1 t. sugar. Lower the heat, simmer 10 minutes. Rub the mixture through a fine strainer. Chill thoroughly. Before serving, stir in the light and heavy cream. Serve chilled and garnished with chopped chives and diced turkey or chicken.
Serves 6-8.

Mrs. Ralph G. Greenlee, Jr.

PUMPKIN SOUP — LA FONDA DEL SOL

2½ lb. pumpkin, peeled and cut into cubes
5 c. chicken stock
1 c. onion, chopped
¾ c. white part of scallion, chopped
2 c. light cream
Salt and pepper to taste
GARNISH:
Thin tomato slices
Whipped cream
Green part of scallions, chopped

In a large kettle combine the pumpkin, chicken stock, onion, white part of scallion. Bring to a boil and simmer until pumpkin is tender. Purée pumpkin and cool well. Stir in light cream and season with salt and pepper. Serve from a pumpkin shell and garnish with tomato slices, whipped cream, and green part of scallions, chopped.
Serves 12-14.

COLD RASPBERRY SOUP

2 pkg. frozen raspberries, defrosted
½ c. sour cream
⅓ c. sugar
2 c. ice water
½ c. dry red wine

Put raspberries through a fine sieve. Add sour cream and sugar. Stir well. Add ice water and wine. Put mixture in blender and blend until well mixed. Chill overnight. Shake before serving. Serve ice cold.
Serves 6.
Note: This soup is good for a ladies luncheon.

Mrs. Peter N. Tart

SENEGALESE

2 T. onions, chopped
2 T. butter
2-3 tart apples, cut up
1 heaping T. flour
2 t. curry powder
3½-4 c. chicken broth
1 t. chicken season stock base
   per can of broth
2 c. heavy cream
White chicken meat, diced

Sauté onions in butter. Add apples and cook for approximately 5 minutes. Add flour and curry powder and cook approximately 5 minutes more. Add chicken broth and chicken season stock base. Cook 30 minutes, then blend at low speed; chill. When ready to serve add heavy cream and chicken.
Serves 6-8.

Mrs. Jere W. Thompson

MOP'S SENGALESE SOUP

2½ lbs. chicken
1 qt. chicken broth
2 T. butter
2 T. flour
2 onions, chopped
2 stalks celery, chopped
2 apples, peeled and chopped
3 or 4 T. curry powder
1 pt. light cream

Boil chicken in water the day before. Skim fat from cooled broth and strain. Sauté onions and celery in butter for 10 minutes; add apples and cook 5 minutes longer. Mix curry powder and flour together and stir into mixture. Add chicken broth and cook over low heat for 40 minutes. Put through a sieve and when cool, add cream. Salt and pepper to taste. Chill. Serve in cups which have been refrigerated. Put 1 T. finely chopped white meat of chicken in each serving.

Mrs. Edward C. Gardere

SQUASH BISQUE

3 T. butter
1 c. onion, minced
¼ c. carrots, minced
Salt and pepper
2 medium potatoes, peeled and
  cubed
2 acorn squash, peeled and
  cubed or frozen winter
  squash
4 c. chicken broth
½ c. milk
½ c. heavy cream
Cayenne

Sauté onions and carrots in butter; add salt and pepper. Add potatoes, squash, and chicken broth and cook until tender. Blend at low speed. Add milk and cream, blend. Correct seasoning and thin with additional chicken broth if too thick. Sprinkle with cayenne when served. Serves 6-8.

Mrs. Jere W. Thompson

COLD TOMATO COB

8 medium tomatoes, peeled and
  chopped
2 small onions, coarsely
  chopped
Salt and pepper to taste
4 T. mayonnaise or sour cream
2 t. curry powder
3 T. chopped parsley

This recipe is excellent when really good, ripe tomatoes are available. Peel and chop coarsely the tomatoes in a bowl. Peel and chop onions into same bowl. There should be hunks of tomatoes and onions and juice. Add salt and pepper. Make a sauce of remaining 3 ingredients and chill. Serve tomato mixture in chilled soup cups and top with generous spoonsful of mayonnaise mixture. Serves 6-8.

Mrs. Paul B. Horton

JELLIED TOMATO BOUILLON

3 c. tomatoes
1 onion, chopped
1 bay leaf
few sprigs thyme
1½ t. minced celery leaf
1½ t. minced parsley
3 bouillon cubes
1 T. gelatin
3 T. cold water
Salt to taste
Paprika to taste

Simmer tomatoes, onion, bay leaf, thyme, and celery until quite soft. Strain. There should be from 2-2½ cups of juice. Add parsley, bouillon cubes, and gelatin softened in water. Stir until cubes and gelatin are thoroughly dissolved. Season to taste with salt and paprika. Garnish with finely shredded green pepper. Serve cold. Serves 8.

Mrs. Henry C. Coke, Jr., 1948 Junior League
of Dallas Cookbook

SLANG-GANG (COLD TOMATO SOUP)

1 14-oz. can whole tomatoes,
  cut in pieces
3 14-oz. cans tomato juice
1 can whole kernel white corn
Juice of ½ lemon
½ green pepper, thinly sliced
½ onion, minced
4 stalks celery, thinly sliced
½ cucumber, thinly sliced
Dash of Tabasco
Salt, pepper, and
  Worcestershire sauce to
  taste

Mix all ingredients and chill for 24 hours before serving. Serve very cold. Serves 6-8.

Mrs. Ronald H. Underwood

FANTASTIC TOMATO SOUP

2 green onions, chopped
½ stick butter
6 medium tomatoes, peeled
1 c. heavy cream
1 c. half-and-half
1 c. milk
Salt and pepper
¼ t. dill weed
1 T. sugar

Sauté onions in butter; put in blender with tomatoes and add all other ingredients. Blend until smooth. Chill and serve with a dollop of sour cream and a touch of caviar.
Serves 8-10 luncheon servings.

Mrs. Searcy Ferguson, Jr.

FROSTED TOMATO SOUP

6 ripe tomatoes, finely chopped
1 large onion, finely chopped
¾ c. mayonnaise
1 t. chopped parsley
½ t. black pepper
2 t. curry powder, or more to
  taste
Add chopped avocado if
  desired.

Mix ingredients, using ¼ cup of the mayonnaise, and chill. Place in soup cups. To the remaining mayonnaise, add the curry powder. Put 1 t. of the curried mayonnaise on each cup. For really frosted tomatoes, pour the mixture into an ice tray; and freeze until ice crystals begin to appear. Then serve the frosty tomato mixture in chilled old fashioned glasses, garnished with a dollop of the curried mayonnaise.
Serves 6.

Mrs. Mark Lemmon, Jr.

VEGETABLE SOUP

1 medium onion, chopped
3 carrots, chopped
2 ears corn, kernels removed
4 ribs celery, chopped
¼ lb. okra, sliced
¼ lb. green beans, sliced
2 T. butter
1 potato, diced
½ turnip, diced (optional)
½ t. garlic salt
2 tomatoes, chopped
Pinch of sugar
2 boullion cubes, chicken or
  beef
1 T. dried parsley flakes
1½ qt. water
½ c. tomato juice
Pinch of thyme
Pinch of marjoram
Salt and pepper to taste

Sauté first six ingredients in butter about 10 minutes over medium heat. Add potato, turnip, garlic salt, and sauté 2 minutes more. Add tomatoes, seasonings, and water. Simmer 1 hour and 15 minutes, covered. Makes 2 qts. Can be frozen.

Mrs. Edward H. Cary, III

"GARDEN FRESH" VEGETABLE SOUP

2 lbs. beef bones with marrow
2-3 qts. water
2 c. onions, coarsely chopped
1 heaping T. dehydrated
  bouillon or 1 beef bouillon
  cube
2 lbs. chuck, in bite-size pieces
Potatoes
Carrots
Tomatoes
Celery
Corn
Green beans
Green peas
Lima beans
¾ c. raw rice
Salt and pepper to taste
3 heaping T. cornmeal
Few drops Tabasco

Simmer bones in water with boullion for 2 hours. Remove bones from broth extracting the marrow. Add chuck and simmer 1 hour. Then add all the vegetables fresh or frozen. Vegetables may vary according to individual preference. Then add rice and simmer for 45 minutes. Then add salt, and pepper to taste. Slowly sprinkle cornmeal in soup to thicken. Add Tabasco. Simmer 15 minutes more. Served with congealed salad, cornbread or hard rolls, this is a complete meal. Keeps 3 to 4 days when refrigerated.
Serves 6-8.

Mrs. Theodore P. Votteler

BREADS

ANGEL BISCUITS

5 c. flour
¼ c. sugar
3 t. baking powder
1 t. baking soda
1 t. salt
1 c. shortening
1 T. dry yeast (1 pkg.)
2 T. warm water
2 c. buttermilk
½ c. butter, melted

Sift flour, sugar, baking powder, baking soda, and salt together and cut in shortening in a large bowl. In a separate bowl dissolve yeast in warm water. Add dissolved yeast and buttermilk to the dry ingredients and mix well. (At this stage the dough may be placed in the refrigerator and kept there for nearly a week before using.) Or, turn out onto a floured board; add more flour if necessary to roll out. Roll to about ⅜″ thickness. Cut with a round cutter, then dip top in melted butter and fold over. Bake on ungreased baking sheets for 15 minutes at 400°. Makes 5 dozen biscuits.

Cook Book Committee

DROP BISCUITS

2 t. baking powder, rounded
½ t. salt
1½ c. cake flour
1 T. shortening, rounded
1 c. sweet milk

Mix baking powder and salt in flour and shortening. Add milk. Drop with spoon on well-greased pan and bake at 350° for 15-20 minutes.
Makes 18 biscuits.

Mrs. Warren Jones, 1924 Junior League
Cookbook

MAYONNAISE BISCUITS

1 c. sifted, self-rising flour
3 T. mayonnaise
½ c. milk

Preheat oven to 425°. Combine all ingredients in a bowl and stir until moistened. Spoon into well-greased muffin tins, filling each about ⅔ full. Bake 10-15 minutes until done. This recipe smells funny while cooking but tastes great. Put butter on top and inside.
Yields 6-8.

Mrs. David C. Smith

SOUR CREAM BISCUITS

2 c. flour
1 T. baking powder
¼ t. soda
1 t. salt
1 c. sour cream
¼ c. milk

Sift together the dry ingredients. Blend in sour cream. Add milk, stirring constantly, and turn out on a lightly floured board. Knead lightly; then roll out to ½" thickness. Cut with a biscuit cutter and bake on ungreased sheets for 10-12 minutes at 450°.

Mrs. Lee F. Wood

BREAD RECIPE

1 c. Crisco
¾ c. sugar
2 t. salt
1 c. boiling water
2 eggs, beaten
1 pkg. yeast dissolved in 1 c. cold water
6 c. flour

Mix first 4 ingredients and let cool. Add eggs and yeast and beat for 5 minutes. Mix in flour. Put a greased plate on top of the bowl and put in refrigerator for several hours. Divide dough into 2 equal parts and let rise until double in 2 greased bread pans. Bake at 375° for 40 minutes.

Mrs. Mark Lemmon, Jr.

HOMEMADE BREAD

2 T. butter
2 T. sugar
1 T. salt
1 c. boiling water
1 c. scalded milk
1 pkg. yeast dissolved in ¼ c. warm water
6 c. flour

In a large bowl, put sugar, butter and salt. Add water and milk. When lukewarm, add yeast mixture. Beat in 3. c. flour, then 2 c. flour. Knead with 1 c. flour. Let rise, covered, until double, knead again, divide into 2 loaves. Put into 2 greased and floured bread pans and let rise until double. Bake at 425° for 10 minutes, then reduce heat to 350° for 15 minutes.

Mrs. G. Duffield Smith, Jr.

NO-KNEAD BREAD

1 qt. whole milk
1 c. sugar
1 c. shortening
9 c. flour
1 t. salt
1 t. soda
2 t. baking powder
2 pkgs. powdered yeast
melted butter

Boil milk, sugar and shortening. Set in a pan of cold water and cool to lukewarm. Add yeast and stir until dissolves. Sift dry ingredients and pour into mixture and stir. Let rise until double, about 1 hour. Work this with a spoon. Pour into 3 large greased loaf pans and let rise until double (pan is about ½ full), about 1 hour. Bake on middle rack of oven at 300° for about 45 minutes. After it starts to brown, brush with melted butter about 3 times before it is done.
Yield: 3 loaves.

Mrs. John Bagwell

BROWN BREAD

2 c. white flour
1 egg
1 c. raisins
2 t. baking powder
2 c. graham flour
2 c. buttermilk
1 c. sugar
1 c. nuts
1 t. salt

Mix all ingredients well. Fill cans about ⅔ full and bake in slow oven 250° about 1 hour.
Makes about 4 1-lb. cylindrical cans with covers.

Mrs. George W. Truett, 1924 Junior League
Cookbook

YEAST BREAD

2 pkgs. active dry yeast
  softened in ½ c. lukewarm
  water
2 c. milk
4 T. sugar
4 t. salt
4 T. shortening
1½ c. lukewarm water
12 c. flour

Scald milk and pour into a large mixing bowl. Add sugar, salt, shortening and water. Cool to lukewarm. Stir in 2 cups flour. Add the softened yeast. Then add 4 cups flour and beat with a wooden spoon until batter is smooth and elastic. Add remaining 6 cups flour to make a dough that is light but does not stick to the hands, beating it in until the beating gets rough, then working it in with the hands. Turn dough out on a lightly floured board, cover and let rest for 10 to 15 minutes, then knead until dough is smooth. Shape dough into a ball and put it in a lightly greased bowl. Brush surface of the dough with melted shortening, cover and let rise 2 hours or until double in size. Punch dough down and divide into 4 equal portions. Shape each part into a smooth ball, cover and let rest 10 to 15 minutes. Shape each part into a loaf, put loaves in greased bread pans, cover and let rise for about 2 hours, or until sides of dough reach top of pans. Bake in a preheated 400° oven for 1 hour. Yield: 4 loaves or 4 dozen rolls or 4 coffee rings.

Mrs. Samuel P. Burford, Jr.

ILSE'S NO-KNEAD FRENCH BREAD

STARTER:
½ c. water
¼ c. milk
2 t. salad oil
1 pkg. dry yeast dissolved in ¼ c. warm water (105°-115°)
2 t. sugar, divided
1¼ t. salt
2⅓ c. flour (about 10½ oz.)

BREAD:
½ c. milk
1 c. water
2½ t. salt
4½ t. sugar, divided
1½ T. salad oil
1 pkg. dry yeast dissolved in ¼ c. warm water
2 T. starter at room temperature
4¾-5 c. flour (approx. 20 oz.)

STARTER: Combine water, milk, salad oil, 1½ t. sugar, salt, and scald. Add ½ t. sugar to dissolved yeast. Cool scalded mixture to warm (105°-115°), add yeast mixture and stir in flour. Let stand in warm place, covered tightly in a slightly greased bowl for 12-24 hours. As it expands push down. This starter can be kept indefinitely. Refrigerate in tightly covered container.

BREAD: Combine milk, water, salt, 4 t. sugar, salad oil, and scald. Add ½ t. sugar to dissolved yeast. Cool scalded mixture to lukewarm and add yeast. Wisk in 2 T. starter. Stir in flour. Do not knead. Place in a slightly greased bowl, cover and let rise in warm place until double in size. Push down and put onto floured board and divide dough into 4 equal parts. Flatten out one part at a time to large rectangle and fold in long sides and then fold in half (put seam on bottom). Shape into long thin loaf 12″ long. Repeat for other 3 portions. Put loaves on ungreased teflon cookie sheet and slash diagonally with knife. Let rise, covered, until doubled in size. Bake at 425° for 10-15 minutes and at 350° for 15-20 minutes more. Place pan of boiling water on lower oven shelf to create steam during cooking. For crustier loaves brush with combination of egg white and water before baking. This bread can be frozen and reheated before serving.
Makes 4 loaves.

Mrs. James Lambert

ICE BOX ROLLS

1 c. milk
1 c. mashed potatoes
¼ c. sugar
1 cake yeast
2 heaping T. lard
1 t. salt
¼ c. tepid water
4½ c. flour

Scald milk and dissolve lard in the hot milk. Add unseasoned potatoes, salt, sugar, and eggs which have been beaten lightly. Soak the yeast in tepid water and add to the above mixture, which should be tepid, not hot. Stir in flour. The dough will be quite soft but will work well with a spoon — do not knead. Let rise in the ice box for 2 hours. Make into rolls and let stand 2 hours out of the ice box before baking. The dough will last a week in the ice box but should be worked every day. Can also make cheese straws and cinnamon buns from the dough.

Makes 36 rolls.

HOT HERB BREAD

1 loaf French or Italian bread
½ c. butter, soften
1 t. parsley flakes
¼ t. oregano, crumbled
¼ t. dill weed
1 clove garlic, minced
Parmesan cheese, grated

Blend butter, parsley, oregano, dill, and garlic. Slice bread and spread slices with butter mixture. Wrap loaf in foil, leaving the top open. Sprinkle the top with cheese and parsley flakes. Heat in a 400° oven for 10 minutes. Freezes well.

Mrs. Larry Higginbotham

WHOLE WHEAT ROLLS

1 qt. milk
1 c. shortening
1 c. sugar
1½ pkgs. yeast
1 qt. white flour
1 qt. whole wheat flour
1 T. salt
1 t. soda
1 t. baking powder

Sift two flours together. Heat milk, shortening and sugar but do not boil. Set aside; when mixture is about 115° on a candy thermometer, add yeast. Sift in 1 qt. flour. Set aside for 2 hours in a warm place to rest. Then sift in remaining ingredients and make a stiff dough. Take as much dough as you need and cut into Parker House rolls, let rise for another 2 hours. Store remaining dough in refrigerator and use when needed. The rolls can be made and frozen on cookie sheets. Allow to thaw for 2 hours before baking. Bake at 350° for 15-20 minutes.

Mrs. David Lide

BACON-CHEESE BREAD

½ c. milk
1 can condensed cheese soup, undiluted
¼ c. butter
3½ c. unsifted flour
1 pkg. dry yeast
1 t. salt
1 large egg
6 slices bacon, cooked and crumbled

Stir milk into soup gradually in a medium-sized saucepan. Add butter. Heat over low heat until lukewarm. Combine 2 cups of flour, undissolved yeast and salt in a large bowl of mixer. Add soup mixture. Beat on low speed until moistened. Add egg and ½ cup of flour. Beat 2 minutes at medium speed, scraping bowl. Remove from mixer, and stir in 1 cup flour and bacon to make the dough firm. Cover bowl with plastic wrap and refrigerate until doubled (approx. 1 hour). Grease a 2-qt. casserole. Shape dough into a ball and place in casserole. Cover with a towel and let rise again until doubled. Bake in a preheated 350° oven for 50 minutes or until golden. Cool on wire rack.

Mrs. William Plack Carr, Jr.

COMPANY SURPRISE BREAD

1 loaf unsliced white bread
Swiss cheese
½ c. butter
½ c. minced onion
1 T. prepared mustard
1 T. poppy seeds
2 strips bacon

Slice off top crust of bread and then make slices from top to bottom 1" apart and stopping 1" from bottom. Place 1 slice of Swiss cheese inside each slice. Mix butter, onion, mustard and poppy seeds and spread on top of bread filled with cheese. Tie bread up and place bacon across length of bread. Bake for 18 minutes at 400°, cut loaf in half lengthwise and serve hot, letting company pull pieces off.

Mrs. Larry M. Nobles

DILLY BREAD

2 T. butter
2 t. salt
4 T. sugar
3 t. dill seed
1 t. dill weed
1 T. minced onion
2 c. cottage cheese
5 c. flour
2 eggs
¾ c. cheddar cheese, grated
½ t. soda
2 pkg. dry yeast dissolved in ½
   cup warm water and ½ t.
   sugar

Melt butter in a saucepan and add the next 6 ingredients. Heat to lukewarm. Put into a warm bowl and add cheese, eggs, soda, and yeast. Mix in flour. Cover and let rise until doubled in bulk. Punch down and divide into 6-8 equal parts. Form into balls and place on greased cookie sheets. Butter tops; cover and let rise until doubled in size. Bake at 350° for 25-30 minutes. Butter tops again when taken from oven. Delicious with gumbo or stews.
Serves 8.

Mrs. James Lambert

EGGNOG BREAD

3 c. sifted, all-purpose flour
¾ c. sugar
1 T. baking powder
1 t. salt
½ t. nutmeg
1 egg, beaten
1½ c. dairy eggnog
¼ c. butter, melted
¾ c. walnuts or pecans, chopped
¾ c. candied fruit, chopped

In a large bowl sift together the flour, sugar, baking powder, salt, and nutmeg. Combine eggnog, egg, and butter; add to the dry ingredients and stir until blended. Add nuts and fruit. Bake in a loaf pan 60-70 minutes in a 350° oven. Cool on a wire rack. Good with Swiss or Cheddar cheeses and cold meats. Makes a nice gift at Christmas. May use all nuts in place of candied fruit for a good nut bread. Freezes well.

Mrs. W. B. Munson IV

MRS. WILCOX'S HERB BREAD

1½ c. lukewarm water
1 T. sugar
2 t. yeast (1 pkg.)
2 t. salt
4 c. flour
1 t. oregano
1 t. basil
½ t. marjoram

Combine in large bowl and let sit 5 minutes: water, sugar, yeast, salt. Then add gradually the flour. Finally, add the oregano, basil, and marjoram. Turn onto floured board and knead 5-8 minutes. Place in greased bowl. Let rise until doubled — about 1-1½ hours. Work down and knead. Put into greased loaf pans or round bowl. Let rise again until double. Bake in loaf pan in preheated 400° oven for 40-45 minutes or until done.

Cook Book Committee

PULLED BREAD

1 c. sugar
½ c. butter
2 c. flour
1 t. soda in 2 T. sour milk
2 eggs, separated
½ c. pecans, chopped
Pinch salt
3 mashed bananas

Cream butter and sugar, adding soda and milk. Add beaten yolks, half the flour, bananas, nuts, remaining flour, and then the egg whites which have been beaten separately. Bake in a loaf pan for 45 minutes at 325°.

Mrs. Earl H. Hulsey

CHILI-CHEESE CORN BREAD

3 ears fresh corn
1 c. yellow corn meal
1½ t. salt
3 t. baking soda
1 c. sour cream
1 stick butter and 2 T., melted
2 eggs, well beaten
¼ lb. Jack cheese in ¼″ cubes
1 4-oz. can peeled green chilies,
   seeds washed out, chopped

Scrape corn off cob, then mix with rest of ingredients. Pour into well-buttered 9-inch square baking dish and bake at 350° for one hour.
Serves 6.

Cook Book Committee

HUSH PUPPIES

¼ c. flour
1 t. baking powder
⅛ t. salt
1 c. corn meal
1 egg, well beaten
½ 14½-oz. can evaporated milk
Fat for frying

Sift flour, baking powder, and salt together. Stir in corn meal. Combine egg and milk into dry ingredients to form a very soft mush. Working with a small amount at a time, form balls and drop by teaspoons into deep hot fat. Cook, turning frequently, for 3 to 5 minutes, until brown. Drain in a colander.
Makes about 12.

Grand Chenier Hunting Lodge, Louisiana —
1948

JALAPENO CORN BREAD

2 boxes Ole Tyme Corn Bread
   Muffin Mix
2½ c. milk
½ c. vegetable oil
3 eggs
3 t. sugar
1 large onion, grated
1 8-oz. can cream-style corn
3-oz. can Jalapeño peppers,
   seeded and cut fine
1½ c. grated cheese — cheddar

Mix all ingredients well and place in a greased baking pan (8x12″) and bake 35-45 minutes in a 375° oven. The cheese can be omitted if the supper is heavy.

Mrs. Spencer Carver

SOUTHERN CORN BREAD

3 T. bacon grease or shortening
2 c. white corn meal
1 t. salt
½ t. soda
2 T. sugar
About 1 ⅔ c. boiling water
1 c. buttermilk
1 egg, beaten
1 T. baking powder

Set oven at 450°. Put bacon grease in a pie pan, rub all around edges, leaving balance on bottom. Put pan in heating oven to melt because pan must be very hot when batter is put in it. Put corn meal, salt, soda, and sugar in bowl. Add enough boiling water to coat the meal (improves texture). Add buttermilk, egg, and baking powder. Mix well. Remove hot pan from oven, pour excess melted fat into batter, mix again quickly and pour batter into hot pan. Bake 20-25 minutes. Brown the top quickly under broiler at the last minute. Serve hot, sliced in wedges. (Omit sugar in this recipe if you are using corn bread for turkey dressing.)

Mrs. L. G. Pondrom

CORN DODGERS

1½ c. white corn meal
1 T. salt
Boiling water (about 1 cup)
Bacon grease

Mix corn meal and salt. Add ¾ cup of boiling water, mix well, and put in a little more if mixture is not workable. If it is too dry, it will not mold well; and if it is too runny, it is hopeless. Let cool until you can handle it. Roll a firm, small ball and flatten it out slightly. A heaping measuring tablespoonful is a good gauge. The flattened dodgers should be about 1½″ in diameter and less than ½″ thick. Put them on a plate or cookie sheet and chill for several hours. Put enough bacon grease in a skillet to make it about ½″ deep when melted. When hot, add as many dodgers as the skillet will hold without crowding. When the bottom is brown, flip to brown both sides. Drain on paper towels. Serve hot with butter. Compulsory with blackeyed peas, also good with fish, hash, or stews. This recipe will make around 20 dodgers and should serve 4, but don't count on it. Addicts can eat 6 with ease.

Mrs. L. G. Pondrom

BANANA APRICOT NUT BREAD

2 c. flour
1 t. baking soda
½ t. salt
1 c. sugar
½ c. dried apricots, chopped
½ c. walnuts, chopped
¾ c. ripe banana, mashed
½ c. milk
1 egg
¼ c. butter, melted

In a bowl stir together the flour, baking powder, soda, salt, sugar, apricots, and nuts. Combine the banana, milk, egg, and butter; stir into the dry ingredients just until well blended. Pour batter into a well-greased 5x9x9½″ loaf pan. Bake at 350° for 1 hour to 1 hour 15 minutes.

Mrs. Walter Sosnowski

Breads of the World

APPLE BREAD

½ c. butter
1 c. sugar
2 eggs
2 T. sour milk
1 t. baking soda
2 c. flour
½ t. salt
1 t. vanilla
2 c. large apples, chopped
½ c. nuts, chopped
TOPPING:
2 T. butter
2 T. flour
2 T. sugar
1 t. cinnamon

Hint: to sour milk, combine 1 tablespoon vinegar with enough milk to fill ½ cup and let stand a few minutes. Cream shortening with sugar; add eggs, one at a time. Put soda in sour milk and add to mixture. Add vanilla and then flour and salt. Add apples and nuts. (Apples will stay light in color, if they are added to mixture immediately after chopping.) Pour into 1 large loaf pan or 2 smaller ones. This can also be baked in soup cans, allowing less cooking time. Sprinkle with topping and bake for 1 hour at 350°. Cool slightly and remove from pan. Can be frozen. For topping, cut butter into flour, sugar and cinnamon. Should be lumpy.

Mrs. Kenneth C. Bernecker

BANANA-BLUEBERRY BREAD

½ c. fresh or frozen blueberries
1½ c. all-purpose flour
⅔ c. sugar
2¼ t. baking powder
½ t. salt
½ c. uncooked oats (quick or old-fashioned)
2 eggs, beaten
⅓ c. melted shortening or salad oil
1 c. ripe bananas, mashed

Sprinkle blueberries with 2 teaspoons flour. Sift together the remaining flour, sugar, baking powder, and salt. Stir in oats. Combine eggs, shortening, and bananas; add to dry ingredients, stirring until just combined. Add the blueberries; stir just enough to distribute them evenly throughout the batter. Pour batter into greased and floured 8x5" loaf pan. Bake at 350° for about 1 hour. Let cool completely. Wrap bread and store 24 hours before slicing. Can be frozen.

Mrs. James G. Aldridge

BANANA NUT BREAD

½ c. butter
1 c. sugar
1 c. bananas, mashed (approx. 2)
2 eggs, beaten
2 c. flour
1 t. soda
½ t. salt
2 t. orange peel, grated
¾ c. pecans, chopped

Cream butter until softened. Add sugar, creaming well. Add bananas and eggs, mixing well. Sift flour, soda and salt together; stir into creamed mixture with orange peel. Stir in nuts. Pour into greased loaf pan and bake about one hour at 350°.
Yield: 1 loaf.

Mrs. M. Weatherby Carr

LEMON BREAD

1 c. butter
2 c. sugar
4 eggs
½ t. salt
½ t. soda
3 c. flour
1 c. buttermilk
Rind of 1 lemon, grated
1 c. nuts, chopped
TOPPING:
Juice of 3 lemons
1 c. sugar

Cream butter and sugar. Add eggs one at a time. Sift dry ingredients and add alternately with buttermilk. Begin and end with dry ingredients. Fold in nuts and grated rind. Pour into 2 7x3x2 loaf pans which have been greased and floured. Bake at 350° for 1 hour.
For topping, combine juice and sugar and let stand. Stir often until sugar dissolves. When bread is done remove from pan and place on foil. Spoon juice over hot loaf. Let cool and then wrap tightly in foil. Freezes well.

Mrs. Maurice E. Moore, Jr.

PRUNE BREAD

8 oz. dried prunes, finely chopped
¼ c. sherry
2 eggs
1 c. buttermilk
½ c. sugar
½ t. salt
1 t. cinnamon
2 c. flour
3 t. baking powder

Marinate chopped prunes in sherry for 24 hours. Mix eggs, milk, sugar, salt, cinnamon, flour, and baking powder. Stir well. Add prunes and sherry. Pour into a well-buttered loaf pan and bake at 350° for 50-60 minutes until top is browned.

Mrs. James Lambert

PUMPKIN BREAD

2½ c. flour
3 c. sugar
2 t. soda
1 t. cinnamon
1 t. nutmeg
1½ t. salt
4 eggs
¾ c. Mazola oil
½ c. water
2 c. canned pumpkin
1 c. nuts, chopped

Sift dry ingredients together. Place eggs, oil and water in a large bowl of mixer. Gradually add dry ingredients to form smooth batter. Add pumpkin, mix well. Fold in nuts. Pour into 2 greased and floured loaf pans or bake in bundt pan as a cake. Bake at 325° for 1½ hours or until firm.
Serves 12 to 14.

Mrs. Maurice E. Moore, Jr.

MOZELL'S STRAWBERRY BREAD

3 c. flour
1 t. soda
1 t. salt
1 T. cinnamon
2 c. sugar
4 eggs, beaten
2 c. frozen strawberries
1½ c. Wesson oil
1¼ c. broken pecans

Sift dry ingredients together. Combine eggs, strawberries and oil and add to sifted ingredients. Add pecans. Pour into 2 greased loaf pans. Bake at 325° for about 1 hour. Cool on wire rack.

Mrs. Spencer Carver

ZUCCHINI BREAD

3 eggs
1 c. oil
2 c. sugar
2 heaping c. zucchini, peeled and medium grated
1 t. vanilla
3 c. flour
2 t. cinnamon
1 t. baking soda
1 t. salt
¼ t. baking powder
¾ c. walnuts, chopped

Beat eggs until light and foamy. Add oil, sugar, zucchini, and vanilla and beat well. Sift flour, cinnamon, baking soda, salt, baking powder and add to creamed mixture. Fold in walnuts. Pour into 2 big loaf pans which are greased and floured. Bake 1 hour at 325 degrees.

Mrs. Larry K. Casey

ORANGE NUT BREAD

2½ c. sifted flour
1 T. baking powder
1¼ t. salt
1 c. nuts, chopped
1 c. milk
2 eggs, beaten
½ c. orange marmalade
2 T. melted butter

Mix and sift flour, baking powder, and salt. Add nuts. Add milk and eggs and stir lightly so as to moisten. Stir in the marmalade and butter. Pour into 2 small, well-greased baking pans. Bake about 1 hour at 350°.
Makes 2 small loaves.

Mrs. Richard K. Marks

BLUEBERRY MUFFINS

1¾ c. cake flour, sifted
2 t. baking powder
½ t. salt
1 c. blueberries or
  huckleberries
¼ c. butter
¼ c. sugar
2 eggs, well beaten
¾ c. milk
Grated rind of ½ lemon

Sift flour, baking powder and salt together 4 times. Sprinkle a little of this flour over blueberries. Cream butter, add sugar, and combine well. Beat in eggs. Add flour alternately with milk. Stir in blueberries and lemon rind. Fill greased muffin tins ⅔ full with batter. Bake at 425° F. for about 20 minutes, or until done.
Makes about 20 small muffins.

Mrs. Joseph H. Bialas — 1948

BLUEBERRY SHORTCAKE MUFFINS

2 c. Bisquick
½ c. sugar
½ t. cinnamon
1 c. sour cream
1 egg, unbeaten
1 c. fresh or other (drained)
  blueberries

Preheat oven to 425°. Lightly grease 12 muffin tins. Combine Bisquick, sugar, and cinnamon; mix well. Make a well in the mixture; add sour cream and egg all at once. Beat with a fork until well mixed. Gently fold in blueberries. Pour into muffin tins and sprinkle with granulated sugar. Bake 20 minutes or until brown.
Makes 12 muffins.

REFRIGERATOR BRAN MUFFINS

2 c. boiling water
2 c. Nabisco 100% Bran cereal
1 c. shortening
3 c. sugar
4 eggs, beaten
1 qt. buttermilk
5 c. flour
5 t. soda
1 t. salt
4 c. Kellogg's All Bran cereal

Pour water over 100% Bran. Set aside. Cream shortening and sugar; add eggs and milk. Add water-Bran mixture. Sift together flour, soda and salt. Add All Bran. Fold all ingredients together only until all dry ingredients are moistened. Bake in greased muffin tins for 20 minutes at 400°. Uncooked batter will keep in the refrigerator in a covered container for 6 weeks. Delicious with butter and honey. Muffins will freeze.
Yields approximately 50 muffins.

Mrs. James G. Aldridge

PINEAPPLE YOGURT MUFFINS

2 c. biscuit mix
½ c. coconut
¼ c. sugar
½ t. soda
¼ c. butter, melted
1 c. pineapple yogurt
1 egg, slightly beaten
½ c. crushed pineapple,
    drained

Mix biscuit mix, coconut, sugar, and soda. Add remaining ingredients. Muffin batter should be slightly lumpy. Pour into muffin cups. Bake at 400° for 15 minutes. May be frozen.
Makes 18 medium-size muffins.

Mrs. Ronald H. Underwood

RAISIN BRAN MUFFINS

1 15-oz. box Raisin Bran
3 c. sugar
5 c. flour
5 t. baking soda
2 t. salt
4 eggs
1 qt. buttermilk
1 c. oil

Combine dry ingredients in a large bowl. Beat eggs, milk, and oil together and add to bran mixture. Mix well. Bake in greased muffin tins, ⅔ full, for 15 minutes at 400°. This batter may be stored in the refrigerator in a covered container for as long as six weeks and used as needed.
Yields approximately 6 dozen.

Mrs. James C. Tubb

CORNBREAD AND RICE DRESSING

2 pans corn bread (can be made
    several days ahead and
    refrigerated)
3 c. chicken stock or 4 T.
    Wyler's Nuggets dissolved in
    3 c. boiling water
½ stick butter
1½ c. raw brown rice, cooked
    and drained
6 c. bread crumbs
3 large onions, chopped
1 bunch green onions, chopped
    (including tops)
4 c. celery, chopped (including
    leaves)
1 c. fresh parsley, chopped
5 T. Lawry's Seasoned salt
2 T. black pepper
2 eggs, beaten

Crumble cold corn bread as well as possible. Melt butter in hot stock and pour it over corn bread, chopping with large spoon to get out all big lumps. Add all other ingredients in order given and mix well. Taste, and add more salt and pepper if needed. If more moisture is needed, add a bit more stock or warm water. Serves about 16. Can be made the day before the turkey is to be cooked, or can be made ahead and frozen as is or in small packages to use for hens or smaller servings. Can be doubled (mix this amount in turkey roaster).

Mrs. L. G. Pondrom

CORNBREAD:
2 c. corn meal
1 c. flour
¼ c. sugar
4 t. baking powder
½ t. salt
2 eggs
1 c. milk
¼ c. vegetable oil
DRESSING:
Corn bread broken up into
  small pieces
4 slices trimmed white toast,
  broken up
2 c. celery, chopped
1 c. onions, chopped
2 t. parsley, chopped
Salt and pepper to taste
2 t. bacon grease
3-4 c. hot chicken broth
3 eggs, beaten

CORN BREAD DRESSING

For corn bread, mix all ingredients in a bowl and beat. Put into a greased 9"-square pan and bake at 425° for about 20 minutes.

For dressing, sauté celery and onions in bacon grease until transparent — about 10 minutes. Add cornbread, bread, parsley, salt and pepper and broth until mixture is moist. Turn off fire, cover and place on back of stove for 3-5 hours. Mix in eggs and put in a casserole, baking 45 minutes at 350°

Serves 8-10.

Mrs. Denys Slater, Jr.

3 slices dry bread (2 to 3 days
  old, cut ¾" thick)
2 eggs
½ c. cream
Pinch of salt
Dash of nutmeg
¼ c. cooking oil
Confectioners sugar
Hot maple syrup

PUFFED FRENCH TOAST

Trim crusts off bread slices and cut each piece across diagonally to make six triangles. In a bowl beat eggs until light and frothy; add cream, salt, and nutmeg. Soak the bread triangles, a few pieces at a time, in the egg mixture until they absorb it thoroughly. In a skillet heat the cooking oil and fry the bread on both sides until each piece is golden brown. Remove bread pieces from the skillet and drain briefly on paper towels to get rid of excess grease. Place the bread on an ungreased baking sheet and allow them to puff up in a hot oven at 400° for about 5 minutes. On heated plates, place 3 triangles of French Toast per portion. Sprinkle generously with confectioners sugar and serve with heated maple syrup.

Recipe will serve 2.

Mrs. George W. Jalonick IV

GERMAN PANCAKES

6 eggs
2 c. milk
2 c. flour
½ t. salt
½ stick butter

Beat eggs very well and stir in milk. Sift flour and measure, then sift with salt. Gradually stir into egg mixture. Melt butter and pour into aluminum foil pie tins. Bake at 500° for 5 minutes; reduce to 450° for 10 minutes. Serve with lemon wedges, powdered sugar, or honey.

Mrs. Clint Josey, Jr.

GIANT PANCAKE

½ c. flour
½ c. milk
2 eggs
Pinch of nutmeg
1 stick butter
2 T. Confectioners sugar
Juice of ½ lemon

Preheat oven to 425°. Mix first 4 ingredients in a blender. Melt butter in rectangular Pyrex dish. When hot, pour in batter. Bake 15-20 minutes until golden brown. Sprinkle with sugar and lemon juice. Serve with jelly or maple syrup. Batter may be made ahead and kept in refrigerator.
Serves 4.

Mrs. John Waggoner

OATMEAL PANCAKES

2 c. buttermilk
1½ c. oatmeal
½ c. flour
1 t. soda
1 t. salt
1 t. sugar
2 beaten eggs

Stir together the buttermilk and oatmeal. Add remaining ingredients and stir well. Cook as ordinary pancakes. Good with applesauce or the traditional syrup and butter.

Mrs. Walter F. Sosnowski

SOURDOUGH PANCAKES

1 yeast cake
2 c. cool water
2½ c. flour
2 eggs
1 T. sugar
1 t. salt
1 t. soda
2 T. butter, melted

Dissolve yeast cake in water. Mix with flour and leave overnight in a large bowl. Add remaining ingredients, adding milk if THIN pancakes are desired. Cook as you would regular pancakes.
Yield: 10 pancakes

Mrs. Edwin L. Cox

WHOLE WHEAT PANCAKES

1½ c. whole wheat flour
3 t. baking powder
¾ t. salt
3 T. brown sugar
1 egg, beaten
1½ c. milk
3 T. melted butter

Combine all dry ingredients. Add egg, milk and butter. Fold in one teaspoon grated tangerine or ½ cup fresh whole raspberries to make these very special.

Mrs. Searcy Ferguson, Jr.

WAFFLES

2 c. flour
1 t. salt
1 T. sugar
3 t. baking powder
2 c. milk
2 egg yolks, well beaten
4 T. butter, melted
2 egg whites, beaten stiff
2 t. syrup

Sift flour once; measure. Add salt, sugar and baking powder, and sift again. Add milk to egg yolks, then flour, beating until smooth. Add butter. Fold in egg white gently, but thoroughly. Just before baking add syrup.
Serves 8.

Mrs. Michaux Nash — 1946

POPOVERS

1 c. flour
¼ t. salt
3 eggs
1 c. milk
1 t. melted butter

Do not preheat the oven. Combine eggs, milk, and melted butter. Mix in flour and salt; stir until smooth. Oil very well ovenproof custard cups and fill half full. Put on a cookie sheet in the oven and bake at 400° about 50 minutes. Or oil an iron popover pan well and bake at 400 for 30 minutes.
Yield: 8-10 in cups or 11 in iron pan.

Mrs. Joe E. Funk,

WHOLE WHEAT POPOVERS

⅔ c. whole wheat flour
½ c. white flour
¼ t. salt
2 eggs
⅞ c. milk
1 T. butter, melted

Sift together the flours and salt. In a bowl, beat until frothy the eggs, milk and butter. Stir liquid into sifted dry ingredients and beat only long enough to blend well. Oil and heat popover or muffin pans, fill ⅓ full and bake at 450° for 20 minutes.

Mrs. Clint Josey, Jr.

SALLY LUNN BREAD

1 c. milk
⅓ c. sugar
5 T. butter, melted
1 egg, beaten
½ yeast cake
2⅔ c. flour, sifted
Pinch of salt

Scald milk and cool until lukewarm. Add sugar, melted butter, beaten egg and crumbled yeast cake and beat. Add flour, salt and beat well. Let rise 3 hours in a warm place then beat for 5 minutes. Pour into a well-greased loaf pan and let rise 30 minutes. Bake 30-45 minutes at 350°. SERVE AT ONCE.
Yield: 1 loaf.

Mrs. M. Weatherby Carr

SOUFFLEED CRACKERS

Soda crackers
Ice water
Butter

Put crackers in a shallow pan and cover with ice water, allowing to stand about 8 minutes. Remove with a cake turner (allowing to drain well on the turner) to a baking sheet. Dot with butter and put into a hot oven. After well puffed, turn heat quite low (250°) and allow crackers to dry thoroughly. Do not use too much butter as it toughens them. Takes from 45 to 60 minutes to dry out. Serve with a soup or salad.

Mrs. Charles Dexter — 1948
Jr. League Cookbook

SOPAPILLAS

6 c. flour
1 t. salt
1 T. baking powder
2 heaping T. Crisco
1 pkg. dry yeast
2 c. water
Hot shortening
Butter
Honey

Sift flour. baking powder, and salt into a mixing bowl: add Crisco and cut in coarsely. Dissolve yeast in warm water and add. Then add 2 c. cold water gradually until dough is kneaded to bottom of bowl and until bowl is clean. Knead until sticky but not dry. Make dough about 3 hours before cooking and cover at room temperature. Roll out thin with a flannel rolling pin and cut into 3" squares. Drop a few squares at a time into deep hot cooking oil (375°). Turn squares over 3 or 4 times to make them puff evenly. Fry about 2 or 3 minutes on each side or until golden brown. Drain on paper and serve hot with honey and butter. If served for breakfast. can be rolled in a mixture of ½ c. sugar mixed with 2 t. cinnamon before serving.

Mrs. Jack Vaughn

YORKSHIRE PUDDING

1 c. flour
½ c. milk
¼ c. water
½ t. salt
2 eggs
1 T. lard

Preheat oven to 350°. Beat eggs until light and add other ingredients. Put 1 T. of lard into a 9-inch square pan and heat pan for 10 minutes. Add mixture and bake for 30 minutes. Serve immediately. Serves 8.

Mrs. Walter N. Kuntz III

EGG DISHES

ASPARAGUS QUICHE

1½ lbs. fresh asparagus or 2 pkgs. frozen asparagus
Pastry for quiche pan or large (11-12" pie plate)
12 slices bacon
½ lb. grated natural Swiss cheese, grated
½ lb. fresh mushrooms (optional)
4 eggs
1½ c. light cream
⅛ t. nutmeg
⅛ t. salt
Dash of cayenne pepper

Cut into 1" pieces and cook fresh asparagus until tender and drain. (Cut into 1" pieces and cook frozen asparagus according to package directions.) Bake pie shell for 10 minutes at 400°. Reduce oven heat to 375°. Cook bacon until crisp and drain on paper towel. Sauté mushrooms in butter. Sprinkle bacon cut into small pieces into the bottom of the pie shell, following with the mushrooms, cheese and asparagus. With a rotary beater, beat eggs, cream, nutmeg, salt and pepper. Beat until just combined and pour into the pie shell. (If you wish, reserve ¼ c. asparagus to decorate the top after the mixture has been poured in.) Bake 40 minutes or until knife inserted 1" from the pastry edge comes out clean. Serve immediately.
Serves 6 as a main dish and 12 as hors d'oeuvres.

Mrs. Yerger Hill III

CURRIED CRAB QUICHE

2 cans (7½-oz. each) or 1 lb. King crab
2 T. lemon juice
2 T. sherry
1 T. onion, finely chopped
1 t. curry powder
1 t. parsley flakes
1 c. Swiss cheese, cubed
Unbaked 10" pie shell
SOUR CREAM CUSTARD:
3 eggs, well beaten
¾ c. milk
½ c. sour cream
¼ t. salt

Bake pie shell in a 400° oven for 10 minutes. Remove from oven. Drain crab, remove cartilage and chop. Combine crab with lemon juice, sherry, onion, curry powder, parsley flakes. Refrigerate 1-2 hours to blend flavors. Cover bottom of pastry shell with cubed cheese. Spread crab and seasoning mixture over cheese. Combine ingredients for custard and pour over all. Bake at 350° for 45 minutes or until custard is lightly browned and set. Cool slightly and cut in wedges to serve.
Makes 8 servings or 24 miniature slices.

Mrs. John J. Kendrick, Jr.

MEXICAN QUICHE

1 9" pie shell, baked
6 thin slices ham
¼ lb. baby Swiss cheese
½ onion, chopped
3 jalapeños, chopped
1 tomato, chopped
4-5 strips cooked bacon,
  crumbled
Dried parsley
¼ lb. sharp Cheddar cheese,
  grated
CUSTARD:
4 eggs
1 t. dry mustard
1 c. whipping cream

Heat whipping cream and add gradually to eggs. Start with ham and layer ½ of all ingredients, making the Swiss with Cheddar cheeses last. Repeat. Pour custard mixture, jiggling pan to settle mixture. Sprinkle with nutmeg and parsley on top. Cook 30-40 minutes at 450°.
Serves 12.

Mrs. Floyd T. Burke

BLENDER ZUCCHINI QUICHE

1 9" pie shell, frozen
1 c. Swiss cheese, grated
1-1½ zucchini, sliced in paper-
  thin rounds
4 small green onions (tops too)
  thinly sliced or finely
  chopped
3 pieces bacon, fried, drained
  and crumbled into bits
1 c. whipping cream (½ pt.)
2 eggs
Salt and pepper to taste

Thaw pie shell. Sprinkle grated cheese on bottom. Arrange zucchini over the cheese and sprinkle onions and bacon over zucchini. Put eggs, cream, salt and pepper in a blender and blend at high speed for 5 seconds. Slowly, pour the mixture into the pie pan (It won't overflow, but it may scare you!) Bake at 350° for 45 minutes or until lightly browned on top and firm to the touch. Allow to rest for 10 minutes before cutting and serving. Good accompanied by broiled tomatoes.
Serves 6-8 for supper, 8-12 for appetizer.

Mrs. James I. Riddle III

BRUNCH EGG CASSEROLE

6 T. butter
6 T. flour
2 c. milk
½ big jar Cheese Whiz
8 oz. sour cream
18-20 eggs, hard boiled
1 lb. bacon, cooked and
  chopped

Cream Sauce: Melt butter and add flour, cook a little. Slowly add milk and cook sauce until thick, stirring constantly. Add Cheese Whiz and sour cream to cooled cream sauce. Slice eggs. Layer cream sauce, eggs, and then bacon in large casserole. Repeat layers ending with bacon. Bake at 350° until bubbly. Serves 12-14.
Note: Can be prepared ahead of time but do not freeze. Could be served on toast points or toasted English muffins.

Mrs. Hobby H. McCall

BRUNCH DISH

Canadian bacon
Swiss cheese
Eggs
Light cream
Parmesan cheese

Line an 8" or 9" Pyrex pie plate or square casserole with Canadian bacon. Place a layer of Swiss cheese over each bacon slice. Break an egg over each slice, then drizzle cream over the eggs until the yolks peek through. Put into a 450° oven for 10 minutes. Take out and sprinkle with Parmesan cheese. Return to oven for about 3-5 minutes. Cut in squares and serve immediately. Delicious with cheese grits, fresh fruit and English muffins.
Serves 4.

Mrs. David W. Tompkins

WELSH RAREBIT

1 lb. Wisconsin cheese, cut up
½ c. beer
Few dashes of Tabasco
1 egg, slightly beaten
1 t. prepared mustard
1 t. Worcestershire
Crackers or toast

Melt cheese over boiling water. Add beer. Add seasonings to egg and combine well with cheese. Let cook for a few minutes until it thickens. Pour over toasted crackers or crisp toast.
Serves 6.

Mrs. Katherine Pitman, 1948 Junior League Cookbook

"EGGS DAY AHEAD"

3 dozen eggs
½ c. milk
¼ lb. butter
¼ lb. Cheddar cheese, grated
2 cans mushroom soup
½ c. sherry

Mix eggs and milk. Soft scramble in a skillet in part of the butter. Heat remaining ingredients in another pan. Layer eggs and sauce in a 3-qt. rectangular baking dish. Cover and refrigerate for one day. Bake at 275° for 50 minutes. Serve with sausages, fruit, muffins, etc., for brunch.
Serves 14-15.

Mrs. Don McIlyar

CHEESE CASSEROLE

2 4-oz. cans green chilies, drained
1 lb. Monterey Jack cheese, grated
1 lb. Cheddar cheese, grated
4 egg whites
4 egg yolks
⅔ c. canned evaporated milk
1 T. flour
½ t. salt
⅛ t. pepper
2 medium tomatoes, sliced

Preheat oven to 325°. Remove seeds from chilies and dice. In a large bowl, combine cheese and green chilies. Turn into well buttered, shallow 2 quart casserole (12x8x2). In large bowl beat egg whites until stiff peaks. In small bowl, combine egg yolks, milk, flour, salt and pepper until well blended. Fold egg whites into egg yolk mixture. Pour egg mixture in casserole and blend it through cheese. Bake 30 minutes. Place sliced tomatoes on top and bake 30 minutes more. Garnish with green chilies.
Serves 6-8.
Great for a brunch and men especially like it.

Mrs. George T. Reynolds, III

CHEESE SOUFFLE

3 T. butter
3 T. flour
½ t. dry mustard
1 t. Dijon mustard
¼ t. salt
Pinch cayenne pepper
1 celery leaf
1 white onion, stuck with 1
  clove
1 c. milk
⅓ c. Parmesan cheese, freshly
  grated
⅓ c. Gruyère, grated
⅓ c. sour cream
4 egg yolks
7 egg whites
¼ c. sherry
½ c. Camembert

Butter the inside of a 6½″ soufflé dish with melted butter. Tie a double band of buttered paper around the top. Butter the paper with a paint brush, using salted butter. Tie with a string just under the rim with a loop knot. Melt butter; stir in off the fire the flour. Mix in dry mustard, Dijon mustard, salt, and pepper. Put in a saucepan milk with small bay leaf and a few peppercorns, celery leaf, and onion. Bring to a boil, strain into cup, stirring into the thickening sauce. Stir over fire until it just begins to boil. Remove and mix in cheeses, sour cream, and camembert (strained.) Beat the 4 yolks with Sherry. Beat until light and fluffy and mix into sauce. Beat egg whites in a large metal bowl by hand with a whisk until bowl can be turned upsidedown and the eggs stay in. Pour cheese sauce (heavy cream consistency) over the whites and fold in. Pour into dish, stand in pan of hot water. Dust the top with Parmesan. Bake 1 hour at 375°.

Mrs. Mark Lemmon, Jr.

BRUNCH EGGS

8 hard cooked eggs
1 pkg. cooked chopped spinach
½ t. onion, grated
1 t. Worcestershire Sauce
Tabasco
2 t. lemon juice
2 T. melted butter
Salt and pepper to taste
1 can cream of mushroom soup
1 small jar cheese whiz
Buttered bread crumbs
Parmesan cheese

Slice eggs in half lengthwise, remove yolks and mash yolks. Combine yolks, spinach, onion, Worcestershire, Tabasco, lemon juice, butter, salt and pepper. Mix all well and pile into whites. Place in buttered, shallow baking dish. Cover with soup and cheese which have been heated in double boiler. Cover with bread crumbs and Parmesan cheese. Bake at 350° until bubbly.
Serves 6-8.

DEVILED EGGS IN CONSOMME RING WITH SHRIMP REMOULADE FILLING

4 hard-boiled eggs, cut in half
   and made into highly
   seasoned deviled eggs
1 can consommé
¾ can water
1 pkg. gelatin
Juice of ½ lemon
1 t. Worcestershire
Onion juice to taste
Salt to taste
SAUCE: for 1 pound of large
   cooked shrimp.
1 c. mayonnaise
½ clove garlic, crushed
1 T. parsley, chopped
1 T. lemon juice
½ t. dry mustard
½ t. anchovy paste
Few chopped chives (optional)
1 t. capers (optional)

Prepare eggs. Mix next 7 ingredients. Cover the bottom of a ring mold with the gelatin mixture. Place deviled eggs around ring with filled side down so that each serving will have an egg. Pour gelatin mixture to the top of the egg white and let gel. Add rest of mixture. Serve with the center filled with shrimp. For each pound of shrimp, the sauce ingredients will make enough to coat it.

Mrs. Wilcox S. Doolittle

CURRIED DEVILED EGGS

12 hard-boiled eggs
1 c. Hellman's mayonnaise
1 t. dry mustard
1 t. salt
Paprika
½ t. curry powder

Put egg yolks through a sieve. Add remaining ingredients and stuff into egg whites. Sprinkle with paprika.
Serves 8-10.

Cookbook Committee

EGGS A LA BELGE

Bread
Butter
Ham
Egg, separated
Gruyère cheese

Cut round slice of bread and sauté it lightly in butter. Top with ham (not too thin) trimmed to fit bread. Separate egg and add enough Gruyère cheese to yolk to make it thick enough to hold shape without running. Pile egg yolk-cheese mixture on top of bread and ham. Whip egg white until stiff, adding pinch of salt. Cover completely with egg white and cook 5 minutes at 400°. Particularly good for non-egg lovers.
Serves one.

Mrs. Mark Lemmon, Jr.

EGGS BRUNCH

SAUCE:
4 slices bacon, diced
½ lb. chipped beef, coarsely
  shredded
¼ c. butter
1 lb. fresh mushrooms, sliced
  and sauteed in butter
½ c. flour
Pepper to taste
1 qt. milk
EGGS:
16 eggs
¼ t. salt
1 c. evaporated milk
¼ c. butter, melted
Reserved mushrooms

Sauté bacon and drain off all but 1 T. grease. Remove pan from heat, add chipped beef, butter and ¾ of the mushrooms. (Reserve remaining for garnish.) Mix well. Sprinkle flour and pepper over bacon-mushroom mixture. Gradually stir in milk. Cook until sauce is thickened and smooth, stirring constantly. Set aside. Combine eggs with salt and milk and scramble in butter in a large skillet. In a 3-qt. rectangular Pyrex dish, alternate layers of scrambled eggs and sauce, ending with sauce. Garnish with reserved mushrooms. Cover and bake 1 hour at 275°. May be fixed the day before, refrigerated, then baked according to directions. Serve platter of sliced tomatoes, little pig sausages, miniature sweet rolls and grits if desired.
Serves 16.

Mrs. Joe B. Neuhoff

EGGS ROYAL CASSEROLE

6 slices Pepperidge Farm
  Bread, trimmed and
  crumbled (use large size not
  sandwich size)
½ lb. sharp Cheddar cheese,
  shredded
4 eggs, beaten
2½ c. milk
1 t. salt
1 t. dry mustard
4-5 T. frozen chives, drained
6-8 slices of bacon, drained and
  crumbled

Put bread and cheese in a greased casserole. Mix eggs, milk, salt, dry mustard, and frozen chives. Pour over bread and cheese. Cover and refrigerate overnight. Add bacon. Bake uncovered in a pan of hot water at 350° for about 50 minutes or until a knife comes out clean. This is a perfect dish for a brunch or breakfast for company. Put in a glass dish a little larger than a square. It is pretty served in a silver liner. Cut eggs in squares and serve while warm.
Serves 6.

Mrs. Joe B. Abbey

EGG TACOS

6 eggs
½ c. milk
2 T. soy grits
2 T. oil
2 fresh hot green chilies or ¼ t.
    dried chilies
½ c. onion, chopped
2-3 t. chili powder
½ t. salt
1 t. cumin
8 taco shells
1 c. cheese, grated
1-2 tomatoes, chopped
Lettuce, shredded
Avocado, chopped (optional)

Beat eggs and milk. Stir in soy grits and let mixture stand. Sauté fresh chilies and onions until onions begin to brown. (If using dried chilies, stir into egg mixture). Add chili powder, salt, and cumin to eggs. Add eggs to onions and scramble them until fairly dry.

Assemble tacos: put generous amount of egg in each shell, cover with cheese, tomato, lettuce, and avocado.

Mrs. Oscar J. Lalla III

POACHED EGGS WITH SHRIMP HOLLANDAISE

6 slices tomato
Seasoned flour
Butter
6 toast rounds
½ lb. cooked shrimp, diced
2 c. Hollandaise sauce
1 T. parsley, minced
6 eggs, poached
Salt and pepper to taste

Cut unpeeled tomato slices ½" thick. Dip in seasoned flour and brown quickly in butter. Keep warm. Spread toast rounds with softened butter. Add shrimp and parsley to Hollandaise. Place a tomato slice on each toast round and top with poached egg. Sprinkle with salt and pepper. Cover with Hollandaise.
Serves 6.

Cookbook Committee

HAM AND CHEESE SOUFFLE

16 slices white bread, crust
  removed lightly buttered
2 c. cooked ham, cubed
8 oz. sharp cheese, grated
7 eggs
3½ c. milk
½ t. dry mustard
1 t. salt
2 c. corn flakes, crushed
½ c. butter, melted

Place 8 slices of bread in bottom of buttered 3 quart rectangular Pyrex casserole. Sprinkle with ham and cheese. Top with remaining 8 slices of buttered bread. Beat eggs, milk, mustard, and salt together. Pour over bread. This should come to top of casserole (if more liquid is needed add 1 more egg and ½ cup milk). Cover with foil and refrigerate overnight. Remove from refrigerator 1 hour before serving. Sprinkle with corn flakes, and pour melted butter over top. Bake at 350° for 1 hour.
Serves 8-10.

Mrs. B. Glenn Graham

CHILIQUILLAS
(A Mexican brunch dish)

1 large tomato, peeled and
  chopped
½ onion, chopped
1 or ½ fresh jalapeño pepper,
  minced
10 or 11 tortillas, cut in bite-
  size pieces
4 eggs
Sour cream
Mozzarella cheese, finely
  grated

Fry the tortillas until crisp in hot oil. Pour off most of the grease, leaving enough to cook the eggs in. Salt the pan of tortillas well. Mix together the tomato, onions, jalapeño, and eggs. Add to the skillet of crisp tortillas and scramble together until the eggs are done. Put the sour cream and grated cheese over each serving. Excellent with a fresh fruit salad and hot coffee or Mexican hot chocolate.
Serves 3-4.

Mrs. Edward James Henry III

MEXICAN TORTE

2 eggs, beaten
2 T. flour
½ t. salt
⅓ c. milk
1 small can (mild) green
   chillies, chopped
½ lb. sharp Cheddar cheese,
   grated
½ lb. Monterey Jack cheese,
   grated

To eggs add flour, salt, milk; beat well. Add remaining ingredients; blend. Pour into a flat greased 9"x13" Pyrex baking dish. Bake 35-40 minutes at 350 degrees. Serves 4-6 as main dish. Serves 12 as appetizer when cut into 1½ inch squares — serve warm. Recipe can be halved successfully. Excellent luncheon or light supper when served with guacamole.

Mrs. William Wilson Bryce

SOUFFLE AU ROQUEFORT

¾ c. Roquefort
2 T. butter
2. T. flour
¾ c. milk
6 eggs, separated
Cayenne '
Nutmeg
Salt and pepper

Mash cheese with a fork. Make a roux of flour and butter by melting butter and stirring in flour until very smooth. Add milk and cook and stir until creamy. Beat egg yolks, two at a time. Add to cream sauce over very low heat or in the top of a double boiler. Add all remaining ingredients except egg whites. Beat whites until stiff and gently fold into cream sauce. Pour into a well-greased 10" soufflé dish and bake at 375° for 20-25 minutes until browned. Don't open oven door to peek!
Serves 6-8.

Mrs. James Lambert

SANDWICHES

ALMOND CHUTNEY CHEESE SANDWICHES

4 oz. cream cheese, softened
2 T. mayonnaise
¼ c. drained chutney, chopped
2 T. almonds, chopped
½ t. orange rind, grated
½ t. mustard
Dash salt
8 slices bread or toast
Sliced cooked chicken for 4
   sandwiches
Iceberg lettuce

Mix cream cheese with mayonnaise, chutney, almonds, orange rind, mustard and salt. Spread on bread. Top 4 bread slices with chicken and lettuce. Close sandwich with remaining bread.
Serves 4.

Mrs. Curtis Sanford, Jr.

BACON AND CHEESE OPEN SANDWICH

8 pieces of bacon, half-cooked
   and cut in half, drained
4 English muffins
2 well-beaten eggs
2 c. Cheddar cheese, grated
1 t. lemon juice
½ t. salt
½ t. paprika
½ t. Worcestershire sauce
⅛ t. pepper
Garlic salt
Celery salt

Toast the muffin. Mix remaining ingredients except bacon and put on top of muffin. Place bacon on top. Cook until cheese melts and bacon is done.
Serves 4 to 8.

Mrs. Joe E. Funk, Jr.

CREAM CHEESE AND CHIPPED BEEF SANDWICHES

1 2½-oz. jar dried beef
2 3-oz. pkgs. cream cheese,
   softened
2 T. milk
1 T. green onions, chopped
½ t. dried dill weed
¼ t. Tabasco sauce
¼ t. salt

Cut beef into slivers and cover with boiling water; let stand 2 minutes. Drain well. Add cream cheese, and remaining ingredients. Mix well, until smooth and let stand at least 30 minutes. Spread on pumpernickle bread.
Makes 8 sandwiches.

Mrs. Clint M. Josey, Jr.

MOZZARELLA CHEESE SANDWICHES

12 thin slices white bread
1 t. oregano leaves
½ c. (⅔ stick) soft butter
6 slices (½ lb.) Mozzarella
  cheese
¼ t. salt
Pinch ground black pepper
Pinch garlic powder
2 T. Parmesan cheese
2 large eggs
Good, light olive oil for frying

Trim crust from bread. Mix oregano with butter and spread on one side of each slice of bread. Cut 6 slices of Mozzarella large enough to cover bread and place one on buttered side of each 6 bread slices. Top with remaining bread slices, having buttered side next to cheese. Press edges firmly together. Combine salt, pepper, garlic powder, Parmesan cheese and eggs and beat well. Dip sandwiches into mixture. Fry on both sides in hot olive oil.
Makes 6 sandwiches.

Mrs. Jack B. Shook, Jr.

PIMIENTO CHEESE

2 lbs. sharp yellow cheese,
  coarsely grated
3 hard-boiled eggs, coarsely
  grated
1 large onion, coarsely grated
2 7 oz. cans whole pimientos,
  coarsely chopped (add juice
  too)
1 pint mayonnaise
3 T. prepared mustard
3 T. Worcestershire sauce
2 t. salt
Coarse grind pepper, paprika,
  onion salt, garlic salt, celery
  salt to taste (approx. ½ t.
  each)

Stir all ingredients in largest mixing bowl until just well mixed. Do not mash or pack down. Should be coarse and loose. It will become firmer when chilled. Can be used to stuff celery, for sandwiches and on Melba rounds. Keeps well when refrigerated — about 3 weeks. Do not freeze.
Makes about 2 quarts.

Mrs. C. Douglas Gill

SPRING SANDWICHES

Black bread
Butter, softened
Hard-boiled eggs, sliced
Radishes, sliced
Chives
Salt and pepper

Spread bread with butter. Layer eggs, radishes, chives, lots of salt and pepper. Top with other slice of black bread which has been spread with butter.
Serves 1.

Mrs. Jack B. Shook, Jr.

HAL'S CHEESE SOUFFLE SANDWICH

6 slices of bread, crust removed
Butter
Cheese
4 eggs
2½ c. milk
Dry mustard, to taste
Paprika, to taste
Worcestershire sauce, to taste

Butter a dripping casserole. Butter bread and make three cheese sandwiches. Place them close together in the buttered dish. Beat eggs and milk. Add dry mustard, paprika. and Worcestershire sauce. Make it tart. Pour over sandwiches. Let stand 2 hours then bake in moderate oven for 45 minutes or longer.
Note: This will hold 20-30 minutes longer if necessary. I've never known it to fail, and I give it to brides.

Mrs. William Wilson Fisher

SUPREME HOT CHICKEN SANDWICH

⅓ c. sifted flour
1 can (10½ oz.) mushroom soup
¾ c. milk
¾ c. cooked chicken, diced
2 T. pimiento, chopped
1 T. onion, minced
8 slices bread, trimmed
3 eggs
¼ c. milk
3 c. potato chips, crushed
3 T. almonds, sliced or chopped

Blend flour into mushroom soup in saucepan. Add ¾ cup milk and bring to a boil, stirring constantly. Remove from heat. Stir in diced chicken, pimiento and onion. Cool slightly. Spread mixture in 8 inch square pan. Chill until firm. Preheat oven to 350°. Cut chicken mixture into 4 squares and place one on each of 4 bread slices. Cover with remaining bread slices. Smooth sides with metal spatula. Cut each sandwich in half to form rectangles. Beat eggs with ¼ cup milk. Dip sandwiches on all sides in egg mixture then in crushed potato chips. Place on greased baking pan. Sprinkle almonds on top and bake for 30 minutes.
Serves 4.

Mrs. Joe Allen Winfield

SANDWICH LOAF

8 slices white bread
8 slices whole wheat bread
Butter
BLACK-OLIVE NUT SPREAD:
1 4½-oz. can chopped black
  olives, drained
1 8-oz. pkg. cream cheese,
  softened
½ c. pecans, chopped
**ALASKA KING CRAB
  SPREAD:**
1 3-oz. pkg. cream cheese,
  softened
2 T. sour cream
1 pkg. green onion dip
  seasoning mix
1 7½-oz. can crabmeat
EGG SALAD SPREAD:
6 hard-cooked eggs, chopped
Mayonnaise
1 T. mustard
Salt and pepper to taste
2 pkg. (8-oz. each) cream cheese
Mayonnaise
Parsley

Remove crusts from bread. Place 4 slices dark bread on platter, butter and spread with black-olive-nut spread. Place 4 slices white bread on top next, butter and spread with crab spread. Place 4 more slices dark bread on top of crab spread and butter and top with egg salad spread. Top with remaining white bread. Beat 2 8-oz. pkgs. cream cheese with enough mayonnaise to soften to spread. Frost top and sides of loaf and sprinkle with parsley. May be made the day before and refrigerated or may be frozen. It is much easier to slice if done either of these ways. For black olive-nut spread, combine all ingredients. For crab spread, place ingredients in blender and blend well, scraping sides often. For egg salad spread, combine all ingredients. (The crab and black olive-nut spreads can be made and served as a dip with crackers.)
Serves 8 generously.

Mrs. William Plack Carr, Jr.

CHEESE-CHUTNEY SANDWICH

2 slices bread
Country Muenster cheese
Chutney

Butter the inside slices of 2 slices of bread. On top of one buttered side, place a layer of cheese and spread top of cheese with chutney. Top with other slice and toast both unbuttered slices.
Serves 1.

Mrs. Charles W. Pace

HOT PIZZA ROLLS — LUNCHEON SANDWICHES

1 15-oz. can tomato sauce
1 large onion, chopped
¼ c. Romano cheese, grated
1 4-oz. pkg. Hard Salami
12 Brown-and-Serve French
  Rolls
Melted butter
Cheddar cheese

Put tomato sauce and onion in a deep pan and boil until it becomes a thick paste, stirring constantly to keep from sticking. Add Romano cheese and remove from heat. Cut salami into small bits with scissors and add to paste. (This much can be done ahead of time and refrigerated. If done this way, reheat in the top of a double boiler.) Slice the top off the rolls, as thin as possible and keep the slice. Using your fingers, pinch out the bread from the middle of the roll, being careful not to break the edges, and making a little boat with sides about ¼" thick. Brush melted butter all over the outside of the boats, including the bottom. Fill with the sauce and top with thin slices of Cheddar cheese. Put the bread top on each roll and brush with melted butter. Set rolls in a 350° oven until brown. These rolls are messy to eat and finicky folks will want a knife and fork. Anyone not on a starvation diet can eat 2, and growing boys will think nothing of eating 4.

Mrs. L. G. Pondrom

CUCUMBER SANDWICH SPREAD

2 8-oz. pkgs. cream cheese
1 pkg. Good Seasons Italian
  Salad Dressing Mix
1 large cucumber, grated
¼ c. chopped onion

Soften cheese to room temperature and cream with dressing mix. Add cucumber and onion, mix and chill at least 4 hours. Soften to spread.
Makes 8 full sandwiches or 12 small sandwiches.

Mrs. W. Bruce Monning

GOURMET TURKEY SANDWICHES

8 slices rye bread, buttered and
  halved
1 cup lettuce, shredded
4 large slices cooked turkey or
  the equivalent of 4 slices
Salt and pepper to taste
16 slices bacon, cooked crisp
2 avocados, sliced
¼ c. dairy sour cream
¼ c. mayonnaise
¼ c. crumbled bleu cheese
2 medium tomatoes, cut in
  eighths
4 hard-cooked eggs, quartered
Paprika and minced parsley

Arrange 1 or 2 slices of buttered and halved bread on each plate. Cover bread with shredded lettuce, then turkey. Season with salt and freshly ground pepper. Top with bacon (broken into appropriate sized pieces) and avocado slices. Combine sour cream, mayonnaise and bleu cheese. Drizzle over top of sandwich. Garnish with tomato wedges and hard-cooked egg wedges. Sprinkle with paprika and minced parsley.
Makes 4 open-faced sandwiches or 8, as appetites demand.

Mrs. John W. McDonough

MEATS

AUNT MARY'S CRAB CAKES FROM THE EASTERN SHORE OF MARYLAND

1 lb. special or claw crab meat
1 slice bread
1 level t. salt or less
1 heaping t. dry mustard
2 well-beaten eggs
⅞ stick butter

Pick shells from crabs and place meat in a bowl. Tear bread into small pieces. Add all ingredients to crab and mix. Form into 8 patties and refrigerate for several hours until firm. Cook in a skillet until brown on both sides.
Makes 8 patties.

Mrs. Lewis Grinnan, Jr.

BAKED CRAB MEAT IN SHELLS

12 slices cubed white soft bread, no crust
1 pt. milk
12 hard boiled eggs, riced
1 pt. mayonnaise
1 c. New York nippy cheese, grated
1 c. celery, chopped
¼ c. pimento, chopped (optional)
½ c. onion, grated (optional)
¼ c. green pepper, chopped (optional)
1 t. Lawry's Seasoning Salt
1½ lbs. lump crab meat, cooked
Crushed corn flakes or fine bread crumbs
Butter

Soak bread in milk while preparing other ingredients. Add eggs, mayonnaise, cheese, celery, pimento, onion, green pepper, and seasoning salt to the bread and milk mixture, blend. Then fold in crab meat. Fill shells or ramekins and cover generously with corn flakes or bread crumbs. Dot with butter. Bake at 350 degrees for 45 minutes. Serve with a sprig of parsley.
Serves 24.
Note: Very rich — do not make large servings.

Mrs. Walter N. Kuntz III

CRAB IMPERIAL

1 lb. lump crabmeat
1 T. butter
1 T. flour
½ c. milk
1 t. instant minced onion
1½ t. Worcestershire sauce
2 slices white bread, cubed
  (crusts removed)
½ c. mayonnaise
1 T. lemon juice
½ t. salt
½ t. pepper
2 T. butter
Paprika

Remove all cartilage from crabmeat. In a medium pan melt butter and mix in flour. Slowly add milk, stirring constantly to keep mixture smooth and free of lumps. Cook until mixture comes to a boil and thickens. Mix in onion, Worcestershire sauce, and bread cubes; cool. Fold in mayonnaise, lemon juice, salt and pepper. In another pan melt butter until lightly browned. Add crabmeat and toss lightly. Combine with sauce. Put mixture into individual shells or ramekins (or greased casserole). Sprinkle with paprika. Bake at 450° until hot and lightly browned on top, 10-15 minutes. This may be made ahead and frozen or refrigerated for a short time.
Serves 4.

Mrs. John Kipp

CRAB AND SHRIMP CHASSEUR

¼ c. butter
1 c. fresh mushrooms, sliced
¼ c. flour
1½ c. half and half cream
½ c. dry white wine
5 oz. cream cheese with chives
1 lb. cooked, clean shrimp
1 lb. king crab meat, cooked
Salt and pepper to taste
Patty shells

In a chafing dish or double boiler melt butter and sauté mushrooms. Sprinkle with flour. Gradually stir in cream and wine. Stir constantly until sauce thickens and bubbles. Add cheese a little at a time, and stir until sauce is smooth. Stir in shrimp and crabmeat. Season with salt and pepper. Serve in patty shells.
Serves 5-6.
Note: Can be made ahead of time and reheated to serve. Do not overheat after the seafood has been added as this will make it tough.

Mrs. Frank W. Perry

MOTHER'S YUMMY COLD CRAB

1 lb. lump crab meat
4 oz. vegetable oil
4 oz. vinegar
1 white onion, chopped or 4
fresh green onions, chopped
Salt and pepper
Green onion tops, chopped

Combine all ingredients and refrigerate overnight before serving. Serve with crackers. Makes over a pint.

Mrs. Larry Higginbotham

CRABMEAT SOUFFLE SUPREME

4 c. King crab or 2 cans lump
crabmeat, diced fine
2 c. medium cream sauce
1 t. Worcestershire
¼ t. Lawry's seasoning salt
Pinch cayenne pepper
Pinch nutmeg or mace
1 c. Cheddar cheese, diced
8 eggs, separated
Truffles

Blend first six ingredients over medium fire until hot. Add cheese and beaten egg yolks and stir until melted. Remove from heat and fold mixture into stiffly beaten egg whites. Place a thin truffle slice in the bottom of each 8-oz. baking dish, pour mixture on top and place dishes in hot water and bake for 25 minutes at 375° or until puffed up and set. Serve with a cheese sauce.

Brook Hollow Golf Club

LOBSTER TART

6 T. butter
3 T. flour
1½ c. cream
4 T. dry vermouth
1 lb. cooked lobster meat
(fresh) or crabmeat
2 c. fresh cracker crumbs
(prefer butter or sesame
seed)
1 t. paprika
2 T. freshly grated Parmesan
cheese
Additional melted butter

In the top of a double boiler melt butter; blend in flour; cook a minute; then add cream and vermouth. Cook, stirring constantly until smooth and creamy. Add the lobster meat, and pour into a low 1½ quart ovenproof casserole. Mix cracker crumbs, paprika, Parmesan cheese, and enough melted butter to make a cohesive mass. Knead a moment and then flatten it out to a thickness of a quarter inch. Cut little biscuits about the size of a silver dollar and arrange them in a pattern on top of the lobster. Bake at 350 degrees for 20-25 minutes.
Serves 4.

Mrs. Mark Lemmon, Jr.

LOBSTER THERMIDOR

2 medium to large lobster tails
  (large preferred)
5 T. margarine
4 T. flour
½ t. paprika
½ t. dry mustard
¼ t. salt
Dash of cayenne
1 c. light cream
1 small can chopped
  mushrooms, drained
4 T. dry sherry
¼ c. Parmesan cheese, grated
Cracker crumbs

Boil lobsters, cool, and cut into bite sized chunks. Save shells to stuff. In skillet, saute lobster in 4 T. margarine for two minutes; stir in flour, paprika, mustard, salt, and cayenne; cook stirring constantly, until bubbly. Stir in cream; continue cooking and stirring until mixture boils for 1 minute. Remove from heat and stir in sherry and mushrooms. Spoon into lobster shells. Melt 1 T. margarine in small sauce pan; add cracker crumbs and cheese; toss lightly to mix and sprinkle over filling in shells. Bake in a hot oven (425 degrees) for 15 minutes or until filling is hot and crumb topping is golden.
Serves 2. Recipe may be doubled successfully.

Mrs. Robert K. Bass

DEVILED OYSTERS

1½ c. finely chopped onions
1 c. finely chopped celery
¼ c. butter
2 slices dry bread, crumbled
  fine
¼ c. oyster liquid
1½ pt. oysters
2 T. lemon juice
Rind of ½ lemon, grated
2 T. Worcestershire
¼ t. Tabasco
Salt and pepper to taste
2 eggs, beaten

Sauté celery and onions in butter. Add bread crumbs, oyster water, oysters, lemon juice and lemon rind. Stir well and add seasonings to taste. Stir 2 minutes over low fire. Remove and add eggs. Pour into greased ramekins or a 1-qt. casserole. Bake 20-30 minutes at 350° or until set and lightly browned.
Serves 4.

Mrs. H. W. Kimmerling

SCALLOPED OYSTERS VIRGINIA

¼ c. butter, melted
2 c. coarse cracker crumbs
1 pt. oysters
¼ c. oyster liquor
¼ t. black pepper
2 T. sherry
4 T. heavy cream
1 T. Worcestershire
¼ t. Tabasco
Dash of cayenne pepper
Salt if needed

Mix melted butter and cracker crumbs. Place ⅓ mixture on the bottom of a greased, shallow 1-qt. baking dish. Add a layer of ½ the oysters. Combine remaining ingredients and cover oysters with ½ the sauce. Repeat layers, ending with the remaining crumbs. Bake for 20 minutes or until brown at 425°.
Serves 4.

Mrs. H. W. Kimmerling

OYSTERS OLEE

1 pt. oysters
3 T. butter
½ c. tomato catsup
Dash of Tabasco sauce
Pinch of salt
2 t. Worcestershire
1 scant T. flour
Cracker crumbs

In a saucepan put oysters and butter and heat until hot. In another saucepan put remaining ingredients except crackers. Stir thoroughly. Take liquor off oysters after heated, add to sauce, and cook until thick. Put oysters in this mixture. Put into shells or ramekins and cover with cracker crumbs. Put in 325° oven just long enough to brown crumbs, about 15 minutes.
Serves 6.

Mrs. Frank Cullinan, 1948 Junior League
Cookbbok

COLD POACHED SALMON

3-4 lb. center cut fresh salmon
1½ c. dry white wine or
  vermouth
1 carrot
2 small white onions, cut into
  pieces
1 t. salt
1 bay leaf
1 c. water
2 T. tarragon vinegar
4 cloves
1½ T. butter
1 t. peppercorns
For garnish: Swedish
  cucumbers, cherry tomatoes,
  sliced lemons, ½ fresh dill

Debone salmon or have butcher prepare for stuffing. Wrap in doubled piece of cheesecloth. Make a court bouillon of the remaining ingredients except garnish. Bring to a boil and simmer for ½ hour, strain, and cool. Lower salmon into cooled bouillon and simmer 6-8 minutes per pound. The fish should be just covered by liquid; if not, add more water. Cook until tender, remove, and cool. When cool, gently remove skin. This much can be done ahead of time. For whole poached salmon, double the bouillon recipe. Serve with Swedish cucumbers, cherry tomatoes, sliced lemons, and fresh dill to decorate the platter. This can be the first course or main course. Also can be served as an hors d'oeuvres served with Melba toast triangles and rye bread rounds.
Serves 4.

Mrs. Steve Summers

SALMON OREGONIAN

Filet of Salmon, to serve your
  needs
Brown sugar
Dill weed
Parsley, fresh
LEMON BUTTER SAUCE:
Juice of 1½ lemons
¼ lb. butter

Make sauce by adding lemon juice to melted butter. Place salmon on foil. Baste with sauce and grill for 5 minutes. Sprinkle salmon with brown sugar and dill weed. Grill for 5-10 more minutes until flaky. Before serving brush again with sauce and sprinkle with fresh parsley.
Serves 4.
Note: fresh salmon is available May-November.

Mrs. Lee R. Slaughter

Spring Cornish Game Hens with Potato Balls, Asparagus, and Tomatoes.

SALMON CROQUETTES

1 8-oz. can salmon
½ stick butter
¼ c. flour
⅔ c. cooked rice
¾ c. milk
Salt, pepper, and lemon juice to
   taste
1 egg
1 T. salad oil
1 T. water
Flour
Bread crumbs
Shortening or salad oil for
   frying

Strain salmon well, reserving juice. Melt butter in a heavy pan and blend in flour. Add milk and salmon juice. Cook, stirring constantly, until sauce is very thick. Add rice and salmon that has been deboned and skinned and mashed. Remove from heat and mix well, stirring in salt, pepper, and lemon juice. Put into a bowl, cover, and chill. Make mixture into croquettes, fingers or pyramids. Should make 12-14. Beat egg with salad oil and water. Dip croquettes in flour, then egg mixture, and then in bread crumbs — being sure they are well-coated all over. Chill for several hours. Heat enough grease or salad oil in a small heavy pan or deep skillet to cover the croquettes. They will brown very quickly so don't crowd them. Drain on paper. Keep warm until all are cooked. Serve with wedges of lemon. Freeze well in foil.
Serves 3-4.

Mrs. L. G. Pondrom

SALMON CHEESE PUFF

3 eggs, separated
¾ c. milk
1 c. soft bread crumbs
1 c. (4 oz.) grated sharp
   Cheddar cheese
1 t. chopped onion
½ t. salt
⅛ t. pepper
2 t. lemon juice
1 can (16 oz.) Red Sockeye
   Salmon, drained, boned, and
   flaked
PARSLEY SAUCE:
3 T. butter
3 T. flour
¾ T. salt
1½ c. milk
1 T. lemon juice
1½ T. fresh chopped parsley

In a mixing bowl beat together egg yolks and milk. Add soft bread crumbs, grated cheese, onion, salt, pepper, lemon juice and salmon. Mix lightly but thoroughly. Beat egg whites until stiff but not dry. Gently fold egg whites into salmon mixture. Turn the mixture into a buttered 1¼ quart shallow baking dish. Bake in a preheated 350° oven for 30-35 minutes, or until knife inserted near center comes out clean. Serve immediately with Parsley Sauce. For sauce, in small 1 quart saucepan melt butter slowly. Stir in flour and salt until well blended. Remove from heat and gradually stir in milk. Cook over medium heat, stirring constantly until sauce thickens. Cook for 2 to 3 additional minutes; add parsley and lemon juice and mix well. Serve immediately while still hot with Salmon Cheese Puff. Both recipes serve 3-4.

Mrs. George W. Jalonick IV

SCALLOPS PARISIANNE

1½ lbs. sea or bay scallops
4 T. butter
1 c. mushrooms, diced
1 t. salt
¼ t. freshly ground pepper
1 can cream of shrimp soup
2 T. dry vermouth
4 T. bread crumbs
3 T. butter, melted

Drain scallops. Slice sea scallops. Leave bay scallops whole. Melt 2 T. butter in skillet. Sauté the scallops 2 minutes. Remove. Melt remaining 2 T. butter in skillet and sauté mushrooms 3 minutes. Add to scallops. Add salt and pepper. Lightly stir soup until smooth and add to the scallop mixture. Add vermouth. Mix. Divide among 8 ramekins. Sprinkle tops with crumbs and melted butter. Bake at 425 degrees for 10 minutes or until heated and delicately brown on the top. Serves 8.

Note: May be assembled ahead of time and then baked.

Mrs. A. C. Black

LEMON-BASTED SCALLOPS

¼ c. butter, melted
2 T. lemon juice
1 small clove garlic, crushed
½ t. Worcestershire sauce
½ t. salt
¼ t. tarragon
¼ t. basil
1 16-oz. pkg. frozen scallops
1 4-oz. jar whole pimientos cut
 into ½" pieces
Watercress
Lemon wedges

Heat oven to broil and/or 550°. Mix first 7 ingredients and reserve. Thread scallops and pimiento on 12-6" skewers. Place on broiler pan and brush with butter mix. Broil kabobs 3" from heat, turning once and brushing with butter, 5-8 minutes. Garnish with watercress and lemon wedges.

Mrs. Floyd T. Burke

SHRIMP AVOCADO BOMBAY

1 small onion, chopped
1 small apple, peeled and
 chopped
2 T. butter
1 can cream of chicken soup
2 c. cooked shrimp or chicken
 pieces
2 T. curry powder
6 ripe avocados, peeled and
 halved
Rice

Sauté onion and apple in butter. Stir in soup. Add shrimp or chicken and curry powder. Place avocado halves on bed of rice and spoon on curry mixture to fill avocados.
Serves 6.

Mrs. James Lambert

SHRIMP-ROLLED FILLETS

1 small onion, minced
¼ c. green pepper, minced
1 clove garlic, peeled and
 minced
¼ c. butter
12 fresh or frozen shrimp,
 shelled, deveined, cooked
¼ c. crumbled day-old bread
 crumbs
1 T. parsley, snipped
¼ t. salt
⅛ t. pepper
4 fillets of sole or flounder
 (about 1½ lbs.)
¼ c. melted butter
HOLLANDAISE SAUCE:
½ c. butter
2 egg yolks
2 T. lemon juice
Dash of cayenne

Sauté onion, pepper and garlic in butter. Dice 8 shrimp and add them with crumbs, parsley, salt, and pepper to skillet. Place shrimp mixture to "bone-side" of fillets. Roll up lengthwise. Pour melted butter over them. Bake at 350° for 25-30 minutes. For sauce, place all ingredients in the top of a double boiler over boiling water and stir constantly until thick. Serve hot over fillets. Fish will freeze without sauce.
Serves 4.

Mrs. James G. Aldridge

CURRIED SHRIMP WITH ORANGE RICE

½ c. butter
2 T. flour
3 c. milk
2 T. curry powder
1 t. salt
½ t. paprika
¼ t. nutmeg
½ t. MSG
2 T. lemon juice
2 T. Sherry
2 t. Worcestershire
1 t. onion juice
2½ lbs. shrimp, cooked

Melt butter, add flour and cook until bubbly. Slowly add milk, stirring constantly. Cook until thick. Add the remaining ingredients and heat. Serve with rice cooked with 3 parts water, 1 part orange juice, 1 T. orange peel and salt to taste.
Serves 8.

Mrs. Ronald H. Underwood

GRILLED EXTRA LARGE JUMBO SHRIMP

2 extra-large, jumbo shrimp per person
1 c. vegetable oil
1 t. salt
¼ t. pepper
2 T. parsley, chopped
⅛ t. garlic powder

Have seafood store split and clean the required number of shrimp. One hour before broiling or grilling, marinate in the remaining ingredients to cover. Turn often.

Mrs. Whit H. Clark

PEEL 'EM AND EAT 'EM SHRIMP

1 lb. butter (not margarine)
1 medium stalk celery, each stem cut in thirds
3 t. celery salt
2 t. garlic salt
Tabasco sauce
2 bay leaves
¼ c. chopped parsley
5 lbs. fresh or frozen shrimp in shells

Melt butter in large pot. Add celery and leaves. Add celery salt, garlic salt, and Tabasco to taste. Add bay leaves and parsley; simmer covered about 45 minutes. Add shrimp in shells and cook covered about 10-15 minutes. Serve with sauce and celery with plenty of paper napkins.
Serves 4-6.

Mrs. Warren A. Weinberg

FRIED SHRIMP AND GREEN ONIONS

2½ lbs. shrimp
8-10 green onions with full
    length leaves
2-3 T. peanut oil
2 t. cornstarch
½ t. MSG
½ t. sesame oil or 2-3 T. toasted,
    crushed sesame seeds

Shell, clean and devein shrimp and place in a paper towel-lined colander to drain well. Wash and trim onions and slice in lengths about ½ the length of shrimp, keeping white stalks and green stalks separate. Have all ingredients at room temperature. Preheat wok and add oil. Sprinkle 2 t. cornstarch over shrimp and toss. Increase flame to high. Put shrimp into swirling hot oil, toss-stir-fry for 1 minute. Add white stalks of onions and continue to stir-fry for 2 minutes. Add green stalks and MSG and stir-fry for 2 minutes. Turn off flame, continue tossing motion another minute. Add sesame seeds or oil and toss to distribute evenly. Remove to a warm shallow platter. Serve at once with steamed rice and steamed wilted spinach.
Serves 4-6.

Miss Byrd Fuertes

MARJORIE PURNELL'S SHRIMP

5 lbs. cooked shrimp
10 white onions, sliced in rings
DRESSING:
1 pt. olive oil
1 8-oz. bottle capers and juice
¾ pt. cider vinegar
Salt
Sugar
Tabasco
Worcestershire

Into a deep flat pan place a layer of shrimp, then a layer of onions, alternating until all are used. Season dressing to taste with salt, sugar, Tabasco, and Worcestershire sauce. Mix ingredients and pour over shrimp and onions. Cover and place in refrigerator for 12 hours, stirring at intervals. To serve, lift out of dressing and place on platter with shredded lettuce. Also serve in shrimp bowl with toothpicks.
Serves 15.

Mrs. Maurice E. Purnell, Jr.

HOT SHRIMP TILLEY

1 lb. shrimp (allow 10-12
   shrimp per person)
½ lb. melted butter
½ c. olive oil
Heaping T. chopped young
   onions
3 cloves garlic, chopped fine
Lemon juice
Salt and freshly ground black
   pepper
1 c. hot dry white wine
Chopped parsley
Thin slices of lemon

Wash shrimp, snip shells and remove all shell and black intestines. Rinse in cold water and dry well. Pour butter mixed with olive oil over the bottom of a rectangular Pyrex dish, sprinkle dish with chopped onions and garlic. Place shrimp on dish, rolling them in butter and oil. Squeeze lemon juice over them and place under a hot broiler 5 minutes. Sprinkle lightly with salt and heavily with pepper. Turn on other side and grill 5 minutes longer. Be sure they are near enough to the flame. Sprinkle again lightly with salt and heavily with pepper. Pour wine over them and place under broiler for just a few seconds. Sprinkle with parsley and lemon slices. Serve with French bread and green salad.

Mrs. Frank Austin, Jr.

SHRIMP A LA McDANIEL

2 lbs. jumbo shrimp, uncooked
   and unpeeled (allow 6
   shrimp per person)
½ lb. butter
1 c. olive oil
Salt and pepper
2 T. green onions, chopped
5 cloves garlic, minced
Juice of 2 lemons
2 c. dry white wine
4 T. chopped parsley

Wash shrimp well; melt butter in a shallow but long pan; add olive oil, onions and garlic. Arrange shrimp in pan. (This can be done ahead of time and refrigerated until ready to cook.) Broil shrimp about 5 minutes in liquid, stirring occasionally. Turn shrimp and add wine and parsley; continue broiling — no longer than 5 more minutes. Add salt and pepper to taste. Serve with lots of sauce over shrimp and let guests peel their own. Accompany with French bread.
Serves 6.

Mrs. Sam Kendrick

SHRIMP A LA CREOLE

4 lb. shrimp, fresh
Water to boil shrimp
¾ c. salad oil
3 T. flour, heaping
1 bunch shallots or 1 large
   onion, sliced thin
½ small pod garlic, sliced
Salt and pepper to taste
1 can Italian tomato paste
2 green peppers, sliced thin
4-5 c. hot water
Tabasco to taste

Clean shrimp and remove vein. Bring shrimp to a boil and immediately drain and set aside. Make a roux with the oil and flour. Brown well, but do not burn. If roux is burned, start over again. Add onions and garlic, cook slowly but do not brown. Add shrimp, salt and pepper. Stir around in roux and onions until each shrimp is coated with the roux and none of the roux and onions stick to the pot. At this point, add a can of tomato paste and green peppers. Stir around for 15 minutes on moderate flame. After all tomato paste is sticking to the shrimp add 1 cup hot water and Tabasco to pot and turn flame low. Let cook 15 minutes more then stir well and add slowly 3 or 4 cups of hot water. If this method is used carefully the rich gravy will cling to the shrimp, but if water is added too fast the shrimp will appear naked and will look more like a stew with no gravy sticking to them. Taste to see if more salt and pepper should be added. Let set 1 hour before serving.
Serves 8.

Mrs. David C. Smith

SHRIMP IN RAMEKINS

4 T. butter
5 lbs. shrimp, peeled
2 t. Worcestershire
1 clove garlic
¼ c. chopped parsley
¼ c. chopped chives
½ t. salt
¼ t. pepper
¼ c. white wine
Parmesan cheese
Dry bread crumbs

Melt butter in skillet. Add shrimp and cook over high heat until they turn bright pink (about 2 minutes — DO NOT OVERCOOK). Add remaining ingredients except cheese and crumbs, mix well and place in individual buttered ramekins. Sprinkle with cheese and crumbs. Put under broiler to brown.
Serves 10.

Mrs. B. Thomas McElroy

S and S SHRIMP SOUFFLE WITH CURRY SAUCE

1½ T. butter
1 T. minced parsley
1 small onion, minced
1 t. salt
Dash of pepper
½ c. cooked rice
1 T. flour
1 c. milk
3 T. tomato soup (canned)
1 c. shrimp, chopped
3 eggs, separated
SAUCE:
2 T. butter
1 T. curry powder
1 t. salt
2 T. heavy cream
½ T. flour
1 c. chicken stock
1 egg yolk

Melt butter in a saucepan, add onion, and cook until soft. Add flour and stir well, gradually adding milk. Cook until thickened and add salt, pepper, soup, shrimp, and rice. Remove from fire, add well-beaten yolks, and blend well. Fold in stiffly beaten egg whites and pour into greased mold. Bake in a pan of water (not allowing water in pan to boil) for about 1 hour or until firm at 350°. Unmold and serve with curry sauce. Melt butter, add flour, curry powder, and salt. Gradually add hot stock and bring to a boil. Let boil about 20 minutes, stirring constantly. Remove from fire, add egg yolk beaten slightly with the cream.
Serves 2.

S and S Tearoom

STUFFED RED SNAPPER

STUFFING:
2 c. Pepperidge Farm stuffing
⅔ c. water
⅓ c. butter
¼ c. onion, chopped
¼ c. celery, chopped
1 T. parsley, chopped
1 t. sage
½ t. poultry seasoning
½ t. black pepper and salt

Remove bones from whole fish, marinate in lemon and lime juice. Black pepper and salt for about two hours. Sauté onion and celery in butter for 8 to 10 minutes under low heat. Add water, stuffing and the other seasonings. Mix well and stuff fish. Bake for 1½ hours at 375°.

Jane Murchison Haber

BEER BATTER FRIED FISH

2-3 lbs. fish fillets
⅓ c. flour
⅓ c. cornstarch
⅓ c. Bisquick
⅓ can beer (or more)
Salt to taste
Lemon juice

Mix all ingredients until the consistency of batter, adding more beer if needed. Marinate 2-3 lbs. fish fillets in lemon juice for 2 hours. Dip in the batter and fry in 1″ of hot oil until crispy brown. Serves 4-6.

Mrs. Virgil Pate

CHARLIE'S FRIED FISH

Any fresh water fish filets
Buttermilk
Tabasco
Salt and pepper
Yellow cornmeal
Oil

Cut fish filets into 1″ wide strips. Soak covered in buttermilk for 30 minutes to 1 hour. Remove from milk and sprinkle with salt, pepper and Tabasco. Roll in yellow cornmeal. Fry in 1½″ of oil that is very hot but not smoking for approximately 4 minutes or until golden brown. Drain and serve immediately.

Mrs. Charles W. Pace

WEB'S "BEST FISH EVER"

Fresh water filets, particularly
   crappie or bream
2 eggs
¼-½ c. skimmed evaporated
   milk
Saltine cracker crumbs
4 T. oil
4 T. butter

(If fish is not to be cooked immediately, soak in any kind of milk in the refrigerator until cooking time.) Beat eggs in evaporated milk. Roll cracker crumbs with rolling pin between 2 pieces of wax paper. Dip filets in milk then roll in crumbs. Heat oil and butter in a skillet and cook filets 4 minutes on each side or until golden brown. Serve immediately and be prepared for people to eat them right from the pan standing over the stove. Delicious!!

Mrs. M. Weatherby Carr

CIOPPINO
A fish stew from San Francisco wharf

2 large onions, cut in wedges
2 bunches green onions, diced
2 green peppers, seeded and
    diced
4 large cloves garlic, crushed
½ c. olive oil
2 c. red wine
1 8-oz. can tomato purée
4 c. water
1 bay leaf
1 t. oregano
1 t. basil
2 dozen clams in shell
2 dozen large shrimp
2 lbs. firm-fleshed fish
½ lb. lump crabmeat or crab
    claws
1 whole lobster (optional)

Sauté onions, green onions, green peppers, and garlic in oil for 5 minutes. Add wine and simmer briskly. Add purée, water, herbs, and seasonings. Cover and simmer 1 hour. Place crabmeat, clams in shells, shrimp, and fish cut in good-sized chunks into a large kettle. Add hot sauce and simmer 20-30 minutes or until clams open. Salt and pepper to taste. The name of this stew comes from the fishermen at the wharf "chippin-in" everything they had caught that day that had not been sold. They would make this marvelous stew, open a bottle of wine, put out some French bread, and have themselves a feast!

Mrs. Robert W. Enholm

LEMON BAKED FILLETS

Fillet of sole to serve 4-6 people
1 onion, chopped
2 T. butter
1 T. flour
1 t. salt
1 t. grated lemon rind
¼ t. nutmeg
⅛ t. pepper
1 c. light cream

Cut fillet in serving-size pieces. Place in greased oven dish. Sauté onion in butter. Blend in the remaining ingredients and cook them until thick. Place over fillets. Cook covered at 300° for 20 minutes. Serves 4-6.

Mrs. David Kelly, Jr.

MIGG'S FISH

¾ lb. fresh mushrooms, sliced
2 T. butter
2 T. shallots or green onions,
   minced
2½ lbs. sole, flounder or redfish
   filets
Salt and pepper
1½ T. butter, cut into bits
1½ c. white wine and water (1
   cup wine and ½ cup water)
2½ T. flour blended to a paste
   with 3 T. softened butter
¾-1 c. heavy cream
Salt and pepper
Lemon juice
¼ c. grated Swiss cheese
1 T. butter, cut into bits

Sauté mushrooms in butter with salt and pepper without browning and set aside. Put half the onions in the bottom of a baking dish. Season filets with salt and pepper. Arrange them in one slightly overlapping layer. Sprinkle filets with remaining onions and all of the mushrooms. Dot with butter. Pour in the liquid — you may need to add more water so fish are barely covered. Bring almost to a simmer on top of the stove. Lay waxed paper over the fish and put in a preheated oven of 350° for 8-12 minutes until fish is done. Drain poaching liquid into a saucepan and preheat broiler. Boil down liquid until it is reduced to about 1¼ cups. Off the heat, beat flour paste into hot liquid and add ½ cup cream. Bring to a boil and thin out the sauce with tablespoons of cream until it coats the spoon. Season sauce with salt, pepper and drops of lemon juice. Spoon over the fish. Sprinkle the cheese over and dot with butter. Run under the broiler for 2-3 minutes. This dish may be done several hours ahead and reheated. After adding the cheese and butter, just set aside. Before serving, reheat to simmer on top of the stove and then run under the broiler to lightly brown the sauce.
Serves 6.

Mrs. David Thompkins

TROUT ALMONDINE

6 trout fillets
Salt and pepper
1½ sticks butter
6 T. onion juice
1½ c. almonds
¾ c. lemon juice

Wash fillets, and salt and pepper. Sauté over low heat in melted one stick of butter and onion juice for approximately 20-25 minutes, depending on size of fish. Remove fish from butter mixture to a warm platter. Add the remaining ½ stick butter to skillet and sauté almonds. Add fish and lemon juice to almond mixture and cook for a few more minutes.
Serves 6.

Mrs. Fulton Murray, Jr.

TUNA FISH SOUFFLE

1 6¾-oz. can tuna, drained
3 T. butter
3 T. flour
1 c. boiling milk
4 eggs, separated
1 c. Swiss cheese, grated
1 small onion, chopped fine
   and sautéed in 1 T. butter
1 t. rosemary
1 t. salt
½ t. pepper

Melt butter over medium heat. Add flour and cook for 3 minutes. Add boiling milk all at once. Stir until thick. Beat in egg yolks (one at a time), then add cheese and seasonings. Add tuna and onion. When cool, fold in stiffly beaten egg whites. Put into a greased souffle dish and bake at 375° for 35 to 40 minutes or until well browned on top.
Serves 4. (This is a great way to get kids to eat tuna.)

Mrs. Searcy Ferguson, Jr.

CHICKEN

CHICKEN BOURSIN

6 boneless chicken breasts,
  pounded thin
7 oz. herbed Boursin cheese
6 slices prosciutto
3 T. butter
1 T. oil
½ lb. sliced mushrooms
4 chopped scallions
2 T. brandy
1 c. chicken stock
½ c. white wine or vermouth
¼ c. parsley, chopped

Season chicken breasts with salt and pepper; dust with flour. Spread 1-2 T. cheese on each breast; cover with prosciutto; roll up; and secure with toothpicks. Brown in the butter and oil. Add mushrooms and scallions to pan and sauté. Add brandy to pan and ignite. Add wine, chicken stock, and parsley. Cover and simmer about 30 minutes until breasts are tender and sauce is slightly thickened. Add salt and pepper to taste. Remove toothpicks before serving. Serve over rice or croutons. Good made the day before and can be frozen.
Serves 6.

Mrs. Edward W. Rose III

BARBECUE CHICKEN

1 T. vinegar
1 t. chili powder
1 t. salt
¾ t. mustard
2 t. sugar
1 T. Worcestershire
⅛ t. red pepper
½ t. Tabasco
1 t. pepper
1 c. water
1 clove garlic, chopped
1 onion, chopped

Combine all ingredients and cook slowly for 15 minutes. Brown one 2½-lb. chicken in ½ cup butter. Pour sauce over chicken in pan with drippings and cook at 350° for 1½ hours. Hot, but excellent. Freezes well.
Serves 4.

Mrs. Norman Smith

BREAST OF CHICKEN WITH SOUR CREAM OVER RICE

4 whole chicken breasts
1 stick butter
3 cloves garlic
1 large onion, chopped
1 bay leaf
½ c. sherry
Salt and pepper
3 T. paprika
1 c. sour cream
RICE:
1 c. uncooked rice
1 4-oz. can mushrooms with
    juice
½ can undiluted consommé
1 4-oz. jar pimientos, drained
Chopped parsley
Butter

Place first seven ingredients in a covered casserole and bake slowly at 300° until very tender — approximately 2½-3 hours. Remove chicken from sauce and debone. Strain sauce and add paprika and sour cream. Place chicken in a 1½-qt. casserole, pour sauce over, and reheat until bubbly at 350° about 20 minutes. Can be done early and reheated. Boil the rice until nearly done. Drain and run cold water over until cool. Add mushrooms with juice, consommé, pimientos and lots of chopped parsley and butter. Mix together and bake at 350° for 25-30 minutes. Serve chicken over rice.
Serves 4.

Mrs. John Lancaster III

BROILED CHICKEN LIVERS

1 lb. chicken livers
Flour
4 strips bacon
Salt and pepper to taste
Oil

Lightly flour livers, add salt and pepper to season. Cover the bottom of a pan with oil; place chicken livers in the pan broil for several minutes, then turn Place strips of bacon on top of livers and broil until bacon is done. Serve on rice o slices of salt-rising bread, toasted.
Serves 4.

Mrs. Gifford O. Touchstor

CALIFORNIA MARINADE FOR CHICKEN

½ c. oil
¼ c. lemon juice
1 T. paprika
2 T. Worcestershire sauce
Dash of Tabasco
2 T. vinegar
1 t. salt
2 t. sugar
2 t. garlic salt

Mix, shake, and refrigerate. Beat well before using. Pour over chicken parts and marinate overnight. Broil chicken on outdoor grill until done. Makes about 1 c.

Mrs. Larry Casey

CHICKEN OR TURKEY PIE

Pastry for a 2-crust pie
2 c. chicken or turkey, cut into bites
2 c. strong stock or gravy
2 T. butter or chicken fat
4 hard-boiled eggs, sliced
4 T. flour
1 c. light cream
Salt and pepper

Line bottom and sides of a deep casserole with pastry, possibly using some of the second crust. Melt butter or fat in a heavy pan. Blend in flour. Add stock or gravy and cream. Let simmer 5 minutes and add salt and pepper to taste. Put chicken in pastry-lined casserole. Place slices of hard-boiled eggs over the chicken. Pour in as much sauce as possible, just covering the egg slices. Place the remaining pastry on top of the pie. Trim and crimp the edges. Cut a large circle in the center, leaving the circle of pastry in place. Set the pie on a cookie sheet to catch any drippings and bake at 375° for 45-50 minutes or until top is lightly browned. About half way along, take the pie out of the oven, lift up the pastry circle and examine the sauce content. If the pie seems to be becoming dry, add some of the remaining sauce through this hole, then replace the circle.
Serves 4.

Mrs. L. G. Pondrom

CHICKEN BREASTS WELLINGTON

6 whole chicken breasts, boned
    and split
Seasoned salt
Seasoned pepper
1 6-oz. pkg. long grain and wild
    rice
¼ c. grated orange peel
2 eggs, separated
3 8-oz. cans refrigerated
    crescent dinner rolls
1 T. water
2 10-oz. jars red currant jelly
1 T. prepared mustard
3 T. Port wine
¼ c. lemon juice

Pound chicken breasts with a meat mallet; sprinkle each with seasoned salt and pepper. Cook rice according to package directions for drier rice; add orange peel and cool. Beat egg whites until soft peaks form; fold into rice mixture. On a floured surface, roll 2 triangular pieces of dinner roll dough into a circle. Repeat with remaining rolls until you have 12 circles. Place a chicken breast in the center of each circle. Spoon about ¼ cup rice mixture over chicken; roll chicken jellyroll-fashion. Bring dough up over stuffed breast. Moisten edges of dough with water and press together to seal. Place seamside down on a large baking sheet. Slightly beat egg yolks with water, brush over dough. Bake, uncovered, at 375° for 45-50 minutes or until breasts are tender. If dough browns too quickly, cover loosely with foil. Heat currant jelly in a saucepan; gradually stir in mustard, wine and lemon juice. Serve warm with chicken.
Serves 12.

Mrs. Howell D. Harralson

CHICKEN BREASTS IN WINE

1 stick butter, melted
Green onion, chopped
4 chicken breasts
Salt and pepper to taste
½ c. Marsala wine
1 c. heavy cream
2 4 oz. cans whole mushrooms
    or 1 c. fresh
1 t. paprika
Sliced ripe olives

In a skillet, sauté green onion in butter. Add chicken and cook until meat is slightly brown. Add wine, cream, mushrooms, paprika, and olives. Cook covered until chicken is tender, approximately 20 minutes.
Serves 4.

Mrs. Spencer Carver

CHICKEN BREASTS IN RED WINE SAUCE

6 large chicken breasts
¼ c. butter
1 onion, sliced
1 clove garlic, minced
2 T. flour
½ t. salt
¼ t. pepper
1 chicken bouillon cube
1 c. hot water
12 small potatoes, cooked
⅓ c. red wine
Parsley, for garnish

Sauté chicken breasts in hot butter on both sides until well browned. Add onion and garlic and simmer about 10 minutes. In a small bowl combine flour, salt and pepper. Slowly stir in bouillon cube dissolved in hot water. Pour over browned chicken. Cook slowly (covered) about a half hour, or until chicken is tender. Add potatoes and wine, heat through. Garnish with parsley.
Serves 6.

Mrs. Charles W. Pace

CHICKEN CACCIATORE

2 3-lb. chickens, cut into
   serving pieces
2 c. flour seasoned with salt
   and pepper
6 T. olive oil
2 onions, finely chopped
2-3 cloves garlic, crushed
8 red ripe tomatoes peeled or 2
   1-lb. cans tomatoes seeded
   and chopped
4 green peppers chopped
4 bay leaves
1 c. white wine
1 lb. mushrooms, sliced
2 4-oz. jars pimientos, sliced
Parsley for garnish
2 T. cornstarch dissolved in 4
   T. cold water

Dry chicken well and dip pieces in seasoned flour. Sauté chicken in hot oil until well browned. Remove chicken from pan. In the same oil, sauté onion and garlic until golden. Return chicken to pan and add remaining ingredients except the cornstarch, mushrooms, pimientos, and parsley. Cover skillet and simmer for 30 minutes until chicken is tender. Add mushrooms and pimientos and cook for 10 minutes. Thicken sauce with cornstarch paste. Garnish with parsley.
Serves 8.

Suggestion: May use 6 boned chicken breasts and 4 boned thighs cut into smaller pieces. This recipe will serve 12.

Mrs. Charles Henry Robertson

CHICKEN PARMESAN

4 chicken breasts or
  drumsticks
½ stick butter, melted
½ c. fine bread crumbs
½ c. Parmesan cheese
Dash of garlic salt

Preheat oven to 350°. Salt and pepper chicken, dip in butter and roll in mixture of bread crumbs, Parmesan cheese and garlic salt. Place in a pan and cover tightly with foil. Bake for 1 hour covered and 30 minutes uncovered. Fix amount of chicken desired per person.

Mrs. Arthur C. White

CHICKEN PATRICIA

3 c. cooked chicken meat
2 avocados, sliced and cubed
  (or scooped into balls)
Slivered, toasted almonds
WHITE SAUCE:
½ stick butter
4 T. flour
1½ c. chicken broth
½ c. heavy cream
1 T. lemon juice
2 egg yolks
Salt and white pepper to taste

Prepare white sauce by melting butter over low heat in a saucepan, add the flour and blend until smooth. Add broth and cream. Blend well and stir over medium heat until sauce is thick. Add the lemon juice very slowly. Beat the yolks slightly and add a little of the hot sauce to the yolks, beating well all the time. The add the yolk mixture to remaining sauce. Add salt and white pepper to taste. Continue cooking over low heat until all ingredients are well blended. Add cooked chicken and avocado slices to the white sauce and heat to serving temperature. Serve over hot white rice and sprinkle generously with almonds.
Serves 6.

Mrs. John W. McDonough

CHICKEN REGAL

3 small chickens, cut in half
2 sticks of butter
Salt and pepper
12 oz. chicken broth
1 c. sherry
8-12 artichoke hearts, boiled
  and sliced
½ lb. mushrooms
Tarragon or thyme

Season chicken with salt and pepper. Fry in butter until brown. Cover with broth and sherry. Add artichokes, mushrooms, and tarragon or thyme if desired. Simmer 45 minutes. Mushrooms can be sautéed in butter before adding to the chicken.
Serves 6.

Mrs. Margaret C. Worsham

CHICKEN WITH OLIVE STUFFING

3-lb. chicken
3½-oz. can pitted black olives,
  minced
3½ oz. goose liver
1 hard-boiled egg
1 raw egg
Salt and pepper
1 t. aniseed (optional)
1 T. orange juice
¾ c. butter

Mash hard-boiled egg and mix with olives, goose liver, and aniseed. Season to taste and mix in raw egg. Stuff and truss the chicken, spread butter over and roast it in a 400-425° oven for 1 hour and 15 minutes. Add orange juice to the drippings after 10 minutes and baste frequently. Salt and pepper the chicken after you take it out of the oven. Serve with rice.
Serves 4.

Geneva Ashby Jones

CHICKEN OREGANO CREAM

6 boned and skinned chicken
  breasts
3 T. butter
2 T. oregano
1 pt. heavy cream
2-3 bay leaves, crushed
Garlic salt
Pepper

Sprinkle breasts liberally with garlic salt and pepper. Sauté lightly in butter. Add oregano, bay leaves and cream. Bring to a boil and place in a casserole. Bake at 350° for 30 minutes.
Serves 4-6.

Mrs. David W. Tompkins

CHICKEN OR TURKEY AND DUMPLINGS

2 c. chicken or turkey, cooked
  and cut into bite-size pieces
  (or left-over chicken or
  turkey)
1 medium onion, chopped
¼ c. butter or chicken fat
2 T. flour
2 c. chicken stock or gravy
1 c. milk
Salt and pepper
Chicken bouillon nuggets, if
  needed
DUMPLINGS:
1½ c. flour
½ t. baking powder
2 t. salt
T. shortening
Ice water

For dumplings mix flour, salt, and baking powder in a bowl. Cut in shortening as for pastry. Add just enough ice water to blend all together. Roll into a ball with floured hands, wrap in waxed paper, and chill for several hours. About 45 minutes before serving time, put butter or chicken fat in a large heavy pan. Add chopped onion and cook slowly until it clarifies but does not brown. Blend in flour. Add stock or gravy and milk. Cover and cook slowly, stirring often. While this is cooking, roll out dumpling dough as thin as possible, less than ¼" thick. Cut into strips about 1" wide and then into squares. Dip each square lightly in flour. When onions are well-cooked, put chicken in pan. Throw the dumplings in one at a time. Cover and cook slowly until dumplings are done — about 15 minutes. Gently scrape the bottom of the pan with a large spoon occasionally, but do not stir dumplings into the bottom as they should cook on top. If pan juices become too thick, a little milk can be added. If too thin, remove chicken and dumplings and boil, stirring constantly until thick. Salt and pepper as needed. If stock needs flavoring, one tablespoon of instant chicken bouillon nuggets will help. Serve immediately. Serves 4.

Mrs. L. G. Pondrom

CREPES DE POLLO

1 c. flour
½ t. salt
½ c. water
½ c. milk
4 T. melted butter, slightly
  cooled
2 well-beaten eggs
FILLING:
3 fryers equalling about 8½ lbs.
4 c. Swiss or sharp Cheddar,
  grated
2 T. onion, grated
8 jalapeños, chopped
3 T. pimientos, chopped
16-oz. whipping cream,
  combined with
16-oz. light cream

Mix first 4 ingredients together and add butter and eggs. In a small skillet put 1 T. of batter and roll it out to the edge of the skillet. Cook like pancakes, turning once. The crêpes should have light brown specks but should not turn completely brown. For filling boil chickens until done in salted water. Bone and chop chicken. Add cheese, chopped jalapeños, grated onion, pimiento, and perhaps more salt. To this add the 16 oz. combined cream. Put filling in the center of each crêpe and roll like small enchiladas. After filling with mixture, lay in a buttered shallow dish and pour rest of cream over the entire dish and sprinkle paprika, a bit of grated cheese, and pimiento on crêpes. Three recipes of crêpes makes 64 crêpes and the filling recipe fills exactly this many. If freezing, wait to pour remaining cream over top when ready to bake. Bake at 350° for 20 mins. or until bubbly.
Serves 20-24.

Mrs. Jack Vaughn

CURRIED CHICKEN CREPES

FILLING:
10 T. butter
½ c. flour
1½ t. salt
3 c. milk
2 t. green onion, chopped
4 c. cooked chicken, cubed
½ c. dry white wine
2 t. curry powder
½ t. Worcestershire sauce
TOPPING:
2 egg yolks
¼ t. salt
8 T. melted butter
4 t. lemon juice
½ c. heavy cream, whipped
Crêpes: for eight

FILLING: Melt 8 T. butter in saucepan; remove from heat. Stir in flour and 1 t. salt until smooth. Gradually stir in milk and cook stirring constantly until sauce thickens. Remove from heat and set aside. In skillet sauté green onion in 2 T. hot butter. Add chicken, wine, curry powder, ½ t. salt, and Worcestershire; cook over medium heat for a few minutes. Stir in two cups of the white sauce. Set aside remaining sauce for topping.

TOPPING: In small bowl beat egg yolk with salt. Gradually beat in 4 T. melted butter. Mix remaining butter with lemon juice; gradually beat into egg yolk mixture. Fold in remaining white sauce until combined. Fold in whipped cream. To assemble crêpes: Preheat oven to 350°. Spoon some filling on each crêpe and fold sides over filling. Arrange in shallow baking dish and cover with foil. Bake 15 minutes or until heated through. Uncover hot crêpes; spoon topping over them and broil several inches from heat until lightly browned. Makes 8 medium crêpes.

Note: to prepare ahead of time, fill crêpes, cover with foil and refrigerate or freeze. Make topping but do not add whipping cream. Refrigerate topping. When ready to serve, heat crêpes, add whipped cream to topping and then broil as directed.

Mrs. Gerard L. Regard

DUSTY'S CHICKEN

8 chicken breast halves
White sandwich bread slices,
   crusts trimmed and bread
   buttered
4 eggs, well-beaten
A little salt
3½ c. milk
8 slices, American or Cheddar
   cheese
2 c. Special K
2 c. Grapenut Flakes
4 T. melted butter

Salt and butter chicken breasts, wrap in foil, and bake 1 hour at 350 degrees. Line 2 quart rectangular Pyrex dish with bread. Cover with diced, cooked chicken. Mix eggs and milk, pour over chicken. Top casserole with cheese. Refrigerate overnight. Mix cereals with melted butter, sprinkle over casserole, bake one hour at 325 degrees. Cut into squares to serve.
Serves 12. Excellent for a luncheon.

Mrs. M. Weatherby Carr

EASY FRIED CHICKEN

BATTER:
1 egg
1 c. half-and-half
1 c. milk
2 t. lemon-pepper marinade
2 garlic cloves, pressed
1 t. salt
COATING:
1 c. flour, salt and pepper to
   taste
2 chickens, cut up
Crisco

Beat egg, cream and milk, add seasoning. Soak chicken for 2 hours. Put salt, pepper and flour in a sack and shake chicken. Fry in hot Crisco (enough to cover chicken). Cook over medium heat until golden. Cover for last 10 minutes.

Cookbook Committee

EASY CHICKEN KIEV

1 stick butter, softened
4 halves of chicken breasts
1 t. onion salt
2 t. dried parsley flakes
1 t. Lawry's Seasoned Salt
½ t. black pepper
2 eggs
2 T. salad oil
2 T. water
Bread crumbs
Flour

Place the breasts on a piece of waxed paper and pound with a wooden mallet. Mix onion salt, parsley, Lawry's Salt and pepper with the softened butter. Put ¼ of the mixture on each breast. Shape it so that it is possible to roll the meat completely around the butter. Place in refrigerator until butter hardens. Beat eggs with oil and water. Put 2 pieces of waxed paper on table and put some flour on one piece and bread crumbs on the other. Take one chicken roll from the refrigerator at a time. Manipulate it so that no butter shows. Dip it first in the flour, then in the egg mixture, then in the bread crumbs. There should be no gaps in the crumb shield. When all 4 have been done, repeat this process, eliminating the flour. Return to refrigerator for several hours. In a heavy deep pan, heat cooking oil to 375°. Ease the rolls into the grease with tongs. Turn heat down as soon as they are in the oil. Cook for 10-15 minutes until brown. Remove with tongs.

Mrs. L. G. Pondrom

GRILLED LIME CHICKEN

4 broiler halves
Lime juice
Paprika
Seasoning salt
½ stick butter
1 t. Worcestershire
Salt and pepper

Squeeze lime juice on each side of broilers. Sprinkle each side with salt, pepper, seasoning salt and paprika. Marinate in refrigerator overnight or for several hours, basting and turning occasionally. Melt butter, add juice of 2 or 3 limes, Worcestershire and marinating juice. Brush chickens with sauce and cook over medium coals on grill, continuing brushing chicken as it cooks.

Mrs. Lewis Lyne

INDIAN CHICKEN

⅓ c. butter
3 small chicken breasts, boned,
  skinned and quartered
1 c. onion, chopped
1 clove garlic, chopped
2 t. salt
1 T. powdered ginger
¼ t. chili powder
½ c. tomatoes, drained
1 c. chicken broth
½ c. flaked coconut
2 T. cornstarch
1 c. heavy cream
½ c. cashews, chopped
Hard cooked egg, chopped
Raisins
Chutney
Toasted Coconut
Rice

In a heavy skillet or Dutch oven, melt half the butter. Brown chicken in butter a few pieces at a time and remove from skillet. Add more butter as needed. Sauté onions and garlic in remaining butter. Return chicken to pan. Add salt, ginger, chili powder, tomatoes, and chicken broth. Mix lightly, cover and cook for 10-15 minutes. Add coconut and heat 5 minutes more. To cornstarch add cream very slowly, then gradually stir this into the chicken mixture. Stir constantly until chicken returns to a boil. If desired, cool and freeze at this point. To reheat, bring to room temperature and reheat slowly. Serve with rice or noodles with chopped cashews on top. Additional condiments may be hard cooked egg, raisins, chutney, toasted coconut.
Serves 10.

Mrs. E. Don Rott

PERSIAN CHICKEN

3 lbs. chicken, cut up, or
  chicken breasts
3 T. milk
3 T. melted butter
¼ c. prepared mustard
½ c. honey
1 t. curry powder
1 t. salt
3 T. toasted sesame seeds

Thoroughly mix milk, melted butter, mustard, honey, curry powder, and salt in a large bowl. Roll chicken parts in this mixture, making sure that each piece is coated well. Place pieces in roasting pan and put in preheated 350° oven. Baste often during cooking with liquid from roasting pan. Bake for one hour and 15 minutes until all pieces are golden brown. After chicken is removed from the oven, sprinkle each piece generously with the toasted sesame seeds.
Serves 4.

Mrs. George W. Jalonick IV

POULET A LA VALLEE D'AUGE
(Chicken with Celery and Apple)

12 chicken breasts
8 T. butter
6 T. hot brandy
2 onions, sliced
6 small stalks celery, sliced
6 sliced apples
8-9 level T. flour
3-4 T. meat glaze
4½ c. chicken stock
Salt and pepper
Bouquet of herbs
3-4 c. thin sour cream
Little grated Parmesan cheese
1 apple, cored and cut in rings
1½ c. sherry

Brown chicken all over in hot butter; pour the ignited brandy over the chicken. Remove the chicken. Place in the pan the onions, celery, and 6 sliced apples; cook slowly until vegetables are soft and nearly cooked. Remove from fire and stir in carefully the flour and meat glaze. Pour in the stock. Stir over the fire until the mixture comes to a boil. Put back chicken with salt, pepper, and herbs. Cover and cook very slowly until tender (approximately 40 minutes). Remove the chicken and arrange in casserole. (This can be prepared ahead to this point.) Strain liquid in which chicken has been cooked and pour over the vegetables in the pan. Bring slowly to a boil. When bubbling, stir in the sour cream and grated cheese. Simmer for 4-5 minutes. Pour over the chicken and garnish top with apple rings, which have been fried until golden in butter, and little bundles of celery, which have been cooked in sherry.
Serves 12.

Mrs. Mark Lemmon, Jr.

SUPREME OF CHICKEN WITH BEL PAESE

4 boned chicken breasts
6 T. butter
1 T. vegetable oil
½ lb. button mushrooms, minced
Salt and pepper to taste
Flour
⅓ c. dry white wine
2 T. Madeira or Port
½ lb. Bel Paese or mozzarella

Sauté mushrooms 4-5 minutes in 2 T. butter. Season with salt and pepper and set aside. Shake breasts in bag with flour, salt and pepper. Heat remaining butter in skillet and cook breasts 3 minutes on one side and 2 on the other. Place in oven dish and cover with mushrooms. Add wines to chicken skillet and boil, then simmer to reduce by one-half. Pour over chicken. Slice cheese and place over chicken then broil 4-5 inches from heat until cheese melts. Serve with potato balls and green beans.

Cookbook Committee

VINEYARD CHICKEN

8 chicken breasts
1 c. cooking sherry
1 T. lemon juice
¼ t. pepper
½ t. paprika
¼ c. melted butter
¼ c. chopped green onions with tops
¼ c. minced parsley or ⅛ c. parsley flakes
2 t. salt

Place chicken breasts in shallow casserole, skin side down. Blend the remaining ingredients and pour over chicken. Cover and bake in 300° oven 1 hour. Turn chicken and bake 30 minutes, then remove top; turn oven up to 375° and let it brown, basting occasionally. This recipe can be cut in half but only with the chicken. Make the entire sauce recipe for four breasts.
Serves 8.

Mrs. Norman Smith

ZUCCHINI AND COLD CHICKEN

2 c. fresh, very tender zucchini,
  cut into noddle size
1 T. butter
1 T. water
1 T. tomato pureé or ketchup
2 t. tarragon vinegar
Salt
Onion salt
1 t. paprika
½ t. monosodium glutamate
Pinch of crushed caraway
2 t. chives, chopped
2 t. brown sugar
1 t. sweet basil
1 t. grated lemon rind
1 T. olive oil or cooking oil
2 t. soy sauce
Bland white cheese
2 c. cold chicken, sliced as fine
  as possible

Sauté zucchini in butter for 2 minutes. Combine water, tomato pureé, vinegar, herbs, spices, and add to zucchini. Cover and cook 2-3 minutes more until zucchini is tender. Sprinkle zucchini with mixture of olive oil and soy sauce. In serving, arrange zucchini in center of dish and surround with a bland white cheese cut into bite-size pieces. Last, sprinkle with grated lemon rind and garnish with slices of cold chicken.

Serves 3-4.

Note: Very tender young kohlrabi sections are equally delicious, but in this case leave out brown sugar and add 2 T. sour cream just before serving.

Mrs. Mark Lemmon, Jr.

GAME HENS WITH WILD RICE AND ORANGE SAUCE

4 Rock Cornish game hens
Salt and pepper
½ c. butter
3 oranges
2 c. wild rice
1 T. soft butter
4 T. Grand Marnier
1 c. chicken broth
1 T. flour
½ c. chopped walnuts
¼ c. soft butter

Preheat oven to 350°. Spread hens with ½ c. butter and sprinkle with salt and pepper. Arrange in a shallow roasting pan and bake for 50-60 minutes, turning the birds and basting frequently with pan juices. Remove birds to warm serving platter and keep warm. Remove the thin orange rind from 1 orange with a vegetable peeler and cut rind into very fine shreds. Cover orange shreds with water, bring to a boil, and simmer for 10 minutes. With a sharp knife, peel other 2 oranges, removing all rind and every trace of the bitter white covering. Cut oranges into sections, free of connecting membranes and add to shredded rind. Pour off excess butter in roasting pan. Add Grand Marnier and ignite. When flame burns out, stir in chicken broth and cook, stirring in all the brown glaze from the bottom and sides of the pan. Stir in flour mixed to paste with 1 T. soft butter and cook, stirring, until sauce is slightly thickened. Add the shredded orange rind and orange sections and simmer for 2 minutes. Toss cooked rice (cooked according to package directions) with walnuts, soft butter and salt and pepper to taste.

Serves 4.

Mrs. Samuel P. Burford, Jr.

BREAST OF TURKEY WITH WHITE TRUFFLES

Breast of 1 young turkey
Butter
Salt and pepper
White truffles (1 large fresh or
  2 canned)
1 T. minced onion
1 T. chopped parsley

Have your butcher bone the breasts of a young (no more than 6 lb.) turkey and carve each breast into 3 flat thin slices. Melt a generous amount of butter in a heavy skillet, add the onions and parsley and salt and pepper to taste. Sauté the turkey breasts in this mixture, the cooking time depending upon the thickness of the slices. Cook them gently as you do not want the butter to burn. When they are done, remove to a hot platter and cover them with thin slices of white Italian truffles.

Serves 4.

Mrs. Mark Lemmon, Jr.

DOVE OR QUAIL

Flour
Salt
Pepper
Sherry or Sauterne
Ice cubes

Flour birds with salt and pepper. Fill skillet with 1" of grease and cook until brown on both sides and half done. Pour off all grease but a bare covering on bottom of the pan. Add one wine glass of Sherry per two doves and 2 cubes of ice per bird. For the quail, do the same, only with Sauterne. Put on top of the stove over low heat and cook until done, about 45 minutes or until falling apart.

Mrs. Joe E. Funk, Jr.

SMOTHERED DOVE OR QUAIL

Doves or quail
Seasoned salt
Salt
Cracked pepper
Lemon-pepper marinade
Garlic powder
Paprika
Flour
½-1 onion, finely chopped
1 can beef broth
4 cans of water

Season birds with salts, peppers, garlic powder, and paprika. Flour lightly and brown in grease. After browning, sprinkle with a little more salt. Set birds aside. Remove all but ¼ inch grease from the pan. Sauté onion in grease. Add flour to grease and brown. Add beef broth and water. Let thicken. When it has thickened a little pour over birds which have been placed in an ovenproof casserole. Cover and cook in oven which has been preheated to 350 degrees for 1-1½ hours. Servings according to number of birds.

Mrs. Jack B. Shook, Jr.

ROAST QUAIL WITH WHITE GRAPES

4 quail
6 T. butter
Salt
Black pepper, freshly ground
About 30 Thompson seedless
  grapes, peeled (if not
  available, use Belgian White
  Muscat or California
  Emperor grapes, peeled,
  halved, and seeded)
2-3 T. cognac
¼ c. dry sherry, white wine, or
  vermouth
1 c. chicken stock
1½ t. arrowroot
1 t. grated lemon rind
1-2 t. lemon juice

Rub quail generously with butter, salt, and pepper. Put a lump of butter, salt, pepper, and 3-4 grapes in the cavity. Sprinkle with cognac. Place in a roasting pan and roast 12-15 minutes at 450 degrees, basting thoroughly 2 or 3 times. While the quail are roasting, gently heat the remaining grapes in sherry and chicken stock in a small saucepan. Remove grapes with a slotted spoon, add to quail, and roast 5 more minutes. Remove quail to heated serving platter. Mix arrowroot into sherry and chicken stock and add to pan juices with grated lemon rind and lemon juice. Stir well, scraping up brown bits on bottom, and simmer until slightly thickened. Check seasoning. Pour sauce over quail and serve immediately.
Serves 4.

Cook Book Committee

QUAIL

6 quail (split down the back)
6 T. butter
1½-2 c. chopped mushrooms
½ c. chopped onion
¼ c. butter
1 c. consommé or beef bouillon
1 c. cream sherry or wine
⅓ c. orange juice

Salt and pepper quail and roll in flour, then brown in the 6 T. butter for about 10 minutes. Remove quail and sauté onions and mushrooms in the ¼ c. butter in the same pan, do not brown. Add browned quail, then consommé and wine. Cover and simmer 20-30 minutes or until quail is tender. (This may be done in the oven or on top of the stove.) Add orange juice and heat to boiling. Serve with wild rice. Spoon some of the gravy over quail before serving. Pass remaining gravy. Serves 4.

Mrs. John P. Boone

QUAIL IN WINE

quail
flour, salt and pepper
stick butter
clove garlic, minced
c. chopped celery
c. chopped onion
c. boiling water
c. white wine

Salt and pepper birds and dust them with flour. Melt butter in a heavy skillet with a cover. Sauté birds until brown on all sides. Add onions, celery and garlic and sauté with the birds (about half the time for the birds). Add boiling water, cover and simmer ½ hour. Add 1 cup of the wine and cook ½ hour covered. Uncover and let the birds cook until tender (another 15 minutes). If necessary add the other ½ cup of wine. Sauce will not be too thick. Check seasonings and serve with wild rice. Serves 3-4.

Mrs. Harold W. Kimmerling

CAJUN DUCK

3 good ducks — skins should be white or yellowish, not pink. (Doves may be substituted)
1 bell pepper
1 onion
1 bunch green onions
4 stalks celery
1 sm. can mushrooms
1 bay leaf
½ t. thyme
½ t. oregano
½ t. cayenne pepper
3 cloves garlic
1 T. parsley
½ can tomato paste
2 T. flour
1 c. hot water
1 c. dry red wine
1 T. Lea and Perrins
1 dash Tabasco

Cut ducks in half; salt, pepper and flour lightly. In heavy iron skillet or dutch oven heat enough grease to cover bottom by 2". Brown ducks, 3 or 4 pieces at a time, on both sides and remove to a platter as browned. When all are browned and removed, pour off all grease but enough to barely cover bottom. Finely chop bell pepper, onion, green onion, celery and garlic. Place in skillet and sprinkle with flour and sauté over medium-low heat until transparent and flour is browned. Add all other ingredients, stirring and blending well. Add ducks, bring to a boil, reduce heat to very low, cover and cook 3 more hours or until tender. Check gravy for seasoning, adding salt and pepper to taste. Serve with plain white rice.
Serves 6.

Mrs. Walter Kilgo

DELECTABLE WILD DUCK

2 ducks, quartered
½ c. flour
1 t. salt
¼ t. pepper
2 T. melted butter
1 can consommé
½ c. sherry
½ medium-sized onion, chopped fine and sautéed in 1 T. butter
½ c. dry red wine
1 T. chopped parsley
1 t. thyme
1 t. marjoram
5 stalks celery and some celery leaves

Place duck in bag containing flour, salt, and pepper. Shake well until duck is well covered. Brown duck in butter, then arrange in a large casserole. Add consommé, wine, onions, herbs. Place celery stalks and leaves over top. Cover and bake at 450° for 20 minutes. Reduce heat to 300° and bake until tender (about 2½ hours). When half done, pour ½ c. dry red wine over ducks. When done, discard celery. The two ducks make 4 servings. Serve with wild rice.

Mrs. Mark Lemmon

Beef Tenderloin Garnished with Mushrooms, Artichoke Bottoms and Bearnaise

ROAST WILD DUCK LITTLE SANDY

6 wild ducks
2-3 apples
2 oranges
2 large stalks celery
2 large onions
Louisiana hot sauce (optional)
1 c. fresh orange juice
1 c. red wine

Clean ducks thoroughly and salt and pepper inside and out. Stuff cavity with unpeeled chunks of apples, oranges, onions, and celery. Stuff cavity very full and plump. Rub breast with a little Louisiana hot sauce if you wish. Lay 2 strips of bacon on each duck. Put in a deep heavy roasting pan and cook uncovered for 30 minutes at 500°. Lower heat to 325°. Mix orange juice and wine together and pour over ducks. Cover with heavy-duty foil and cook 2-3 hours more until done, depending on size of ducks. Baste ducks frequently. When ducks are done, remove from pan and use drippings for gravy. Excellent with wild rice, sliced water chestnuts, and mushrooms.
Serves 8.

Mrs. Tom M. Moore

BEEF

1½ lb. ground beef
3 large onions, chopped
1 bell pepper, chopped
¼-½ head cabbage, chopped
3 carrots, sliced thin
3 pieces celery, sliced thin
1 large can tomatoes
1 c. rice, raw
1¼ c. water
Curry powder to taste
½ t. cinnamon
Garlic salt
Salt and pepper

AFRICAN STEW

Brown ground beef. Add onions and bell pepper and sauté. Add other vegetables, rice and water. Add enough curry powder to turn rice yellow and cinnamon. Cover and simmer for about 30 minutes or until rice is tender. Add salt, pepper, and garlic salt to taste.
Serves 6.

Mrs. E. Don Rott

BEEF BIRDS

4-lb. eye of round roast
1 medium-sized onion,
    chopped fine
1 c. bread crumbs
1 stick butter (or ½ cup beef
    grease)
Seasoning salt
Pepper
1 t. Wyler's Instant Beef
    Bouillon
¼ c. hot water
1 c. flour
GRAVY:
1 small onion, chopped
¼ c. flour
3 c. hot water
1 T. Wyler's Bouillon
1 t. salt
½ t. pepper
Sour cream (optional)

Slice the center of the roast into 8 thin slices. Trim fat and membrane and pound with a mallet on both sides to increase its size and make as thin as possible. Sauté onion in half the butter or grease until clarified. Remove pan from heat and add bread crumbs and bouillon that has been dissolved in ¼ cup hot water. Add salt and pepper to taste. Spread crumbs on center of each piece, dividing it evenly. Roll the meat up tightly and secure at both ends with toothpicks. Moisten the rolls slightly with cold water, using your fingers, and then roll them in flour, coating all sides well. Heat the remaining butter or grease (you may need to add more) and sauté the rolls quickly, turning them so that all sides will be a light brown. Transfer to a baking dish that is large enough to hold them all, uncrowded, with space for a gravy around them. The grease left in the pan will be used for the gravy. Put the small chopped onion into the grease and let it clarify. Blend in flour. Add hot water, bouillion, salt, and pepper. As this bubbles, stir vigorously to scrape the bottom of the pan. Pour gravy around, not on top, of the birds. Can be refrigerated or frozen at this point. From room temperature they require 1 hour at 350°, lightly covered with foil. If still cold, give them about 1 hour and 15 minutes. Watch the gravy and add water if it becomes too thick. Half a cup of sour cream can be mixed with ¼ cup water and added to the gravy about 15 minutes before serving time.
Serves 8.

Mrs. L. G. Pondrom

BEEF BOURGUIGNON

4 lbs. lean sirloin
2 cloves garlic
1 c. flour
4 c. fresh beef consommé or canned
2 bay leaves (crushed)
1 t. thyme leaves
6 slices chopped bacon
2 lbs. fresh mushrooms
¾ c. butter
1 c. burgundy
2 T. chopped parsley
Salt and pepper

Fry bacon until crisp. Set aside cut beef into ½ inch pieces and sauté in bacon drippings turning frequently until brown. Remove beef, add t T. butter to beef consommé. Sauté sliced mushrooms and garlic until brown. Remove mushrooms set aside. In the same pan make a roux by adding remaining butter and flour and cook slowly to a light tan. Add consommé, and Burgundy. Stir and cook until slightly thickened. Add bay leaves, parsley, thyme, salt, and pepper. Add beef, mushrooms, and bacon. Cover and simmer until beef is tender about one hour. Adjust seasoning add more burgundy if needed.
Serves 8 to 10.

Jane Murchison Haber

MARJORIE PURNELL'S CADILLAC STEW

3 lbs. beef tender, cut in 1″ cubes (eye of round or sirloin can be used)
Flour, salt, and pepper
6 strips bacon
½ c. diced salt pork
Oil, if needed
12 mushrooms, sliced
12 small onions
6 carrots, diced
4 whole cloves
1 bay leaf
2 T. parsley, chopped
Pinch of marjoram and thyme
1 c. beef bouillon
1½ c. dry red wine
2 oz. brandy

Fry bacon and salt pork in a heavy skillet. Remove bacon and cut it into pieces and put it in a large casserole. Discard salt pork. Flour, salt, and pepper the beef cubes and brown them quickly in the bacon fat. You may need to add oil. Put beef cubes in the casserole and pour warmed brandy over them and flame. Add more fat, if necessary, to the skillet and sauté the onions, carrots, cloves, bay leaf, parsley, and thyme for 10 minutes. Add mushrooms and sauté 5 more minutes. Add all to casserole and pour bouillon and red wine over all. Bake at 300° for 3 hours.
Serves 8.

Mrs. Maurice Purnell, Jr.

BEEF CURRY

3 sliced onions
2 T. oil
2 chopped apples
1 16-oz. can applesauce
3 T. flour
2½ lbs. stewing beef, browned
½ c. stock or consommé
Salt and pepper
2 T. curry powder
1 c. raisins

Sauté onions in oil. Add apples, apple-sauce, flour, browned beef, stock, salt, pepper, curry powder, and raisins. Cook for 3 or 4 hours at least. Serve over rice. Offer condiments such as: chopped peanuts, crushed pineapple, shredded coconut, cubed avocado, chopped cucumber, chopped hard-cooked eggs, cooked and crumbled bacon, chutney.

Mrs. Curtis Sanford, Jr.

ORIENTAL BEEF

1½-2 lbs. beef tenderloin, sliced thin
Teriyaki Marinade
½ lb. fresh mushrooms, sliced
2 T. salad oil
4 or 5 green onions, sliced or 1 small onion, chopped
1 c. water chestnuts, thinly sliced
1 pkg. frozen green peas or snow peas
3 fresh ginger root, thin slices, chopped, or 1 t. powdered ginger
1 t. salt
2 T. soy sauce
4 T. dry sherry
2 T. cornstarch (add another t. if sauce proves too thin)
1½ c. beef broth or 1 c. broth and ½ c. pinot noir or similar red wine
Chopped parsley

Sprinkle the sliced beef with the Marinade and allow it to marinate a half hour or so. Sauté the beef and mushrooms in oil until mushrooms are soft and beef has about lost its pink color. Add onions and sauté briefly. (If using regular onion, it will need to be sautéed before the beef or in a separate pan and added at this time.) Add chestnuts, peas, ginger, and salt. Stir to combine. Combine soy sauce, cherry, cornstarch, and some of the beef broth. Mix well, add to the meat mixture, then add the remaining broth (and wine), and stir carefully as it heats and thickens. If the peas have been thawed beforehand, they cook quickly. These can be cooked ahead of time and added at the last moment just to heat through. Transfer the mixture to a serving dish, sprinkle with chopped parsley, and serve with rice. Freezes successfully.
Serves 6 generously.

Mrs. John W. McDonough

BEEF PROVENÇAL

2½ lb. top sirloin, cut in 1½-2"
  squares
5½ oz. salted butter, divided
⅓ c. brandy
3 t. fresh garlic, finely chopped,
  divided
1 t. meat glaze, heaping
2 t. tomato paste
4 t. potato flour
2¼ c. chicken stock
1 c. red wine
2 t. red currant jelly
Salt and pepper to taste
18 baby white onions, blanched
12 baby carrots, blanched
Pinch of sugar
12 mushroom caps
1 t. lemon juice
1 red pepper, pitted, cut into
  eighths
1 green pepper, pitted, cut into
  eighths
2 tomatoes, skinned, cut into
  eighths

Heat 1½ oz. salted butter in heavy pan, when about to color put in about 8 pieces of meat at a time and do not let them touch each other. Brown the pieces, remove and repeat. Put together in a pan when all are brown and flame with brandy. Remove meat and add 1 oz. butter and 2 t. finely chopped garlic. Stir in, off the fire, meat glaze, tomato paste, potato flour. When smooth, mix in chicken stock and red wine, add red currant jelly, little salt, and fresh black pepper. Stir over fire until it comes to a boil and put back beef. Place in a 375 degree oven on top shelf for 1¼ hr. or until tender. Baste occasionally. Brown carrots and onions in 1½ oz. hot butter, salt and pepper. When they begin to brown sprinkle with a little sugar. Place mushroom caps in 1½ oz. foaming butter. Turn in butter and add lemon juice, salt, and pepper to taste. Cook briskly for 3 minutes. Add 1 t. chopped garlic, red and green pepper and cook 2 minutes. Then add to onions and carrots. Add mix to beef 10 minutes before it is done. Five minutes before it is ready add tomatoes. Serve in casserole with French bread and red wine. Better the next day.
Serves 6.

Mrs. Mark Lemmon, Jr.

RAGOUT

1 lb. beef (eye of round),
   trimmed free of fat and
   gristle, cut into chunks
1 large onion, chopped
¼ c. bacon grease
1 c. flour
1 ripe tomato, peeled and
   chopped with juice
2 carrots, chopped or sliced
3 c. hot water
1 T. Wyler's Instant Beef
   Bouillon
1 T. seasoned salt
1 t. pepper
2 T. dried green pepper flakes
1 c. celery, chopped
1 pkg. frozen green beans
Potatoes for 4
½ c. sour cream
¼ c. dry red wine or water

Melt bacon grease in a heavy pan. Dredge beef in flour and brown lightly in hot grease. Remove meat with a slotted spoon, transferring it to a Dutch oven or baking pan. Put onion in grease; add ¼ cup of remaining flour to onions and blend. Put in hot water, bouillon, salt, pepper, green pepper flakes, chopped carrots, tomato, and celery. Bring this to a boil and pour over meat, scraping the pan out well. Cover with foil and bake at 350° for 2½ hours. Stew can be readied for oven hours ahead and refrigerated. If this is done add 30 min.-1 hr. cooking time. Peel enough potatoes for 4 and cut them into large chunks. Put the potatoes and beans in the stew for the last hour of cooking. Add more water if needed. Spoon gravy over the tops of the potatoes if they are not submerged. Beat sour cream and wine together and add this to the gravy for the last 15 minutes. Adjust salt and pepper before serving.
Serves 4.

Mrs. L. G. Pondrom

SUGARED STEAK

5-6 lb. porterhouse steak
1½ c. sugar
½ lb. butter
Salt and pepper

Have butcher cut the steak about 2½" thick with ample surrounding fat and chuck end left on. Work into the steak with the heel of the hand ¾ cup of sugar on each side until steak has absorbed all sugar and meat shows red again. Use wooden skewers to hold steak together, sear steak for 5 minutes on each side to seal it. The shrinkage will be terrific. Keep turning for about 30 minutes. Do not salt while cooking. Put butter, salt, and pepper on a platter, place steak on the butter and cut on the bias.
Serves 4.

Mrs. W. W. Overton, Jr.

BEEF STROGANOFF

1½ lb. round steak or beef
  tender
3 T. butter
2 T. flour
½ t. salt
1 t. pepper
1 T. paprika, heaping
½ t. nutmeg
1 t. sugar
1 c. sour cream
½-¾ c. mushrooms, sliced (may
  use dried mushrooms)
Rice, brown rice, or noodles

Brown round steak in 1 T. butter. Remove from skillet. Let cool and then slice or cut with scissors into 2x½" pieces. In the same skillet melt 2 T. butter and add flour. Make a light roux. Then add salt, pepper, paprika, nutmeg, and sugar. Stir until combined then, add sour cream. In another skillet brown mushrooms in additional butter. Then add mushrooms and meat to sour cream mixture. Serve over rice, brown rice, or noodles.
Serves 4.

Mrs. Clint M. Josey, Jr.

BEEF STROGANOFF
(This recipe is from a Dallasite's Russian grandmother.)

1½ lb. sirloin steak, trimmed
  and boned
2 T. butter
1 onion, chopped
½ lb. fresh mushrooms, thinly
  sliced
1 pt. sour cream
1 t. dry mustard
Flour
Salt (about 1 t. to 1 lb. meat)
Pepper, Accent,
  Worcestershire
Bouillon if needed

Cut meat into strips about the size of your first finger. Take sour cream out of the refrigerator when you begin to cut up the meat. Brown onions in butter for 10 minutes. Add mushrooms and cook about ½ hour. Remove from skillet. Put meat in skillet with 2 T. butter and sauté over a high fire, stirring constantly, about 10-15 minutes. Add salt, pepper, Accent, dry mustard and Worcestershire to taste. Add mushrooms and onions. Shake on a little flour, then add sour cream. (Add ¾ of the sour cream at first. Blend in well and then add remainder.) Stew on top of the stove, covered, about 1 hour. If the mixture is too thick, add a little bouillon (about ¼ cup,) enough to make sauce flow. Serve over wild rice.
Serves 4-6.

Mrs. Harold W. Kimmerling

THE WYNNE FAMILY SPICED ROUND

3 lbs. suet
2 T. red pepper
24 T. black pepper
6 T. allspice
6 T. cayenne pepper
6 T. ground cloves
4"-5" beef, first cut of the round with the bone in, about 20-25 lbs.
1 mop or broom handle, sharpened to a fine point
3 yds. heavy twine for tying the meat
1 yd. new white domestic
Heavy thread for sewing meat in domestic
½ c. saltpeter
1 box kosher salt
1 raw egg
1 large crock stone container
1 screen to cover top of crock
1 brick

Preparation time: 2 days plus 2 weeks curing brine.

Render suet the night before stuffing meat. When liquified, add spices and stir until well mixed. Pour into shallow jelly roll pan and refrigerate over night. (This may be done the same day you stuff meat and put in freezer if you prefer one day preparation). The next morning take sharpened broom stick and punch deep holes in beef at 2" intervals, or wherever there is a strategic place for stuffing. The suet will have hardened and may be cut into pencil thin strips and slipped into holes. Stuff holes as tightly as possible. This adds flavor to the meat, so liberally spice. Turn beef; stuff the other side. Tie a string as tightly as possible a couple of times around circumference of meat and bone. If there is suet mixture remaining, warm it and ice meat. Sew round of beef securely in the domestic. Fill clean crock ¾ full with water. Add enough kosher salt to float whole raw egg. Add ½ c. saltpeter to water. DO NOT leave this out as it gives meat a nice red color. Place beef in brine and weight down with clean brick (not a painted one.) Cover crock with piece of screen. After one week turn meat and after second week remove meat from brine. DO NOT remove cloth. Place in large pot and cover with fresh water. Boil 3½ hours for 20-20½ lbs. meat. Turn meat after 1½ hrs. Remove from liquid; do not allow beef to cool in water. Remove cloth when meat is cool enough to handle. When cold, slice off top layer and discard.

Serving suggestions: Spiced round should be sliced paper thin, served on soda crackers, little beaten biscuits or hot biscuits with cooked salad dressing or homemade mayonnaise. Keep meat wrapped in damp cloth to prevent drying.

Special Notes: Spiced round cannot be made except during cold weather or meat will spoil in brine. One hot winter a local grocer was kind enough to store it for us in his cooler.

Margaret Wynne Harrison

BEST ROAST BEEF

3-7 lb. rolled rib or standing rib
   roast
Salt and pepper

Rub the roast with salt and pepper. Place, fat side up, in a shallow pan and roast in a pre-heated oven at 375° for 1 hour. Turn off the heat, but don't open the oven door. No matter how long it is until dinner time, don't open door or remove roast. Turn it on to 375° again 30-40 minutes before serving time. Does not matter about the size of roast.

Mrs. J. Brevard Haynes

BOEUF A LA MODE EN GELEE
(Beef à la Mode in Aspic)

4 lbs. well-shaped piece of
   larded beef
2 T. butter
5 c. water
½ c. white wine
2 carrots cut in small pieces
6 small onions
1 t. salt
¼ t. black pepper
4 whole cloves
BOUQUET GARNI:
4 sprigs parsley
1 small bay leaf
¼ t. thyme
SAUCE:
4½ c. reserved broth from meat
2 envelopes unflavored gelatin
¼ c. cold water
GARNITURE:
4 carrots, freshly cooked, cut in
   perfect rounds
1 8-oz. can tiny whole peeled
   onions, drained and
   marinated in pickle brine
Parsley
Dijon mustard

Sear meat on all sides in butter. Add water, wine, salt, pepper, cloves, carrots cut in pieces, small onions, and Bouquet Garni. Bring to boiling point on top of stove. Remove to 300 degree oven, cover and cook 3 hours. Place meat on heated platter. Sauce: Strain broth, chill and remove all fat. Reserve 4½ cups of broth. Soften gelatin in cold water. Stir gelatin into the hot reserved broth until well mixed. Garniture: Arrange thin slices cold beef on platter. Cover with rounds of carrots and surround with marinated onions. When gelatin broth has cooled to syrupy stage, pour over meat and vegetables carefully so as not to disturb pattern you have made. Place platter in refrigerator. When aspic is stiff, garnish with parsley and serve with Dijon mustard. It is important that this dish look very decorative.
Serves 6.

Mrs. Mark L. Lemmon, Jr.

BEEF TIPS IN WINE

2-3 lbs. round or sirloin steak
  cubed
2 T. flour
Cooking oil
1 can beef bouillon
1 c. red wine (more if needed)
1 medium green pepper, cut
  into strips
1 small onion, chopped
2 medium very ripe tomatoes,
  chopped
Salt and pepper to taste

Dredge meat in flour and brown quickly in electric skillet. Add bouillon and wine and cook for 1 hour. Add remaining ingredients and simmer until tender. Delicious served over parsleyed rice or noodles.
Serves 6 to 8.

CHINESE PEPPER STEAK

4 c. hot cooked rice
1½ lb. lean round steak,
  pounded and sliced
1 T. paprika
3 T. butter
1 t. garlic, minced
1½ c. beef broth
½ lb. mushrooms, sliced
1 large green bell pepper, cut in
  strips
1 medium zucchini, sliced
1 c. green onions, sliced
1 c. celery, sliced
2 T. cornstarch
¼ c. water
¼ c. soy sauce
1 6-oz. can water chestnuts,
  sliced
2 large fresh tomatoes, cut in
  eighths (optional)

While rice is cooking, slice steak into ¼″ wide strips. Sprinkle meat with paprika and allow to stand while slicing vegetables. In a large skillet or wok brown meat in butter. Add garlic and broth. Cover and simmer 30 minutes. Stir in mushrooms, bell pepper, zucchini, onions, and celery. Cover and cook 5 minutes. Blend cornstarch, water, and soy sauce. Stir into meat mixture. Cook, stirring until clear and thickened — about 2 minutes. Add tomatoes, if desired, and water chestnuts and stir. Serve over fluffy rice with extra soy sauce.
Serves 6.

Mrs. John T. Kipp

COMPANY POT ROAST

4-5 lb. beef pot roast
2 onions, sliced
4 carrots, cut in sticks
½ c. water
¼ c. chili sauce
⅓ c. dry sherry
1 clove garlic, minced
1 bay leaf
¼ t. dry mustard
¼ t. marjoram
¼ t. rosemary
¼ t. thyme
1 8-oz. can sliced mushrooms, undrained

Dredge meat in flour seasoned with salt and pepper and brown slowly in oil in a Dutch oven. When almost browned, add onions and carrots and cook in the same fat for a few minutes. Stir in remaining ingredients except for mushrooms. Cover and cook at 300° for 2½-3 hours. Add mushrooms with their liquid and cook for 30 minutes longer. For gravy, blend 1½ t. cornstarch with ¼ c. cold water. Stir into pan juices, stirring constantly until thickened. Do not strain gravy, serving it with carrots, onions and mushrooms in it.
Serves 8.

Mrs. James Mason

GREEK STEW

lbs. stew beef, cubed
½ c. butter
small can tomato paste
⅓ c. red table wine (burgundy)
small stick cinnamon
½ t. whole cloves
T. brown sugar
clove garlic crushed, optional
bay leaf
¼ t. cumin
2½ lbs. tiny onions
salt and pepper

Melt butter and lightly sauté beef cubes. Mix other ingredients and pour over beef. Simmer in oven in a heavy covered casserole at 200-250 degrees 3-4 hours, or until tender. Freezes well.
Serves 6.

Mrs. E. Don Rott

FILET OF BEEF WITH GREEN PEPPERCORNS

4 lb. filet, trimmed and tied
2 T. oil
Salt and pepper to taste
3 T. Cognac
1½ c. brown stock or bouillon
1 c. heavy cream
3 T. green peppercorns, well
  drained
Lemon juice, salt, and pepper
  to taste
3 T. butter

In a large, heavy skillet, brown the filet well on all sides in the oil over moderately high heat. Transfer the meat to an oval gratin dish and roast uncovered 20-25 minutes in a 450° oven for rare (140° on a meat thermometer). Transfer the meat to a serving platter and let it rest for 10 minutes. Meanwhile make the sauce. Pour off fat from the skillet, add Cognac and flame, shaking the pan until the flames go out and stirring in the brown bits. Add the stock and cream. Reduce over moderately high heat to 2 cups. Add the peppercorns, lemon juice, salt and pepper to taste. Remove pan from heat and swirl in butter, softened and cut into bits. Slice meat and re-form into filet. Pour some of the sauce over, then serve remaining in a sauce boat. The sauce may also be served with sautéed steak, à la steak Diane or steak au poivre.
Serves 6.

Mrs. Harold W. Kimmerling

FLANK STEAK

4 flank steaks sprinkled with
  coarse ground pepper
5 oz. Kikkoman Teriyaki Meat
  Marinade Sauce
2 c. Wesson oil
4 cloves garlic, smashed
1 piece ginger root, sliced
1 onion sliced

Mix all ingredients and marinate steaks overnight, turning occasionally. Cook on a hot grill 3-4 minutes to the side. Slice paper-thin, against the grain, on the diagonal. Count on one flank for 2-3 people. Serve on small onion buns with a hearty Bearnaise sauce, accompanied by mushroom soup and spinach and bacon salad. Great "after-tennis" supper.
Serves 8-10.

Mrs. Stephen J. Summers

GRILLED FLANK STEAK WITH RED WINE AND SHALLOT SAUCE

Flank steak
Soy sauce
Salt
Black pepper, freshly ground
Meat Tenderizer
1 t. thyme
SAUCE:
1¼ c. shallots, chopped or green onions, chopped
1¼ c. red wine
1 stick butter
2 T. parsley, finely chopped

Brush flank steak with soy sauce and sprinkle well with salt, pepper, meat tenderizer, and dried thyme, crumbled. Let stand for 1 hour or so. Brush again with soy sauce and grill over brisk fire, 3 to 4 minutes on each side for rare steak. Carve with sharp knife in thin slices on the diagonal. Serve with sauce. Sauce: Combine shallots or green onions and red wine. Bring just to boiling. Add butter and salt to taste and stir well, until butter is melted. Add parsley. Spoon over steak slices and pass remaining sauce.

Note: Sauce only tastes good as a complement to the meat, does not taste as well on its own.

Mrs. John J. Kendrick, Jr.

GREEK POT ROAST

4 to 6 lb. roast
1 med. eggplant (firm and heavy for its size)
3 onions, cut in large pieces
1 1-lb. can tomatoes, drained (reserve liquid)
4 to 6 zucchini squash
1 bay leaf
1 t. oregano
3 cloves garlic, chopped

Preheat oven to 350°. Salt, pepper and flour roast. Heat grease in dutch oven to fill 2″ from bottom. On top of stove, brown roast over medium heat till well browned on all sides. Pour off all grease to another skillet and reserve. To roast, add onions, garlic, bay leaf, oregano and cover. Place in oven. Slice unpeeled eggplant and zucchini in 1″ slices. Salt and pepper and brown a few at a time in reserved grease over medium heat. Remove browned pieces and drain on paper towel. After roast has cooked for 1 hour, add remaining ingredients and continue cooking until meat is tender, about another 1½ hours. If more liquid is needed, add tomato juice and salt and pepper to taste.
Serves 6.

Mrs. Walter Kilgo

HAWAIIAN BEEF

3 c. water
1 T. chicken-seasoned stock
  base
1 t. butter
1½ c. rice
2 T. vegetable oil
¼ t. garlic powder
1 lb. sirloin (cut into ¼″ strips)
1 c. diagonally sliced celery
1 medium onion, sliced
1 t. Mei Yen seasoning
2 t. cornstarch
¼ c. soy sauce
½ c. water
½ c. cubed green pepper
6 cherry tomatoes, halved
½ c. toasted slivered almonds
  (optional)

Bring water to a boil with stock base and butter. Stir in rice, cover and cook over low heat for 20 minutes or until rice is tender. Heat oil and garlic powder in a skillet. Stir in sirloin strips and brown; remove from skillet. Add celery and onion, cover and heat 1 minute. Mix cornstarch and soy sauce and add along with Mei Yen seasoning, water, beef, green pepper, cherry tomatoes and almonds. Heat, covered 1 minute or longer if preferred, and serve over rice. Makes 4 servings.

Mrs. Don McIlyar

CALF'S LIVER VENETIAN

½ lb. calf's liver
1 large onion, sliced
1 T. butter
1 T. olive oil
2 T. dry wine
Salt and pepper to taste
1 t. chopped fresh tarragon
Few drops lemon juice

Cut liver into small, very thin strips. Sauté onion in butter and oil. Add wine and reduce the sauce over a high flame. Add liver and over a good hot fire, brown the strips briefly on both sides. Add salt, pepper, tarragon and lemon juice. Serve immediately.

TENDERLOIN MARINADE

2-3 lb. beef tenderloin
Fresh cracked pepper
1 5-oz. bottle Worcestershire
  sauce
1 5½-oz. can unsweetened
  pineapple juice
1 T. soy sauce
¼ c. butter or margarine,
  melted
½ c. red cooking wine

Press cracked pepper into tenderloin on all sides. Combine Worcestershire sauce, pineapple juice and soy sauce in pan. Let tenderloin marinate in this mixture about one hour before cooking. When ready to charcoal, combine the marinade with melted butter and wine. Baste meat while cooking to desired doneness. Gives meat an unusual but delicate flavor.
Serves 4. This is also delicious on pieces of boned skinned chicken breast — just place on skewers and grill 6 minutes.

Mrs. James F. Mason

STEAK ROQUEFORT

¼ lb. Roquefort cheese
¼ c. olive oil
1 clove garlic, crushed in 1 T.
  brandy
Steak of your choice

Blend cheese with olive oil and garlic. Broil steak to desired doneness. Spread steak with cheese mixture and put it back on the grill again just long enough to melt the cheese.
Serves 1.

Mrs. J. Murray Smith

BEEF SHORT RIBS ANISE

Beef short ribs, cut into
  serving-size pieces for 6
  people
12 anise seeds
2 T. soy sauce
½ c. dry red wine
1 garlic pod
⅛ t. ground ginger
2 t. beef stock base
2 t. powdered mushrooms
1 c. hot water
¾ t. bouquet garni for beef

Place ribs in pyrex container. Crush anise seeds thoroughly. Combine with soy sauce, wine, garlic pod, and ginger. Pour over ribs. Marinate for several several hours or overnight. Remove beef from marinade and brown in heavy frying pan. Pour off excess fat and add beef stock and mushrooms to hot water. Pour over ribs. Crush bouquet garni and sprinkle over meat. Cover tightly and simmer slowly for 2 hours or until ribs are very tender. Thicken sauce, if desired, with 2 t. arrowroot or cornstarch mixed with 1 T. cold water.
Serves 6.

Mrs. R. Stewart Campbell

SHORT RIBS OF BEEF BURGUNDY

3 lbs. beef short ribs
3 T. butter
1 large onion, sliced
1 clove garlic, chopped fine
4 sprigs parsley
1 carrot, chopped
1 small bay leaf
1 pinch thyme
2 T. flour
1 c. dry red wine
1 c. water
1 beef bouillon cube
¼ t. Worcestershire
¼ t. brown gravy color
Salt and pepper to taste

Brown short ribs in a shallow pan at 450° 30-40 minutes, turning once. In a big pot melt butter and add onion, garlic, parsley, carrot, bay leaf, and thyme; sauté until the onion yellows. Stir in flour, mixing well. Add wine, water, and bouillon cube. Mix well. Bring to a boil, stirring often, then simmer; add ribs to pot, cover, and simmer about 2 hours. Remove meat, skim fat off, and strain gravy. Add Worcestershire and gravy color, salt, and pepper. Return meat to gravy and serve.
Serves 4.

Cookbook Committee

SIRLOIN TIPS RAGOUT AU VIN

3 lbs. sirloin tips, cut into 1-
   inch cubes
3 T. butter
3 oz. tomato paste
2 T. red wine vinegar
1 c. Burgundy
1 stick cinnamon
2 bay leaves
2 lbs. tiny whole onions, peeled
1 t. salt
¼ t. pepper
1 t. cornstarch

Place cubes of meat in deep saucepan with butter. Simmer meat over medium heat, stirring constantly until meat is brown and tender. Mix tomato paste, vinegar and wine with browned meat. Add cinnamon, bay leaves and onions to mixture. Season with salt and pepper. Simmer covered for 1 hour over low heat. Mix cornstarch with ¼ cup water and blend into sauce. Serve hot. Better if made the day before and reheated.
Makes 6 servings.
Serve with rice and green salad.

Mrs. Walter N. Kuntz III

SAUTEED BEEF AND SPINACH

1 lb. beef tender, cut 1 inch
   cubes
3 T. soy sauce
1 T. sesame oil
1 T. sugar or Sugar Twin
½ onion, finely chopped
Dash of cayenne
1 pkg. fresh spinach
2 T. toasted sesame seed

Marinate beef in all ingredients except last two. Sauté beef in 1-2 T. sesame oil and remove from heat. Sauté spinach quickly in the same pan and add beef and sesame seed. Serve alone or over rice.
Serves 2-3.

Mrs. Charles Pierce, Jr.

SALISBURY STEAK

1½ lbs. lean ground beef
1½ c. fresh bread crumbs
1-2 t. salt
4 medium onions
3 T. butter
2 T. cornstarch
1½ c. water
2 beef bouillon cubes
1 or 2 t. Worcestershire

Mix the beef, crumbs, and salt. Shape into 6 oval patties. Set aside. Cut onions into rings. Melt butter in a 10″ skillet. Cook onion until tender; mix cornstarch with the water and add to onions along with bouillon cubes and Worcestershire. Broil patties to the desired doneness. Place patties on a warm platter and pour the onion sauce over all. Garnish and serve. The onion mixture can be made ahead of time and frozen, then reheated. Serves 6 or 4 extremely hungry people.

Mrs. Edward James Henry III

PHIL'S CHILI

10 lbs. cheap cut beef steak put through grinder one time *or* chili ground meat
6 T. paprika
8 T. chili powder
1 T. cayenne
2 T. salt
6 T. garlic powder
9 T. round comino seed (cumin)
Flour and water paste
4 lb. pinto beans

Cover beef with water and simmer 2 hours. Bring simmer slowly so that juices from the meat are extracted by the slowly cooking water. Mix seasonings in a bowl and stir into meat. Cook 45 minutes more. Lower the fire and thicken with flour and water paste to desired consistency. Cook pinto beans as package directs adding salt to taste after they are cooked. Serve chili and beans separately so each person may add beans as desired.
Serves 20-25.
Recipe divides successfully. Keeps well refrigerated or frozen.

Mrs. L. L. May, Jr.

PEPPER STEAK
(Steak Au Poivre)

2 Delmonico steaks
Butter
2 T. white pepper
1 T. black pepper freshly
    crushed in pestle and mortar
Watercress
Béarnaise sauce

Clarify salted butter, cool and brush it heavily on 1 side of the steak. Put it in the refrigerator to set, repeat on the other side and put to set. Cover one side of the steak with both peppers. Put under broiler 4 minutes on each side. Brush with melted butter twice before turning. Remove, put on a serving dish and garnish with watercress and serve with béarnaise sauce.

Mrs. Mark Lemmon, Jr.

OUACHITA STEW

2 lbs. boneless stew meat (or
    cut-up chuck roast)
1 16-oz. can peeled, whole
    tomatoes
1 T. sugar
2½ t. salt
3 T. tapioca
1 c. diced celery
4-5 carrots, sliced
2 medium potatoes, sliced
Handful of croutons
2 medium onions, sliced

In a huge bowl, mix the meat and all other ingredients except the last four. Dump the mixture into a baking dish and arrange the remaining four ingredients on top. Sprinkle generously with lemon-pepper marinade. A little red wine (¼-½ cup) may also be added. Cover the pan with a tight-fitting lid and bake for 6-7 hours at 250°.
Serves 5-6.

Mrs. Peter R. Thompson

SAVORY STUFFED FILET OF BEEF

3 lg. onions thinly sliced
6 T. olive oil
4 T. Butter
2 cloves garlic minced
18 coarsely chopped pitted
   black olives
Salt
1 t. fresh ground pepper
½ c. chopped cooked Virginia
   or Country Ham
1 t. thyme
2 egg yolks beaten
2 T. chopped parsley
1 filet (about 7 lbs.)

Saute onions in oil and butter until just limp, add garlic, ham, 1 t. pepper, thyme, 1 t. salt, cook til well blended. Stir in beaten egg yolks and parsley. Cook for 3 minutes. Cut filet cross wise not quite through in rather thick slices and spoon stuffing in between. Tie securely. Place on rack, brush with oil or butter and roast in 300° oven for about 50 minutes or until internal temperature 225°. Let rest 10 minutes. Salt lightly and place on hot platter, with garnish of perfect sprigs of watercress, tiny glazed carrots. Serve with bordelaise sauce and tiny buttered new potatoes.

Mrs. Anthony N. Briggle

MEAT SAUCE

1 medium onion, chopped fine
2 cloves garlic, chopped fine
¼ medium bell pepper,
  chopped fine
3 T. butter or olive oil
1 lb. chopped meat (½ beef, ¼
  veal, ¼ pork)
1 1-lb. 13-oz. (#2½) can
  tomatoes, chopped fine
1 6-oz. can tomato paste
½ t. powdered thyme
1 bay leaf
2 t. salt
¼ t. pepper
1 t. sugar
3 T. grated Parmesan cheese
¼ c. heavy cream

In large pan, sauté onion, green pepper, garlic in butter or olive oil until onion yellows. Add meat and stir until red is gone. Add tomatoes, tomato paste, bay leaf, thyme, salt, sugar, and pepper. Simmer slowly until very thick, about 1 hour; stirring often. Skim off fat, remove from heat, extract bay leaf, add cheese and cream and mix well. Add more salt and pepper if necessary.
Serves 4.

Cook Book Committee

ITALIAN MEAT LOAVES IN SQUASH BOWLS

3 medium acorn squashes
2 T. melted butter
Salt and pepper
1½ lb. ground beef
1½ c. soft bread crumbs
1 egg, beaten
⅓ c. catsup
1 t. salt
1 T. oregano
2 T. Parmesan cheese, grated

Halve squashes; scoop out seeds, but do not pare. Brush hollows with melted butter and sprinkle lightly with salt and pepper. Combine ground beef, bread crumbs, egg, catsup, salt, and oregano and mix lightly. Heap into squash halves, dividing evenly. Sprinkle with cheese. Stand squashes in a shallow baking pan and bake uncovered at 375° for 45 minutes. Cover with foil and bake 1 hour longer or until squashes are tender.
Makes 6 servings.

Mrs. John D. Williamson, Jr.

MEAT LOAF WITH GRAVY

2 16-oz. cans tomatoes
1 T. Kitchen Bouquet
1 c. chopped onions
1 c. chopped celery
1 T. dried green pepper flakes
1 pkg. Lipton's Onion Soup
1 t. salt
1 t. pepper
2 eggs
2 lbs. ground round steak
¾ c. bread crumbs
1 T. salt
1 t. pepper
2 T. dried parsley flakes
½ c. bread crumbs
⅓ c. flour
2 c. hot water

Mix first 8 ingredients and let simmer, stirring often, for about 30 minutes, adding water if it becomes too thick. Let cool and pureé in blender. Beat eggs in a large bowl and add beef, ¾ c. bread crumbs, salt, pepper, and ¾ cup of the sauce from the blender. Mix well, using your hands. Add salt and pepper as needed. (The only way to check seasoning is to cook a small sample on a hot skillet.) On a piece of foil shape the meat into a loaf firmly. Crumple the foil around the loaf to form a boat. Mix parsley with bread crumbs and pat into top of loaf. Set in an open roasting pan. Pour the remainder of the blender sauce around it. Mix flour and hot water, blending well with a whisk. Pour over loaf. Cover lightly with foil and bake at 350° for 2 hours, adding water if the gravy becomes too thick. Remove foil for the last 15 minutes to let the top brown. Season gravy with salt and pepper before serving. The loaf is good cold; it also reheats well. Store loaf and gravy separately. Reheat loaf wrapped in foil and gravy on top of the stove. Serves 6-8.

Mrs. L. G. Pondrom

LOUISIANA MEAT PIES

Preparation Time: Approx. 1½ hours

MEAT MIXTURE:
2 T. flour
1 T. shortening
1½ lbs. lean ground beef
½ lb. ground pork
2 large dry onions, chopped fine
6 green onions, chopped fine (tops and bottoms)
3 T. parsley, chopped
Salt, red and black pepper to taste

MEAT PIE DOUGH: 3½-4 c. all-purpose flour
2 t. baking powder
1 t. salt
½ c. melted shortening (NOT liquid)
2 eggs, at room temperature
½-⅔ c. milk, at room temperature

Meat Mixture: Make a roux of the shortening and flour. Add the other ingredients and cook thoroughly, stirring quite often. The amount of beef and pork can be reversed, depending on taste. Skim as much of the fat off as possible when finished cooking. Let cool. (If not cool, it will tend to melt your dough!)

Pie Dough: Sift flour, baking powder, and salt. Add the melted shortening, then the beaten eggs and milk. (Add milk to beaten eggs until liquid measures 1 cup.) Mix well until dough is stiff. Roll on floured board until paper thin. Cut out dough the size of a coffee cup saucer. Fill with the cooled meat mixture, fold over and dampen dough and press together with fork which has been dampened. Fry pies in deep fat until golden brown, about 3 minutes. Makes 22-26 meat pies. Pies can be frozen between sheets of waxed paper *before* frying. To cook after freezing, remove from freezer, separate pies, and thaw. Then fry as above.

Note: This dough is very difficult to work with so do not be discouraged. The more you make the easier it gets! I find it more successful to roll out one pie at a time.

Mrs. Larry M. Nobles

LEFT-OVER BEEF OR LAMB

1 onion, chopped
½ green pepper, chopped
1 2-oz. can B and B mushrooms, drained
2 T. ripe olives, minced
3 T. butter
2 T. flour
1 t. Kitchen Bouquet
1 c. water or beef bouillon
1 c. cooked beef or lamb, diced
3 T. sour cream
2 oz. wine, red or white
Salt and pepper to taste

Sauté onion, green pepper, mushrooms, and olives in butter. Stir in flour and brown. Gradually add water mixed with Kitchen Bouquet. Cook until thick gravy is made. Add meat, then sour cream and wine. Serve over rice, noodles, or toast. Serves 3-4.

Mrs. Maurice E. Purnell, Jr.

LARCHMONT CREOLE BEEF OR VEAL

1½-2 lbs. beef sirloin or veal (across the grain) cut into finger strips about ¼" thick
2 t. cornstarch
½ t. salt
¼ t. coarsely ground pepper
1 T. peanut oil
2 T. butter
2 large onions, finely chopped
2 large green peppers, seeded and cut into strips
2 stalks celery, sliced thinly on the slant
4 cloves garlic, minced
2 T. peanut oil
3 T. butter
1 16-oz. can peeled tomatoes, drained, cored, seeded, and minced
2 bay leaves
1 can beef bouillon
1 soup can of water
1 6-oz. can B and B mushrooms
¼ c. dry sherry
Sliced water chestnuts
2 T. cornstarch
1 T. butter

Shake the meat in a bag with cornstarch, salt, and pepper. Sauté the prepared meat in peanut oil and butter (or 3 T. clarified butter). In a separate skillet, sauté onions, green peppers, celery, and garlic in peanut oil and butter. Add tomatoes, bay leaves, bouillon, water and mushrooms. Bring the onion-green pepper mixture to a boil, lower heat, and cook uncovered while preparing meat. When meat is done, combine it with the onion-pepper mixture and place over low heat. Add sherry and water chestnuts. Thicken with cornstarch that has been blended with butter. Serve over rice or grits.
Serves 4.

Geneva Ashby Jones

HOMEMADE CORNED BEEF

**4-6 lbs. fresh beef (brisket,
    rump, eye of round)**
4 qts. cold water
1½ c. salt
1 T. brown sugar
2 T. pickling spice
6 bay leaves
½ oz. saltpeter
6 cloves garlic, sliced
1 onion, sliced

Combine all ingredients except beef, garlic, and onion and bring to a boil. Reduce heat and simmer 5 minutes. Let cool. Put beef in a crock (or any container which is not metal). Add the liquid, garlic, and onions. Cover with a plate or something that will keep meat submerged. Store in a cool corner 14-16 days. A brine of mold may develop but this is a normal part of the curing process. To cook, rinse beef thoroughly. Cover with cold water and simmer 2-2½ hours.

LAMB

SHISH-KEBABS ST. JOHNS

1 c. olive oil
¼ c. lemon juice
1 bay leaf, crumbled
¼ t. oregano
1 t. salt
¼ t. pepper
3 lbs. lean lamb, cut in 1″ cubes
1 small basket cherry tomatoes
2 green peppers, cut in 2″ strips
24 small onions (pickling-size)
24 fresh mushrooms, small

Soak small onions for about 3 hours in water before beginning recipe. Clean and trim fresh mushrooms, tomatoes, and green peppers. Prepare marinade as follows: combine olive oil, lemon juice, bay leaf, oregano, salt, and pepper in a large baking pan. Place lamb, tomatoes, green pepper strips, onions, and mushrooms each together on its own skewer. (This is done because each item has a different cooking time and cannot all be cooked equally.) Put skewered ingredients into the marinade and let stand 4-6 hours, turning occasionally. On a covered outdoor grill, cook the skewers over medium heat for the following time periods:

Lamb: cook close to heat 25-30 minutes
Onion: cook close to heat 15-20 minutes
Green pepper: cook distant to heat 15-20 mins.
Mushroom: cook distant to the heat 15-20 mins.
Tomato: cook distant to the heat 10 mins.
Remove all skewers from the grill at the same time. Pull meat and vegetables from the skewers and mix all together in a ring, around a mound of hot saffron rice.
Serves 6.

Mrs. George W. Jalonick IV

GINGERED LAMB ROAST

5-lb. leg of lamb
½ c. flour
¾ t. cracked black pepper
5 t. ground ginger
1½ t. salt
¼ c. melted butter
½ T. Worcestershire
Juice of 1 lime
Raisins (optional)
1 onion

Preheat oven to 450°. Remove the lamb from the refrigerator at least ½ hour before cooking. Remove the papery outer covering and rub the meat with flour to which has been added pepper, ginger and salt. Secure slices of onion over the roast with toothpicks. Pour over the lamb a sauce made of butter, Worcestershire and lime juice. Brown in hot oven for 15 minutes. Reduce heat to 350° and cook about 2½ hours. Serve with pan gravy to which raisins have been added.

Mrs. Allen L. Oliver, Jr.

SENECA LEG OF LAMB

5½-lb. leg of lamb with *all* fat
    removed
Marinate in:
1 qt. dry white Sauterne
2 cut up carrots
1 onion
6 peppercorns
3 cloves
2 bay leaves

Marinate meat at least 8 hours or more, turning every hour or so. Preheat oven to 350°, place lamb in roasting pan. Cook a total of 1½ hours, it should be pink, meat thermometer reading 140°. Put marinade in pan on top of stove and reduce for about 15 minutes. Strain and then baste roast with it quite often. Turn oven up to 500° for last 10 minutes or until brown. When lamb is done, remove to a warm platter, take off any fat from the juice in the pan and you will have a wonderful thin gravy.
Serves 8.

Mrs. Searcy Ferguson, Jr.

BROILED BUTTERFLIED LEG OF LAMB

Leg of lamb
2-4 garlic cloves
Salt and pepper
Rosemary
Melted butter
Béarnaise sauce

Have the butcher bone the leg and butterfly it, cut it, open and spread it flat, so that the meat is approximately the same thickness all across, about 2½-3″. It will resemble a thick steak with some fat on one side. Spread out the butterflied lamb. Cut garlic cloves into small slivers and insert them into the meat by making tiny incisions with the point of a knife. Season the lamb with salt and pepper and rub rosemary into the flesh. This can be cooked inside or out on a charcoal grill. Outside, cook it about 15 minutes on each side for rare. Brush the meat with butter several times during cooking. Inside, place lamb on broiling rack with the inner, fleshy side up and broil about 6″ from heat for about 15-18 minutes. Brush it with butter and turn it. Broil it another 14-16 minutes for rare or 20 minutes for medium rare. To serve, slice the meat in thin slices and serve with béarnaise sauce.

Serves 6 well or 8 moderately.

Mrs. Jack Shook

BOBBIE'S BUTTERFLIED LEG OF LAMB

1 6-lb. leg of lamb (boned and butterflied)
½ t. fresh ground pepper
½ c. red wine vinegar
1½ c. oil
2 cloves garlic, minced
1 t. rosemary
½ t. salt
2 bay leaves, crumbled

Combine all ingredients and marinate lamb overnight or longer, covered and refrigerated. One hour before serving, remove. Put on grill, fat side up. Cook 40-50 minutes, basting often with marinade. Cut across grain.

Mrs. Edward W. Rose III

BARBECUED LEG OF LAMB

6 lh. leg of lamb, boned and
  flattened
MARINADE:
2 T. vinegar
½ c. olive oil
1 clove garlic, mashed
1 t. salt
½ t. pepper
SAUCE:
2½ c. chili sauce
1 t. chili powder
¾ c. olive oil
½ c. lemon juice
1 T. brown sugar
2 T. tarragon vinegar
1 bay leaf
2 t. Tabasco
1 t. dry mustard
½ c. water
2 c. finely chopped onion
2 cloves garlic, minced
1 t. salt

Marinade: Combine all ingredients and marinate lamb 2 hours. Sauce: Combine all ingredients and boil, then reduce and simmer 15 minutes. Charcoal lamb 1½-2 hours, turning frequently and basting every 5 minutes with sauce.

Serves 6-8.

Note: Sauce is good with lamb, chicken, spare ribs.

Cook Book Committee

LAMB NOISETTES WITH ROSEMARY

6 lamb Noisettes
½ t. powdered rosemary
Peanut oil
Salt

Brush both sides of chops with oil. Sprinkle them with rosemary. Cook to your taste under the broiler or pan-broil them in a large and heavy frying pan that has been sprinkled with a very thin layer of salt and heated before putting in the chops.

Noisettes are lamb chops without the bone.

Serves 2

Mrs. Geneva Ashby Jones

JUDY GLAZER'S MARINATED LAMB

⅔ c. olive oil
3 T. lemon juice
1 t. salt
½ t. pepper
1 t. oregano
3 bay leaves, crumbled
3 c. onions, sliced
3 cloves garlic
Leg of lamb

Marinate lamb in a mixture of all ingredients for at least 12 hours, turning occasionally. Cook for 1½-2 hours, basting occasionally with marinade.

Cookbook Committee

BAKED LAMB SHANKS

6 lamb shanks
Salt and pepper
2 T. butter or margarine
4 shallots or green onions (use some of the green part), chopped
1 garlic clove, crushed
½ c. burgundy
6 c. rich brown stock, made with beef bouillon powder or cubes
12 medium mushrooms, sliced
2 medium tomatoes, peeled and diced
Additional salt and pepper, to taste
Parsley, chopped

Trim the excess fat from the lamb shanks and season them with salt and pepper. Brown them on all sides in a skillet or roasting pan in the butter. Stir in the shallots (or onions) and garlic and simmer the mixture briefly for 2-3 minutes. Add the burgundy and cook the mixture until the wine is reduced by half. Add the beef stock and bring the sauce to a boil. Cover the skillet or roasting pan tightly and place in a 350 degree oven for 1-1½ hours or until it is tender when tested with a fork. Add the mushrooms about 20 minutes before the meat is done. Remove the lamb shanks from the skillet and put them on a heated serving dish. Stir the tomatoes into the sauce in the pan and cook it, uncovered, on top of the stove until it is reduced by half. Season it to taste with salt and pepper and pour it over the lamb. Sprinkle dish with chopped parsley before serving. Serve with rice pilaf or noodles.

Serves 6.

Note: This freezes well. If time permits it is nice to start this dish the day before and take it up through the addition of the mushrooms and oven cooking. Refrigerate it overnight and remove any hardened fat that has formed on top before finishing the dish the next day. Then proceed with the tomatoes, et cetera.

Mrs. John W. McDonough

VENISON CHILI

5 c. canned tomatoes
1½ lbs. onions, chopped
1 lb. green pepper, chopped
2 cloves garlic, crushed
½ c. parsley, chopped
½ c. butter
1 lb. ground lean pork
2½ lbs. deer meat, ground for chili
½ c. chili powder or to taste
2 15-oz. cans red kidney beans with juice
2 T. salt
1½ t. cumin seed
1½ t. pepper
1 ½ T. salad oil

Simmer tomatoes 5 minutes in their own juices. Add onions, green peppers, and cook until tender, stirring often. Add garlic and parsley. Melt butter in a large skillet and sauté meat for 15 minutes. Add meat to tomato mixture; stir in chili powder; and cook 10 minutes. Add beans and spices and water if needed. Simmer covered 1 hour. Cook uncovered for 30 minutes. Recipe can also be used for beef chili.
Serves 8-10.

Mrs. Harold W. Kimmerling

PARTY VENISON

2 lbs. boneless venison stew meat with fat and fibers trimmed off
½ c. fresh bacon drippings
1 can beef broth (not bouillon)
1¾ c. California Burgundy
3 medium onions, sliced
1 lb. fresh mushrooms, sliced
4 T. flour
Generous pinch of thyme and marjoram
Freshly ground pepper and salt to taste

Sauté onions in ¼ cup of bacon drippings in a 4-qt. Dutch oven until golden. Remove to a bowl. Add bacon fat as needed; brown venison cubes in small portions to avoid too much liquid. When all are browned, return to the pan and stir in the flour. Add the wine and about ¾ of the broth, marjoram, thyme, salt, and pepper. Cover and simmer gently for about 3 hours. Add onions and mushrooms and cook for another hour. Serve over hot noodles. Can be prepared a day or two ahead which improves the flavor and can be frozen.
Serves 8-10.

Mrs. Henry V. Campbell, Jr.

BARBECUED VENISON ROAST

4-lb. venison roast or larger
  venison ham
Barbecue sauce
1 c. chopped celery
2 cloves garlic, chopped
3 T. Worcestershire
½ onion, sliced thin
Freshly grated pepper
2 pieces bacon

Combine your favorite barbecue sauce with celery, garlic, Worcestershire, and onions. Grate pepper over the top of the roast which is on a trivet in a roasting pan or rectangular cake pan. Pour sauce mixture over the roast. Lay 2 pieces of bacon, cut in half, over the roast. Cook on an outdoor smoker with regular charcoal for 3 hours if a 4-lb. roast, about 4 hours if larger. Slice ½″ thick and serve with the pan juices. Serve Jalapeño jelly on the side, a cranberry apple salad, and baked potatoes.
Serves 8-10.

Mrs. Norman Spencer, Jr.

MOUSSAKA

3 eggplants
2 T. oil
¼ c. butter
1 onion, finely chopped
1 clove garlic, chopped
2 lbs. ground lean veal
½ c. red wine
2 tomatoes, peeled, chopped,
  and seeded
⅓ c. chopped parsley
¼ t. cinnamon
¼ t. nutmeg
Salt and pepper to taste
BECHAMEL SAUCE:
¼ c. butter
¼ c. flour
3 c. scalded milk
1 t. salt
3 eggs, beaten
⅛ t. nutmeg
2 T. grated Parmesan

Pare and dice the eggplant; cover with water; and bring to a boil. Cook 5-10 minutes until done and drain. Sauté in oil and set aside. Cook onions in butter until browned. Add garlic and veal and brown. Heat wine and tomatoes together and add to veal mixture. Add parsley, cinnamon, nutmeg, salt, and pepper; and simmer 30 minutes. Begin béchamel sauce by melting butter. Blend in flour and cook until bubbly. Stir the milk in gradually. Add salt and cook, stirring, until thick and smooth. Add 3 T. to the veal mixture. With a whisk, combine remaining sauce with eggs and nutmeg. Put veal into a 2-qt. rectangular casserole and pour over béchamel sauce. Sprinkle with Parmesan and bake at 350° for 45 minutes or until top is golden brown. Serve with a spinach salad with Greek olives and Feta cheese and a spice nut cake.
Serves 8.

Mrs. Norman Spencer, Jr.

VEAL OR CHICKEN CORDON BLEU

4 veal scallopini *or* 4 halves of
  boneless chicken breasts
4 thin slices of baked ham
Swiss cheese
Kitchen Bouquet
Salt and pepper
Flour
Oil for frying
2 T. butter
¼ c. flour
½ c. onion, chopped
1 can chicken bouillon
1 T. Wyler's Instant Chicken
  Bouillon Nuggets
Salt and pepper
½ pt. sour cream
½ c. white wine

Since veal has no pronounced taste just about the same effect is achieved with either scallopini or chicken breasts, and the latter are both cheaper and easier to find. The veal will be paper thin, but the breasts will have to be pounded with a kitchen mallet. Use the packaged baked ham that comes in very thin slices. Lay one slice on each piece of chicken or veal. Trim the ham to fit the other meat. Cut a finger of Swiss cheese about a half an inch from the outer edges of the center of the meat, going across the narrower part. Roll the meat around the cheese, securing the roll in several places with toothpicks, especially the two ends. Rub Kitchen Bouquet all over the outside of the rolls. Sprinkle them with salt and pepper, and roll them in flour, being sure to coat them well. Heat some oil in a small pan, and brown the rolls, one or two at a time, on both sides. As they brown lay them in a flat baking dish. Drain off most of the oil. Put 2 T. butter in the frying pan and blend in flour. Add chicken bouillon, with either chicken or veal, onion, Wyler's Nuggets, and a little salt and pepper. Let this simmer until well mixed. Pour it over the chicken or veal rolls. The rolls should be baked an hour. If the baking dish is covered and refrigerated several hours, or overnight, the rolls should be baked 1½ hours. Cover them lightly with foil. Add water if gravy becomes too thick. For the last 15 minutes of baking add the sour cream and wine which has been blended well with a wire whip. Before serving, taste gravy and adjust salt and pepper. Rice or thin noodles should be served with the Cordon Bleu. Remove toothpicks before serving.
Serves 4.

Mrs. L. G. Pondrom

Shrimp Curry with Condiments

VEAL PICCATA

2 T. flour
½ t. salt
¼ t. pepper
1 lb. veal scallops
½ c. butter
¼ c. dry white wine
1 lemon, sliced thin
¼ c. chopped parsley
SAUCE:
1 T. butter
1 egg yolk
¼ c. dry white wine

Combine flour, salt and pepper and use to coat veal. In hot butter in a medium skillet sauté veal until well browned. Add wine, lemon slices, and parsley and simmer covered 10 minutes. Remove veal to a warm serving platter and discard lemon slices. Make a sauce by slowly heating butter in the same skillet. Beat egg yolk with wine. Slowly add to butter in skillet, stirring constantly. Cook over low heat, stirring constantly, until sauce is thickened and hot. Pour over veal. Garnish with parsley and lemon. Makes 4 servings.

Mrs. Harold W. Kimmerling

VAGLIETTE ALLA PERUGINA
(Little Veal Suitcases)

12 small veal scallops
12 thin slices prosciutto or ham
12 slices Mozzarella cheese (or
   Fontina cheese)
2 T. butter
2 T. olive oil
1-2 T. finely chopped parsley
1 T. lemon juice
½ c. Marsala (dry) wine (more if
   needed or desired)
Flour
Salt and pepper

Place one ham slice and one cheese slice on each veal scallop. Fold them and close them with toothpicks on all open sides. Season with salt and pepper and dip in flour, shaking off excess flour. Brown in butter and olive oil, removing them to a plate as browned. Add wine to remaining juices and replace veal in skillet. Simmer until tender. Add lemon juice and parsley. Continue simmering 1-2 minutes. Serve sauce over veal. Serves 6.

Mrs. James E. Lambert

LOW-CALORIE VEAL PARMESAN

1 8-oz. can tomato sauce
1 t. basil
¼ t. salt
1 bay leaf
4 veal cutlets
1 egg, beaten
¼ c. bread crumbs
¼ c. Parmesan cheese
3 T. olive oil
4 squares Mozzarella cheese

Simmer first four ingredients in a saucepan while preparing the veal. Dip each cutlet in beaten egg, then in bread crumb-Parmesan cheese mixture. Brown on both sides in olive oil. Put into oven pan, pour sauce mixture over veal (removing bay leaf). Top each veal with a square of cheese. Cook 15 minutes at 350°. Excellent with fresh asparagus and tossed green salad. May be frozen. Serves 4.

Mrs. M. Weatherby Carr

ESCALOPES DE VEAU FLAMBEES AUX RAISINS
(Veal Flambéed with Grapes)

4 thin veal cutlets or chops (¼ lb. each)
3 T. butter
⅔ c. dry white wine
1 large bunch seedless grapes
4 t. Cognac
Salt and pepper to taste

Heat butter in a skillet and brown the cutlets on each side. Add the wine and season with salt and pepper. Cover and cook for 30 minutes over low heat. Ten minutes before the end of cooking time add the grapes. Just before serving, add the Cognac and ignite. Serves 4.

Mrs. John P. Boone

VEAL STROGANOFF

3 lb. veal stew meat
2 T. butter
1 T. olive oil
2 T. flour
2 c. sour cream
1 c. chicken broth
1 t. salt
½ t. paprika
3 T. chopped onion
½ lb. sliced mushrooms
2 T. butter

Sauté meat in butter and oil until lightly browned. Add flour and stir until smooth and cook for 1 minute. Add sour cream, broth, salt and paprika. Heat but do not let boil. In a separate pan, sauté onion and mushrooms in butter and add to meat. Pour into a shallow dish that can be used for serving and cover to freeze or bake at 325° for 1 hour. Serve with rice cooked in bouillon. Serves 12.

Mrs. George S. Watson

STATE FAIR OF TEXAS CORN DOGS

6-8 hot dogs
⅔ c. cornmeal
1 c. flour
2 T. sugar
1½ t. baking powder
1 t. salt
2 T. oil
¾ c. milk
1 egg, slightly beaten

Combine all ingredients for batter. Boil hot dogs, put stick in end of each hot dog, dip in batter. Cook in deep fat at 360° until brown.
Serves 6-8.

Mrs. Gary Utkov

APPLE BRANDY PORK CHOPS

6 thick center-cut pork chops, about 8 oz. each
12-15 large fresh basil leaves, finely minced or 2 t. dried basil
3 T. shallots or onion, minced
¼ c. green pepper, very finely minced
¼ c. butter
6 T. (3 oz.) apple brandy
Bread crumbs
Salt and pepper
Flour
2 eggs
Cooking oil

Preheat oven to 350°. Cut a lateral pocket in each pork chop 2" long and 1" deep. Sauté shallots and green peppers in butter until vegetables are merely tender. Add apple brandy and set ablaze. When flames disappear, add ½ cup bread crumbs and basil. Mix well. Add salt and pepper to taste. Stuff pork chops with bread crumb mixture. Dip chops in flour, Beat eggs with 4 teaspoons oil. Dip chops in beaten eggs, coating thoroughly. Dip chops in bread crumbs; pat crumbs on chops to make firm coating. Close pockets shut with several toothpicks (cut ends of picks with scissors). Heat ¼" oil in skillet. Sauté chops until medium-brown on both sides. Place chops in a shallow baking pan — stacking them upright. Bake for 1 hour.
Serves 6.

Mrs. Ernest F. Kennedy, Jr.

BARBECUED PORK CHOPS

4 pork chops
½ stick butter
3 T. catsup
4 T. vinegar
1½ T. Worcestershire
1½ T. prepared mustard
1 T. Tabasco
1 t. brown sugar
¼ t. salt
⅛ t. pepper
Dash of: paprika
          garlic powder
          onion powder

Boil chops in water 45 minutes until done. Combine remaining ingredients in a saucepan to make sauce. Bring sauce slowly to a boil. If too thick, thin with water. Baste chops generously with sauce. Broil until chops are brown.
Serves 4.

Mrs. Robert S. Addison

CHINESE BARBECUED PORK STEAKS

6 pork steaks or chops, cut ¾ to 1" thick
¼ c. bottled lemon juice
¼ c. mustard
¼ c. soy sauce
¼ c. honey
2 t. Worcestershire sauce
½ t. ginger

Marinate pork overnight in the refrigerator in a mixture of the remaining ingredients, turning occasionally. To grill, place meat on grill about 5" from glowing coals. Cook about 30 or 45 minutes, or until done, turning occasionally and basting with additional sauce.
Serves 6.

Mrs. Charles W. Pace

CRISPY PORK CHOPS

Seasoned bread crumbs:
6 pieces dry bread
1 T. parsley flakes
½ clove garlic
½ t. dried oregano
¼ t. dried sweet basil
½ t. Lawry's seasoning salt
Salt, to taste
Pepper, to taste
⅛ t. cayenne pepper
½ t. Tony's Creole Seasoning (optional)
12 small pork chops
¾ c. butter, melted
¼ t. garlic salt

Make seasoned bread crumbs in blender by adding bread, a few pieces at a time, and parsley, garlic, oregano, sweet basil, seasoning salt, salt and pepper, cayenne pepper, and Tony's Creole Seasoning. Blend well. Set aside. Melt butter and add garlic salt. Remove from heat. Coat pork chops in melted butter then dredge in bread crumb mixture. Arrange pork chops in foil-lined pan large enough for all, not touching. Pour any left-over butter over chops. Bake at 350 degrees for 1 hour (uncovered) or until chops are crisp and brown.
Serves 6.
Note: Chicken can be substituted for pork chops.

Mrs. Edward H. Cary III

BARBECUED RIBS

4 lbs. pork ribs (have the butcher cut them in serving pieces)
2 lemons, sliced
2 medium onions, chopped
1 c. ketchup
3 T. Worcestershire
1 t. chili powder
1 t. salt
Dash of Tabasco
1 c. water

Heat oven to 425°. Place ribs, meaty side up in roaster or baking dish. Place slice of lemon on each piece and roast 30 minutes. Combine remaining ingredients and pour over ribs. Reduce heat to 350° and bake 2 more hours, basting 2 or 3 times. (This sauce is also delicious on hamburgers.)
Serves 4.

Mrs. George Searcy Watson

ROAST PÓRK TENDERLOIN

Pork tenderloin
Sauerkraut with caraway seeds
Sour cream or light cream
Paprika

Place the pork tenderloin uncovered in a 350° oven. When about ⅔ done, score it, heap the kraut on top, and dust it liberally with paprika. Pour on the sour cream and continue cooking until the pork is done. Commercial sour cream sometimes will curdle so light cream may be substituted.
Serves 3.

Mrs. Henry V. Campbell, Jr.

HAM AND CHEESE CREAM CREPES

8 crêpes
FILLING:
⅓ c. cream cheese, softened
6 T. sour cream
⅔ c. heavy cream
¼ c. grated aged Swiss cheese
Salt, white pepper, and nutmeg
8 very thin slices cooked
   boneless ham

Lay crêpes out flat. Mix remaining ingredients except ham together. Spread a small amount of cream mixture on each crêpe; lay ham on top, and more cream mixture on ham. Roll loosely and place in a buttered dish. Spoon remaining cream over crêpes and bake at 400° for 5 minutes or until brown.
Serves 4.

Mrs. J. Thomas Hedrick

HAM BAKED IN BEER

Ham
1 can black molasses
4 qts. weak tea
2 qts. water
1 c. catsup
3 T. mustard
1 bottle of beer
Brown sugar

Wash ham and put in boiler, end side up. Soak all night in 1 can black molasses and weak tea. The next day, drain and put in steamer, fat side up, and add water. Bake three or four hours (twenty minutes to the pound). Take out and skin. Cover with paste made from catsup and mustard. Return to oven and let cook half an hour with 1 bottle of beer. Baste, sprinkle brown sugar on top, and bake until sugar melts.

Mrs. Webster Atwell, 1948 Junior League
Cookbook

BARBECUED HAM

Large slice of ham
⅛ c. melted butter (about 2 T.)
1 c. sherry
1 t. powdered cloves
⅛ c. dry mustard (about 2 T.)
2 T. brown sugar
1 t. paprika

Mix all ingredients and marinate ham slice or slices for 2 hours, turning once. Broil for 20 minutes, turning frequently and basting with marinade. Can be done on a charcoal grill. One ham slice serves 2.

Mrs. William Plack Carr, Jr.

APRICOT GLAZED HAM

½ c. apricot preserves
2 T. mustard
1 T. water
2 t. lemon juice
1 t. Worcestershire sauce
⅛ t. cinnamon
1 center slice of ham 1″ thick

Combine first six ingredients and heat until preserves melt. Pour over ham in a shallow dish, refrigerate 12 hours, turning several times. Grill ham over charcoal fire five minutes on each side, brush with marinade, grill five more minutes on each side. Serve sauce with ham. Serves 4-5.

Mrs. Frederick W. Burnett, Jr.

CASSEROLES

ARTICHOKE AND CRAB CASSEROLE FROM EVERHOPE PLANTATION, MISSISSIPPI

3 T. butter
3 T. flour
1 t. salt
1½ c. milk
1 t. Worcestershire sauce
⅓ c. fresh Parmesan cheese, grated
⅛ t. coarse black pepper
Tabasco to taste, needs a lot
Prepared mustard to taste, needs a lot
4 hard-boiled eggs, shelled and sieved
1 lb. can artichoke hearts, drained
2 c. fresh crab meat, cooked
¼ c. Parmesan cheese, grated

Make a roux with the butter, flour, and salt; and add the milk 1 tablespoon at a time. Cook until thick. Add Worcestershire sauce, ⅓ c. Parmesan cheese, pepper, Tabasco, mustard, eggs, artichoke hearts, and crab meat. Mix well. Check for seasoning. Pour into a greased baking dish. Sprinkle with ¼ c. Parmesan cheese. Bake at 350 degrees for 30-45 minutes or until brown on top. Makes an excellent first course when prepared in small individual servings. Serves 4.

Geneva Ashby Jones

CRABMEAT AND BROCCOLI CASEROLE

1 pkg. frozen broccoli, cooked
 and drained
½ lb. fresh or one 6½-oz. can
 crabmeat
1 c. sour cream
½ c. bottled chili sauce
1 small onion, finely chopped
1 c. sharp Cheddar cheese,
 grated
2 T. lemon juice
1 T. lemon peel, grated
Salt and pepper

Put broccoli in the bottom of a 1½-qt. or 9″ square casserole. Reserve enough cheese to sprinkle on top of casserole. Mix ingredients and pour over broccoli. Sprinkle with grated cheese. Bake at 350° until lightly browned on top.
Serves 6.

Mrs. Pat Guillot

SPINACH-SHRIMP PARMESAN

1 pkg. chopped spinach,
 cooked and drained
¾ lb. cooked shrimp
3 T. butter
3 T. flour
1 c. light cream
½ c. Parmesan cheese
¼ c. sherry

Place spinach in the bottom of a 1-qt. baking dish or individual shells; and put shrimp on top. Make a cream sauce by melting butter, adding in flour, and stirring in cream. Cook over medium heat until thick; add cheese and sherry. Pour over shrimp, and place under broiler 5-6 minutes until brown and bubbling.
Serves 6 in individual ramekins and 4 in a casserole.

Mrs. Frederick W. Burnett, Jr.

CHICKEN SPAGHETTI

1 4-lb. chicken
1 lb. spaghetti
1 c. onion, chopped
1 c. celery, chopped
1 c. green pepper, chopped
1 garlic button, pressed
4 T. butter
1 can tomato soup
2 8-oz. cans tomato sauce
1 t. sugar
1 t. chili powder
Salt and pepper to taste
Dash of Tabasco
¾ lb. Cheddar cheese, grated

Cook chicken in salted water until tender; bone and cut into small pieces. Cook spaghetti according to package directions in the same water used for boiling chicken. Sauté onions, celery, green pepper, and garlic in butter in a large saucepan. Add other ingredients and mix well. Add cooked chicken and spaghetti to mixture. Pour into 2 2-qt. casseroles. Top with grated cheese. Bake uncovered in a 350° oven for about 30 minutes. Can be prepared the day before serving.
Makes 12 servings.

Mrs. William Livingstone III

ACAPULCO ENCHILADAS

2 c. chicken, diced
½ c. ripe olives, chopped
1 c. almonds, slivered
6 T. flour
3 c. water
6 T. catsup
2 heaping T. chili powder
Salt and pepper
12 corn tortillas
Salad oil for frying tortillas
1½ c. shredded sharp Cheddar
  cheese
2 c. sour cream
4 T. green onions, minced

Make the filling by combining chicken, olives, almonds, and ⅓ c. of sauce made up of flour, water, catsup, chili powder, salt, and pepper. Fry tortillas in hot oil for a few seconds to soften. Drain and dip into sauce. Spoon some chicken mixture into center of tortilla and roll, placing flap side down in a shallow, ungreased baking dish. Top with remaining sauce and sprinkle with cheese. Bake uncovered in a 350° oven for 15-20 minutes, or until heated through. Mix sour cream with onions and serve cold as a sauce. Makes 12 enchiladas.
4-6 servings.

Mrs. John Bagwell

CLAIRE'S CHICKEN TETRAZINNI

5 c. cooked chicken, chopped
  (reserve stock)
1 lb. thin spaghetti
1 stick butter
1 green pepper, chopped
1 large onion, chopped
1 garlic clove, crushed
5 T. flour
2 c. milk, room temperature
2 cans golden mushroom
  soup
2 small jars pimiento, minced
1 T. Worcestershire
½ c. sherry
1 4-oz. can mushrooms (sliced)
1 c. chopped celery
6 c. mild Cheddar cheese,
  grated
1 c. Parmesan cheese, freshly
  grated
Salt and pepper to taste
1 c. almonds, shaved

Cook spaghetti in chicken stock. Rinse and pour a little of the stock over the spaghetti. Melt butter and sauté pepper, onion, and garlic. Slowly add flour and milk. Stir until thickened. Add mushroom soup. Let simmer. Add pimiento and a little garlic salt, then the Worcestershire, sherry, mushrooms, and chicken. Add 5 cups Cheddar cheese, then the Parmesan. Cook over low heat until well blended. Salt and pepper, then put in ½ cup almonds. Simmer 5 minutes. Layer spaghetti, sauce; spaghetti, sauce. The top with 1 cup cheese and almonds. Bake at 350° for 15 minutes or until bubbles appear.
Serves 18. Freezes well.

Mrs. B. Thomas McElroy

PAELLA

¼ c. olive oil
1 clove garlic
1 onion, chopped fine
2-2½-lb. frying chickens, skinned, boned, and cut in pieces
½ lb. pork, trimmed and cubed
1 lb. German smoked sausage (1 inch diameter) cut in thin slices
2 c. white rice, uncooked
1 lb. ripe tomatoes, peeled and chopped
6 c. chicken broth
2 t. salt
1 t. white pepper
1 t. saffron
1½ lb. fresh raw shrimp, peeled all but the tail
1 doz. clams, mussels, or oysters
6-8 large shrimp, about 5"-6" long, one per person — leave in the shell
4 T. pimiento, sliced
½ c. parsley, chopped

In a heavy, deep skillet or pan heat the oil. Add the onion and garlic; cook until onion is clear. Remove from oil. Cook the chicken and pork until lightly browned. Remove from the pan. Add the rice and the sausage; cook over medium heat until lightly browned. Add the tomatoes, the seasonings, the onion, the broth, the chicken, and the pork. Cook covered about 25 minutes. Add the seafood; cook 6-10 minutes uncovered until shrimp turns pink. Stir occasionally. Add the pimiento. Taste for seasonings. Serve immediately.

Serves 6-8.

Serving suggestions: Place the Paella on a large platter, reserving the large shrimp and the mussels to decorate the top of the paella. Put the parsley around the sides. Serve with spinach salad with or without mandarin oranges and French bread.

Miss Patricia M. Barr

CHICKEN AND MUSHROOM CASSEROLE FOR A CROWD

36 pieces chicken (breasts, thighs, drumsticks)
Salt
Pepper
Paprika
¾ c. butter or margarine
¾ lb. fresh mushrooms, sliced
4 T. flour
1½ c. chicken broth
6 T. sherry
3 sprigs fresh rosemary *or* ½ t. dried rosemary, crumbled

Sprinkle chicken pieces with salt, pepper, and paprika. Brown the chicken in half of the butter and remove to a casserole or shallow baking pan. Add remaining butter to drippings and sauté mushrooms until tender. Sprinkle flour over mushrooms and stir in chicken broth, sherry, and rosemary. Cook until thickened then pour over chicken. Cover and bake in a moderate over (350°) for 45 minutes.

Serves 18.

Note: May be prepared a day in advance and refrigerated.

Mrs. Robert Norris, Jr.

CHICKEN TETRAZZINI

5 lbs. chicken pieces
8-10 green onions (tops too),
  chopped
10-12 medium fresh
  mushrooms, sliced
4 stalks celery, sliced
  diagonally
1 stick butter
½ c. flour
2 c. milk (or 1 pt. light cream)
4 oz. spaghetti
4 oz. American cheese, grated
4 oz. Old English cheese, grated
1 can cream of mushroom soup,
  undiluted
1 2¼-oz. can sliced ripe olives
1 4-oz. jar sliced pimientos
1 small pkg. sliced blanched
  almonds
Buttered bread or cracker
  crumbs
Fresh or dry parsley flakes for
  garnish

Boil chicken until tender (with a quartered onion and a piece of celery and whatever other seasonings you like to use for chicken broth). When cooked, bone, and cut into bite-size pieces. Reserve chicken broth to cook spaghetti in. In a large saucepan or dutch oven sauté briefly the green onions, mushrooms and celery in butter. Add flour and cook for a few minutes. Add the milk or cream and stir constantly with a wire whisk until the cream sauce thickens. Stir in the grated cheeses and soup. Blend until smooth and well-mixed. Add the olives, pimientos, almonds, and chicken pieces and mix well. To this add the spaghetti which has been cooked in the chicken broth (slightly undercook according to pkg. directions, then drain). Mix everything well and put into a buttered 3-qt. casserole dish. Top with buttered crumbs. Bake uncovered at 375° for about 30 minutes. Can be prepared ahead and refrigerated or frozen.
Serves 12.

Mrs. James I. Riddle III

SHRIMP-BROCCOLI CASSEROLE

1½ lbs. shrimp, cooked and
  cleaned
4 boxes frozen broccoli,
  chopped
1 stick butter
6 3-oz. pkgs. cream cheese with
  chives
2 cans cream of shrimp soup

Cook broccoli 5 minutes; drain well. Let butter and cream cheese come to room temperature; blend and add soup. (A blender can be used for this.) Place broccoli and shrimp in layers in a buttered 3-qt. casserole and top with sauce. Bake at 350° for 30 minutes, until hot and bubbly.
Serves 8-10.

Mrs. George W. Jalonick III

ENCHILADAS VERDES DE MERCEDES

3 chicken breasts, cooked and shredded
24 tortillas, fresh not frozen
7 green tomatoes
1 clove garlic, crushed
3 jalapeños, seeded
2 c. sour cream
⅓ c. light cream
1½ c. Monterey Jack cheese, grated
1 large onion, sliced and separated into rings
3 cubes chicken bouillon

Dip each tortilla in hot oil, keeping it smooth and stack them. Fill and roll each tortilla with approximately 1 T. shredded chicken. Cover and refrigerate. Peel green tomatoes, mix them with garlic, and fry in a little oil. Put this mixture in a blender with the bouillon cubes and jalapeños and blend a few seconds to make the sauce. When ready to serve, top the enchiladas with the sauce, then onion rings (halved), next cheese, and last a mixture of the two creams. Heat in a preheated 400° oven for 10 minutes or until bubbly hot.
Serves 6.

Mrs. Horace R. Nash, Jr.

DOVE AND ARTICHOKE HEARTS CASSEROLE

1 20-oz. can artichoke hearts, drained
10-12 doves
4 T. butter
½ lb. fresh or canned mushrooms, drained
3-4 c. cream sauce
1 T. Worcestershire
1-2 drops Tabasco sauce
¼ c. dry sherry
½ c. Parmesan cheese, grated
Salt and Pepper
Paprika

Dust the doves with flour and sauté in melted butter until brown. Remove from pan and add mushrooms, sautéing for 5 minutes. In a deep baking dish, which has been buttered, arrange artichoke hearts on bottom. Next add the doves and sprinkle the birds with mushrooms. Mix Worcestershire, Tabasco, sherry, salt, and pepper with cream sauce and pour into baking dish. (Birds need to be covered in sauce.) Sprinkle top with Parmesan cheese and paprika. Bake 45 minutes to 1 hour at 350°. Serve over plain or wild rice.
Serves 4.

Mrs. Rhodes R. Bobbitt

CASSOULET

4 lbs. pork loin
4 lbs. leg of lamb or lamb
  shoulder
2 wild ducks or 1 domestic one
2 lbs. Polish sausage
2 lbs. dry white beans (Great
  Northern)
½ lb. salt pork
1 c. sliced onion
Bouquet garni (1 cut garlic
  clove, 8 parsley sprigs, 2
  cloves, ½ t. thyme, and 2 bay
  leaves tied in cheesecloth)
6 t. tomato paste
½ t. thyme
2 c. dry white wine
Salt and pepper to taste
1 c. bread crumbs
½ c. parsley, chopped

Cook pork loin and lamb separately until done. Save cooking juices and cube pork and lamb. Cook duck and cube, saving cooking juices. Rinse beans and put into a large kettle. Add two quarts of water or enough water to cover beans; cover and bring to a rolling boil. Remove pot from stove and let stand one hour. When beans are plump, add one quart chicken broth, Polish sausage, whole salt pork, onions, and bouquet garni. Bring to a boil, spooning off scum. Reduce heat and simmer 30 minutes uncovered. Remove Polish sausage and continue cooking beans 30 minutes or more until barely tender. Remove bouquet garni and discard. Remove salt pork and save. Drain beans and reserve liquid. Add pork, lamb, and duck cooking liquids to bean liquid. To this add tomato paste, thyme, and white wine and bring to a boil. Simmer for 15 minutes. Add salt and pepper to taste. Slice Polish sausage ⅛″ thick and cube the salt pork into small pieces. To assemble, use an 8-quart fireproof casserole five or six inches high. First, put a layer of beans, then meats (lamb, pork, duck, sausage, salt pork), layer of beans, layer of meat, and end with beans. Pour the cooking juices over until they come to the top layer of beans. Spread on bread crumbs mixed with parsley. May be prepared to this point ahead of time. (Save extra liquids to add if it dries out during cooking.) When ready to cook, bring to a simmer on top of the stove. Place in the upper third of a preheated oven at 375° for 20 minutes. Add reserved liquid if too dry. Turn oven down to 350° and cook for another hour.

Mrs. Denys Slater, Jr.

CHALUPAS

2 lbs. pinto beans
2 lbs. pork roast, Boston butt
1 jalapeño pepper
1½ T. chili powder
1 t. comino seeds
1 large garlic clove
½ t. oregano
½ t. red pepper
Salt to taste, Hot Sauce
Fritos, Guacamole
2 lbs. cheese, grated
3 onions, chopped
6 tomatoes, chopped
1 head lettuce, shredded

Put beans, pork roast, jalapeño pepper, chili powder, comino seeds, garlic, oregano, red pepper, and salt in a large pot and cover with water. Cook about 6 hours or until the consistency of chili. In large casserole layer fritos, beans, cheese, onions, lettuce, tomato, and guacamole on top. Pass hot sauce.
Serves 12.

Mrs. Wade C. Smith

DELUXE MEAT CASSEROLE

2 lbs. ground round
1 6-oz. can tomato paste
1 6-oz. can tomato sauce
2 t. oregano
2 t. basil
2 t. salt
2 T. olive oil
2 8-oz. cartons small curd
cottage cheese
1 lb. Mozzarella cheese, grated
1 c. Parmesan cheese, freshly
grated
1 pkg. dry onion soup mix
1½ c. water
½ lb. THIN noodles

Brown meat in oil; drain most of oil off. Stir in everything except cheeses and noodles. Cover and simmer over medium heat 30 minutes. Boil noodles in salted water and drain. Lay in following order in 9″ × 12″ pyrex dish: Noodles, mozzarella cheese, meat, cottage cheese, meat, Parmesan cheese, noodles, cottage cheese, meat, Parmesan cheese, meat, remaining cheese on top. This can be frozen easily. Bake at 350° for 30 minutes.
Serves 12.

Cookbook Committee

OYSTERS ROCKEFELLER CASSEROLE

1 lb. fresh spinach, half cooked,
chopped and well drained
2 bunches green onions,
minced (green tops included)
½ c. parsley, minced
½ c. celery, minced
1 clove garlic, minced
½ oz. Pernod
¾ t. Tabasco
1 t. Worcestershire
1 T. anchovy paste
1 c. bread crumbs
Salt and pepper to taste
1½ pt. oysters
¾ stick butter, melted
¼ c. Parmesan cheese
Butter

Mix the first 9 ingredients well. Add ¾ cup of bread crumbs and salt and pepper to taste, stirring well. Mix in well drained oysters and melted butter. Place mixture in a well-greased 1½-qt. casserole or individual ramekins. Top with ¼ cup crumbs and Parmesan cheese, mixed together. Dot with butter and bake at 350° for 45 minutes.
Serves 4.

Mrs. H. W. Kimmerling

PECAN CUPLETS

PASTRY:
2 c. flour
1 t. salt
¾ c. shortening
5 T. cold water
PECAN FILLING:
1 c. sugar
1 c. light corn syrup
3 eggs
1 t. vanilla
3 T. butter, melted
1 c. pecans, chopped

Cut together shortening, flour and salt. Sprinkle water over mixture. Mix with fork. Form into ball. Roll pastry out, cut with 6-oz. juice can. Place circles in small muffin tins. Fill each with 1 t. pecan filling. Bake 10 minutes at 400°, reduce heat to 350°, bake an additional 15 minutes.

Filling: combine ingredients except pecans and beat lightly. Add pecans last. Makes about 4 dozen.

Mrs. David Grafe

SHERRY WINE CHIFFON PIE

1 c. milk
½ c. sugar
3 eggs, separated
1 c. sherry wine
½ t. nutmeg
½ t. salt
1 c. heavy cream, whipped
1 T. gelatin, soaked in 4 T. cold milk

Combine milk and sugar; heat to boiling point. Put in top of double boiler, add well-beaten yolks, nutmeg and salt. Stir constantly; add wine slowly and soaked gelatin. Cook until it coats the spoon. Cool slightly; fold in stiffly beaten whites. Cool until firm; blend with whipped cream. Place mixture in cooked pastry shell, cover with sweetened whipped cream. Chill before serving.

Mrs. K. N. Hapgood

FRESH STRAWBERRY PIE

2 pints fresh strawberries washed and stemmed)
1 c. sugar
3 T. corn starch
1 8-oz. pkg. cream cheese, softened with 1 T. cream
1 half pint whipping cream
1 9 or 10″ rich pie crust, cooked

Mash 1½ pints berries (reserve ¼ pint to top pie) in sauce pan; add sugar and corn starch. Cook over low heat, stirring constantly, for 10 minutes or until thickened. Cool. Spread cream cheese over bottom of pie shell, top with cooled strawberry mixture. Whip cream, cover pie, and top with whole strawberries. Pie may be prepared the day before serving, but must be covered well with saran wrap. It may be prepared without whipping cream the day before, then whip cream and top 2 hours before serving.

Serves 8 or 9.

Mrs. Ralph D. Gibson, Jr.

HAM AND ARTICHOKE CASSEROLE

4 T. butter
4 T. flour
2 c. milk
Generous dash seasoned salt
  and cayenne pepper
¼ t. nutmeg
Paprika, Pepper to taste
⅔ c. Swiss cheese, grated
4 T. sherry
2 14-oz. cans artichoke hearts,
  drained
12 thin slices ham
⅔ c. buttered bread crumbs
½ cup grated Parmesan

Melt butter, stir in flour, then milk, and heat to boiling, stirring constantly until thickened. Add cheese and seasonings and stir until melted. Stir in sherry. If artichoke hearts are large, cut in half and wrap two halves in a slice of ham. Arrange in a buttered casserole with sides touching. Pour sauce over all and sprinkle with bread crumbs and Parmesan combined. Bake at 350° for 25-30 minutes.
Serves 6.

Mrs. Virgil Pate

MANICOTTI

SAUCE:
2 lbs. ground meat
1½ c. onion, chopped
1 clove garlic, chopped
2 - 1 lb. cans Italian tomatoes,
  undrained
6 oz. tomato paste
2 T. parsley, chopped
1 T. salt
1 T. sugar
1 t. dried oregano leaves
1 t. dried basil leaves
½ t. pepper
1-1½ c. water
SHELLS:
6 eggs, at room temperature
1½ c. flour
¼ t. salt
1½ c. water
FILLING:
3 lbs. ricotta cheese (or cottage
  cheese)
1 lb. mozzarella cheese, grated
⅔ c. Parmesan cheese, grated
3 eggs
1½ t. salt
¼ t. pepper
1½ T. parsley, chopped
½ c. Parmesan cheese, grated

Sauce: Brown meat in large skillet and drain off most of the fat. Add onions and garlic; cook until onions are clear. Add rest of the sauce ingredients. Simmer 1 hour covered.

Shells: Combine a l ingredients and beat until smooth. Let stand 30 minutes. Heat a 6″ skillet, brush with oil, pour in 2 T. of batter, and rotate skillet quickly to spread batter evenly over bottom. Cook over medium heat until bottom is dry but not brown. Turn out on wax paper to cool. Makes 24 shells.

Filling: Combine all ingredients *except* ½ c. Parmesan cheese and mix with wooden spoon. Spread 2-3 T. filling in each shell and roll as you would a crêpe. Place 8 rolled manicotti seam side down in a 12″ × 8″ pyrex dish in a single layer. Cover with sauce and sprinkle with reserve Parmesan cheese. Bake at 350 degrees for 30 minutes. Makes 24 manicotti.
Serves 12.

Mrs. Virgil Pate

QUICK LASAGNE

1 lb. ground beef
2 T. olive oil
2 6-oz. cans tomato paste
3 6-oz. cans water
1 T. oregano
1 pkg. Italian Sauce mix
1 pkg. lasagna noodles
1 pt. cottage cheese
12 oz. mozzarella cheese
Parmesan cheese

Brown meat in olive oil. Combine paste, water, oregano, and Italian mix. Simmer for 30 minutes. Add meat to mixture and heat 15 minutes. Cook noodles in boiling, salted water according to package directions. Add noodles one at a time to the water. Cook until tender, drain. Put in 2-qt. rectangular baking dish in the following order: sauce with meat, noodles, cottage cheese, mozzarella cheese. Repeat in that order. Sprinkle with Parmesan cheese. Bake at 325° for 30 minutes. Serves 6-8.

Mrs. John R. Lee

LASAGNE CASSEROLE

MEAT SAUCE:
1 lb. Italian sausage or ground
    meat
1 clove garlic, minced
1 T. basil
1 1-lb. can tomatoes
2 6-oz. cans tomato paste
10 oz. lasagne noodles
CHEESE FILLING:
3 c. ricotta or creamy cottage
    cheese
½ c. Parmesan or Romano
    cheese, grated
2 T. parsley flakes
2 beaten eggs
2 t. salt
½ t. pepper
1 lb. mozzarella, sliced thin

For meat sauce brown meat slowly; spoon off fat. Add remaining ingredients except lasagne; simmer, uncovered, 30 minutes, stirring occasionally. Cook lasagne until tender in large amount of boiling, salted water 15 to 20 minutes. Drain and rinse in cold water. For the cheese filling mix first six ingredients. Place one-half of noodles in a 13″ × 9″ baking dish; spread with one-half of cheese filling. Cover with one-half of the mozzarella and one-half of the meat sauce. Repeat the layers. Bake at 375° for 30 minutes. Before cutting into squares, let stand 5 minutes so filling will slightly set. May be made the day before and heated. Also may be frozen.
Yields 10 servings.

Mrs. Paul Varner Tate

LASAGNE VERDE

BOLOGNESE MEAT SAUCE
6 T. butter
2½ T. olive oil
1 garlic bud mashed
1 onion, finely chopped
1 carrot, finely chopped
1 stalk celery, finely chopped
⅔ c. bacon, finely chopped
1 lb. ground beef
1 lb. ground sausage
⅔ c. dry white wine
4 t. tomato paste
1¼ c. stock
4 T. light cream or milk
Salt and pepper
1 lb. fresh mushrooms
2½ T. oregano and 2½ T. sweet basil

BECHAMEL SAUCE
6 T. butter
6 T. flour
1 t. salt
5 cups milk
1 box green lasagne noodles
3 T. butter
1 c. fresh Parmesan cheese, grated
1 c. mozzarella cheese

Heat half the butter and all the olive oil in a deep heavy skillet. Add onion, carrot, celery, garlic, and bacon and sauté until softened. Add the beef and sausage and sauté until brown and crumbly. Drain thoroughly. Moisten with wine and cook until it evaporates. Season to taste with salt and pepper and spices. Dilute the tomato paste with a little stock, stir into sauce, cover and cook slowly, stirring from time to time, gradually adding the rest of the stock. After the sauce has cooked for about 1½ hours, stir in the cream and mushrooms and continue to cook until reduced. Finally add the remaining butter, stirring until melted and thoroughly blended.

Melt butter in a heavy pan, stir in flour and salt to make a roux. Cook gently without letting it brown, then gradually add the hot milk, stirring constantly until sauce is thick and smooth and the raw taste of the flour is gone. Pour sauce into a bowl and beat it lightly. Additional flavorings may be added at this time — grated Parmesan cheese, egg, tomato paste, oysters, shrimp, parsley or capers.

Cook noodles according to package directions. Grease a lasagne casserole with 1 T. butter. Cover the bottom with a layer of noodles spread thinly with Béchamel Sauce and Bolognese Meat Sauce, and sprinkle with about 1 T. Parmesan and mozzarella. Continue layering. The top layer should be lasagne sprinkled with the remaining Parmesan and dotted with the remaining butter. Bake at 375° for 1 hour or until the top is golden brown.
Serves 6-8.

Mrs. Searcy Ferguson, Jr.

MEXICAN CASSEROLE

1½ lb. ground beef
1 c. onion, chopped
1 clove garlic, minced
3 cans condensed minestrone
  soup
1 31-oz. can pork and beans in
  tomato sauce
1½ c. celery, chopped
1 T. Worcestershire sauce
½ t. dried oregano

In large saucepan cook beef, onion, and garlic until beef is brown and onion is tender. Stir in all other ingredients. Simmer covered for 20 minutes.
Serves 8.
Note: Freezes well.

Mrs. John D. Carr

FRIJOLES REFRITOS A LA MEXICANA
(Refried Beans, Mexican Style)

1 lb. pink or red beans
¾ qts. water
¾ qts. beer
Salt to taste
½ c. bacon drippings or lard

Soak beans overnight in beer and water. The next day add more water to cover and salt. Cook slowly until very tender. Mash with a potato masher, add ¼ cup bacon drippings (very hot), and continue cooking for 10 minutes. Add remaining fat to a frying pan and add beans. Fry beans, stirring until beans are piping hot. Optional: You may add cubed Monterey Jack cheese, let cheese melt, and then serve immediately. This is good as an appetizer, on tacos, tostados, or chalupas.
Serves 6-8.

JALAPENO PIE

2 cans mild jalapeños
6 eggs, beaten
1 lb. Cheddar cheese, grated
⅓ lb. Swiss cheese, grated
Muenster cheese, sliced

Wash and seed jalapeños. Put in the bottom of a greased 9″ pyrex pie plate. Combine eggs and cheeses and pour over jalapeños. Top with slices of Muenster cheese. Bake at 350 degrees for 45-50 minutes. Serve with a green salad.
Serves 6.

Mrs. Don McIlyar

POLISH SAUSAGE AND LENTILS

1 c. rinsed lentils
2 T. vegetable oil
2 medium onions, chopped
3 garlic cloves, crushed
1 medium carrot, chopped
2-3 tomatoes, chopped
2 lbs. sausage (venison or
   Kielbasa)
1 t. sugar
½ t. pepper
1 bay leaf
Salt to taste

Put lentils in a large saucepan with salted water to cover. Bring to a boil, lower heat, and simmer 20 minutes. Drain and reserve liquid. Heat oil in an ovenproof casserole. Stir in onions and garlic and cook until onions are tender. Mix in carrot and tomatoes and cook until liquid is almost gone. Peel casing from sausage and cut meat into ½" pieces. Toss sausage into lentil and tomato mixture and add sugar, pepper, bay leaf, and salt to taste. Stir and bake in a 350° oven for 30 minutes. Add lentil liquid if it gets too dry.
Serves 4 generously.

Cookbook Committee

SAUSAGE CASSEROLE

1 lb. pork sausage
½ onion, chopped
½ green pepper, chopped
½ c. uncooked rice
2¼ c. boiling water
1 pkg. dried chicken noodle
   soup

Brown meat and pour off excess fat. Put meat in 1½ quart casserole. Add onion, green pepper, and rice. Completely dissolve soup in boiling water and add to meat mixture. Bake uncovered at 375° for 45 minutes. Stir twice while baking.
Serves 4.

Mrs. Robert P. Lancaster

TACOS

1½ c. shortening
12 tortillas
½ t. cumin seed
2 cloves garlic
1 lb. ground meat
2 T. chili powder
Salt and pepper
1 large head lettuce, shredded
2 medium tomatoes, peeled and
   diced

Heat shortening in a large skillet until very hot. Drop tortillas in, a few at a time, and fry for 1-2 minutes until they begin to get crisp. Fold each over in half and continue to cook until crisp and browned. Drain well on paper towels. Mash cumin seeds and peeled garlic together with a fork. Mix with meat and chili powder. Add salt and pepper to taste. Sauté until brown. Fill tortillas with meat, lettuce, and tomatoes.
Serves 4-6.

Mrs. Frank Austin, Jr.

FRENCH SPAGHETTI

1 c. olive oil
4 large onions, chopped
4 large green peppers, chopped
1 lb. ground beef
2½ c. tomatoes, drained
1 4-oz. can mushrooms,
  drained
Salt and pepper to taste
Cayenne to taste
1 lb. New York cheese, grated
1 12-oz. pkg. long spaghetti

Pour oil in a heavy skillet and add onions. Cook until soft but do not brown. Add bell peppers and cook until they lose their green color. Pinch meat off and drop into mixture. Cook until done. Add tomatoes, mushrooms, salt and cayenne pepper to taste. Turn to low and simmer covered while cooking spaghetti according to package directions. After draining spaghetti, fold into mixture and heat to boiling. Add cheese 15 minutes before serving.
Serves 6-8.

Mrs. Raymond A. Williams, Jr.

TAMALE PIE

¼ lb. pork sausage (hot)
1 lb. ground beef
1 c. onion, finely diced
½ c. green pepper, finely diced
½ c. celery, chopped
2½ c. sieved (blended) tomatoes
1¼ c. whole kernel corn,
  drained
2 t. chili powder
1 t. salt
¼ t. MSG
¼ t. black pepper
1 c. cold water
½ c. yellow corn meal
1 c. ripe olives, sliced
1 c. sharp Cheddar cheese,
  grated

Place sausage into a large, cold skillet and break meat into small pieces. Add 1½ T. cold water, cover, and cook slowly about 8 minutes. Remove cover, pour off excess fat, and mix in beef. Brown, stirring occasionally, and pouring off fat as it collects. When meat begins to brown, add onion, celery, and green pepper; continue to cook slowly until vegetables are soft. Mix in tomatoes, corn, chili powder, salt, MSG, and pepper. Cover and simmer slowly for 15 minutes. Mix together water and corn meal and gradually blend into meat mixture. Continue to cook slowly until thickened. Mix in sliced olives and turn into a greased 2-quart baking dish. Bake 1 hour at 350°. Remove from oven; sprinkle with grated cheese and return to oven until cheese melts. Garnish with whole ripe olives and parsley.
Serves 8.

Mrs. John Bagwell

SPAGHETTI ALLA MATRICIANA

1 large onion, chopped
1 carrot, grated
½ of a lb. pkg. bacon, chopped
1 qt. tomatoes, mashed
½ of a 6-oz. can tomato paste
½ c. Pecorino cheese, grated
Spaghetti (12 oz.)

Sauté onion and carrot with bacon until bacon is cooked. Add tomatoes and tomato paste and cook quickly while spaghetti is cooking according to package directions. Toss drained spaghetti with sauce and Parmesan cheese and serve immediately.
Serves 4-6.

Mrs. James Lambert

POLISH SAUSAGE DISH

2 lbs. sauerkraut, drained
½ c. carrots, diced
2 apples, peeled and diced
1 c. bacon, diced
½ c. onion, chopped
1 c. raw potato, grated
1½ c. soup stock plus ½ c.
   sauterne *or* 2 c. soup stock
2 lbs. Polish sausage

Place all vegetables and bacon in a 3 quart casserole in layers. Combine soup stock and wine and pour over vegetables. Cut Polish sausage into 4 to 6 pieces and put on top of vegetables. Bake in covered casserole at 350° for 2 hours. If after 2 hours there is too much liquid, remove cover and cook an additional 15 minutes.
Serves 6 generously.

Mrs. Walter F. Sosnowski

VEGETABLES

VEGETABLE STEAMING GUIDE
A vegetable steamer is a pan with a rack and a tight fitting cover. Place enough water in steamer to form sufficient steam, but do not let water touch rack. Place vegetables on the rack after the water has begun to boil. Since the vegetables are cooked entirely by steam, the required cooking times are somewhat longer. The following cooking times allows for variances in individual tastes from crisp to tender. When vegetables are done, season as desired or use one of the suggested tossables.

FRESH VEGETABLES	APPROXIMATE COOKING TIME IN MINUTES	SUGGESTED TOSSABLES
Artichokes	40-50	Toss in buttermilk dressing

Asparagus	10-20	Pour melted lime butter and grated lime rind over asparagus
Beets		
Young, whole	30-45	Toss in fresh orange
Old, whole	45-90	juice, orange and
Sliced or diced	15-25	lemon rind
Broccoli	10-20	Sliced toasted almonds and butter
Brussels Sprouts	10-20	Fresh dill mayonnaise
Cabbage		
Shredded	3-10	Toss in olive oil
Quartered	10-15	and caraway seeds Cointreau
Carrots		
Young, whole	15-25	brown sugar and butter
Old, whole	20-30	
Sliced	10-20	
Cauliflower		
Whole	10-12	Toasted sesame seeds and
Flowerets	9-10	butter or Spice Islands Salad Seasoning
Corn-on-cob	6-12	Steam with slices of bacon
Eggplant	10-12	Ro-tel tomatoes and green chiles
Okra	10-20	Butter and lemon peel, coarse ground pepper or hot pepper vinegar and butter
Onions	15-30	Toss in sour cream and chives
Pea, English	10-20	Fresh mint and butter
Potatoes, sweet or Irish	30-40	Shredded baby Swiss cheese
Squash, summer	10-15	Fresh lavender and butter
Turnips		
Whole	20-30	Mashed with fresh parsley
Cut in pieces	10-20	and coarse pepper
Zucchini	10-15	Olive oil, basil and oregano, or Parmesan

APPLE-YAM CASSEROLE

2 cans (24-oz. each) dry pack
   yams or sweet potatoes,
   drained
1 can (22-oz.) apple pie filling
2 t. lemond rind, grated
⅓ c. honey
1 t. cinnamon
Raisins (optional)

Put yams in a buttered 2-qt. casserole. Mix remaining ingredients and pour over the yams. Bake uncovered at 350° for 30 minutes.
Serves 4-6.

Mrs. Ellis C. Buckley

ARTICHOKE HEARTS ZANTE

2 T. lemon juice
2 T. olive oil
¼ c. water
¼ t. salt
¼ t. crushed, dired mint or 1 T.
   fresh
2 scallions, sliced
¼ c. currants or raisins
1 pkg. frozen artichoke hearts

Put all ingredients in a skillet and bring to a simmer. Cook slowly until tender, 10-15 minutes. Stir gently once or twice.
Serves 4.

Cookbook Committee

ARTICHOKES

Artichokes
1 lemon, sliced
1 onion
1 bay leaf
1 stalk celery
8-10 cloves
White pepper
Dash Tabasco

Soak artichokes in salted water. Simmer together for 30 minutes in a large pot: heavily salted water, lemon, onion, bay leaf, celery, cloves, pepper, and Tabasco. Add artichokes; bring to a boil and cook, uncovered, 35-45 minutes or until tender. Drain and serve cold, stuffed, or with seasoned mayonnaise.

Mrs. Geneva Ashby Jones

GOURMET ARTICHOKES

4 large (or 8 medium) artichoke
   bottoms
½ lb. mushrooms, sliced
2 T. butter
Juice of ½ lemon
1 c. heavy cream
Parmesan cheese (or grated
   Swiss cheese)

Rinse the artichoke bottoms thoroughly. Sauté thinly sliced mushrooms in butter and lemon. Reduce juices and add cream. Cook over low heat until much of the cream has been absorbed, but leave enough to be saucy. Remove from heat. Fill hearts, pouring remaining sauce over them. Sprinkle with Parmesan cheese (or grated Swiss). Place under broiler to brown.
Serves 4.

Mrs. Alan K. Stewart

ARTICHOKES WITH MOUSSELINE SAUCE

6 artichokes
SAUCE:
3 egg yolks
1 egg white
1½ T. lemon juice
1 stick butter, hot and melted
2 t. scallions, chopped

Wash and trim artichokes. Simmer gently for 45 minutes in covered pot. Drain and serve with sauce. Sauce: Blending egg yolks with lemon juice. Add the hot, melted butter drop by drop, blend at medium speed. Beat egg white until stiff. Discard 2 T. of beaten egg white and add blended ingredients and scallions. Blend gently with spatula. This may be made hours before serving. Do not refrigerate. Delicious with asparagus and poached fish.
Serves 6.

Mrs. Gerard L. Regard

ARTICHOKE AND SPINACH CASSEROLE

2 10-oz. pkgs. frozen chopped
   spinach
1 8-oz. pkg. cream cheese,
   softened
1 stick butter, softened
1 6-oz. can water chestnuts,
   sliced and chopped
1 14-oz. can artichoke hearts,
   rinsed and drained
Salt and pepper to taste
Buttered bread or cracker
   crumbs to cover top

Slightly cook spinach and drain in sieve. Squeezing out excess moisture with back of large spoon. Return spinach to pan; add softened butter and cream cheese. Let mixture heat enough to melt and blend, stirring constantly. Add water chestnuts, salt, and pepper. Grease or butter a 1½ or 2-qt. baking dish. Rinse artichoke hearts under cold water. Drain and pat dry with paper towel. Quarter artichokes, removing any tough fibers. Line bottom of baking dish with artichokes. Pour the spinach mixture over artichokes. Sprinkle enough buttered bread crumbs or cracker crumbs to cover top of casserole. Heat casserole in 350° oven for 30-45 minutes. May need to lightly cover with foil the last 5 or 10 minutes to prevent crumbs burning.
Serves 8.

Mrs. James I. Riddle III

ARTICHOKE TOWERS

2 pkgs. frozen spinach
1 4-oz. can mushrooms or ¼ lb.
 fresh
1 T. butter
1 pkg. Holland rusk crackers
¼ c. lemon juice
1 c. sour cream
2 cans artichoke hearts packed
 in water (each 8½-oz. dr. wt.)
1 T. flour
1 T. butter
1 c. milk

Cook spinach according to package directions and drain very well. Sauté mushrooms in butter. Make a white sauce of flour, butter, and milk. Combine mushrooms, spinach, and white sauce. On crackers place 3 artichoke hearts. Top with 1-2 heaping spoons of spinach-mushroom mixture. Top with sour cream-lemon juice mixture. Bake 15 minutes at 325°. May be prepared ahead and refrigerated, adding sour cream-lemon juice mixture just prior to baking. Serves 6-8.

Mrs. Frank W. Perry

ASPARAGUS PUDDING OR SOUFFLE

1 14-oz. can cut asparagus
1 c. sharp Cheddar cheese,
 grated
¼ c. light cream
½ stick butter
3 eggs
1 T. Wyler's Instant Chicken
 Bouillon Nuggets
About ½ t. cayenne pepper
Salt to taste

Put asparagus with its juice into a blender and purée. (If you are making a pudding, the eggs go into the blender also. If a soufflé, just the yolks as the whites will be added later. These will taste the same but the soufflé will have a more dramatic appearance.) Put cheese, butter, and nuggets into a heavy pan with the cream and heat slowly to melt butter and cheese. Stir often but do not let boil. Add this to the asparagus mix. For soufflé let cool before adding egg whites which have been beaten stiff. Butter the 1½-qt. casserole for the pudding but not the soufflé dish. This much can be done the day ahead, minus the egg whites. For soufflé add whites and bake at 375° for 1 hour. For pudding bake at 350° for 1 hour. For garnish cut some bacon with scissors and cook in a heavy skillet. Drain. Melt approximately ¼ stick of butter and add bacon and bread crumbs to it. Scatter this on top of the pudding or soufflé for the last 5 minutes of cooking. Serves 6-8.

Mrs. L. G. Pondrom

ASPARAGUS SOUFFLE

1 can cream of asparagus soup
4 eggs, separated
Cut asparagus, optional

Heat soup and add, one at a time, the egg yolks. Cool; beat whites and fold into mixture. Bake at 350° for 30 minutes or until firm. More cut asparagus may be added.
Serves 4-6.

Mrs. Jack P. Brown

ASPARAGUS TORTE

2 pkg. frozen asparagus,
  cooked according to package
  directions
3 T. melted butter
¼ c. grated Gruyère
¾ c. ham, shredded
3 eggs, beaten
3 T. Parmesan cheese, grated

Chop asparagus into big pieces and season with salt, pepper, and nutmeg. Add butter. Put into a 9″ pie pan and cover with Gruyére cheese and ham. Pour beaten eggs over and top with Parmesan. Bake 30-40 minutes at 350°.
Serves 6-8.

Mrs. James Lambert

SOUTHERN BAKED BEANS

3 16-oz. cans Ranch-Style pinto
  beans
1 12-oz. jar chili sauce
8 pieces bacon
1½ c. brown sugar
1 T. dry mustard

In a 2-qt. casserole layer beans, chili sauce, 4 strips of bacon, brown sugar, and mustard. Top with 4 strips of bacon. Bake at 250° for 5 hours.
Serves 8-10.

Mrs. J. Kyle DuVall

GREEN BEAN AND MUSHROOM CASEROLE

3 pkgs. frozen French-style
  green beans
1 lb. fresh mushrooms, sliced
  or 4 oz. canned
3 c. light cream
½ c. butter
¼ c. flour
¾ lb. sharp Cheddar cheese,
  grated
1 t. Worcestershire sauce
1 t. salt
½ t. pepper
1 t. soy sauce
1 medium onion, chopped
1 5-oz. can water chestnuts,
  sliced thin
Few dashes Tabasco
Almonds, toasted and slivered

Cook beans until barely tender and drain. Sauté onion in butter with mushrooms; add flour, and cook for 1 minute. Add cream which has been heated; stir until smooth. Add grated cheese and remaining seasonings. When cheese is melted, mix sauce with beans and water chestnuts. Bake in a 3-qt. rectangular casserole in a 350° oven until hot and bubbly, approximately 20 minutes. Sprinkle with toasted almonds before serving. Freezes well.
Serves 12.

Mrs. Robert G. Hallam

BEANS PARMESAN

1 pkg. frozen baby lima beans
1 pkg. frozen green beans,
  French cut
1 c. water
1 t. salt
½ stick butter, melted
3 T. flour
1½ c. light cream
½ t. dry mustard
¼ t. cayenne
1 t. onion salt
½ c. Parmesan cheese
1 T. Wyler's Instant Chicken
  Boullion Nuggets

Cook lima beans till done, and salt. Add frozen green beans and cook 5 more minutes. Drain. Remove beans. In the same pan without washing it, melt ½ stick butter. Blend in flour and add cream. Stir out all lumps. Add cheese, mustard, cayenne, onion salt, and Wyler's. Cook slowly, stirring continually, until sauce thickens a little. Put beans in casserole. Pour sauce over them. Cover the top with a mixture of melted butter, bread crumbs, Parmesan cheese, parsley flakes, and paprika. Add more of each if necessary to cover top. Cover and refrigerate this for hours or even overnight. Bake uncovered about 30 minutes at 325°.
Serves 6-8.

Mrs. L. G. Pondrom

MOLLY'S SOUR CREAM GREEN BEANS

2 cans (16-oz. each) drained
   whole Blue Lake green beans
4 T. oil
4 T. vinegar
1 large onion, sliced
½ pt. sour cream
¼ t. dry mustard
1 T. lemon juice
1 T. horseradish, ground
½ c. mayonnaise
1 T. onion purée
Salt and pepper

Marinate beans in first 3 ingredients up to three days. Blend remaining ingredients together and refrigerate until needed. Before serving, drain marinade from beans, pour sauce over beans, and blend until all are well coated.
Serves 6-8.

Mrs. Joe E. Funk, Jr.

PLUM BEANS

½ t. dried basil
1 t. coriander
2 T. parsley
¼ t. cayenne pepper or to taste
½ t. salt
1 small clove garlic, minced
6 T. plum jam, melted over low
   heat and rubbed through a
   sieve
2 T. red wine vinegar
3 c. red kidney beans, cooked
   and cooled or canned red
   kidney beans, washed under
   cold running water and
   drained

In a bowl put the basil, coriander, parsley, cayenne pepper, salt, and garlic and mash to a paste with a wooden spoon. Beat in the jam and vinegar. Add beans and toss gently. Let marinate 2-3 hours or overnight. Serve at room temperature sprinkled with additional parsley.
Serves 4-6.

Mrs. Edward W. Rose III

BAKED BEETS IN ORANGE SAUCE

6 large beets, sliced
3 T. brown sugar
¼ stick of butter, cut in bits
1½ c. fresh orange juice
½ t. salt

Layer beets in pyrex pan, cover with rest of ingredients. Bake covered at 350° for 45 to 60 minutes.
Serves 4 to 6.

Cookbook Committee

BROCCOLI PUDDING

2 pkgs. frozen chopped
  broccoli
2 T. melted butter
½ c. mayonnaise
2 T. flour
3 eggs, beaten
1 c. light cream
½ t. salt

Cook broccoli according to directions on package and drain. Add butter, mayonnaise, flour, eggs, and cream. Pour into greased individual casserole dishes or medium ring mold and place in a pan of hot water. Bake at 375° for 50 minutes or until a knife comes out clean (a little less time for the individual dishes). Serve directly in casseroles or unmold and serve immediately.
Serves 8.

Mrs. M. Weatherby Carr

NANCY ANN'S MOCK BROCCOLI SOUFFLE

1 pkg. frozen chopped broccoli
1 c. mayonnaise
1 can mushroom soup
3 eggs, well-beaten
1 T. onion, grated
Salt and pepper to taste

Cook broccoli until tender. Drain well and blend in other ingredients. Pour into greased 1 quart casserole. Bake at 325° until set in center, approximately 45 minutes. This can be mixed in the morning and baked for dinner.
Serves 6.

Mrs. Theodore P. Votteler

BRUSSELS SPROUTS IN CREAM

2 c. Brussels sprouts
Water
1½ c. heavy cream
¼ t. nutmeg
½ t. salt
½ stick butter
¼ c. Parmesan cheese, freshly
  grated

Parboil sprouts in water for 6 minutes. Drain thoroughly and place in 1½-qt. casserole and cover with cream, spices, and butter. Sprinkle cheese on top. Bake covered at 350° for 30 minutes.
Serves 4.

Mrs. Searcy M. Ferguson, Jr.

PHILADELPHIA CABBAGE

1 medium head cabbage,
  chopped
3 oz. pkg. cream cheese
2 T. milk
½ t. celery seed
Dash pepper

Cook cabbage in salted water. Mix cream cheese, milk, celery seed, and pepper and stir into hot cabbage.
Serves 6.

Mrs. Robert P. Lancaster

STIR-FRY CABBAGE

1 medium head green cabbage
3 T. bacon drippings
1 8-oz. carton sour cream
Salt and pepper to taste

Slice cabbage paper thin. Sauté in bacon drippings in a heavy large skillet. Season to taste. Add sour cream and serve immediately.
Serves 8-12.

Mrs. Steve Summers

SWEET AND SOUR RED CABBAGE

1 head red cabbage (about 3
  lbs.)
3 T. bacon drippings or oil
1 large onion, chopped (1 c.)
2 medium size apples, peeled
  and diced
½ c. red wine vinegar
1 T. sugar
1 t. salt
1 bay leaf
½ c. red currant jelly

Shred cabbage, rinse in colander, and drain. Heat bacon drippings or oil in large covered pot. Sauté onion until soft. Add cabbage and cook over low heat, stirring often, for 10 minutes. Add apples, wine vinegar, sugar, salt, and bay leaf. Mix well. Cover kettle, lower heat. Simmer two hours, stirring several times. Add jelly, stir until melted and blended. Bring to boiling and simmer 10 minutes more. Cover and simmer 4-5 minutes.
Serves 8.

WILTED CABBAGE

1 head cabbage
Salt and pepper to taste
2 garlic cloves, chopped
½ c. diced lean bacon
2½ T. oil
1½ T. wine vinegar

Shred the cabbage very finely, removing the core and heavy ribs. Sprinkle it with salt and pepper and add chopped garlic cloves. In a heavy skillet heat bacon, oil, and vinegar over moderate heat until the bacon has rendered its fat and is tender. Put the cabbage in a warmed salad bowl, pour the bacon mixture over it, and toss it well. Serve at once.
Serves 8-12.

CARROTS WITH ARTICHOKES

½ lb. fresh mushrooms, cut in
  quarters
1 T. olive oil
1½ T. butter
Salt and pepper
2 T. green onion, chopped
1 pkg. frozen artichoke hearts,
  cooked according to pkg.
  directions
1½ lbs. carrots, cooked until
  just barely tender
⅓ c. beef stock
2 T. minced parsley

Sauté the mushrooms in olive oil and butter until very lightly browned. Add salt and pepper to taste. Stir in the green onions and artichoke hearts; toss for 2 or 3 minutes over medium high heat. Add carrots and beef stock. Cover and cook slowly for 5 minutes. Serve sprinkled with minced parsley.
Serves 6.

Mrs. Yerger Hill III

CARROTS IN COGNAC

1 lb. carrots
1 stick butter
½ t. salt
½ t. powdered sugar
1 oz. Cognac

Scrape or peel carrots and cut them into very thin slices. Melt butter in a heavy 9″ iron skillet and season with salt and sugar. Add carrots and Cognac, mixing well. Cover tightly and cook for 1 hour (or less, depending on the maturity of the carrots) over the lowest possible heat. Do not stir after the original mixing. The carrots will have absorbed all the liquid and will not be dry.
Serves 8.

Mrs. L. Franklin Beard

MARINATED CARROTS

2-3 lbs. sliced carrots, cooked
   in salted water and drained
1 green pepper, chopped
1 onion, chopped
1 can tomato soup
⅓ c. oil
¾ c. sugar
1 t. dry mustard
1 t. Worcestershire sauce

Mix marinade ingredients well and pour over carrots. Refrigerate overnight. This is a great vegetable to serve with Mexican food. Can be kept in refrigerator for several weeks.

Serves 6-8.

Mrs. Floyd T. Burke

CARROT PUDDING

8 large carrots
2 T. onion, chopped
2 T. fresh parsley, chopped
6 T. butter
1½ T. flour
1 T. sugar, or less, to taste
Salt and pepper to taste
1 c. hot milk
1 c. fresh bread crumbs
   (optional)

Peel and cook carrots. Drain and mash. Sauté onion and parsley in 4 T. of the butter. Add flour, sugar, seasonings, and hot milk. Cook until thickened. Combine mixtures. Pour into buttered 1½-qt. baking dish, cover with crumbs, and dot with remaining 2 T. butter. Bake in 350° oven for 30 minutes.
Serves 6-8.

Mrs. Ralph Wood, Jr.

CARROT RING

2 bunches of carrots, grated
   (approx. 20 carrots)
3 eggs
½ c. butter
1 c. light cream
1 T. brown sugar
½ t. salt
1 oz. Cointreau

Mix all ingredients together and pour into a 1½-qt. greased ring. Place ring in pan of water and bake at 350° for 40 minutes. Alternate method of preparation: Cook the carrots in small amount of water, drain, and mash them. Add all other ingredients and bake at 350° for 20 minutes. The ring could be filled with peas or watercress.
Serves 8.

Eggplant Stuffed with Vegetables

CHEESY CARROT SOUFFLE

1 c. carrots, finely grated
1 small onion, grated
1 c. soda crackers, crushed
1 c. processed American
   cheese, grated
2 eggs, well beaten
1½ c. light cream
1 t. salt
Dash of pepper
Bacon, cooked and crumbled

Combine the ingredients in the order given. Bake in a 1-qt. buttered dish in a shallow pan of hot water in a 350° oven for 1 hour or 1 hour 15 minutes or until a knife comes out clean. Serve with slices of crumbled bacon on top.
Serves 4-6.

Mrs. Tom Turner

FROM FINLAND — CARROT AND TOMATO DISH

2 lbs. carrots
Sugar, salt, and pepper to taste
1 large onion, sliced
2 T. butter
3-4 large tomatoes, sliced
Swiss cheese, sliced
2 c. white sauce
WHITE SAUCE:
4 T. flour
4 T. butter
2 c. milk
Sherry to taste
¾ of a 6-oz. can tomato paste

Peel carrots and cook them until almost done. Slice thin. Cover the bottom of 2-qt. pan with a generous layer of carrots; sprinkle with sugar, salt and pepper. Sauté onion slices in butter. Place a layer of onion rings on carrots. Cover the onion layer with tomato slices; sprinkle with sugar, salt, and white pepper. Place slices of Swiss cheese on tomatoes. Make white sauce by cooking the flour and butter and gradually adding milk. Cook until thickened. Add sherry and tomato paste; stir until blended. Pour sauce over casserole. Bake for 45 minutes at 325° or until hot and bubbly. It is best made the day before serving; bring to room temperature and heat slowly at 300°.
Serves 8.

Mrs. H. Leslie Moore II

COPPER PENNIES

2 lbs. carrots, sliced and
   cooked
1 green pepper, chopped
¼ c. vinegar
1 c. sugar
1 t. prepared mustard
½ c. Wesson oil
Dash of salt
1 can tomato soup
1 medium onion, chopped
1 t. Worcestershire

Boil vinegar with sugar until sugar dissolves. Then add remaining ingredients and refrigerate at least 8 hours. Serve cold. Keeps in the refrigerator for several weeks.
Serves 6.

Mrs. Michael Boone

CAULIFLOWER MORNAY

1 head cauliflower
1 c. Cheddar cheese, grated
⅔ c. buttered bread crumbs
CREAM SAUCE:
2 T. flour
2 T. butter
⅓ t. salt
½ c. milk
½ c. light cream

Wash cauliflower, remove outer leaves, and break into flowerlets, cutting away heavy stems. Steam flowerlets in 1″ of boiling water in a covered saucepan. Cook until crispy tender. Drain thoroughly. Transfer flowerlets to a greased, 1½-qt. shallow baking dish. Make a cream sauce by melting butter, adding flour and salt. Add milk and cream, cooking until thick (add more milk or cream if too thick.) Add ½ cup of the grated cheese to the sauce. Pour over the cauliflower and top with remaining ½ cup grated cheese and bread crumbs. Bake at 350° for 20 minutes or until hot and bubbly.
Serves 6-8.

Mrs. Yerger Hill III

CELERY AND ALMONDS IN CREAM

4 c. celery, cut in pieces
1 t. salt
White pepper to taste
4 T. butter
1 T. onion, grated
1 T. chives, fresh or frozen
1½ T. flour
1 c. light cream
½ c. chicken bouillon (2 cubes)
¾ c. slivered blanched almonds

Cook celery. salt, pepper in butter in tightly covered pan. Shake well until crispness is lost. Add onion and chives. Cook a bit more. Stir in flour, then cream and bouillon. Let just come to a boil, then add almonds and serve immediately.
Serves 4.

Mrs. Lewis L. May, Jr.

CELERY AU GRATIN WITH ALMONDS

2 T. butter
2 T. flour
¾ c. chicken stock or broth
¼ c. light cream
Salt and pepper
2 c. celery, cut and parboiled
½ c. chopped, blanched
    almonds
American cheese, grated
Buttered bread crumbs

Make a cream sauce with the butter, flour, chicken stock, cream, salt, and pepper. Add celery and chopped almonds. Put in a buttered 1½-qt. casserole dish, top with cheese and crumbs, and bake uncovered at 350° until brown, approximately 30 minutes.
Serves 4 and can successfully be doubled for 8.

Mrs. Kenneth C. Bernecker

SCALLOPED CELERY

4 c. celery, coarsely chopped
¼ c. almonds, slivered and
    blanched
1 6-oz. can water chestnuts,
    sliced
½ c. canned mushroom pieces
    or ½ c. fresh mushrooms,
    sliced
5 T. butter
3 T. flour
½ c. light cream
1 c. chicken broth
½ c. dry bread crumbs
½ c. Parmesan cheese
Salt and white pepper to taste

Boil celery for 5 minutes in salted water and drain. Mix with almonds, chestnuts, and mushrooms. Melt the butter in a saucepan; add the flour and cook roux until it bubbles; add the cream and chicken broth and cook until thick. Blend celery mixture into the sauce, salt and pepper, then pour into a butterd 2-qt. ovenproof casserole. Top with bread crumbs and cheese, dot with butter, and heat in a 375° oven for 20-25 minutes or until hot and bubbly.
Serves 8.

Mrs. Yerger Hill III

CHINESE STIR-FRY

4 T. oil
1 clove garlic, finely minced
1 large yellow onion, sliced
   razor thin
2 stalks celery, sliced
   diagonally
2 large fresh zucchini, cut thin
½ head cabbage, thinly sliced
3 carrots, sliced diagonally
1 green pepper, cut in thin
   julienne strips
¼-½ lb. mushrooms, sliced
4 water chestnuts, thinly sliced
4 T. soy sauce

Heat oil in a deep skillet. Cook garlic and onions 2 to 3 minutes; add celery, zucchini, cabbage, carrots, and green pepper. Cook 2 or 3 minutes and add mushrooms, water chestnuts, and soy sauce. Stir and cook for 3 or 4 minutes. Crunchy and good with any meat.
Serves 6.

Mrs. Gifford Touchstone

BROWNIE'S CHINESE NOODLES

1 c. onions, diced
1 c. celery, diced
2 T. oil
¾ c. salted, toasted cashews,
   chopped or whole
1 can mushroom soup
1 c. mushrooms, sliced
1 7-oz. can water chestnuts,
   drained and sliced, reserving
   juice
1 16-oz. can chow mein noodles
Cooked rice
Soy sauce
OPTIONAL:
Bean sprouts
Chinese vegetables

Sauté onions and celery (can also use green pepper) in oil for 5 minutes. Combine soup and water from chestnuts (if you use canned mushrooms, use that juice too.) Combine all ingredients, except noodles and rice, and heat but do not cook. Serve over rice and top with noodles. A sweet and sour dish goes well with this.
Serves 6-8.

Mrs. William H. Marsh III

CORN CUSTARD

3 eggs, beaten
2 pkgs. (10-oz. each) frozen
   corn
2 c. light or heavy cream
1¼ T. salt
1 T. sugar
1¼ t. white pepper
⅓ c. flour
⅛ t. nutmeg
⅛ t. mace
3 T. melted butter

Butter a 2-qt. casserole dish. Mix eggs and corn; then add remaining ingredients. Bake for approximately 2 hours at 325°. Two jalapeño peppers, seeded and chopped fine can be added if you like a spicier corn dish.
Serves 8.

Cookbook Committee

CORN FRITTERS

1 No. 2 can cream-style corn
1 c. flour, sifted
1 t. baking powder
2 t. salt
¼ t. paprika
2 egg yolks, well beaten
2 egg whites, beaten stiff
Fat for frying

Add dry ingredients to corn. Mix in egg yolks. Fold in egg whites. Drop from a tablespoon into deep fat heated to 380°. Cook, working with a few at a time, until golden brown. Drain on absorbent paper. Serve with maple syrup.
Serves 6.

Mrs. Dan C. Williams, 1948 Junior League
Cookbook

CORN PUDDING

½ c. butter
¼ c. flour
2 t. salt
1½ T. sugar
1¾ c. milk
3 c. corn (canned — if using frozen, follow directions on package)
3 eggs, beaten

Melt butter, stir in flour, salt, sugar, and milk. Cook until thick, then add corn and beaten eggs. Pour into greased 3 qt. casserole and place in pan of hot water. Bake at 350° for 45 minutes. Serve immediately.
Serves 8-10.

Mrs. John B. Cowden, Jr.

CORN SOUFFLE

2 T. butter
½ large green pepper, chopped
3 T. flour
2 c. milk
Salt and pepper to taste
3 eggs
1½ c. corn (fresh or vacuum packed)
1 c. Cheddar cheese, grated

Melt butter in saucepan and sauté pepper slightly. Add flour, milk, salt, and pepper. Cool slightly, then add beaten eggs, corn, and cheese. Pour into buttered 2-qt. soufflé dish and cook about 35 minutes in rather slow oven (275-300°).
Serves 4-6.

Mrs. Lawson Long, 1948 Junior League
Cookbook

PAN DE ELOTE (CORN-CHEESE CASSEROLE)

1 lb. can cream style corn
1 c. biscuit mix
1 egg, beaten
2 T. melted butter
1 T. sugar
½ c. milk
1 4-oz. can green chiles, chopped
½ lb. Monterey Jack cheese, sliced thin

Combine first six ingredients. Pour half of batter into a greased 8″ × 8″ glass baking dish. Cover with chiles and then cheese. Cover cheese with remaining batter. Bake at 400° for 20 minutes. Serves 6.

Mrs. John Kendrick, Jr.

NATHANIEL BARRY'S EGGPLANT CASSEROLE

4 large eggplants, peeled and diced
1 pt. good chicken broth
4 slices white bread, diced and crusts removed
4 whole eggs, beaten
1 c. diced American cheese
Salt and pepper to taste
½ lb. bacon chopped
1 medium onion, chopped
American cheese, grated
Parmesan cheese, grated
Butter

Soak eggplant in salt water for 15 minutes. Drain, then cook in lightly salted water until tender. Drain and add broth, bread, eggs, cheese, salt and pepper. Sauté onion and bacon together and add to above mixture. Pour into buttered casserole and sprinkle with equal parts of the grated cheeses. Dot with butter and bake at 350° for 20-30 minutes or until brown. Serve hot.

Brook Hollow Golf Club

EMERY'S BAKED EGGPLANT

1 1-lb. eggplant, peeled
½ to ¾ box seasoned croutons
1 small can Pet evaporated milk
¼ c. whole milk
¼ c. finely chopped onions
¼ c. finely chopped green pepper
¼ c. finely chopped celery
½ stick (2 oz.) butter
Salt to taste
2 eggs, slightly beaten
Dash of pepper and sage
1 t. chopped pimiento
2 oz. grated Cheddar cheese
Dash of Accent

Peel and soak eggplant in salt water for 6 to 12 hours, overnight if possible in the refrigerator. Soak bread crumbs in milk. Sauté onions, celery and pepper in butter for 15 minutes. Place eggplant in a large pan, cover with water and cook until almost done. Mix bread crumbs, sautéed ingredients and eggplant together. Add eggs, pimiento and seasonings. Blend well. Place in a baking dish and top with cheese. Bake at 350° for 30 minutes or until golden brown. Serves 6-8.

Mrs. George W. Jalonick III

ITALIAN EGGPLANT

1 eggplant
1 egg
1 T. milk
Cracker crumbs
Fat for frying
1 onion, chopped
2 c. tomatoes, peeled, seeded,
    and chopped
1 t. salt
Pepper, few grains
1 t. sugar
1 c. mozzarella cheese, grated

Peel eggplant and cut into half inch slices. Beat egg and add milk. Dip slices in beaten egg and then in cracker crumbs. Fry in small amount of fat until golden brown on both sides. Place slices in a greased shallow baking dish. Brown onion in a little fat, and add tomatoes, salt. pepper. and sugar. Season more if desired. Add ⅔ cup cheese. Pour the tomato mixture over the eggplant and sprinkle top with remaining cheese. Bake in a moderate oven (350°) about 20 to 30 minutes or until the eggplant is tender. Serves 6.

Mrs. Henry C. Coke, Jr., 1948 Junior League
Cookbook

EGGPLANT SOUFFLE

2 c. medium white sauce
3 egg yolks, well beaten
1 onion, chopped
1 c. eggplant, cooked and
    sieved
1 t. Tabasco
3 egg whites, beaten stiff
Salt and pepper to taste

Pour hot white sauce into egg yolks while stirring constantly. Add onion. Cool. Thoroughly mix in eggplant and seasoning. Fold in egg whites. Place in a greased 2-qt. casserole and set in a pan of hot water. Bake at 375° for 45 to 50 minutes, or until firm. Serves 8.

Mrs. Burton Gilliland, 1948 Junior League
Cookbook

STUFFED EGGPLANT

1 large eggplant
½ medium onion, chopped
2 T. butter
3 T. chopped parsley
1 can cream of mushroom soup
Salt and pepper to taste
Butter crackers (not saltines),
    crumbled
Butter

Cut off eggplant top and cut in half length-wise. Scrape out, leaving ¼" around sides and bottom of shell. Boil eggplant meat in salt water until tender (approximately 10 minutes.) Drain thoroughly in a colander and chop. Sauté onion in butter and add parsley. Mix eggplant, soup, and crumbled crackers to make a good stuffing consistency. Pile filling into eggplant shells and sprinkle cracker crumbs on top, dot with butter, and bake at 375° for 30 minutes. (If you like spicy taste to eggplant, add a few drops of Tabasco.)
Serves 6 to 8.

Mrs. Carey G. King, Jr.

LA LOUISIANE STUFFED EGGPLANT GALATOIRE

1 1-lb. eggplant
¼ c. onion, minced
1 T. parsley, chopped
½ stick butter
Salt and pepper to taste
½ c. crabmeat, chopped and
    cooked
½ c. shrimp, chopped and
    cooked
½ c. béchamel sauce
Parmesan cheese, freshly
    grated
Butter bread crumbs

Halve lengthwise the eggplant and put the halves cut-side down into a baking pan just large enough to hold them. Cover the pan with foil and bake the eggplant in a preheated 375° oven for 50 minutes or until tender. Scoop out the pulp, leaving the shells intact, reserve the shells, and chop the pulp. In a skillet sauté onion and parsley in butter until browned. Stir in eggplant, salt, and pepper to taste. Cook, covered, over moderate heat for 5 minutes or until the eggplant is very soft. Add crabmeat, shrimp, and béchamel sauce. Put the reserved shells in a baking dish just large enough to hold them. Divide the stuffing between the shells and sprinkle each shell with 2 T. each of cheese and crumbs. Bake in a 425° oven for 10 minutes or until topping is golden.
Serves 4.

Mrs. Michael M. Boone

ENDIVE OR LETTUCE SOUFFLE

1 qt. green outer leaves of
Western iceberg lettuce or
limestone, shredded
4 T. butter
1 t. onion salt
3 T. flour
1 c. milk, scalded
1 t. salt
⅛ t. pepper
1 t. Worcestershire sauce
4 eggs, separated, plus 1 more
white (4 yolks, 5 whites)
1 c. sharp Cheddar cheese,
shredded
¼ t. cream of tartar
1 pinch salt
Buttered crumbs or grated
cheese

Wash and drain lettuce; preheat oven to 400°. Steam lettuce, covered, in very little water. Drain, and chop very fine. Melt 1 T. butter; add lettuce and onion salt. Cook, stirring, over medium heat to evaporate liquid. Set aside. Melt remaining 3 T. butter and blend in flour. Blend in milk, salt, pepper, and Worcestershire. Cook, stirring, over medium heat until thickened, about 1 minute. Beat in egg yolks one at a time. Blend in cheese and stir in lettuce mixture. This much can be made in advance. Whip egg whites at low speed until foamy. Add cream of tartar and salt; then whip at high speed until stiff but not dry. Stir about ¼ of the whites into the lettuce mixture; fold in remaining whites. Heavily butter the bottom and sides of a 1½-qt. casserole and, if desired, sprinkle with Parmesan cheese. Pour in the lettuce mixture. Sprinkle with buttered crumbs. Place in the middle of the oven and reduce heat to 375°. Bake 25-30 minutes and do not open oven door during the first 20 minutes.
Serves 4.

Cookbook Committee

CARAWAY FRENCH FRIES

French fried potatoes for 6
servings
1 t. salt
⅓ c. parsley, finely chopped
⅓ c. butter, melted
2 t. caraway seed

Spread fried potatoes in a single layer in a 13″×9″×2″ baking dish; heat at 450° for 15 minutes. Sprinkle with salt and parsley. Combine butter and caraway seed; pour over potatoes. Heat 5-8 minutes longer, stirring occasionally, or until French fries are crisp and golden brown. Serves 6. Frozen potatoes can be used.

Mrs. Mark Lemmon, Jr.

ETHELEEN BROWN'S JALAPENO CHEESE GRITS

4½ c. water
1 t. salt
1½ c. regular grits
1 roll garlic cheese
1 stick butter, cut into bits
1 c. milk
3 eggs, beaten
3 jalapeño peppers, chopped

Cook grits in water with salt until done. In the top of a double boiler cook cheese, butter, milk, and eggs until mixed. Add this and peppers to grits. Pour into a 2-qt. casserole and bake at 325° for 45 minutes.
Serves 8-10.

Mrs. Searcy Ferguson, Jr.

HOMINY CASSEROLE

2 1-lb. 13 oz. cans hominy
2 4-oz. cans peeled green chiles
4 T. sour cream
salt to taste
butter
½ c. heavy cream
1½ c. shredded Monterey Jack
  cheese

Drain and wash the hominy. Butter a 2½ to 3 quart casserole. Remove seeds from green chiles and chop finely. Alternate layers of hominy and chiles in the casserole, dotting each layer with butter, sour cream and salt. Make the top layer hominy, dot with butter, and add the heavy cream. Top the casserole with the shredded cheese and bake at 350° for 25 to 30 minutes or until the ingredients are blended and piping hot. The amount of green chiles may be reduced according to your taste.
Serves 6 to 8.

Mrs. Yerger Hill III

LIMA BEAN CASSEROLE

½ lb. Velveeta cheese
¼ c. milk
1 4-oz. can sliced mushrooms,
  drained
½-1 T. jalapeño pepper juice
2 T. Worcestershire sauce
4 pkgs. frozen lima beans,
  cooked and drained

Melt cheese in top of double boiler. Add milk, stirring constantly. Add mushrooms, seasonings, and lima beans. Pour all into casserole and bake at 350° for 25 minutes.
Serves 8-10, easily. This is delicious with baked ham.

Mrs. Earl Fain III

LIMA BEAN PUREE

1 lb. dried lima beans
2 strips bacon
1 garlic clove
1 green onion, minced
Janmil's Crazy Mixed Up Salt
White pepper
4 T. minced fresh parsley
½ stick butter, melted

Cover limas with water and soak over night. Drain beans and cover with fresh water. Add bacon, garlic, onion and salt. Simmer for several hours — until beans are soft — then drain off most of liquid. Pour beans and remaining liquid into blender and purée. Check seasoning. Butter a 2 quart casserole dish and pour purée into casserole. Sprinkle with parsley and half stick of melted butter and bake at 350° for 30 minutes. This can be done hours ahead.

Mrs. Seary Ferguson, Jr.

MUSHROOMS BAYHEAD

1 lb. mushrooms, chopped fine
1-2 T. onions, grated
4 T. butter
Salt and pepper to taste
8 oz. pkg. cream cheese

Sauté mushrooms and onions in butter. Salt and pepper to taste. When most of the liquid is absorbed, add cream cheese. Mix and put into casserole dish. Bake at 350° for 25 minutes.

Mrs. Bruce Swenson

MUSHROOMS IN CREAM

20-24 large mushrooms
½ cup butter, softened
2 T. fresh parsley, chopped
1½ t. chives, chopped
1½ shallots, minced
Salt to taste
¼-½ t. lemon juice
1 c. heavy cream

Remove stems from mushrooms and stuff caps with a mixture of the butter, parsley, chives, shallots, salt and lemon juice. Put in a shallow baking dish and pour the cream over all. Bake at 450° for 10 minutes.
Serves 8.

Mrs. Edward W. Rose III

MUSHROOMS IN SOUR CREAM

1 lb. mushrooms, washed
4-6 T. butter
1 c. chopped green onions
½ t. freshly ground pepper
½ t. salt
1 c. sour cream

Slice mushrooms lengthwise, stems and all. This can be done the day before and refrigerated in a plastic bag. Melt butter and sauté onions for 10 minutes. Add mushrooms and saute 3-4 minutes. Add seasonings and sour cream, serving immediately.
Serves 2-4 depending upon how lavish you want to be!

Mrs. Cyrus M. Johnston

MUSHROOMS L'SLATER

4 c. mushrooms, sliced
1 medium onion, sliced thin
3 T. butter
1 t. marjoram
½ t. caraway seeds
½ t. salt
pepper to taste
2 T. flour
½ c. milk
½ c. sour cream
3 T. bread crumbs
2 T. fresh parsley

Sauté mushrooms and onion in butter for 10 minutes or until onions just begin to get soft. Add marjoram, caraway seed, salt, and pepper. Sprinkle flour on top and stir for about 3 minutes, then add milk and cook until thick. Add sour cream and put in an au gratin dish. Sprinkle the top with toasted bread crumbs and parsley. Or add butter to bread crumbs and run under broiler after heating a few minutes.
Serves 6.

Mrs. Denys Slater, Jr.

STUFFED MUSHROOMS SUPREME

18 large fresh mushrooms
1 pkg. frozen chopped spinach
1 can cream of mushroom soup
1 8-oz. pkg. cream cheese
1 3-oz. can French fried onions
1 stick butter
1 4-oz. pkg. saltine crackers, crushed

Wash and stem mushrooms. Cook and season spinach according to package directions and drain well. Heat soup and cheese together. Add spinach and fold in onions. Stuff mushrooms with spinach mixture. Top with cracker crumbs mixed with butter. Place in a greased baking dish and heat at 350° for 25 minutes. Allow 2 mushrooms per person. This is a great accompaniment for steaks. Spinach can also be served as a casserole dish without mushrooms. Can be made ahead and refrigerated before cooking.
Serves 8.

Mrs. Lee R. Slaughter, Jr.

MUSHROOM SOUFFLE

1 lb. fresh mushrooms
3 T. butter
3 eggs separated plus 1 extra
    egg white
1 c. milk
1 heaping T. flour

Peel mushrooms, chop fine, and cook in 2 tablespoons butter. Melt 1 tablespoon of butter in the top of a double boiler, stir in flour, then milk, and cook until thick. Add beaten egg yolks and cook 3 minutes. Remove from fire and fold in egg whites, beaten very stiffly, and the mushrooms. Bake in a buttered casserole at 350° for 30 minutes.
Serves 2-3.

Mrs. George Gardere, 1948 Junior League
Cookbook

NOODLES ROMANOFF FOR A CROWD

2 8-oz. pkgs. egg noodles
3 c. large-curd cottage cheese
2 cloves garlic, minced or
    mashed
2 t. Worcestershire
1 pt. sour cream
1 bunch green onions, finely
    chopped
½ t. Tabasco
1 c. Parmesan, grated or
    shredded

Cook noodles in boiling, salted water until tender and drain. Combine cooked noodles, cottage cheese, garlic, Worcestershire, sour cream, onions, and Tabasco. Turn into a greased 3-qt. casserole and sprinkle cheese over the top. Bake for 25 minutes at 350° (30-35 mins. if refrigerated.) May be prepared a day in advance.
Makes 18 servings.

Mrs. J. Robert Norris, Jr.

HUNGARIAN NOODLES AND PEAS

2 c. noodles
½ c. onion, chopped
3 T. butter
1 c. sour cream
½ c. cottage cheese
1 T. poppy seed
¾ t. salt
Dash of pepper
1 pkg. cooked green peas
Parmesan cheese

Cook noodles according to package directions; drain. In a large pan, saute onion in butter until tender. Combine sour cream, cottage cheese, poppy seed, salt and pepper — add to onions. Stir in noodles and green peas. Heat through and sprinkle with Parmesan cheese.
Serves 6.

Mrs. J. Brevard Haynes

OKRA AND TOMATOES

1½ lbs. okra, sliced
¼ c. bacon drippings
2 medium onions, chopped
1-1 lb. 15 oz. can tomatoes,
   chopped
1 green pepper, chopped
⅔ c. water
2 T. basil
2 bay leaves — optional
Salt and pepper to taste

Sauté okra in bacon drippings for 30 minutes. Add onions and cook 10 minutes. Add all remaining ingredients and simmer for 30 minutes or until done. Remove bay leaves.
Serves 8.

Mrs. M. Weatherby Carr

STUFFED ONIONS

6 large onions
1 c. rice, boiled
1 c. blanched almonds
½ c. pecans
½ t. salt
¼ t. pepper
¼ t. sugar
1 T. heavy cream
1 egg, well beaten
1 c. white sauce, well seasoned

Boil onions in water 30 minutes. Drain, and remove outside skin. Take out centers and mix with boiled rice, almonds, pecans. salt. pepper, and sugar. Add cream and egg. Stuff back into onions, and place in baking dish. Put dash of butter on each, and bake twenty or thirty minutes. Pour 1 cup well-seasoned white sauce over onions and serve piping hot.

Mrs. Julius Runge, 1948 Junior League
Cookbook

ONION TART

1¼ c. Ritz cracker crumbs
10 T. butter
4 c. onions, sliced thinly
4 T. flour
1 c. hot milk
½ c. hot chicken stock
½ c. sour cream
1 egg yolk, beaten
1-1½ c. grated Colby Longhorn
   cheese

With fingers, mix cracker crumbs with 4 T. softened butter. Press into bottom and sides of a 9-inch pie plate. Saute onions in 2 T. butter in a heavy-bottomed pan until tender. Melt 4 T. butter, stir in flour, cook 1 minute. Take off heat and stir in hot milk and chicken stock. Return to heat and stir until thickened. Add sour cream mixed with egg yolk. Season to taste with salt and pepper. Mix sauce with onions: pour into crust. Spread cheese over top and bake at 350° about 25-30 minutes. Good with roast beef, pork tender, leg of lamb. Can be made ahead and baked when ready to serve. Can also be frozen.
Serves 8.

Mrs. Edward W. Rose III

MADOLYN'S PEAS WITH CHESTNUTS

1 pkg. frozen peas
½ c. water
1 chicken bouillon cube
1 c. light cream
1 T. flour
1 t. cornstarch
1 6-oz. can water chestnuts
⅛ t. black pepper
3 T. butter
Salt to taste

Cook peas in water with bouillon cube. Combine cream and enough drained liquid to make 1½ cups. Melt butter over low flame, remove from heat, stir in flour and cornstarch. Add liquid and cook over low heat until smooth and thick. Add peas, thinly sliced water chestnuts, pepper, and salt. Reheat and serve. Serves 6.

Mrs. M. Weatherby Carr

GREEN PEA SOUFFLE

1 qt. peas
2 T. butter, melted
3 eggs, beaten
1 pt. milk
Salt, pepper, and sugar to taste

Cook peas until tender. Mash them with melted butter and add eggs which have been beaten lightly with milk. Season with salt, pepper, and sugar. Beat hard and bake in a greased baking dish. Cover for 20 minutes, then brown and serve immediately. Serves 6-8.

1948 Junior League Cookbook

STIR-FRIED PEA PODS

2 T. chopped green onion
1 T. oil
½ lb. fresh pea pods OR 7 oz. pkg. frozen pods defrosted
½ c. sliced water chestnuts
½ c. bean sprouts
¼ t. salt
⅓ c. chicken stock
1 T. soy sauce

Sauté green onion in oil for 1 minute. Add pea pods and sauté an additional 2 minutes. Add remaining ingredients. Cover and steam 1½ to 2 minutes or until pea pods are barely tender. Serves 4.

Miss Byrd Fuertes

PEPPERS STUFFED WITH GUMBO

1 large onion, chopped
2 buds garlic, chopped
½ c. okra, chopped
4 T. olive oil
1 T. chili powder
1 20 oz. can tomatoes
⅔ c. rice, uncooked
6 bell peppers
Salt and pepper to taste

Fry onion and garlic with okra in olive oil. Add chili powder and tomatoes; simmer two hours. Cook rice, drain, and mix with gumbo. Season with salt and pepper. Wash peppers and scoop them out. Stuff with rice and gumbo mixture, which should be very thick. Arrange peppers in a pan with a little water in it. Bake slowly until peppers are tender. Serves 6.

Mrs. L. G. Pondrom, 1948 Junior League Cookbook

CHEESE POLENTA PERUGIA

1 c. corn meal
1 t. salt
1 c. cold water
3 c. boiling water
2 T. butter
4 T. Parmesan cheese, grated
4 T. olive oil
1 c. onion, thinly sliced
¼ lb. fresh mushrooms, thinly sliced
1 large clove garlic, minced
20-oz. can Italian tomatoes, coarsely chopped
6-oz. can tomato paste
2 T. parsley, minced
Salt, pepper, paprika
¼ lb. mozzarella, sliced thin

Mix corn meal with salt and cold water, very slowly add mixture to boiling water, stirring constantly, and simmer 20 minutes over lowest flame, stirring frequently. Stir in butter and 2 T. Parmesan; then pour into greased shallow pan and chill in refrigerator 4 hours or overnight. Pour 2 T. olive oil into heavy saucepan, add mushrooms, onion, and garlic, sauté until mushrooms are just tender; add tomatoes and tomato paste and simmer 10 minutes. Add parsley and salt and pepper to taste. Cut chilled polenta into ½" slices and place half of them in greased shallow casserole, top with mozzarella. Pour one-half of sauce over cheese and rest of polenta on top, then sauce. Sprinkle with Parmesan cheese, 2 T. olive oil and paprika. Bake at 350° for 30 minutes.

Mrs. Searcy Ferguson, Jr.

POLENTA RING FILLED WITH ZUCCHINI

1 box polenta
3 eggs, beaten
½ c. butter
¾ c. Parmesan cheese
2 T. parsley
1 clove garlic, minced
Salt and pepper to taste
Nutmeg
½ lb. prosciutto, thinly sliced
8 oz. mozzarella, thinly sliced
TOMATO SAUCE:
2 lbs. fresh tomatoes
1 onion, chopped
1 stalk celery, chopped
2 carrots, diced
2-3 basil leaves, crumbled
3 T. oil
2 T. butter
1 garlic clove, minced
3 T. parsley, chopped
½ t. oregano

Cook polenta according to package directions. Stir in butter, parsley, cheese, garlic, salt, pepper, nutmeg and eggs. Line an oiled mold with prosciutto overlapping; pour in half the polenta mixture. Bang mold to settle polenta. Put cheese on top and cover with remaining polenta, drape prosciutto on top and bake at 350° for 25 minutes in a hot water bath. Serve with sautéed zucchini and mushrooms in the center of the mold and pass fresh tomato sauce. For sauce, sauté in oil and butter, the onion, celery and carrots. Add seasonings and tomatoes and simmer uncovered for 30 minutes.

Mrs. Mark Lemmon, Jr.

CARMEN'S DOUBLE BOILER CREAMED POTATOES

4 large potatoes
2 T. onion, grated
1 small clove garlic, mashed
Salt and pepper to taste
1-1½ c. heavy cream
¼ c. salted pistachio nuts,
   chopped

Peel and shred potatoes on grater. Squeeze out liquid and put in double boiler. Beat in onion, garlic, salt, pepper, and 1 cup heavy cream. Cook, covered, over boiling water until tender and thicker, stirring frequently. It might need more cream. Sprinkle in serving dish with nuts.
Makes 4 servings.

Cook Book Committee

POTATOES IN CREAM

15 to 20 small new potatoes —
   sliced thin
2 c. cream
1 t. nutmeg
Salt and pepper
½ stick butter

Layer potatoes in flat 13½" × 9" casserole dish, cover with cream and season. Dot with butter and bake at 350° for 50 minutes or until brown on top.
Serves 6-8.

Mrs. Searcy Ferguson, Jr.

POTATOES DAUPHINAISE

6 potatoes, cut into thin slices
Salt and pepper to taste
1 clove garlic
2 T. butter
1 c. grated Gruyère
2 eggs
2 c. heavy cream
¼ t. nutmeg

Season potatoes with salt and pepper and place them in baking dish which you have rubbed with garlic and greased with butter. Alternate potatoes in layers with Gruyère. Then beat eggs with cream and nutmeg and pour this over potatoes and cheese. Bake 1 hour at 350°. Serves 8-10.

Mrs. James Lambert

DELMONICO POTATO TORTE

6 T. butter
6 Idaho potatoes, peeled and
   thinly sliced
1 c. Parmesan cheese
Salt and pepper
½ t. nutmeg
½ c. grated Gruyère or Swiss
   cheese
¼ c. thick cream
2 T. fresh chives

Thickly butter a 2-quart mold or heatproof bowl. Layer potatoes in mold, sprinkling each layer with Parmesan cheese, salt, pepper, and nutmeg. Cover tightly with lid or foil. Bake at 400° until potatoes are done, about 1 hour. Unmold on serving dish. Sprinkle with Gruyère and brown quickly under broiler. Pour cream slowly into center of potatoes. Sprinkle with chives.
Serves 6.

Mrs. Mark Lemmon, Jr.

SWEET POTATOES ALEXANDER

12 T. sweet butter
½ c. sugar
½ c. orange juice
3 oz. Grand Marnier
1 c. apples, sliced
2 c. sweet potatoes, cooked and
   sliced
1 c. peaches, sliced
2 medium bananas, sliced
2 oz. roasted almonds

Prepare Angel Sauce: melt butter and sugar in a saucepan over low heat. When they are completely melted, add orange juice and bring to a boil. Remove saucepan from heat and stir in Grand Marnier. This makes approximately ½ pint sauce. Spread sauce on the bottom of a baking dish and add one thin layer of apples, sweet potatoes, peaches and bananas. Spread almonds on top. Bake in a 350° oven for 25 minutes. Serve as a garnish for baked ham, roast pork, roast duckling, or roast turkey.

SWEET POTATO RUM CASEROLE

4-5 large sweet potatoes
1 T. butter
1 c. black walnuts, chopped
1½ c. brown sugar
2 eggs, well beaten
2 oz. rum or bourbon

Boil potatoes in jackets. Peel while hot and mash. Add remaining ingredients and place in orange cups or greased casserole; top with marshmallows and bake at 325° for 25-30 minutes.
Serves 4-6.

Cookbook Committee

PUMPKIN ORANGES

1 T. gelatine
3 eggs, separated
½ t. salt
¾ c. sugar
½ c. milk
1 T. brandy
Whipping cream
1¼ c. canned pumpkin
½ t. cinnamon
½ t. nutmeg
1 t. ginger
¼ t. cloves

Soak gelatin in ½ c. cold water. Beat egg yolks. ½ c. sugar, pumpkin, milk, salt, cinnamon, nutmeg, ginger and cloves. Cook and stir these over hot water until thick. Stir in gelatine. Add the brandy. Cool. Beat egg whites with salt and remaining ¼ c. sugar. Fold into cooled pumpkin mixture. Hollow out 6 oranges and fill. Decorate with whipped cream (use pastry tube) and a sprig of mint.
Serves 6.

Mrs. Julian A. Wells

MOZZARELLA AND POTATO PIE

2 lbs. potatoes, peeled
¼ c. butter, softened
Salt and pepper to taste
½ lb. mozzarella cheese
3 tomatoes, peeled
1 t. oregano
1 t. basil
Salt and pepper to taste
½ c. Parmesan cheese, freshly
  grated
¼ c. butter, melted

Boil peeled potatoes in salted water to cover until they are tender. Drain and mash them. Stir in softened butter and season with salt and pepper. Butter and lightly flour a deep 9½" pie plate. Spread in the mashed potatoes. Cut the mozzarella cheese into ¼" thick slices. Arrange half of the cheese on the potatoes and top it with the peeled tomatoes cut into ½" thick slices. Sprinkle with oregano, basil, salt and pepper. Top the tomatoes with remaining mozzarella, Parmesan, and melted butter. Bake the pie in a 425° oven 20-25 minutes or until cheese is melted and lightly browned. Can be made ahead and refrigerated until baking time.
Serves 4-6.

Mrs. Searcy Ferguson, Jr.

PARTY POTATOES

8-10 medium-sized potatoes
1 8-oz. pkg. cream cheese
¼ c. sour cream
Salt and pepper
Butter
Paprika

Pare potatoes and boil until tender. Beat softened cream cheese and sour cream at medium speed on electric mixer until well blended. Add hot potatoes, gradually beating until light and fluffy. Season to taste with salt and pepper. Spoon into a buttered 2-qt. casserole. Brush the top with softened butter and sprinkle with paprika. Brown in a 350° oven for 30 minutes. Can be prepared ahead of time and heated just before serving.
Serves 6-8.

Mrs. Yerger Hill III

SCALLOPED HASH BROWN POTATOES

4 c. hash brown potatoes (16-oz. pkg. frozen)
1 c. (4 oz.) grated sharp processed American cheese
¼ c. sliced green onions
½ c. sour cream
½ t. salt
1 chicken bouillon cube
½ c. boiling water
1 T. butter
Sliced American cheese to cover

In a 1½-qt. casserole, combine hash brown potatoes, grated cheese and onions. Then add sour cream and salt. Dissolve the bouillon cube in boiling water and pour over the potato mixture. Dot with butter, cover and bake at 375° for 30 minutes or until potatoes are tender. Stir casserole gently once or twice while baking. Remove from oven; top with slices of cheese and bake several minutes longer or until cheese melts.
Serves 6.

Mrs. John W. McDonough

SPINACH-STUFFED POTATOES

6 baked potatoes
¾ stick butter
1½ c. mornay sauce
1 c. cooked spinach, chopped and drained
1 c. Gruyère cheese, grated

Scoop out potatoes and place pulp in mixer with butter, mornay sauce, spinach, and seasonings. Mix well. Heap into potato shells, sprinkle with cheese, and bake in 350° oven for 20 minutes or until brown. This can be done ahead.
Serves 12.

Mrs. Searcy Ferguson, Jr.

ARROZ AMARILLO

2 T. butter
2 T. olive oil
2 T. onion, finely chopped
2 T. celery, finely chopped
1 t. salt
½ t. white pepper
1 T. lemon juice
2 c. long grain rice
¼ t. powdered saffron
3½ c. hot chicken broth
½ c. California Sauterne

Melt butter in a skillet and mix with the olive oil. Add onion, celery, salt and pepper to the skillet and cook until the onion is limp. Add the lemon juice and stir well. Add the rice and cook, stirring to coat the rice well, for about 10 minutes. Add the powdered saffron to the hot chicken broth and dissolve. Add the rice mixture and transfer to a covered casserole. Cook at low heat for about 20 minutes. Remove from the heat, uncover and pour the sauterne over the rice. Cover and let stand about 20 minutes before serving.
Makes 6-8 servings.

Cookbook Committee

BAKED RICE

1½ c. raw rice
1 green pepper, chopped
1 onion, chopped
3 T. margarine or butter
1 c. parsley, chopped (can use dried — put in water to soften)
2 c. milk
3 eggs, beaten
2 c. sharp cheese, grated
1½ t. salt
⅛ t. pepper
2 t. or more to taste Picante sauce

Cook rice according to directions on box. Sauté green pepper and onion in margarine. Add all ingredients to rice, mix and bake in a greased 1½ qt. casserole at 350° for 45 minutes to 1 hour. Can be fixed in the morning then refrigerated. Take out 2 hours before putting it in oven.
Serves 8.

Mrs. Leland Clemons

RICE CASSEROLE

1 c. raw rice, cooked
1 8-oz. carton sour cream
1½ slices Muenster or Monterey Jack cheese
Cheddar cheese, shredded on top
½ can green chiles (4 oz. can)

Put half of the cooked rice in the bottom of a casserole, half of the sour cream, all of the Muenster and all of the chiles. Repeat Rice and sour cream, top with shredded cheddar cheese and warm in 350° oven.

Mrs. Clint M. Josey, Jr.

CURRIED RICE

1 c. converted rice
2 chicken bouillon cubes
1½ t. curry powder
1 t. instant minced onion
½ t. salt
½ t. parsley flakes
½ t. green onion flakes
⅛ t. paprika
1 T. butter

Combine all ingredients with 2½ c. cold water. Turn burner to high. When mixture boils, turn to simmer 15 minutes. Stir once with fork.
Serves 4-6.

Mrs. David Kelly, Jr.

EDAM RICE RING

2½ c. long grain white rice
Salted water with lemon slice
½ lb. Edam cheese, grated
½ stick butter

Wash uncooked rice through 5 different water rinses. Bring a large kettle of salted water with a lemon slice added to a rapid boil. Sprinkle the rinsed rice a little at a time into the kettle of boiling water. Cook rice according to package directions for cooking time. When rice is tender, strain in a colander and rinse with boiling water. Put hot, well-drained rice in a warm mixing bowl and add the cheese and butter. Toss well until cheese and butter are completely melted and well distributed through the rice. Pack the rice mixture into a buttered 10″ ring mold. (This much can be done ahead and refrigerated.) Two hours before serving, remove from refrigerator and let warm to room temperature. Set rice ring in a pan of boiling water and bake for 30 minutes at 350°. Serve immediately after turning ring out onto a serving plate. Fill center with fresh green peas with sliced mushrooms.
Serves 10-12.

Mrs. George W. Jalonick IV

FRUITED RICE PILAF

2 T. currants
4 T. butter
¼ c. dried apricots, cut into
  narrow strips
¼ c. finely chopped, blanched,
  untoasted almonds
1 T. honey
1 c. long-grain raw brown rice
1 t. salt
3 or 4 very thin slices of lemon
  (optional)

Soak the currants in a bowl of warm water for 15 minutes; then drain and pat them dry with paper towels. Melt the butter in a 10- to 12-inch skillet or casserole over high heat and add the apricots, currants, and almonds. Reduce the heat to low, and cook uncovered for 3-4 minutes or until the nuts are lightly colored. Stir in the honey, rice, and salt and cover with 2¼ cups of water; bring to a boil over high heat. Reduce the heat to low, cover the pan and simmer 50 minutes or until the liquid has been absorbed. Serve hot as a main course for lunch or an accompaniment to lamb, beef, or wild game.
Serves 4.

Mrs. Edward W. Rose III

FLUFFY RICE

1 t. salt
1 c. long grain rice

Fill a 2-qt. pot with water. Bring to a boil; add salt and rice, cooking about 20 minutes. Put rice into a colander and pour cold water through until well rinsed. (Rice may be held at this point. Don't put it into the oven until you are almost ready to serve it.) Place in a pyrex dish and put into the upper part of a 400° oven for about 10 minutes. The rice will be very fluffy.
Serves 6-8.

Mrs. Margaret C. Worsham

GOLDEN RICE

1 c. converted rice
2 T. butter
2 c. boiling water
2 bouillon cubes (beef or
   chicken)
5 scallions (or to taste)
2 T. soy sauce
Salt to taste

Start oven at 350°. Sprinkle rice on cookie sheet and bake about 5 minutes, until lightly browned. Dissolve bouillon cubes in water, add butter and rice. Bring to a boil, reduce heat to very low, cover with a tight-fitting lid and cook for 25 minutes or until just tender. Pour off any excess liquid, stir in finely chopped scallions and soy sauce. Remove from heat, cover tightly and let stand until serving time.

Mrs. Spencer Carver

RICE AND MUSHROOMS

½ c. butter
2 T. onion, chopped
½ c. mushrooms, sliced
1 green pepper, chopped
Dash garlic powder
1 c. rice — Uncle Ben's
3 c. chicken broth
Salt and pepper to taste

Melt butter and sauté onions, mushrooms, green pepper, and garlic. Add raw rice. When rice is yellow, add chicken broth, salt, and pepper. Pour into 1½ qt. casserole, cover and bake at 350° for 1 hour. Stir once.
Serves 6.

Mrs. Don McIlyar

ORANGE RICE

3 T. butter
⅔ c. celery, diced
2 T. onion, chopped
2 c. water
2 T. orange peel, grated
1 c. orange juice
1½ t. salt
1½ c. uncooked rice

Melt butter in a saucepan with a cover, add celery and onions, and brown. Cook until tender. Stir in water, orange peel, orange juice, and salt. Bring to a boil. Add rice, cover, and steam over low heat for 20-25 minutes.

Mrs. Walter F. Sosnowski

OREGANO RICE

2 c. rice
1 can beef broth plus enough
    water to make 4 c. liquid
    total
1 T. oregano
1 t. salt
2 T. butter
Juice of ½ lemon

Mix ingredients together in a heavy casserole. Cover tightly with foil and bake at 350° for 40-45 minutes.
Serves 8.

QUICK SAFFRON RICE

¼ c. onion, diced
2 T. butter
1/16 t. powdered saffron
1½ c. chicken stock
2 c. quick-cooking rice
½ t. salt

Cook onion in butter until soft but not brown. Add saffron and stock; mix well. Stir in rice and salt. Bring to a vigorous boil; cover and simmer 5 minutes or until rice is tender and all liquid is absorbed.
Serves 4.

Mrs. J. B. Griffith, Jr.

SPANISH RICE

c. uncooked rice
c. onion, chopped
T. bacon grease
No. 2 can tomatoes
t. salt
t. pepper
c. water
½ T. bottled meat sauce
c. green pepper, sliced

Sort rice but do not wash. Place rice, onion, and bacon grease in skillet and brown lightly over low heat. Stir frequently. When browned, add tomatoes, salt, pepper, and water. Cook slowly for 25 minutes, stirring occasionally, until all liquid is absorbed and rice is tender. Add meat sauce and sliced green pepper. Cook for 3 minutes.
Serves 8.

Mrs. Marion B. Solomon, 1948 Junior League
Cookbook

SUMMER DRESSING

. cooked rice
ggs, barely beaten
. milk
b. Velveeta cheese, grated
    parsley flakes
mall onion, chopped
. salt
. Wesson oil

Mix all ingredients and bake at 325° for 30 minutes or until set. Good with a baked hen or turkey in place of stuffing.
Serves 4-6.

Mrs. H. Dunlap Weichsel

WILD RICE WITH GRAPES

1 c. wild rice
2 T. bacon grease
1 10½-oz. can hot consommé
1 c. water
1 4-oz. can seedless white
    grapes, drained

Fry rice in bacon drippings until brown. Add hot consommé diluted with water. Place in casserole and bake at 350° for 45 minutes. Add grapes and continue cooking for 15 minutes or until rice has absorbed all liquid and is crusty on top. Serves 6.

Mrs. Tom Shartle, 1948 Junior League
Cookbook

WILD RICE WITH WALNUTS

Raw wild rice
Melted butter
Salt
Chopped walnuts

Wild rice is actually a grass seed and must never be boiled. Rather it is prepared by a soaking method such as the following.

Cover raw rice with boiling water. Place tightly fitting lid on the heavy pot holding the rice. Let stand 1 hour and pour off water. Repeat this process 3 more times, the last time allowing the rice to stand in the water for several hours or preferably overnight. Next, drain the rice in a colander for at least 2 hours before using in a recipe as you would cooked rice. Heat prepared rice in melted butter. Salt and add chopped walnuts. Stir and serve.

Geneva Ashby Jones

CHANDLER'S BARLEY PILAF

1¼ c. barley
3 T. butter
1 onion, chopped
3½ c. chicken broth
¼ c. slivered almonds
1 c. fresh mushrooms, sliced
2 T. butter
Salt and pepper to taste

Brown barley lightly in 3 T. butter. Add onion and sauté. Place in casserole with chicken broth. Cook at 325° for 1½ hours or until barley is cooked. Sauté almonds in 2 T. butter until slightly brown. Remove. Add mushrooms and sauté. Mix mushrooms and almonds with cooked barley. Can be made ahead and then warmed. Serves 8-10.

Cookbook Committee

SAUERKRAUT

20 lbs. cabbage
½ lb. Kosher salt
Caraway seeds, if desired

Wash, quarter, core and shred fully-matured cabbage. Thoroughly mix cabbage (20 lbs.) and salt. Firmly pack in a large crock. Cover cabbage with a heavy china plate or glass pie plate. Fill a large jar with water and use to hold plate under brine, which forms as salt draws juice from cabbage. Start curing in a temperature of about 85°. When fermentation starts, move to a cooler place (around 65-70°). Remove scum each day. It is ready to can in 2-4 weeks, when sauerkraut is yellow-white and free of white spots. Pack in hot sterile jars, leaving ½″ head space. If there is not enough juice to cover, add brine made by dissolving 2 T. salt in 1 qt. water. Add caraway seed in cured cabbage if desired. Seal and process pints and quarts 30 minutes in boiling water bath.
Makes 6 to 7 quarts.

Mrs. Leo F. Corrigan, Jr.

SPINACH AND ARTICHOKES au GRATIN

3-16 oz. jars marinated
  artichokes
3-10 oz. pkgs. frozen chopped
  spinach, thawed
3-3 oz. pkgs. cream cheese
4 T. soft butter or margarine
3 T. milk
1 c. grated Parmesan cheese

Drain artichokes. Save a few to use as garnish. Distribute the rest over the bottom of a shallow 1½ quart casserole. Squeeze as much moisture as possible from thawed spinach and arrange evenly over artichokes. Beat cream cheese and butter until smooth and fluffy. Gradually blend in milk. Spread this mixture over spinach. Sprinkle with Parmesan cheese (add more if needed). Bake uncovered at 350° for 40-45 minutes.
Serves 8.

Mrs. Mark Lemmon, Jr.

SPINACH FINGERS

2 pkgs. frozen chopped spinach
2 T. butter
4 oz. ricotta cheese
½ c. Parmesan cheese
1 egg yolk
Salt and pepper to taste
Dash of nutmeg
Flour
1 8 oz. can tomato sauce

Cook spinach according to package directions; drain and squeeze out moisture. Place in skillet with melted butter. Saute over medium heat until moisture has cooked away. Add ricotta, Parmesan cheese, egg yolk, salt and pepper, and nutmeg to spinach and mix well. Shape mixture into fingers, roll in flour and place on greased cookie sheet. Dribble tomato sauce over fingers before baking. Bake at 350° for 15-20 minutes.
Serves 6.

Mrs. James Lambert

JALAPENO SPINACH

2 pkgs. frozen chopped spinach
4 T. butter
2 T. flour
½ c. evaporated milk
2 T. onion, chopped
½ t. pepper
½ t. celery salt
½ t. garlic salt
½ t. salt
1 t. Worcestershire sauce
1 6-oz. pkg. Jalapeño cheese
Bread crumbs to cover

Cook spinach and drain well, saving liquid. Make sauce of butter, flour, milk, and ½ cup vegetable liquid. Add onion and seasonings. Cut cheese into pieces and stir into mixture until melted. Add spinach. Pour into greased 1 quart casserole and chill 6 hours or longer. Top with bread crumbs and bake for 30 minutes at 350°.
Serves 4-6.

Mrs. Floyd T. Burke

SPINACH SOUFFLE

1 lb. fresh spinach
1 onion
3 T. butter
3 T. flour
¼ t. salt
¼ t. pepper
Nutmeg, optional
1 c. thin cream or whole milk
3 egg yolks, beaten well
½ c. Parmesan cheese, grated
3 egg whites, beaten stiff
Crumbs, buttered and
    seasoned
Hollandaise or mushroom
    sauce

Prepare spinach in usual way, adding onion to water while cooking. Remove onion and drain spinach very dry. Put through a purée strainer; there should be 1 cup. Melt butter, add flour, salt, pepper, and nutmeg, if desired. Add gradually cream or milk, spinach pulp, and egg yolks. Fold in cheese and egg whites. Turn into a buttered baking dish; sprinkle with buttered, seasoned crumbs. Set in pan of hot water and bake 25 minutes at 350°. Serve with Hollandaise or mushroom sauce.
Serves 6.

Junior League Cookbook Committee, 19

QUICK SPINACH SOUFFLE

2 pkgs. Stauffer's Spinach
  Soufflé, thawed
2 T. onion, grated
1 large bud garlic, pressed
Lawry's Salt to taste
Artichoke hearts, cut in half
Parmesan cheese

Put the spinach in a buttered casserole and add remaining ingredients except cheese. Top with cheese and bake according to directions on the package. Can be fixed but not cooked early in the day.
Serves 4.

Mrs. John Lancaster III

SPINACH SUPREME

2 pkgs. frozen chopped spinach
3 T. butter
3 T. flour
1 t. salt
½ t. pepper
Juice of one lemon
2 eggs, beaten
1 c. freshly grated Parmesan
  cheese
Dash nutmeg
Flick cayenne pepper

Cook the spinach and drain, reserving 1½ c. of the liquid (you may add water if necessary). Make a sauce with the liquid, flour, butter, salt and pepper. When thick, remove from heat and add lemon juice and eggs. Put back on heat for a minute, stirring constantly. Remove from heat and add cheese, spinach, nutmeg and cayenne to the sauce. Pour into ring mold and bake 30 minutes at 350° or until set. Unmold and place buttered carrots in the center before serving. Can be made early in day, then baked for dinner.
Serves 8.

Mrs. Theodore P. Votteler

SORCI VERDI

2 pkgs. frozen chopped spinach
1 lb. ricotta cheese
1 egg
2 egg yolks
Pinch of nutmeg
Salt and freshly ground pepper
   to taste
½ c. freshly grated Parmesan
   cheese
4 T. melted butter

Cook spinach according to package directions. Drain and cool. Squeeze out all moisture by hand. Drain the ricotta and place in a mixing bowl with the spinach, egg and yolks, nutmeg, and salt and pepper. Mix well and chill in refrigerator. Half an hour before serving, bring a large kettle of salted water to a boil. Dust your hands with flour and form the spinach mixture into small balls the size and shape of a walnut or just a bit larger. Place in baking pan and bake at 350° for 30 minutes. After baking, sprinkle with grated Parmesan, pour the melted butter over them and serve immediately.
Serves 6.

Mrs. A. G. Hill, Jr.

SQUASH AU GRATIN

3 c. zucchini, sliced
3 c. yellow squash, sliced
6 T. butter
2 small onions, chopped
1 T. green pepper, chopped
1 T. pimento
1 t. paprika
1 t. oregano
½ pint sour cream
½ lb. cheddar cheese, grated
Salt and pepper to taste

Cook both kinds of squash in boiling water until it is done, but not mushy. Sauté onion and green pepper in butter. Add paprika and oregano. Heat sour cream and cheddar cheese in frying pan with onion and pepper, stirring to a sauce consistency. Do not boil. Strain *all* water off the squash and put in buttered casserole. Add pimentos to sauce and pour over the squash. Bake in 350° oven until bubbly.
Serves 6-8.

Mrs. Ralph Wood, Jr.

SQUASH CASSEROLE

1½ lb. yellow summer squash
½ c. butter
1 egg
½ onion, chopped
Salt and pepper to taste
6 Ritz crackers, crushed
¾ c. (2 wedges) Gruyère cheese, grated

Boil squash, drain and add butter. Beat egg and add. Add onion, salt, pepper, and crackers. Place mixture in a buttered casserole. Sprinkle grated cheese on top and bake at 350° until it bubbles around the edges (20-25 minutes).
Serves 6.

Mrs. Gifford O. Touchstone

YELLOW SQUASH CASSEROLE

4 medium-sized yellow squash, grated (should yield about 2-3 cups)
1 c. Ritz cracker crumbs (24 crackers)
2 eggs, slightly beaten
2 T. onion, grated
4 T. green pepper, chopped
1 t. salt
¼ t. pepper
½ c. milk
½ c. sour cream
1 c. Cheddar cheese, grated

Combine all ingredients and mix well. Check for seasonings. Bake in a 350° oven until set — about 35-40 minutes.
Serves 6.

Mrs. John W. McDonough

LOLA'S SQUASH

6 medium yellow squash, sliced
2 medium onions, sliced
½ cup butter
1 T. sugar
1 t. salt
Pepper to taste

Melt butter in large skillet. Add onions and squash. Sauté all ingredients in butter until soft but not mushy.
Serves 6-8.

Mrs. Searcy Ferguson, Jr.

SQUASH PUDDING

1 c. yellow squash, mashed
¾ c. milk
2 eggs
½ t. salt
¼ t. white pepper
2 t. sugar
2 t. cornstarch dissolved in 3 t. milk
4 c. Velveeta cheese

Put all ingredients into blender, blending until smooth. Pour into buttered 2 quart shallow casserole and bake at 350° for 30-45 minutes.
Serves 6-8.

Mrs. Denys Slater, Jr.

MOTHER'S SQUASH SOUFFLE

2 lbs. white or yellow squash
1 T. salt
½ lb. Longhorn cheese, grated
3 eggs
½ c. light cream
1½ t. salt

Boil squash with 1 T. salt until tender. Drain well and mash. Place in buttered casserole. Add cheese and mix well. Break eggs into mixture, beating with a fork. Add cream and 1½ t. salt mixing well. Bake at 350° for an hour or until set. It can be made ahead and refrigerated.
Serves 8. *Mrs. John A. Alexander*

STUFFED CREAMED SQUASH

3 medium yellow crookneck
  squash
1½ T. butter
2 T. flour
¼ t. salt
Dash of white pepper
½ c. milk
1 T. grated onion
4 slices cooked bacon
1 c. Cheddar cheese, grated
½ c. buttered bread crumbs
Dash of paprika

Boil whole squash until almost tender. Melt butter over low heat and add flour, salt and pepper. Stir until well blended and remove from heat. Gradually stir in milk and return to heat, stirring constantly until thick and smooth. Drain squash. Cut in half lengthwise and scoop out pulp. Mash and add white sauce, onion, 3 slices crumbled bacon and ½ c. cheese. Season to taste and fill shells. Sprinkle with bread crumbs, remaining slice of bacon crumbled, cheese and paprika. Place in a shallow baking dish with a small amount of water. Bake at 375° for 25-30 minutes or until browned. Serve immediately.
Serves 6.
Mrs. E. Don Rott

APPLE-FILLED SQUASH

3 acorn squash
2 T. butter, melted
1   1 lb. 2 oz. can pie-sliced
  apples
¾ c. brown sugar
1 t. lemon juice
¼ t. ground ginger
3 T. butter

Halve squash lengthwise and remove seeds. Brush with melted butter and sprinkle with a little salt. Place, cut-side down, in a large baking dish. Bake in a 350° oven for 35 minutes. Combine apples, brown sugar, lemon juice and ginger. Place squash cut-side up and fill centers with apple mixture. Dot with butter. Continue baking 25 minutes more, or until squash is tender. If desired, sprinkle with ground cinnamon before serving.
Serves 6.

Mrs. Harold W. Kimmerling

ACORN SQUASH STUFFED WITH VEGETABLES

Acorn squash
Carrots
Cauliflower
Green beans
Turnips
Green peppers
French dressing
Pickled green tomatoes

Boil acorn squash halves in water till tender. Steam desired vegetables for stuffing till tender but quite crisp. Marinate stuffing vegetables overnight in French dressing. Drain and fill squash and garnish with strips of the green tomatoes. Chill.

Cookbook Committee

SQUASH-GREEN CHILES CASSEROLE

1 8-oz. jar Cheese Whiz
1 large onion, chopped
1 4-oz. can whole-roasted green chiles
2 lbs. yellow squash
2 eggs

Wash, slice, and simmer squash until tender; drain. Sauté chopped onion in butter. Drain can of chiles and chop fine. Beat egg thoroughly. Mix squash that has been mashed with onions, green chiles, and beaten eggs. Put Cheese Whiz in bottom of 1-qt. casserole and put squash mixture on top. Bake in 350° oven for 30 minutes or until cheese comes to the top and bubbles and browns. After 15 minutes of baking, poke knife in casserole several times to help cheese come to the top. Can be made several hours ahead and cooked just before eating.

Mrs. Donald R. Howe

BAKED TOMATOES PARMESAN

4 large tomatoes
1 c. Hellman's mayonnaise
2 T. onion, chopped
4 T. Parmesan cheese
Fines herbes
Onion salt

Halve the tomatoes, sprinkle with onion salt and fines herbes, and warm in oven. Cool. Mix mayonnaise, onion and Parmesan cheese and spoon over tomatoes. Just before serving, place in 500° or 550° oven until puffed and lightly browned. Serves 8.

Mrs. Searcy Ferguson, Jr.

PIQUANT BROILED TOMATOES

Firm small tomatoes
Salt
Accent
Green onions, sliced thinly
Brown sugar
Bread crumbs
Butter

Slice off about a fourth of the stem end of tomato. Remove the core, taking out enough pulp to hold the filling. Salt and Accent each tomato, and put a layer of green onions in the cavity. Over this layer place about 1 T. brown sugar. Sprinkle a thick layer of bread crumbs over the top and place a pat of butter on each. Place in a baking dish and bake at 375° for 25-30 minutes, or until the tops bubble.

Mrs. Robert F. Zech

TOMATO PIE

9″ pie pastry
Tomatoes, firm, ripe, peeled
Salt and pepper
Sweet basil
½ c. Gruyère cheese (or Swiss), grated
Parmesan cheese
Butter

Prick pastry with a fork and bake at 400° until it starts to brown; let cool. Slice tomatoes in thick slices. Let drain on paper towels and sprinkle with salt, pepper, and basil. Cover bottom of pie crust with grated Gruyère. Place tomato slices on top of cheese. Put a generous amount of Parmesan cheese on top and dot with butter. Bake at 375° or 400° until cheeses are melted and crust is brown.
Serves 8.

Mrs. Bill Temple Spencer

SALSIFY-STUFFED TOMATOES

6 medium tomatoes
1 can miniature French carrots, drained
1 can salsify, drained
1 c. chicken broth
1 t. dill
Salt and pepper to taste
2 c. hollandaise sauce

Remove pulp of tomato, invert and drain for 20 minutes. Sauté carrots, salsify, and dill in chicken broth. Simmer 20 minutes. Salt and pepper insides of tomatoes. Drain liquid from carrot mixture and stuff into tomatoes, alternating carrots, and salsify into decorative designs. Bake at 300° for 20 minutes or until hot. Remove from oven. Before serving, pour hollandaise on the top of each tomato.
Serves 6.

Mrs. Denys Slater, Jr.

SOUFFLE IN TOMATO SHELLS
(Allow one whole tomato per person)

6 tomatoes
4 cloves
3 T. onion, grated
2-3 leaves basil
2 T. butter
2 T. flour
¾ c. hot milk or cream
3 eggs separated
Salt and pepper to taste
1 t. Cognac

TOMATO SOUFFLE. Cut a 1″ slice from the tops of the 6 tomatoes and scoop out the pulp. Save the pulp and set the tomato shells to drain, saving any further juice also. Simmer the pulp and the juice with the cloves, grated onion, and basil until reduced to slightly more than 1 cup. Put through a strainer, mashing so that you get everything but the seeds. Melt the butter, and stir in the flour. When smooth, add the hot milk or cream; and cook and stir until thick and smooth. Beat the egg yolks until light in color. Put a little of the hot cream sauce into the egg yolks, then a little more, and then the lot, stirring briskly between additions. Add the tomato purée, season to taste with salt and pepper, and add the Cognac. Cool. Beat the egg whites until stiff but not dry. Stir ¼ of the whites into the sauce; and then pour the sauce over the rest of the whites, folding in lightly. Cut the tiniest slice from the bottom of each tomato so that it may stand upright in the pan. Fill tomatoes ¾ full, place them in a shallow pan, and bake in a preheated 375° oven for 25-30 minutes. Surround with Mornay sauce, and season sauce with a little Worcestershire. Other vegetable Soufflés may be substituted if wished.

Cook Book Committee

ZUCCHINI STUFFING CASSEROLE

4 medium zucchini
¾ c. carrots, shredded
½ c. onion
6 T. butter
2¼ c. herbed croutons
1 can cream of chicken soup
½ c. sour cream

Cook zucchini and drain. Cook carrots and onion in 4 T. of the butter. Remove. Stir in 1½ c. of herbed croutons, soup, and sour cream. Stir in zucchini. Pour into 1½ quart casserole. Melt remaining butter. Put remaining croutons on top of casserole and pour butter over it. Bake at 350° for 30-40 minutes.
Serves 6-8.

Mrs. George T. Reynolds III

SEVRE ZUCCHINI CASSEROLE

6 medium zucchini squash —
   1½ lb.
3 T. butter
3 T. flour
2 c. canned or fresh tomatoes
1 small bell pepper, chopped
1 small onion, chopped
1 t. salt
1 T. brown sugar
½ bay leaf
2 whole cloves
½ c. cheddar cheese, grated
Parmesan cheese

Slice and place the zucchini in a buttered au gratin dish or casserole. Melt butter, blend in flour and add tomatoes. Add bell pepper and onion. Season with salt, brown sugar, bay leaf and cloves. Cook sauce 5 minutes. Remove bay leaf. Pour over zucchini, dot with butter and cover with grated cheese. Sprinkle with Parmesan cheese. Bake at 350° for 45 minutes.
Serves 6-8.

Mrs. Clint M. Josey

ZUCCHINI AND CHEESE CASSEROLE

3 c. zucchini, finely grated
1 c. cracker crumbs
1 c. Cheddar cheese, grated
2 eggs, beaten
2 T. onion, chopped

Combine all ingredients and put into a well-buttered 2-qt. casserole. Bake for 1 hour at 350°.
Serves 6.

Mrs. Yerger Hill III

ZUCCHINI CASSEROLE

Fresh zucchini, sliced
Fresh tomatoes, sliced
Fresh onions, sliced
Garlic salt
Salt and pepper to taste
New York State cheese, grated
Bacon, cooked and crumbled

Layer in a casserole zucchini, tomatoes and onions. Season each layer with garlic salt, salt and pepper. Top with cheese and sprinkle with bacon. Bake uncovered for 1 hour at 375°.

Mrs. M. Weatherby Carr

ZUCCHINI BEAUTIFUL

3 large zucchini
1 onion, chopped
1 lb. ground chuck
½ c. mushrooms
3 c. your favorite spaghetti
   sauce
1 lb. mozzarrella cheese, grated
Salt and pepper to taste

Parboil the zucchini until partially done and scoop out pulp. Mash and set aside. In a frying pan, sauté onion until tender. Add meat and cook until tender. Drain excess fat. Add squash pulp, mushrooms, and sauce; simmer 10 minutes. Pile meat mixture in zucchini case and place cheese on top. Cook in a 300° oven until heated and cheese melts.
Serves 6.

Mrs. Curtis Sanford, Jr.

ZUCCHINI MAISON

6 large zucchini squash
¼ c. onions, thinly sliced
4 T. olive oil
2 T. chopped parsley
2 large tomatoes, peeled and
   thinly sliced
Dash of salt and pepper to taste
Parmesan cheese

Wash and slice squash ½″ thick. Cook in salted water to cover until tender, about 5 minutes. Sauté onion in olive oil until yellow. Add parsley and remove from heat. Drain squash; put into casserole dish in layers with tomatoes and olive oil and onions. Sprinkle salt and pepper and cheese on top. Bake for 30 minutes at 375°.
Serves 4-6.

Mrs. Ray McKown

ZUCCHINI WITH SOUR CREAM

8 medium zucchini
½ c. sour cream
2 T. butter
2 heaping T. Old English
   cheese, grated
Salt and pepper
Paprika
1 T. chopped chives
Bread crumbs for topping
Cheese for topping

Slice zucchini into thin rounds — do not peel. Simmer zucchini in small amount of water, and cook until tender. Drain. Cool slightly. Combine sour cream, butter, cheese, salt, pepper and paprika. Stir over low heat to melt cheese. Remove from heat and mix in chives, add zucchini, tossing lightly to coat with sour cream mixture. Place in greased 1-qt. baking dish. Top with crumbs and dot with butter. Sprinkle with more grated cheese. Brown in 375° oven for about 10 minutes. If prepared in advance and refrigerated, increase baking time to 30 minutes.
Serves 4.

Mrs. Judy Weatherford

JAN'S STUFFED TOMATOES

1 pkg. frozen spinach
6 tomatoes
3 strips bacon
¼ c. onion, chopped
1 c. sour cream
Salt and pepper to taste
Tabasco
2 slices mozzarella cheese, chopped
Squares of mozzarella cheese

Blanch spinach and drain well. Shell tomatoes and chop insides finely. Drain shells well. Salt and drain upside down on paper towels. Cook bacon until crisp, drain and crumble. Save 2 T. drippings. Saute onion in drippings. Add onion and bacon to spinach and tomatoes. Add sour cream, salt, .pepper and Tabasco to taste. Stir. Add chopped cheese and let heat through. Fill shells with mixture. Top with squares of cheese. Heat in buttered pan until cheese on top is melted. May be made a day ahead.
Serves 6.

Mrs. W. Plack Carr, Jr.

TOMATO TIMBALES

4 eggs, well beaten
1 c. tomato juice
1 T. onion juice
Salt and pepper to taste
SAUCE:
1 No. 2 can tomatoes (2½ cups)
1 T. tomato paste
1 stalk celery, chopped
1 onion, chopped
1 whole clove
1 T. parsley, chopped
Salt and pepper
3 T. tomato catsup
Dash of Worcestershire sauce
4 T. butter
4 T. flour

TIMBALES: Add tomato juice, onion juice, salt and pepper to eggs. Fill greased custard cups ⅔ full with this mixture. Set in a pan of hot water. Bake at 325° for about 20 minutes, or until firm.

Serve with the following sauce: Simmer tomatoes, tomato paste, celery, onion, clove and parsley together for 15 minutes. Strain. Season with salt and pepper. Stir in catusp and Worcestershire. Melt butter, blend in flour, and add tomato mixture. Cook, stirring constantly, until thickened.
Serves 4 to 6.

Mrs. W. M. Lingo, Jr. — 1948
Junior League Cookbook

CAKES

BANANA NUT CAKE

2 c. flour, sifted
1 t. baking powder
½ t. salt
2 eggs
2 bananas, mashed
1 c. white sugar
1 c. light brown sugar, packed
½ c. butter
1 t. soda (dissolve in
   buttermilk)
¾ c. buttermilk
1 t. vanilla
½ c. nuts, chopped
ICING:
2 bananas, mashed
1 box powdered sugar
½ t. vanilla
1 stick butter
½ c. nuts

Mix all ingredients well in large bowl with a huge spoon. Oil a tube or Bundt pan (do not use Wesson Oil), pour mixture in and bake at 350° for about 1 hour. Then mix icing ingredients and pour over cake. Will freeze.

Mrs. John D. Carr

COFFEE CAKE

2½ c. sifted flour
¾ c. granulated sugar
1 c. light brown sugar (packed)
¾ c. salad oil
1 t. nutmeg
½ t. salt
1 egg
1 t. baking powder
1 c. buttermilk to which 1 t.
   soda has been added
1 c. broken pecans
2 t. cinnamon

Mix first six ingredients. Reserve ¾ c. for topping. Then add egg, baking powder, and buttermilk with soda and mix well. Pour into greased 12"x18" baking pan. Add pecans and cinnamon to reserved mixture and mix with hands; it will be crumbly. Sprinkle topping on batter in pans. Bake at 350° for 30-40 minutes. May be prepared ahead and frozen. Is good heated.
Serves 12-16.

Mrs. Tom Andrews

BEAUTIFUL FILLED ANGEL FOOD CAKE

1 cooked angel food cake
COFFEE FILLING:
1 large package of large
   marshmallows
1 c. perked coffee (hot or cold)
1 c. toasted almonds
3 c. cream, whipped
STRAWBERRY FILLING:
1 large pkg. large
   marshmallows
1 pkg. frozen strawberries —
   reserve juice
½ c. plain almonds
2 c. whipped cream

Remove cake from oven and turn upside down to cool 1 hour. When cool, remove from pan and freeze for about 2 hours. Slice into three layers and fill between layers and frost on top and sides with filling.

Coffee Filling, Put marshmallows and cup of coffee into top of double boiler over hot water and heat until melted. Remove from stove and set aside until well cooled. Add ½ c. almonds and fold in whipped cream. Fill cake and cover with ½ c. almonds. Put in refrigerator or freezer until set.

Strawberry Filling, Put juice from frozen strawberries and marshmallows into top of double boiler over hot water and heat until melted. Remove from stove and cool until very cool. Mix in strawberries, almonds, and cream. Fill cake and put in refrigerator or freezer until set.

Mrs. Joe B. Abbey

CHOCOLATE ANGEL FOOD CAKE

¾ c. sifted cake flour
¾ c. plus 2 T. sugar
¼ c. cocoa
1½ c. egg whites (about 12)
1½ t. cream of tartar
¼ t. salt
1½ t. vanilla
¾ c. sugar
CHOCOLATE FLUFF ICING:
1 c. sugar
¾ c. cocoa
⅛ t. salt
3 c. heavy cream

Preheat oven to 375°. Sift first three ingredients together 3 times. Beat until foamy egg whites, tartar, salt, and vanilla. With last ¾ cup of sugar, add 2 T. at a time, beating about 10 seconds after each addition. Continue beating until meringue is firm and holds stiff peaks when mixer is lifted out. Sift 3 T. flour mixture over meringue. Fold gently with wire whisk 8 to 10 strokes until flour mixture disappears, turning bowl after each addition or stroke. Repeat until all has been folded in. Scrape down sides of bowl with rubber scraper and fold 8-10 more strokes or until completely blended. Batter will be very thick. Then carefully push into ungreased 10-inch tube pan. Cut through batter 5 or 6 times with a knife. Level batter. Bake 30-35 minutes at 375° or until top springs back when lightly touched. Immediately turn upside down to cool, placing tube over neck of a bottle. Ice when cool.

For icing, mix all except cream in a chilled bowl. Stir in cream and whip to a spreading consistency. Split cooled cake crosswise into 3 even layers, and spread layers, top and sides with chocolate fluff. Store cake in the refrigerator.

Mrs. William W. Wigley

WHOLE WHEAT APPLE CAKE

1 c. cooking oil
1½ t. vanilla
2 eggs
½ c. honey
1 c. brown sugar
2⅓ c. whole wheat flour
1 t. baking soda
1 t. salt
1 t. cinnamon
½ c. walnuts, chopped
3 c. apples, peeled and diced

Combine oil, vanilla, eggs, honey, and sugar and mix well. Mix whole wheat flour with soda, salt, and cinnamon and add to oil and egg mixture. Stir in apples and nuts. Pour into a 9"x13" pan and bake at 325° for 40-50 minutes. Can be served with a hard sauce.

Mrs. Clint Josey, Jr.

APPLESAUCE CAKE

1 c. butter (2 sticks)
2 c. white sugar
2 eggs
3 c. flour
1½ t. nutmeg
1 T. cinnamon
1 t. salt
1 t. ground cloves
1 T. soda
2½ c. applesauce
2 T. corn syrup, white
1 c. pecans or walnuts,
   chopped

Cream butter and add sugar. Add unbeaten eggs one at a time, beat after each addition. Sift together flour, soda, and spices. Add flour mixture alternately with combined applesauce and syrup. Fold in nuts. Bake in well-greased angel food cake pan or Bundt pan for 1½ hours at 300 degrees. Cool and serve with whipped cream. (Can serve warm).

Mrs. Ray McKown

BUTTERMILK SPICE CAKE

¾ c. butter
¾ c. sugar
¾ c. brown sugar (packed)
3 eggs
1 t. vanilla
2¾ c. flour
2 T. baking powder
1 t. soda
½ t. cinnamon
½ t. nutmeg
¼ t. ground cloves
1¼ c. buttermilk
1 c. pecans or walnuts,
   chopped
ICING:
1 3-oz. pkg. cream cheese
¼ c. butter
1½ t. instant coffee
3 c. sifted powdered sugar

Cream butter and sugars. Add eggs and vanilla and beat 5 minutes at high speed. Sift dry ingredients together. Add to creamed mixture alternately with buttermilk. Stir in nuts. Pour batter into two greased and floured 9″ cake pans. Bake at 350° for 40 minutes. Cool and frost with icing.

For icing, cream cheese and butter. Blend in coffee and powdered sugar.

Mrs. Peter M. Tart

CARAMEL CAKE AND ICING

4 eggs, separated
1 c. butter
2½ c. flour
2 c. sugar
1 c. milk
2 heaping t. baking powder
1 t. vanilla
ICING:
2½ c. sugar
1 T. flour
1 c. milk
1½ c. sugar
½ c. cream
4 T. butter
1 t. vanilla
1-1½ c. chopped pecans

Cake: Beat whites. In another bowl cream butter, 1 T. flour, and sugar. Add egg yolks one at a time and then other ingredients. Last fold in the egg whites. Pour into 2 greased and floured 9" pans and bake at 325° for 40-45 minutes.

Icing, In a saucepan, bring to a slow boil 2½ c. sugar mixed with flour and milk. In a heavy iron skillet brown 1½ c. sugar until golden brown. Pour in boiling ingredients from saucepan to browned sugar and cook a few more minutes until it forms a soft ball in cold water. Remove from heat and add cream, butter, and vanilla and beat. Fold in pecans and spread on cake.

Mrs. David M. Lide, Jr.

CARROT CAKE

2 c. flour
2 c. sugar
4 eggs
3 c. carrots, grated
1 t. vanilla
1½ c. corn oil
2 t. cinnamon
½ t. salt
1 t. baking powder
2 t. baking soda
FROSTING:
1 c. chopped pecans
1 box powdered sugar
1 8-oz. pkg. cream cheese
1 stick butter, softened
1 t. vanilla

Mix all dry ingredients. Add oil, eggs, and vanilla and blend well. Bake in 3 9" pans at 350° for 30 minutes or until done. *For frosting,* cream cheese and butter. Add remaining ingredients and blend well. Add milk if necessary.

Mrs. Gary S. Utkov

RUM CAKE

½ c. pecans, chopped
1 pkg. butter cake mix
1 pkg. instant vanilla pudding
   (regular size)
½ c. light rum
½ c. water
½ c. salad oil
4 eggs
RUM GLAZE:
1 c. sugar
1 stick butter
¼ c. light rum
¼ c. water

Grease and flour bundt pan. Sprinkle nuts in bottom of pan. Mix cake mix, pudding, rum, water, oil, and eggs together. Mix for 2 minutes. Pour into bundt pan. Bake at 325° for 50-60 minutes. Remove cake and immediately pour on hot glaze.

For glaze, place ingredients in a saucepan and boil for 2-3 minutes.

Mrs. T. M. "Mack" Strother

CREAMY CHEESECAKE WITH BLUEBERRY TOPPING

CRUST:
16 graham crackers, crushed
2 T. sugar
6 T. melted butter
1½ t. cinnamon
CHEESECAKE:
3 8-oz. pkgs. cream cheese
3 eggs
1 c. sugar
1½ pts. sour cream
3 T. sugar
TOPPING:
1 16-oz. can blueberries
¼ c. + 2 T. corn starch
Juice from blueberries plus
   enough water to make one
   cup
1 c. sugar

For the crust, mix all ingredients and press into a springform pie pan. Refrigerate until ready to fill. For the cheesecake, beat cream cheese until soft. Beat eggs until fluffy in another bowl. Add sugar to eggs gradually. Beat until pale yellow color and silky smooth consistency — about 10 minutes. Combine cheese mixtures and mix thoroughly. Pour into crust and bake 20 minutes at 375°. Take out of oven and, while hot, pour 1½ pints sour cream mixed with 3 T. sugar over top. Run in 500° oven 5 minutes (put cookie sheet under).

For the topping, make a paste of corn starch and 2 T. of the juice. Add the rest of the juice and sugar. Cook until thick, about 10 minutes, on medium heat. After juice cools, add berries. Spoon carefully on top of cheesecake and chill overnight.

Mrs. James B. Francis

OLD-FASHIONED CHOCOLATE CAKE

1 stick butter
4 T. cocoa
¼ c. shortening
1 c. water
2 c. flour
2 c. sugar
3 eggs
½ c. buttermilk
1 t. baking soda
1 t. vanilla
ICING:
1 stick butter
4 T. cocoa
½ c. evaporated milk
1-lb. box powdered sugar
3-oz. cream cheese, softened
1 c. pecans
1 t. vanilla

In a saucepan put butter, cocoa, shortening, and water and bring to a boil. Pour over the sifted flour and sugar. Add eggs, buttermilk, baking soda, and vanilla and beat well. Grease and flour the bottom of a 9"x12" pan and bake at 350° for 40 minutes.

For icing, bring butter, milk, and cocoa to a boil. Sift powdered sugar and pour liquid over it. Beat with cream cheese. Add pecans and vanilla and pour over hot cake.

Mrs. Searcy Ferguson, Jr.

ENGLISH CLOVE CAKE

1 c. butter
2¼ c. sugar
6 eggs, well-beaten
3½ c. flour
1 T. ground cloves
1 T. ground cinnamon
1 t. baking soda
Pinch of salt
1 c. buttermilk
Sifted confectioners sugar

Cream butter until smooth; gradually add sugar and continue beating until blended. Add eggs and mix thoroughly. Sift dry ingredients together and add to above mixture alternately with buttermilk. Pour into an oiled 10" tube pan and bake at 350° for 50-60 minutes. Invert cake over a wire rack and remove pan. When cake is almost cool, sprinkle with confectioners sugar.

Cookbook Committee

MAMA'S FIG PRESERVE CAKE

2½ c. sugar
¾ c. margarine
4 eggs
3 c. flour
1 t. soda
1 c. buttermilk
1 t. each cloves, nutmeg, cinnamon, vanilla
2 c. fig preserves
1 c. pecans, chopped
Pinch salt

Cream sugar and margarine; add eggs, one at a time, beating well after each addition. Sift dry ingredients and add to creamed mixture with buttermilk. Add vanilla, nuts, and preserves. Pour into a greased bundt pan and bake at 325° for about 1 hour 20 minutes or until done.

Mrs. Peter M. Tart

HAZEL'S FRESH COCONUT CAKE

2 c. sugar
1 c. butter
5 eggs
3 c. flour
3 t. baking powder
⅔ c. milk
¼ c. orange juice
½ t. orange peel
1 t. vanilla
FROSTING
1 c. sugar
½ c. water
½ t. cream of tartar
Pinch of salt
2 egg whites, stiffly beaten
Grated fresh coconut

Cream sugar and butter. Add eggs one at a time and mix well. Sift flour with baking powder and add alternately with milk. Blend in orange juice, orange peel, and vanilla. Bake at 350° for 35-40 minutes in 2 round pans. Cool and frost.
For frosting, boil sugar, water, cream of tartar, and salt until it spins a thread. Beat egg whites into the mixture. Add freshly grated coconut.

Mrs. Mark Lemmon, Jr.

½ stick butter, softened
2 c. sugar
2 eggs
1½ c. milk
Pinch of salt
2 c. flour
2 t. baking powder
3 1-oz. squares bitter chocolate
2 t. vanilla
FILLING:
1 6-oz. pkg. semi-sweet
    chocolate bits
¼ stick butter
3 T. light cream
Pinch of salt
4 T. powdered sugar
1 t. vanilla
1 c. toasted, chopped pecans
ICING:
2 egg whites
1½ c. sugar
½ c. water
Pinch of salt
1½ c. miniature marshmallows
2 t. baking powder
1 t. vanilla
1 t. almond flavoring

BIRTHDAY SURPRISE CHOCOLATE CAKE

Set chocolate in a Pyrex custard cup, put cup in a pan of warm water and let chocolate melt. Do not let water boil. When butter is soft, cream it with a large spoon. Cream in sugar and vanilla. Add eggs one at a time, beating well after each addition. Sift flour, salt, and baking powder, and add alternately with milk. Stir well; add meltechocolate that is still warm. Prepare 2 cake pans, either round or square, by greasing them lightly with salad oil and covering the bottoms with pieces of waxed paper cut to fit. Grease the waxed paper by pressing it down in the greased pan and then turning it over so that the greased side is on top. Put batter in pans and bake in a preheated 350° oven until the centers are just barely done when tested. This will take about 25-30 minutes. Run a knife around the edges, invert cakes on racks covered with waxed paper, remove the bottom paper and let cool.

For the filling, put everything but the pecans in the top of a double boiler and let it heat to melt butter and chocolate. Stir often. When completely blended, add pecans and let cool before spreading between layers.

For icing, put egg whites, water, sugar and salt in the top of a large double boiler. When water in bottom pan is boiling, set the top pan on it and begin beating. Beat continually. When the mixture turns white and is warm begin adding the marshmallows, a few at a time, until all have been melted and absorbed. Add baking powder and flavorings and beat until well mixed. If points will remain when raising the beater, the icing is done. Remove from heat and let cool. Taste when cool. If it tastes grainy, it was cooked a bit too long. But do not panic. Add 2 T. boiling water and beat again. The grains should disappear. Spread on top and sides of cake.

For garnish, sprinkle with freshly grated coconut. Or you can melt 2 squares bitter chocolate with 1 T. butter in the top of a double boiler. Spread this over the icing after it has set for an hour or so. Sprinkle toasted, chopped pecans on top. Though this cake is time consuming what a lovely treat for a special birthday.

Mrs. L. G. Pondrom

CHOCOLATE ROLL:
⅓ c. flour
⅓ c. cocoa
½ t. baking powder
Pinch of salt
¾ c. sugar
4 eggs, separated
1 t. vanilla

STRAWBERRY FILLING:
1 10-oz. pkg. frozen
    strawberries, thawed
¼ c. sugar
¼ c. cornstarch
¼ c. light cream
Pinch of salt
1 pt. whipping cream

CHOCOLATE STRAWBERRY ROLL

Sift together flour, cocoa, baking powder, and salt. Beat egg whites until very stiff. Gradually fold in sugar. Add well-beaten yolks. Fold into flour mixture and add vanilla. Line a cookie sheet (with low sides) with greased waxed paper. Spread batter on paper and bake at 400° for 12 minutes. Do not overcook. Sprinkle powdered sugar on waxed paper. Turn the roll out on this, remove the baking paper and trim edges with a sharp knife. Roll while still warm on sugared paper. Cool. When roll is cold, fill with strawberry filling.

For filling, mix sugar and cornstarch in a heavy pan. Set a strainer over this pan and put strawberries in this pan, leaving them there until all juice has drained into the pan. Set strainer aside, add light cream to liquid and cook the sauce, stirring constantly until very thick. Add strawberries, put in a bowl and chill. Whip half of the cream and fold it into the chilled berries. Gently unroll the cake. Spread the strawberry mixture over it and roll up again, on a serving plate. About an hour before serving time, whip the other half of the cream and cover the roll with it.

For garnish, some plump fresh strawberries dipped in powdered sugar, chopped toasted pecans or almond slivers, or tiny chocolate bits.
Serves 8-10.

Mrs. L. G. Pondrom

FRENCH COFFEE CAKE

½ c. butter
½ c. margarine or Crisco
1½ c. sugar
5 eggs
1 t. vanilla
3 c. flour
2 t. baking powder
1 t. baking soda
1 c. sour cream
STREUSEL:
1 t. cinnamon
½ c. sugar
2 squares baking chocolate,
   grated

Cream butter, shortening, and sugar. Add eggs, one at a time, beating well after each one. Add vanilla. Sift dry ingredients and add them alternately with sour cream to above mixture and beat well. Mix together streusel ingredients. Put half of batter into greased 10″ tube pan. Sprinkle half of streusel over batter. Pour rest of batter on top and sprinkle with rest of streusel. Run knife around to marbleize. Bake 55 minutes in preheated 350° oven. Turn upside down on plate. May be frozen.
Serves 12-16.

Mrs. David Kelly

KITTY'S FRUIT CAKE

8 oz. candied cherries, chopped
8 oz. candied pineapple,
   chopped
16 oz. dates, chopped
6 c. pecans, chopped
2 cans Eagle Brand Milk
2 — 3½ oz. cans coconut

Mix all ingredients with hands. Set for 1 hour. Mix again. Pack into tube pan or two loaf pans. Bake 1½ hours at 275° or till firm and brown. Can be divided into smaller loaf pans with baking time lowered accordingly. Can be frozen.

Mrs. M. Weatherby Carr

ITALIAN CREAM CAKE

2 c. sugar
1 stick butter
½ c. shortening
5 egg yolks, beaten
2 c. flour, sifted then measured
1 c. buttermilk
1 t. soda, mixed with milk
1 c. coconut
5 egg whites, beaten
ICING:
1 8-oz. pkg. cream cheese
1 stick butter
1 1-lb. box powdered sugar
1 t. vanilla
1 c. chopped pecans

For cake, cream sugar, butter and shortening. Add egg yolks, flour and buttermilk, alternating the latter two. Add coconut.Fold in egg whites. Cook at 350° for 25 minutes in 3 round layer pans.
For icing, combine all ingredients and ice when cool.

Mrs. Roy A. Kull

AUNT BETTY'S DEVILS FOOD CAKE

9 T. butter, softened
¾ c. white sugar
½ c. light brown sugar, packed
1 c. sifted cake flour
¾ c. sifted regular flour
2 eggs
1 t. vanilla
¼ t. salt
1 t. soda
1 c. buttermilk
½ oz. unsweetened chocolate, melted
ICING:
5 egg whites at room temperature
1 c. boiling water
2 c. sugar
1 t. vanilla

For cake, cream butter and sugars together until light and fluffy. Sift dry ingredients together 3 times. Add vanilla and chocolate to butter mixture. Add eggs one at a time quickly. Alternately, add dry ingredients and buttermilk to butter mixture as quickly as you can — do not overbeat. Pour batter into two 8″ diameter cake pans which have been greased and floured. Bake at 350° for 25-30 minutes. Cool on racks.

For icing, put sugar and boiling water in heavy saucepan. Don't stir after it has dissolved. Cook until it spins a heavy hair. Remove from heat. Beat egg whites until stiff and dry. At medium speed on mixer, slowly pour sugar syrup into whites, scraping sides of bowl often. Add vanilla, and beat at high speed until very stiff. Spread on cake.

Mrs. George E. Seay, Jr.

DIVINE DEVIL'S FOOD CAKE

BATTER:
2½ c. sugar
1 c. butter
1 c. buttermilk
1 t. soda (dissolved in milk)
5 eggs, separated
2½ c. flour (measure before sifting)
4 oz. chocolate, melted
2 t. vanilla
FILLING:
1½ c. milk
½ c. sugar
3 egg yolks
2 oz. chocolate
2 heaping T. flour (more if necessary to make thick)
1 t. vanilla
ICING:
2½ c. sugar
1 c. whole milk
4 oz. chocolate
½ t. soda
Small piece butter
2 t. vanilla
Salt

For batter, cream butter and sugar together well. Add yolks which have been well-beaten. Add buttermilk and flour alternately. When thoroughly mixed, add melted chocolate and vanilla. Fold in well-beaten whites. Bake in 2 9x13 inch layers about 20-30 minutes at 350°.

For filling, melt chocolate in the top of a double boiler. Heat milk and pour into chocolate. Add well-beaten yolks, sugar and flour, mix well together. Add butter, vanilla, and a pinch of salt. Cool thoroughly and spread between layers.

For the icing, mix well the sugar, milk, grated chocolate, soda, and salt. Boil until it forms soft ball in cold water. Add butter and vanilla, and beat until right consistency to spread on cake.

Mrs. Julius Runge

EGGNOG CAKE

BATTER:
1 c. butter
2 c. sugar
8 egg whites
3¼ c. flour
1 c. milk
1 level T. baking powder
1 t. vanilla

FILLING:
1 c. sugar
½ c. butter
8 egg yolks
1 heaping T. flour
4 oz. whiskey
1 c. chopped pecans
1 c. raisins
1 c. coconut

ICING:
2 c. sugar
½ c. water
½ t. cream of tartar
2 egg whites
1 t. vanilla

For batter, cream butter and sugar until smooth. Add flour with baking powder well mixed. With last cup of flour add alternately with milk. Add vanilla and fold in well-beaten whites. Grease and flour 2 9" cake pans and bake for 30 minutes at 350°.

For filling, cream butter, sugar, and flour. Add to the well-beaten egg yolks. Cook mixture in the top of a double boiler until thick enough to cut. Cool thoroughly and add whiskey, pecans, raisins, and coconut. Spread between layers.

For icing, cook sugar, water, and cream of tartar until it ropes. Whip into well-beaten egg whites. Add vanilla and beat until cool enough to place on cake. This cake tastes like cakes used to taste — and well worth the time.

Mrs. Julius Runge

PINEAPPLE UPSIDE DOWN CAKE

1 c. sugar
6 T. hot milk
2 egg yolks, well beaten
1 generous c. flour, sifted
1 t. vanilla
2 egg whites, beaten stiff
½ c. butter
1 c. brown sugar
5 slices pineapple
¼ c. pecans, chopped

Gradually add ½ c. of the sugar and milk to the egg yolks. Beat well. Mix in the remaining ½ c. sugar, flour and vanilla thoroughly. Fold in egg whites. Melt butter in a large skillet. Add brown sugar and blend well. Arrange pineapple and nuts in a symmetrical pattern on the butter and sugar. Cover pineapple with batter. Bake at 350°F. for 25 to 30 minutes, or until done. Invert immediately onto a serving dish.
Serves 8.

Mrs. W. T. Slaton, 1948
Junior League Cookbook

MINCE MEAT UPSIDE DOWN CAKE WITH HOT RUM SAUCE

CAKE PAN:
½ stick butter
½ c. sugar
1 c. pecans, chopped
¼ c. rum
1 lb. jar prepared mince meat

CAKE BATTER:
1 stick butter
1 c. sugar
2 eggs
1 t. vanilla
2 c. flour
Pinch of salt
2 t. baking powder
1 c. milk

RUM SAUCE:
½ stick butter
¼ c. flour
¾ c. sugar
Pinch of salt
1 pt. whipping cream
½ c. rum

Set out butter for batter to soften in large mixing bowl. While that is taking place, prepare the pan. Of course, this cake can be baked in a 9″ cake pan, but there will be a better crust on it if it is baked in a 9″ heavy iron skillet whose handle will withstand the heat of the oven.

For the pan: melt the butter in the skillet. Scatter the sugar around the bottom of the pan and then distribute the pecans. Mix rum with mince meat and dab it around the bottom of the pan as evenly as possible. The pan is now ready for the cake batter.

Cake batter: When butter is soft, cream it in mixer. Add sugar at low speed, cream well, turn speed up and add eggs one at a time. Add vanilla. Mix again. Sift flour, salt, and baking powder together. Add this mixture alternately with milk, turning mixer to lowest speed, always, when adding flour. Pour batter in prepared skillet. Bake at 350°F. until the middle tests done. Run a spatula around cake, scraping the bottom of the skillet carefully. Put a cookie sheet or a serving plate over the top of the skillet, with pot-holders in both hands, and invert. Cake should drop out nicely. It is best served hot, but it can be kept warm, covered with foil, if not served immediately.

Rum sauce: Melt butter in a heavy pan. Blend in flour. Add sugar, salt and whipping cream. Cook slowly, stirring constantly, until sauce thickens. Add rum. Taste and see if it needs more sugar or rum. Keep hot over warm water, if necessary, uncovered. Serve over slices of cake.

Suggested substitutions: Canned pineapple or apricots can be substituted for the mince meat, everything else remaining the same, except that the ¼ c. rum in the mince meat is omitted.

Serves 8-10.

Mrs. L. G. Pondrom

SHORT CAKE

1 c. flour
2 T. butter
1 t. baking powder, rounded
1 egg
1 t. sugar
1 T. milk
Fruit
Whipped cream

Mix all ingredients. Divide dough in half, roll thin, and cut into rounds. Spread half the rounds lightly with butter. Stack an unbuttered round on a buttered round. Bake at 425° for 12 min. Split. Put fruit or berries between rounds and top with whipped cream.

Serves 6.

Mrs. George Dexter, 1924 Junior League
Cookbook

FUNNEL CAKES

2 beaten eggs
1½ c. milk
2 c. sifted flour
1 t. baking powder
½ t. salt
2 c. cooking oil
Sifted confectioners sugar

In a bowl combine eggs and milk. Sift together flour, baking powder, and salt. Add to egg mixture. Beat until smooth. Test to see if mixture flows easily through a funnel. If too thick, add milk; if too thin, add flour. In an 8" skillet, heat oil to 360°. Cover bottom opening of funnel with finger and pour a generous ½ cup batter into funnel. Remove finger and release batter into hot oil in spiral shapes, initials, etc. Fry until golden brown, about 3 minutes. Using a wide spatula and tongs, turn carefully and cook 1 minute more. Drain on paper towels and sprinkle with sifted confectioners sugar. Serve hot with syrup.
Serves 4-6.

Mrs. Ben D. Jenkins

HERSHEY BAR CAKE

8 plain Hershey bars
2 sticks melted butter
2 c. sugar
4 eggs
1 c. buttermilk
2½ c. sifted flour
2 t. baking powder
2 t. vanilla
1 c. Angel Flake coconut
1 c. chopped pecans
GLAZE:
½ plain Hershey bar
1 T. butter
½ c. powdered sugar
2 T. milk

Melt Hershey bars in melted butter. Cool, then add sugar. Add eggs, one at a time, mixing well after each addition. Add buttermilk. Sift flour and baking powder together and mix a small amount at a time with above mixture. Add vanilla, coconut, and pecans. Bake in a tube or bundt pan for 1 hour 15 minutes at 325°.

For Glaze, melt the Hershey bar in butter. Add powdered sugar and milk. Stir over low heat until smooth. Pour over cooled cake.

Mrs. James M. Hudnall, III

MISSISSIPPI MUD

2 sticks butter
2 c. sugar
4 eggs
2 T. cocoa
2 t. vanilla
1½ c. flour
1⅓ c. coconut (4 oz.)
1½ c. chopped nuts
1 large jar marshmallow cream
FROSTING:
1 1 lb. box powdered sugar
1 stick butter
½ c. evaporated milk
⅓ c. cocoa
1 t. vanilla

Cream butter and sugar. Add eggs, cocoa, and vanilla. Then add flour, mixing well. Fold in coconut and nuts. Bake in greased and floured 9"x13" pan at 350° for 30-40 minutes. Spread with marshmallow cream and let cool. Then frost. Mix all frosting ingredients and beat until smooth. Spread over top of brownies and marshmallow cream. Cut into 1" to 1½" squares.
Makes 4-5 dozen.

Mrs. Larry M. Nobles

CHRISTMAS NUT CAKE
(A 4-generation family recipe)

½ lb. butter
1 lb. flour (approx. 4 c.)
1 jigger brandy
1 lb. pecans
1 nutmeg, grated
2 c. sugar
6 eggs
¼ t. salt
½ lb. seeded raisins

Before starting cake, salt and flour nut meats and raisins. Cream sugar and butter; add eggs, one at a time, and beat well after each addition. Add a little flour. Continue adding one egg and flour until all six eggs and all the flour are used. Then add brandy, floured nuts, raisins, and grated nutmeg. Bake at 300° for about an hour or until done.

Mrs. Mark Lemmon, Sr.

WHIPPING CREAM POUND CAKE

2 sticks butter
3. c. sugar
6 eggs
1 t. vanilla
1 t. lemon extract
3 c. flour
Pinch salt
½ pint heavy cream, whipped

Cream butter and sugar. Add eggs, one at a time, beating well after each addition. Add flavorings. Then slowly blend in flour and salt. Beat cream and fold into mixture. Bake in a lightly greased and floured tube pan or two loaf pans. If tube pan is used, do not fill more than two thirds full. Place cake in a *cold* oven; then turn thermostat to 325°. For the tube pan, bake for 1 hour and 30 minutes. The loaf pans take about 1 hour and 20 minutes.

Mrs. E. Don Rott

LEMON AND ORANGE POUND CAKE

2 sticks butter, softened
2 c. sugar
6 eggs, room temperature
2 c. flour
Juice of 1 large orange
1 t. almond extract
1 t. lemon extract
ICING:
Juice of 1 lemon
1 t. grated lemon peel
2 T. orange juice
1 c. powdered sugar
3-4 jiggers Cointreau

Cream butter, add sugar and cream again. Add eggs, one at a time, mixing well after each addition. At lowest speed, add flour gradually. When all is added, turn to medium speed and beat for 10 minutes. Add 2 T. orange juice and both extracts. Pour mixture into a greased and floured Bundt pan. Bake in a pre-heated oven of 350° for about 1 hour. For the first 30 minutes of cooking put a pan of water under the cake. Let cake cook in the pan on a rack for 20 minutes. Turn out and ice while still hot.

For icing, combine all ingredients except Cointreau, adding more sugar if needed for thickness. Sprinkle liquor over cake then spread icing over warm cake. Keep covered — wait a few hours to serve.

Mrs. L. G. Pondrom

PRUNE CAKE

2 c. sugar
2 c. cake flour
2 t. baking powder
1 t. soda
1 t. nutmeg
1 t. ground cloves
2 t. cinnamon
1¼ t. allspice
1 c. cooking oil
1 c. buttermilk
3 eggs
1 t. vanilla
1 c. chopped prunes
1 c. chopped pecans
ICING:
2 c. sugar
1 c. buttermilk
1 t. soda
5 T. butter
2 t. maple syrup

For cake, stir and mix first 8 ingredients. Add oil, buttermilk, then eggs one at a time, and vanilla. Mix well. Add chopped prunes and nuts. Mix well. Turn into tube pan and bake at 325° for 1 hour or until done.

For icing, mix soda with buttermilk. Combine all ingredients in a heavy saucepan and boil slowly, stirring occasionally. Cook for 30 minutes while cake is baking. Remove cake from oven when cooked. Pour hot icing over cake. Jab holes in cake so icing will seep through cake. A rich delicious cake which keeps for a long time providing it isn't eaten in one day.

Mrs. Fulton Murray, Jr.

SAWNIE'S CHOCOLATE MINT ROLL

6 eggs, separated, room
   temperature
½ t. cream of tartar
1 c. sugar
1½ t. vanilla
¼ c. cocoa
¼ c. flour
½ t. salt
CREAM MIXTURE:
2 c. whipping cream
¼ c. sugar
1 t. peppermint extract
**SAWNIE'S CHOCOLATE
   MINT SAUCE:**
4 oz. German chocolate
½ c. boiling water
2 c. sugar
¼ stick butter
7 oz. evaporated milk
1½ t. peppermint extract

Cream ½ cup of sugar and egg yolks; add vanilla and sift in dry ingredients. Beat egg whites until stiff and slowly add ½ cup of sugar. Fold in egg white mixture. Line a 15"x12" cookie sheet with foil. Grease foil and sides of pan with butter. Pour in batter and bake at 325° for 25 minutes. When done, turn out on a tea towel which has been covered with powdered sugar. Peel off foil and roll up as in a jelly roll. Let cool for about ½ hour. Unroll and fill with whipped cream mixture (see recipe for this.) Serve with chocolate mint sauce. For a special occasion put some of the whipped cream mixture in a pastry tube and decorate accordingly and sprinkle with shaved chocolate.

For cream mixture beat ingredients to desired consistency — fairly thick. For mint sauce place chocolate and water in the top of a double boiler. Add sugar and cook until it dissolves. Add remaining ingredients and cook until sauce is smooth. This sauce can be put on almost any dessert and will be a favorite.
Serves 8.

Mrs. Searcy M. Ferguson, Jr.

SQUASH CAKE

½ c. shortening
1 c. brown sugar
1 c. white sugar
2 eggs, beaten
1 c. cooked yellow squash
3 c. cake flour
4 t. baking powder
½ t. soda
½ c. milk
1 c. black walnuts, chopped
1 t. maple or vanilla extract

Cream shortening and slowly add sugars, beaten eggs, and cooked squash. Sift together flour, baking powder, and soda and add alternately to creamed mixture with milk. Add chopped nuts and extract. Pour into 3 wax paper lined 8" layer pans. Bake 30 minutes at 350°. Cool and ice with Harvest Moon Caramel Seven Minute Frosting.

Cookbook Committee

CARAMEL SEVEN MINUTE FROSTING

3 egg whites
1¼ c. brown sugar
Dash salt
⅜ c. water
1 t. vanilla

In top of double boiler combine egg whites, sugar, salt, and water. Beat well with rotary or electric beater. Place over rapidly boiling water and cook seven minutes, beating constantly or until frosting stands in peaks. Remove from water, add vanilla and beat until thick enough to spread.

Cookbook Committee

SIMPLE CHOCOLATE FUDGE ICING

1 egg white
1½-2 c. powdered sugar
1 T. butter, melted
1-2 T. heavy cream
2 squares unsweetened
   chocolate, melted

Beat egg white until stiff. Add powdered sugar until thick. Add chocolate and butter, then more sugar. Add cream and more powdered sugar to attain desired consistency. Do not make too stiff. Covers two cake layers.

Mrs. T. V. Murray, Jr.

WHITE CAKE AND ICING

1 c. butter
2 c. sugar
8 egg whites or 4 whole eggs
Pinch of salt
3 c. flour
3 t. baking powder
1 c. milk
1 t. lemon or vanilla extract
ICING:
3 egg whites
¾ c. light corn syrup
¾ c. sugar
1½ T. water
Coconut, freshly grated
   (optional)

Have all ingredients at room temperature. Cream butter and sugar, adding sugar gradually. Put eggs in one at a time if using whole eggs. If using whites, beat separately, adding salt. Beat mixture stiffly and set aside. Sift flour 6 times and measure after sifting. Mix flour and baking powder, milk and vanilla alternately into the creamed mixture, adding flour last. If egg whites are used, fold in last. Oil and flour two 8" cake pans and bake at 350° for 45-50 minutes. Or use greased loaf pans and bake at 325° 40-45 minutes.

For icing, combine egg whites, syrup, sugar, and water in the top of a double boiler. Cook over rapidly boiling water while beating. When icing will stand in peaks, remove from fire. Ice cake and sprinkle with coconut.

Mrs. Trammel Crow

COOKIES

APRICOT BALLS

1 lb. dried apricots
1 medium-sized orange
2 c. sugar
1 c. coconut, shredded
Powdered sugar to cover

Grind together apricots and whole orange (including peel) in the fine part of a meat grinder or Cuisenart. Add sugar and cook in a double boiler over boiling water until sugar is dissolved. Add shredded coconut. Remove from heat and set aside to cool. When well cooled, with buttered fingers, roll apricot mixture into balls about the size of a small walnut. Then roll in powdered sugar until the balls are well covered. Store in refrigerator in tightly closed container until ready to use. Before serving, re-roll in powdered sugar.
Recipe yields about 75 apricot balls.

Mrs. John W. McDonough

BEACON HILL COOKIES

1 c. (6 oz.) semi-sweet chocolate
 chips
2 egg whites
Dash of salt
½ c. granulated sugar
½ t. vinegar
½ t. vanilla

In the top of a double boiler melt chocolate chips over hot water. Beat egg whites with salt until foamy. Gradually beat in sugar. Continue beating until stiff peaks form. Beat in vinegar and vanilla and fold in melted chocolate. Drop by teaspoonfuls on greased baking sheets and bake 10 minutes at 350°. (Cookies will be crisp, chewy, and come out of the oven slightly cracked.
Makes 4-5 dozen.

Mrs. John H. Bissell

CHOCOLATE TURTLES

1 c. brown sugar
2 squares semi-sweet
 chocolate, melted
1 c. flour
¼ c. butter, melted
1 egg
½ lb. whole pecans

Mix all the ingredients except the pecans. For each cookie, place 4 whole pecans on the greased cookie sheet, drop a teaspoon of the dough on pecans. Bake for 10-12 minutes in 350° oven.
Makes 24.

Mrs. Theodore P. Votteler

FORGOTTEN CHOCOLATE KISSES

3 egg whites
½ t. cream of tartar
1 c. fine granulated sugar
2 T. unsweetened cocoa
    powder
1 c. pecans
½ t. vanilla

Beat egg whites in a small bowl with mixer until foamy. Add cream of tartar and beat until soft peaks are formed. Gradually beat in sugar. Fold in cocoa 1 T. at a time. Fold in nuts and vanilla. Use level teaspoon to drop meringue mixture on nonstick or ungreased cookie sheet. Place in a 350° oven and immediately turn off oven. Forget until the next morning or at least 8 hours later. Don't peek! Makes about 2 dozen.

Mrs. George Wilkin, Jr.

CHOCOLATE MINT SQUARES

½ c. butter
1 c. sugar
2 eggs
½ t. peppermint extract
2 squares sweetened chocolate,
    melted
½ c. flour
ICING:
1 c. powdered sugar
2 T. butter
1 T. cream
½ t. peppermint extract
2 squares chocolate, melted
½ c. toasted almonds, slivered

Cream butter and sugar. Beat in eggs. Blend in chocolate and peppermint. Stir in flour. Bake in 8"x8" pan for 30 minutes in 350° oven. Cool.

For icing, combine ingredients and spread on top. Sprinkle with slivered, toasted almonds.

Makes 12 squares. Doubles easily.

Mrs. Searcy Ferguson, Jr.

BLENDER LACE COOKIES

1¼ c. quick-cooking oatmeal
1½ c. brown sugar, firmly
    packed
1 egg
1½ t. vanilla
½ t. salt
1⅓ c. butter, melted

Place oatmeal in a blender. Combine all the remaining ingredients; place in blender and blend until smooth. Drop by teaspoonful on greased cookie sheets 3" apart. Bake 14 minutes at 350°. Remove from sheets after 2 minutes while still warm. Store in airtight container. Makes about 4 dozen.

Mrs. Searcy M. Ferguson, Jr.

COWBOY COOKIES

1 c. butter
½ c. granulated sugar
1½ c. dark brown sugar
2 eggs
2 c. flour, sifted
½ t. salt
1 t. baking soda
1½ t. vanilla
2 c. rolled oats
2 3½-oz. cans coconut
1 12-oz. pkg. semi-sweet
    chocolate bits

Cream butter and sugars. Add eggs, flour, salt, and soda. Add vanilla, oats, coconut, and chocolate bits. Drop by teaspoonful onto a greased cookie sheet and bake at 350° for 15 minutes.

Mrs. David C. Smith

CHRISTMAS CUT-OUT COOKIES

½ c. butter
1 c. sugar
2 eggs
1 T. milk
½ t. vanilla
2½ c. cake flour
2 t. baking powder
¼ t. salt
FROSTING:
4 egg whites
½ t. cream of tartar
½ t. vanilla
5 c. sifted powdered sugar

Cream butter. Add sugar gradually. Add well-beaten eggs, milk, and vanilla. Sift flour, measure, and sift again with baking powder and salt. Add to the first mixture gradually. Chill thoroughly. Roll out very thin on a lightly floured board and cut in shapes. Bake on a greased cookie sheet about 10 minutes at 350°. Cool and frost.

For frosting, beat egg whites with cream of tartar and vanilla until foamy. Gradually beat in sugar. Put the frosting in several different bowls and add the food coloring of your choice.

Makes 4 dozen.

Mrs. Arthur C. White

DATE BARS

1½ c. dates, quartered and
    sprinkled with 1½ t. lemon
    juice
1 c. sugar, sifted
¾ c. butter
2 eggs
1 t. vanilla
1 c. flour
1¼ t. baking powder
½ t. salt
2 T. milk
1 c. nuts, chopped
Powdered sugar

Cream butter and add sugar gradually. Beat in eggs and vanilla. Sift flour, baking powder, and salt, and add to butter mixture in 3 parts with the milk. Add dates and nuts. Bake in a 9" square pan which has been lined with waxed paper at 325° for 40 minutes. When cool, cut into bars and roll in powdered sugar.

Makes 24.

Mrs. Walter N. Kuntz III

BROWNIES

¼ lb. butter
4 oz. unsweetened chocolate
2 c. sugar
4 eggs
¼ t. salt
1 c. flour
1 c. pecans
1 T. vanilla

Melt butter and chocolate in the top of a double boiler. Add sugar and eggs, one at a time. Add remaining ingredients. Put into a 13"x9" pan and bake at 325° for 30 minutes.
Serves 24.

Mrs. Thomas M. Andrews

THREE-LAYER BROWNIES

COOKIE LAYER:
1 sq. unsweetened chocolate
¼ c. margarine
1 egg
½ c. sugar
¼ c. flour, sifted
¼ c. pecans
FILLING:
2 T. soft margarine
1 c. confectioners sugar
1 T. heavy cream or evaporated
   milk
¼ t. vanilla
GLAZE:
2 squares unsweetened
   chocolate
2 T. margarine

Preheat oven to 350°. Grease an 8" square pan. For cookie layer, melt chocolate and margarine in double boiler. Cool slightly. In bowl, beat egg until frothy. Stir in chocolate mixture and sugar. Add flour and nuts. Put in pan. Bake 20 minutes. Cool thoroughly.
Mix all filling ingredients together and spread over cookie layer. Chill in refrigerator for 10 minutes.
Melt glaze ingredients together and spread over filling. Can be frozen.
Serves 9-16, depending on size of squares.

Miss Jane Hays

BLONDE BROWNIES

1½ c. sifted flour
2 T. baking powder
½ t. salt
½ c. butter
1 c. granulated sugar
½ c. brown sugar
2 eggs
1 t. vanilla
1 c. Almond Roca, crushed

Sift flour, baking powder, salt. Cream butter with sugar. Add eggs and vanilla. Beat until fluffy. Stir in crushed candy. Blend in dry ingredients. Spread over bottom of a well-greased 9"x13" pan. Bake at 350° for 30 minutes. When cool, frost with chocolate butter cream icing (see icings). Sprinkle with more candy.

Mrs. Curtis Sanford, Jr.

BROWNIE DROPS

2 4-oz. pkgs. Baker's German
  Chocolate
1 T. butter
2 eggs
¾ c. sugar
¼ c. unsifted flour
¼ t. baking powder
⅛ t. salt
¼ t. cinnamon
½ t. vanilla
¾ c. walnuts

Melt chocolate and butter in the top of a double boiler over hot water. Stir and cool. Beat eggs until foamy. Add sugar (2 T. at a time). Beat until thickened. Blend in the chocolate. Add flour, baking powder, salt, and cinnamon. Stir in vanilla and chopped nuts. Drop by teaspoonfuls onto greased baking sheets. Bake at 350° until cookies feel "set" when touched, approximately 8-10 minutes. Can be frozen.
Yields 3 dozen average size or 5 dozen tea size.

Mrs. James G. Aldridge

CHOCOLATE BALLS

1½ c. butter
¾ c. granulated sugar
1 t. vanilla
½ c. cocoa
2 c. flour
⅛ t. salt
2 c. pecans, chopped

Cream butter and sugar until fluffy. Sift together flour, salt, and cocoa. Gradually add sifted ingredients to creamed mixture. Blend in pecans and vanilla. Refrigerate 6 hours. Roll into 1" balls and place on ungreased cookie sheets about ½" apart as they do not spread. Bake for 20 minutes at 350°. Then roll in powdered sugar.
Makes 6-7 dozen.

Mrs. Richard Thomas

LACE COOKIES

¼ c. butter
¼ c. shortening
⅔ c. brown sugar, firmly
  packed
½ c. light corn syrup
1 c. flour
2 T. quick oatmeal
1 c. almonds, chopped

Melt butter and shortening in pan. Stir in brown sugar and corn syrup and bring to a boil, stirring frequently. Remove, and stir into it flour, oatmeal, and almonds. Drop by half teaspoons, 3" apart, onto oiled baking sheets. Bake at 325° for 8-10 minutes. Let cool one minute and lift off.
Makes 72.

Mrs. Jack Vaughn

GOODIE COOKIES

1 stick oleo
1 c. graham cracker crumbs
12-oz. pkg. chocolate chips
12-oz. pkg. butterscotch chips
1 can Eagle Brand milk
1 c. pecans, finely chopped

Pour the melted oleo into 9"x13" Pyrex or metal pan. Sprinkle the graham cracker crumbs evenly over the oleo. Sprinkle the chocolate chips and then the butterscotch chips. Spread Eagle Brand milk evenly over the mixture. Top with crushed pecans and take spatula and press mixture. Bake 20-25 minutes at 350°. Be sure to cut into desired squares while it is still warm; but leave in the pan until completely cooled.
Makes about 3 dozen.

Mrs. Kenneth W. Anderson

MOTHER'S GUM DROP COOKIES

1 c. gum drops
4 eggs, beaten
1 T. cold water
2 c. light brown sugar
2 c. flour
½ t. salt
1 t. cinnamon
GLAZE:
1 c. powdered sugar
2 T. butter, melted
2 T. orange juice

Cut gum drops, using scissors which you can dip in warm water to keep from sticking. Then combine all cookie ingredients. Pour on cookie sheet. Bake at 350° for 30 to 35 minutes. While warm, spread glaze over cookies; cut in squares when slightly cooled. For Christmas, use red and green gum drops and a few drops food coloring in glaze.

Mrs. Arthur C. White

JUDY GLAZER'S COOKIES

1 c. large-curd cottage cheese
2 sticks butter
2 c. pastry flour, sifted
½ stick butter
¾ c. light brown sugar
¾ c. pecans, chopped

Combine cottage cheese, butter; add flour. (The dough will be a little lumpy). Divide into 2 balls, wrap in waxed paper, and place in the refrigerator for 4 hours. Roll out one ball to a 12-15" circle. Combine remaining 3 ingredients for a filling and spread half of the filling on top of the circle. Press into dough with a rolling pin. Cut into wedges and roll up from big end to little. Do the same with the remaining ingredients. Bake at 350° for 20 minutes or until golden. These should be eaten immediately — or surely within 24 hours. They can be prepared ahead and baked while your guests are eating.

Mrs. Searcy Ferguson, Jr.

1 c. raisins
½ c. non-fat dried milk powder
¼ t. baking powder
¼ t. baking soda
¾ t. salt
¾ c. whole wheat flour
⅓ c. wheat germ
½ c. butter
1 c. brown sugar, firmly packed
1 egg
1 t. vanilla
½ c. sunflower seeds
1 c. granola
½ to ⅔ c. applesauce
1 t. cinnamon
¼ t. allspice
¼ t. nutmeg

HI-ENERGY RAISIN COOKIES

Mix all ingredients well. Drop in small teaspoons on cookie sheet. Bake at 350° for 10-12 minutes or until soft brown on top.

Mrs. Stephen J. Summers

1 c. butter
¼ c. honey
2 c. flour, sifted
½ t. salt
2 t. vanilla
1 c. pecans, chopped
Powdered sugar

HONEY BALLS

Cream butter and honey until light and fluffy. Add flour, which has been sifted with salt, slowly. Add vanilla and nuts. Form into balls, place on ungreased cookie sheets. Bake at 300° until light brown, approximately 30-40 minutes. Do not overcook. When warm, roll in powdered sugar. Let cool. Roll in powdered sugar again.
Makes 45-50.

Mrs. Donald R. Howe

CRUST:
1½ c. flour
1½ c. brown sugar
½ c. butter or margarine
FILLING:
2 eggs, beaten
1 c. brown sugar
1½ c. coconut
1 c. pecans, chopped
2 T. flour
½ t. baking powder
¼ t. salt
½ t. vanilla
FROSTING:
1 c. powdered sugar
1 T. butter, melted
Juice of one lemon
1 t. orange juice

LEMON COCONUT SQUARES

Crust: mix flour, brown sugar, and butter; pat into well buttered 9″ x 13″ pan. Bake at 275° for 10 minutes.
Filling: combine ingredients and spread over baked mixture. Bake at 350° for 20 minutes or until done.
Frosting: combine ingredients, spread on warm cookies. Cut into squares.
Makes about 24-30 squares.

Mrs. E. Don Rott

LEMON BARS

1 c. butter
¼ t. salt
½ c. powdered sugar
2 c. flour
4 eggs, slightly beaten
4 T. lemon juice
2 c. sugar
4 T. flour
Grated rind of 1 lemon

Blend first 4 ingredients well and press into a greased 10"x13" baking dish. Bake at 350° for 20-30 minutes. Mix remaining 5 ingredients together and pour over first mixture. Bake for 20-30 minutes at 325° or until firm. Dust with powdered sugar and cut when cool. Keep in the refrigerator.
Makes about 5 dozen.

Mrs. Alan Schoellkopf

MAPLE NUTTIES

2 c. flour
⅔ c. soft margarine
1 T. water
1 t. mapleline (maple flavoring)
1 c. nuts
1 c. powdered sugar

Mix all ingredients well. With fingers pull off small pieces of dough and roll into cylinders about 1"x½". Place on ungreased baking sheet. Bake at 275° for 1 hour. When done, roll in additional powdered sugar, usually about 1 cup.

Mrs. E. Don Rott

BETSY'S MINT MERINGUES

2 egg whites
Pinch of salt
¾ c. sugar
½ t. cream of tartar, scant
½ t. vanilla
½ t. mint flavoring
1½ c. chocolate chips

Beat egg whites until stiff. Add salt, cream of tartar, and sugar gradually. Add flavorings to beaten egg whites. Carefully fold in chocolate chips. Drop by small spoonfuls on slightly greased heavy cookie sheets. Preheat oven at 375° for 15 minutes. Turn off oven and immediately place cookies in oven. Leave for 5 hours or overnight.
Makes 50-60 meringue cookies.

Mrs. Charles M. Best II

NANCY'S POTATO CHIP COOKIES

1 lb. butter
1 c. sugar
3 c. flour
1 t. vanilla
1½ c. crushed potato chips

Cream butter and sugar. Add flour and vanilla. Fold in potato chips. Drop by teaspoonfuls on ungreased cookie sheets. Bake at 350° for 15 minutes.
Makes 4 dozen.

Mrs. Searcy M. Ferguson, Jr.

Chocolate Mousse, Chocolate Mint Roll, Poached Pears with Chocolate Sauce.

ORANGE PECAN ICE BOX COOKIES

1 c. butter
½ c. brown sugar
½ c. white sugar
1 egg
2¾ c. flour
¼ t. soda
2 T. orange juice
1 T. orange rind, grated
½ c. pecans, chopped

Cream butter and sugar; add egg, orange juice, and rind. Sift flour, mix with soda, and add to first mixture. Add pecans. Chill overnight. Slice thin and bake 10 minutes at 350°.

Mrs. K. N. Hapgood

PECAN BARS

1 c. margarine
1 c. sugar
1 egg, separated
2 c. flour
1 t. cinnamon
1 T. milk
1 c. pecans, chopped

Cream margarine and sugar; add egg yolk; add flour, cinnamon, and milk. Mix well. Pat dough out in a greased 13x9x2 inch pan; beat egg white slightly, brush over top; sprinkle with pecans and press lightly into dough. Bake at 350° for 35 to 45 minutes. Cut into bars while hot. Makes 30 cookies.

Mrs. Justin S. McCarty, Jr.

PECAN WHATNOTS

1 stick butter or margarine
3 oz. cream cheese
1 c. flour
FILLING:
¾ c. brown sugar
1 egg, beaten
1 T. butter, melted
1 t. vanilla
¾ c. pecans, chopped

Melt together the butter and cream cheese. Add flour and knead together until smooth. Divide into 20-24 balls. Using thumbs, line bottom and sides of 1″ size muffin pan.
Filling: Mix all ingredients and warm over low heat for about 5 minutes. Fill lined cups and bake for 30 minutes at 350°. These freeze well.

Mrs. Margaret C. Worsham

RUSSIAN ROCKS

1½ c. brown sugar
1 c. butter
3 eggs, beaten separately
2¾ c. flour
Pinch of salt
2 t. cinnamon
¾ t. cloves
2 c. pecans, chopped
1 lb. seeded raisins

Combine all ingredients and drop by teaspoons onto well-greased cookie sheets. Bake at 350° for 12-15 minutes or until browned.
Makes about 5 dozen.

Mrs. P. C. Baird, 1948 Junior League Cookbook

CHRISTMAS MINCEMEAT COOKIES

1 pkg. mincemeat
1 c. boiling water
3½ c. all-purpose flour
1 t. salt
¼ c. brown sugar
1 t. soda
1 t. cinnamon
1 c. shortening
2 eggs
¾ c. honey or maple syrup
1 c. seeded raisins
1 c. nuts, chopped

Break up package of mincemeat; add boiling water. Let stand until soft and dissolved. Sift together flour, salt, brown sugar, soda, and cinnamon. Cream shortening with honey or maple syrup. Add eggs and beat well. Blend with mincemeat, mixing thoroughly. Stir in dry ingredients. Add raisins and nuts. Drop from spoon onto cookie sheet. Bake for 15 minutes at 350°.

Makes 100 small cookies.

Mrs. George Searcy Watson

SCOTCH SCONES

2 c. flour
½ t. salt
3 T. sugar
2 t. baking powder
1 T. butter, heaping
2 T. dried currants or raisins
¾ c. milk or a little more, but
   not a cupful

Sift together flour, salt, sugar, and baking powder. Rub in the butter. Add fruit. Mix to a soft dough with milk. Turn out on floured board, divide in two, and make into round cakes about ¾" thick. Press down the tops and moisten with a little milk. Sprinkle with sugar or cinnamon-sugar. Cut each cake into four and bake on a greased and floured pie plate at 400° until brown, about 10-12 min. When done split and butter generously.

Makes 8 scones.

Mrs. Lewis N. May, Jr.

IRISH OATMEAL COOKIES

½ lb. butter or margarine
1 T. of Tates Golden Syrup
   Lyles
1 c. plain flour
1 c. sugar
2 c. quick-cooking oats
1 t. baking soda
1 pinch of cream of tartar

Slowly melt butter and golden syrup in sauce pan. Mix all dry ingredients in a bowl. Put soda and cream of tartar in last. Pour margarine and syrup over dry ingredients. Place small lumps (one teaspoon) on greased tray. Space them widely. Bake for 12-15 minutes at 250-300°. Slip off baking tray with spatula. Leave to cool on cardboard or brown paper. Very light and crisp cookie.

Mrs. Robert W. Ryan, Jr.

OATMEAL COOKIES

1 c. margarine
1 c. brown sugar
1 c. white sugar
2 eggs, well-beaten
1 t. vanilla
1½ c. flour (or whole wheat)
1 t. cinnamon
½ t. nutmeg
1 t. salt
1 t. soda
3 c. oatmeal (3 minute)
½ c. pecans, chopped *or* ½ c.
　raisins

Cream shortening, brown sugar, and white sugar. Add eggs and vanilla; beat well. Sift flour, cinnamon, nutmeg, salt, and soda together. Add to creamed mixture and blend well. Stir in oats and pecans or raisins. Drop from a spoon on to greased cookie sheet and bake in 350° oven for 10 minutes or until brown. Makes 5 dozen.

Mrs. Ronald Howell Underwood

TASSIES

¼ lb. butter
1 3-oz. pkg. cream cheese,
　softened
1 c. flour
1 egg, slightly beaten
¾ c. brown sugar
1 T. melted butter
1 t. vanilla
½ c. pecans, finely chopped

Mix first 3 ingredients until smooth, then chill. Roll a little piece out, and shape to fit miniature tart pans. May also use miniature muffin tins. Mix remaining ingredients together and drop by tsp. into unbaked tassie shells. Bake 25 minutes at 350°. These may be frozen before or after baking.
Makes about 30-36.

Mrs. Jerry C. Jenkins

TOFFEE BARS

c. butter
½ c. brown sugar
½ c. white sugar
egg yolks
c. flour
c. rolled oats
1-oz. Hershey bars
T. butter
½ c. nuts

Cream butter and sugars. Beat in yolks. Add flour and oats. Mix and spread over the bottom of a 9"x13" greased pan. Bake at 350° for 30 minutes or until done. Cool 10 minutes. Melt Hershey bars and 2 T. butter in a double boiler and spread over cooled layer. Sprinkle the top with nuts and cut into 1½" squares.
Makes 48 bars.

Mrs. Ray McKown

SAND TARTS I

1 lb. butter
1 lb. pecans, chopped fine
1 egg, beaten
2 c. sugar
4 c. flour
Vanilla to taste

Mix all ingredients well and shape dough into crescents. Bake on a greased cookie sheet at 350° for 15 minutes. When cool, roll in powdered sugar.
Makes about 8 dozen.

Mrs. Edwin L. Cox

SAND TARTS II

½ lb. butter (not margarine)
½ c. confectioner's sugar, sifted
2 c. cake flour, sifted
1 c. pecans, chopped
1 t. vanilla

Cream butter; add sugar. Stir well and add flour, nuts, and vanilla. Shape into balls or crescents (just drop them from spoon — the more you handle them the harder they will get) and bake on ungreased cookie sheet at 325° for 20 minutes or until a light brown. Roll in powdered sugar while warm.
Makes 4 dozen.

Mrs. Sterling P. Bush
Mrs. Tom Maswath

SCOTCH BREAD

2 sticks butter, room
    temperature
2½ c. flour, not sifted
¼ c. sugar

Mix all ingredients together. Press into an 8-inch square buttered Pyrex dish. Cook in a 300° oven for 1 hour. Take out, cut into long narrow strips, then cool. Serve with afternoon tea or coffee.
Serves 6 to 8.

Mrs. Julian A. Wells

SESAME COOKIES

½ c. sesame seeds, toasted in an
    iron skillet
1 c. unsifted flour
¼ t. baking powder
⅛ t. salt
¾ c. soft butter
1 c. brown sugar
1 egg
1 t. vanilla

Sift flour, baking powder, and salt. Mix butter, brown sugar, egg, and vanilla at medium speed until smooth. With a wooden spoon add flour and seeds. Refrigerate for 2 hours, covered. Drop lightly rounded teaspoons on a cookie sheet. Flatten with a spatula. Bake 10-12 minutes. Let stand. Cool completely.
Yield: 5 dozen.

Mrs. Mark Lemmon, Jr.

CANDY
TOFFEE

1 c. butter
1 c. sugar
¼ c. water
½ t. salt
¼ bar German Sweet Chocolate
1 c. sweet chocolate chips
Chopped nuts

Over medium heat combine butter, sugar, water, and salt and cook stirring constantly to 300° about ½ hour. Immediately pour into ungreased 9"x13" pan. Tilt pan quickly until it reaches edges. Work fast. Cool until hard. Melt chocolates together. Spread over cooled toffee and sprinkle with chopped nuts. Pat nuts into the icing. Let it set overnight. Break into pieces and store in tight fitting cans.

Mrs. Larry K. Casey

MY GREAT-GRANDMOTHER'S CANDIED GRAPEFRUIT PEEL — MY FAVORITE CHRISTMAS CANDY

2 or 3 grapefruit
1 c. sugar, per grapefruit
½ c. water, per grapefruit

Remove pulp and inner skin from grapefruit. Cut peel into long strips ½" wide. Soak peel 24 hours in water to cover, changing water several times. Put peel in fresh cold water and boil 5 minutes; repeat twice. The third time, boil peel until tender — it can be easily pierced with a fork. Drain and let rest. Make a heavy syrup using the sugar and water per grapefruit. Cook syrup to 238° (soft ball stage). Add grapefruit and simmer until most of the syrup has evaporated — about ½ hour. Watch pan to prevent grapefruit sticking. Drain in a sieve. Roll the peel, a few pieces at a time, in sugar. Cool and store in a covered container. Better in 1 week.

Mrs. Charles M. Best II

MOCK PRALINES

1 c. butter
1 c. brown sugar
1 c. nuts, chopped
Honey graham crackers

Bring butter, brown sugar, and nuts to a boil; cook 5-10 minutes. Spoon over cookie sheet which has been filled with graham crackers (8"x10" sheet). Cook in 350° oven for 10-15 minutes. Cool slightly and cut into squares.

Mrs. Mark Lemmon, Jr.

POPCORN BALLS

2 quarts unsalted popcorn
1 c. light corn syrup
1 t. vinegar
2 T. butter
1 t. vanilla
Food coloring (optional)

Place popcorn in a large greased bowl. Combine syrup and vinegar in saucepan. Boil slowly until candy thermometer registers 260°F. (Hard ball stage). Remove syrup from heat and stir in butter, vanilla and food coloring, if desired. Pour syrup over popcorn in bowl and toss until it is well coated. Shape into balls. Makes 7 — 3" balls.

Mrs. Mark Lemmon, Jr.

CREAMY FUDGE

2 1-oz. squares chocolate
2 c. sugar
1 c. milk
2 T. butter
1 t. vanilla
Chopped pecans, if desired

Melt chocolate, stir in milk and mix well. Add sugar, bring to a boil and cook until soft ball forms, stirring occasionally. Remove from stove and set pan in ice water. Add butter and vanilla. When slightly cool, add nuts and beat until color turns dull. Pour onto greased plate. Makes 20 pieces.

Mrs. George W. Jalonick III

CHOCOLATE CANDY BALLS

1 stick margarine (not butter), softened
1½ boxes (1 lb. each) powdered sugar
1 c. Eagle Brand milk
½ t. vanilla
1 8-oz. can coconut
1 lb. pecans, chopped
3 12-oz. pkgs. chocolate chips
¼ lb. parafin

Mix first four ingredients. Stir in coconut and nuts. Roll into balls the size of large marbles. Chill overnight. Melt chocolate chips and parafin over hot water. Use a toothpick to dip ball into chocolate mixture and let dry on waxed paper.

Mrs. Theodore Votteler

CLAIRE'S PEANUT BRITTLE

¼ c. water
½ c. Karo syrup
1 c. sugar
2 c. raw peanuts
1 t. soda
Pinch of salt

Bring all ingredients, except soda, to a boil. Then add peanuts. Stir constantly until candy thermometer registers 290° or hard crack stage. Remove from fire and add soda, stirring quickly. Candy will foam up when soda is added; then stir down and pour into buttered sheet. When cold, break into pieces.

Mrs. Theodore Votteler

2 c. sugar
1 c. whipping cream (may
    substitute half-and-half if
    less richness desired)
Pinch of salt
2 squares unsweetened
    chocolate
1 t. vanilla
1 T. butter
1 c. pecans, chopped (optional)

GEORGE'S FUDGE

Mix sugar, salt, and whipping cream together in a large saucepan. Bring mixture to a boil over medium-high heat. Add chocolate and reduce heat back to a medium-low setting. Stir as little as possible at this point, mixing only often enough to keep the chocolate from sticking to the bottom of the pan. Let mixture cook until it forms a soft ball in a glass of tap water. (Use a candy thermometer just to double check the cooking. If it cooks too long it will harden in the pan and be sugar; if it doesn't cook long enough it will never harden, but will make super chocolate sauce!). When mixture has cooked long enough to the soft ball stage, remove pan from heat and add butter and vanilla. Tilt pan on its side with the base resting on a damp dishcloth to keep pan from slipping, and start to beat the mixture with a large spoon. When you first start to beat you will notice that the chocolate is fairly thin and has a shiny look to it. As you beat, it should begin to thicken and lose its lustre. Do not add the pecans to the mixture until just before it is ready to pour out. You can tell it is ready when the fudge becomes very dull in appearance and when dribbles from the spoon stand on the surface of the mixture and don't blend back in. Add the pecans and pour fudge out onto a buttered dish. Refrigerate for about two hours before attempting to cut into squares.

Should yield about 25 to 30 medium-size pieces.

Mrs. George W. Jalonick IV

DIVINITY

2 c. granulated sugar
½ c. light corn syrup
¼ t. salt
½ c. water
2 egg whites
1 t. vanilla
¾ c. candied cherries or 1 c.
    chopped nuts

Dissolve sugar, syrup, and salt in water over low heat, stirring. Cook, without stirring, to 248°F., or to firm ball stage (or light crack stage 265°F.). Wash down with a damp cloth any crystals that may form on the sides of the pan during cooking. Remove from heat and pour gradually over the stiffly beaten egg whites. Add vanilla and continue beating until mixture will hold its shape when dropped from a spoon. Add nuts or fruit if used. Drop by spoonfuls on wax paper. Makes 30 servings.

Mrs. Sam P. Burford, Jr.

ORANGE SUGARED PECANS

3 c. sugar
1 c. water
⅓ c. strained orange juice
1 packed and heaping t. grated orange peel
4 c. pecan halves

Cook sugar, water, and orange juice until it makes a soft ball in water. Add rind and nuts and remove from fire. Stir until it begins to sugar, then pour on unbuttered board.

Mrs. Charles W. Pace

PIES

ANGEL PIE

CRUST:
1⅓ c. chocolate cookie crumbs
2 T. sugar
¼ t. cinnamon
5 T. melted butter
½ c. blanched almonds, finely chopped
FILLING:
1 qt. coffee ice cream
TOPPING:
⅔ c. sugar
⅓ c. water
2 egg whites
½ c. whipping cream
2 t. cocoa
⅛ t. salt
¼ c. blanched almonds, chopped

For crust mix crumbs, sugar, and cinnamon. Stir in butter and almonds. Press in a 9-inch pie pan. Chill in freezer. When crust has chilled, spoon in softened coffee ice cream. Return to freezer.

For the topping, combine sugar and water in a 1-qt. saucepan. Boil and cook until syrup spins a thread (about 7 minutes). Meanwhile, beat egg whites until stiff. Continue beating while adding sugar mixture slowly until meringue holds its shape. Chill. In a chilled bowl whip cream, cocoa, and salt until firm consistency. Fold cream mixture and almonds into chilled meringue. Mound on pie. Top with chocolate curls or additional sprinkling of cookie crumbs. Return to freezer. Can be made up to 48 hours in advance.
Serves 8.

Mrs. Richard W. Ince

DUTCH APPLE PIE

1 T. flour
Dash of cinnamon, cloves, allspice
1 c. sugar
¾ c. heavy cream, dotted with butter
Pie crust
4 c. tart apples

Line a pie dish with a good crust and fill with thin, sliced tart apples. Blend flour, cinnamon, cloves, and allspice with sugar. Pour over apples. Over all pour cream dotted with butter. Bake with one crust only in a slow oven (325°) for 45 minutes.
Serves 6 to 8.

Mrs. Charles Witchell, 1948 Junior League of Dallas Cookbook

DEEP DISH APPLE RAISIN PIE

Pastry for 1 crust pie
1 1-lb. 4-oz. can pie sliced
   apples, well drained
1 c. brown sugar
3 T. flour
½ t. cinnamon
¼ t. nutmeg
3 T. rum
⅓ c. heavy cream
1 1-lb. 4-oz. can raisin or
   mincemeat pie filling
1 egg yolk
3 T. rum

Make pastry from your favorite recipe and refrigerate until ready to use. Turn well drained apples into bowl and toss with sugar, flour, and spices. Add the rum and cream. Mix well. Turn into a buttered shallow 2 quart casserole. Spread raisins or mincemeat pie filling over the apple filling. Roll out pastry and fit over top of pie. Flute edge. Make a few vents in top for steam. Brush with egg yolk, beaten, and 3 T. rum. Bake in pre-heated oven at 400 degrees for about 1 hour, or until crust is golden and apples are tender. Serve warm with ice cream, whipped cream, hard sauce, or plain cream.
Serves 8.

Mrs. William Plack Carr, Jr.

COCONUT CREAM PIE

4 T. cornstarch
2 egg yolks
½ c. sugar
1½ pts. sweet milk
1 fresh coconut, grated
1 t. vanilla
2 egg whites, beaten stiff
2 T. sugar
1 thin but deep baked pie crust

Mix the cornstarch, egg yolks, and sugar; then add milk and cook until very thick. When cool, add most of the coconut and vanilla. Beat the egg whites until stiff and add 2 T. sugar. Fold egg whites into custard. Pour into shell and sprinkle with remaining coconut. Brown quickly in hot oven (475°). Serve at once.
Serves 6-8.

Mrs. A. A. Green, 1924 Junior League
Cookbook

PUMPKIN ICE CREAM PIE

¾ c. pumpkin, grated
1 c. milk
1 pt. heavy cream
1 c. sugar
1 t. cinnamon
½ t. cloves
1 t. vanilla
1 baked pie crust
MERINGUE:
4 egg whites
¼ c. sugar

Combine pumpkin, sugar, spices, milk, and cream; then freeze. When cream is frozen, place in the baked pie crust. Cover with meringue made from egg whites and sugar. Brown quickly in a very hot oven (475°). Serve at once.
Serves 6-8.

Mrs. E. M. Reardon, Jr., 1924 Junior League
Cookbook

LADYFINGER PIE CRUST

16 ladyfingers
1 stick of butter or margarine, softened
¼ c. sugar

Split the ladyfingers, place them on a cookie sheet and put them in a very slow oven (200°-225°) to dry out. When crumbly, remove them from oven and pulverize them in the blender, or, place in a plastic bag and roll into fine crumbs with a rolling pin. Blend the crumbs thoroughly with the butter and sugar. Line a 10″ pyrex pie plate with the mixture, pressing down firmly. Do not extend out over lip of the plate as this makes it more difficult to remove when ready to serve. Chill until ready to fill. Use as you would a graham cracker crust. Excellent with chiffon pies.

Mrs. John W. McDonough

PASTRY FOR PIES

2 c. flour, sifted
1 t. salt
¾ c. shortening
5 T. ice water (or more if necessary)

Combine flour and salt in a bowl. Cut in shortening with 2 forks until it is the consistency of coarse cornmeal. Sprinkle a small amount of water over the mixture and stir lightly with a fork. Continue adding the water gradually until the dough holds together but is not sticky. Shape the dough into a smooth ball and half it. It can be refrigerated until ready to fill and bake.
Makes two 9″ pie shells.

Mrs. Horace R. Nash, Jr.

THE VERY BEST CHESS PIE

1 stick butter
1½ c. sugar
1 T. flour
1½ t. vinegar
1 t. vanilla
3 eggs
Prepared pastry shell

Melt butter, add all other ingredients and mix well. Pour into pastry shell and bake at 350° for 35 minutes.
Serves 6.

Mrs. J. Brevard Haynes

BEST BLUEBERRY PIE

4 c. fresh blueberries
¾ c. sugar
½ c. water
2 T. cornstarch
1 T. butter
¼ c. slivered, toasted almonds
1 T. Cointreau or orange
  Curacao
Baked 9″ pastry shell
TOPPING:
½ pt. whipped cream
¼ t. almond extract
Little sugar

Put 1 c. blueberries, sugar and water into pan, bring to boil and cook until soft, about 10 minutes. Cool. Mix cornstarch with a little water, add to blueberry mixture and cook until thick. Stir so it won't stick. Add butter and let cool. Add remaining blueberries, almonds, and Cointreau, and pour into pastry shell. Mix topping ingredients and spread over pie.
Serves 6-8.

Mrs. Oscar J. Lalla III

BUTTERSCOTCH PECAN PIE

3 eggs, room temp.
1 c. light corn syrup
⅛ t. salt
1 t. vanilla
1 c. light brown sugar, packed
2 T. butter, melted
1 c. pecans
9″ unbaked pie shell

Preheat oven to 400°. In a medium bowl, beat eggs slightly. Add corn syrup, salt, vanilla, brown sugar and melted butter. Mix well, then stir in nuts. Pour into pie shell. Bake 15 minutes, then reduce heat to 350°. Bake an additional 30-35 minutes or until outer edge of filling seems set. Let cool completely.

Mrs. William B. Madden

CARAMEL PIE

1 heaping t. flour (more if
  needed)
1 c. sweet milk
2 eggs, separated
  (reserve whites for meringue)
1 c. sugar
1 heaping t. butter
½ t. vanilla
1 pie crust
4 T. sugar
Few drops vanilla

Mix flour and milk with well-beaten yolks. Melt sugar in saucepan, stirring constantly. To this, add milk, eggs, and flour mixture. Keep stirring to dissolve each ingredient. Cook until very thick; then add butter and vanilla. Bake pie crust separately. Pour custard into crust. Beat egg whites very fine; add sugar and vanilla. Spread over pie. Bake very slowly 30-40 minutes at 250-300°.

Mrs. Dabney White, 1948 Junior League Cookbook

CHOCOLATE ANGEL PIE

4 eggs, separated
½ t. cream of tartar
¼ t. salt
½ t. vanilla
1½ c. sugar
1 1-oz. square bitter
   chocolate, grated
1 pint heavy cream, whipped

Allow egg whites to come to room temperature in large bowl. Beat with cream of tartar, salt, and vanilla until soft peaks form. Gradually beat in 1 c. sugar, one fourth at a time, and continue beating until soft peaks form. Spread into greased 9" pie pan, building edges a little higher than center. Bake at 250° 1 hour to 1 hour 10 minutes. Turn off oven and leave pie in with door ajar for 1 hour. Then cool to room temperature. Beat together yolks and remaining sugar until thick. Add chocolate. Cook over hot water, stirring until very thick and smooth. Cool to room temperature. Fold in 1 c. whipped cream and spoon into shell. Chill several hours, cover with remaining whipped cream, and garnish with grated or curled chocolate.

Mrs. Robert W. Enholm

DEVONSHIRE LEMON PIE

1 unbaked 8-inch graham
   cracker pie shell
FILLING:
1 8-oz. pkg. cream cheese
⅓ c. sugar
1 egg
½ c. sour cream
1½ t. lemon rind
1 T. lemon juice
¼ t. vanilla
LEMON GLAZE:
¼ c. sugar
1 T. cornstarch
Pinch of salt
¼ c. water
1 egg yolk
½ t. grated lemon rind
1½ T. lemon juice
1½ t. butter
¼ t. vanilla

For filling, soften cream cheese and beat in sugar until fluffy. Beat in egg, then sour cream, lemon rind, and juice. Add vanilla. Bake in crust at 375° for 20 minutes or until set and crust is lightly golden. Cool completely and glaze.

For glaze, mix sugar, cornstarch, and salt in a small saucepan. Stir in water, beat in egg yolk. Cook slowly, stirring constantly, until thickened and boiled for 3 minutes. Remove from heat. Stir in lemon rind and juice, butter and vanilla. Cool in bowl. Spread over top of pie and chill.

Serves 6.

Mrs. Thomas M. Dunning

CREME DE MENTHE PIE

CRUST:
20 chocolate wafers, crushed
5 T. butter
FILLING:
20 marshmallows
⅔ c. crème de menthe
1 pt. heavy cream, whipped

Crust: Melt butter and add cookie crumbs. Pat into lightly buttered pie plate. Bake at 350° for 12 to 15 minutes. Cool.
Filling: Melt marshmallows in crème de menthe in a double boiler. Cool and fold in whipped cream. Pour into crust. Crumble extra cookies on top of pie. Freeze. Serve frozen.
Serves 8.

Mrs. Robert W. Enholm

GREEN PARROT CHOCOLATE FUDGE PECAN PIE

4 whole eggs
2 c. sugar
3 squares, bitter chocolate, melted
5⅓ T. margarine, melted
1 t. lemon juice
1 c. pecans broken in pieces
Two 9" unbaked pie shells

Blend egg yolks and whites. Slowly blend in sugar and then other ingredients. Pour into unbaked pie shells. Bake at 375 degrees for 35 minutes. The pie should still be somewhat shaky when removed from oven. Do not chill. Top with whipped cream if desired.
Serves 12.

Mrs. L. Franklin Beard

FROZEN CHOCOLATE PIE

1 prepared crust (chocolate wafers, graham crackers, or cooked pastry)
FILLING:
1 c. powdered sugar
½ c. butter, softened
4 oz. semi-sweet chocolate, melted
1 t. vanilla
3-4 eggs
TOPPING:
1 c. chilled whipped cream
2 T. powdered sugar
½ c. nuts, chopped

For filling: blend on low speed the powdered sugar and butter; add melted chocolate and vanilla; on high speed add eggs, one at a time. Pour into pie shell and put into freezer. Add 2 T. powdered sugar to the whipped cream. Remove pie from freezer, cover filing with chopped nuts, and pile whipped cream onto pie. Garnish with chocolate chips. Return to freezer. Remove 15 minutes before serving.

Mrs. John D. Bertrand

FUDGE PIE IN WALNUT SHELL

½ c. margarine
1 c. sugar
2 oz. baking chocolate, melted
Pinch salt
¼ c. flour
2 eggs, beaten
1 t. vanilla
½ c. pecans, chopped
**CHOPPED WALNUT PIE
   SHELL:**
¼ c. margarine, softened
1 T. flour
¼ c. sugar
1 c. walnuts, finely chopped

Cream margarine and sugar. Add chocolate, salt, flour, eggs, and vanilla. Blend thoroughly. Fold in nuts. Pour filling into baked walnut pie shell. Bake at 325° for 30 minutes. Let cool.

Pie shell: Combine margarine, flour, sugar, and walnuts; mix well. Put in a 9″ pie pan and bake at 325° for 10 minutes. Will freeze.

Mrs. Larry M. Nobles

NANA'S BLACK BOTTOM PIE

1⅓ c. graham cracker crumbs
5 T. melted butter
1 T. gelatin
4 T. cold water
½ c. sugar
2 T. flour
4 eggs, separated
2 c. milk
1½ sq. unsweetened chocolate, melted
1 t. vanilla
1 c. whipping cream
2 T. powdered sugar

Mix crumbs and butter and pat in the bottom of a Pyrex baking dish (11¾x7½). Bake 10 minutes at 300°.

Soak gelatin in cold water and set aside. In top of a double boiler, combine sugar, flour, egg yolks and milk. Cook until custard is thick. Take out 1 cup of the custard and add to the melted chocolate and vanilla. Spread this chocolate layer on top of cooled graham crust. To the remaining cooled custard, add the gelatin and stiffly beaten egg whites to which ½ c. sugar and 1 t. vanilla have been added. Spread custard layer over chocolate layer.

Whip cream and add sugar. Spread whipped cream over custard layer and grate chocolate on the top. Refrigerate.

Can be made the day before and add whipped cream before serving.

Serves 10-12.

Mrs. Frederick W. Burnett, Jr.

KENTUCKY DERBY PIE

4 eggs, beaten
½ c. butter, melted
1 c. white corn syrup
1 c. white sugar
1 t. vanilla
1 c. pecans, chopped
½ c. chocolate chips
1 9-inch unbaked pie shell

Stir the eggs, butter and corn syrup together. Add the sugar and stir well. Add vanilla and pecans. Add the chocolate chips. Pour into pie shell. Bake for 45 minutes in 350 degree oven.

Mrs. John D. Williamson

JEANNE HAYS' GRASSHOPPER PIE

CRUST:
30 Hydrox cookies
½ stick butter, melted
FILLING: 30 large
   marshmallows
⅔ c. milk
1 T. crème de cocoa
1½ T. crème de menthe
4 drops green color
½ pt. whipped cream (perhaps
   more if want to top pie)

For crust, roll cookies and mix with butter. Put into a greased 9-inch pie pan and refrigerate. For the pie filling, melt marshmallows in milk in a double boiler. Remove from heat and add crème de cocoa, crème de menthe and color. Refrigerate until cool. Fold mixture into whipped cream. Pour into pie crust and dab with whipped cream. Refrigerate.

Mrs. Lawrence H. Wilson, Jr.

MARIAN'S HEAVENLY LEMON PIE

MERINGUE:
1 c. granulated sugar
¼ t. cream of tartar
4 egg whites
FILLING:
8 egg yolks, slightly beaten
1 c. sugar
6 T. lemon juice
2 T. grated lemon rind
2 pts. heavy cream

For the meringue, sift together sugar and tartar. Beat egg whites until stiff but not dry. Gradually add sugar mixture, continually beating until thoroughly blended and meringue falls back into folds. Line bottom and sides of a 9-inch greased pie pan — DO NOT SPREAD OVER RIM — But build up on sides as it expands. Bake at 275° for 1 hour. Cool. (Individual meringues may be used.)

For the filling, stir in sugar with yolks, add juice and rind. Cook in the top of a double boiler until very thick. Remove from heat and cool. Whip one pint of cream and combine with lemon mixture. Fill shell. Chill in refrigerator for 24 hours. When ready to serve, whip the other pint of cream and cover the top. Serves 8.

Mrs. Frederick W. Burnett, Jr.

HERSHEY BAR PIE

CRUST:
1 c. crushed graham crackers
½ c. Angel Flake coconut
⅓ c. melted butter
¼ c. powdered sugar
PIE FILLING:
7½-oz. almond Hershey (1 lg. and 1 small)
2 t. instant coffee
1 large carton Cool Whip
1 T. rum (optional)

For crust, combine ingredients and press into a 9-inch pie pan and bake at 350° for 10 minutes. Cool.

For filling, dissolve coffee in 2 T. water in a saucepan. Melt Hersheys in coffee mixture over low heat. Remove from heat and add Cool Whip and rum. Put into crust and freeze.

Serves 8.

Mrs. Virgil Pate

MINCE CUSTARD PIE

1½ c. prepared mincemeat
3 eggs plus 1 yolk
½ c. sugar
¼ t. salt
1¾ c. milk, scalded
1 t. vanilla
1 unbaked pie shell
¼ t. nutmeg

Spread mincemeat over the bottom of the pie shell. In a bowl, beat eggs and yolk with sugar and salt. Blend in milk and vanilla. Pour the custard over the mincemeat, sprinkle a little grated nutmeg on top and bake at 350° for 1 hour or until the custard is firm. Let the pie cool on a wire rack.

Serves 6-8.

MINCEMEAT PIE

1 pkg. Nonesuch mincemeat
6 T. sugar
1¼ c. water
¼ c. raisins
1 apple, peeled and chopped fine
¼ c. dark rum
2 unbaked pie shells, one of them cut into pastry strips

Break up the mincemeat into small pieces; add sugar, water, raisins and chopped apples. Bring to a boil and boil briskly for 3 minutes, making sure that the mincemeat is completely broken up and all ingredients are well mixed. Remove from heat and add dark rum. Mix thoroughly. Pour mixture into an unbaked pie shell and cover with pastry strips. Bake at 425° for 30 minutes.

Serves 6-8.

Mrs. John W. McDonough

MOCHA CHIFFON PIE

One 9" vanilla wafer crumb
  crust or Nabisco Chocolate
  Cookie crumb crust
1 c. semi-sweet chocolate chips
1 8-oz. pkg. cream cheese
6 T. brown sugar
4 T. granulated sugar
2 T. instant coffee
½ t. salt
1 t. vanilla
2 eggs, separated
1 c. cream, whipped

Melt chocolate and cool. Combine cream cheese, sugars, coffee, salt and vanilla. Beat in egg yolks. Add the melted and cooled chocolate. Beat egg whites until stiff and fold into chocolate mixture. Fold in whipped cream. Turn into prepared pie shell. Garnish with additional whipped cream.
Serves 8.

PEANUT PIE

20 Ritz crackers, rolled out
  fine
½ c. sugar
¾ c. salted peanuts, finely
  chopped
3 egg whites, stiffly beaten
¼ t. cream of tartar
½ c. sugar
1 t. vanilla
½ pt. cream, whipped
Bittersweet chocolate, grated

Mix Ritz cracker crumbs, sugar, and chopped peanuts. Fold this mixture into the following: egg whites, cream of tartar, sugar and vanilla. Bake in 8" pie pan for 20 minutes at 350°. Let cool. Top with whipped cream and grated bittersweet chocolate. Refrigerate 3-4 hours before serving.
Serves 6-8.

Mrs. J. Michael Brown

PUMPKIN PIE WITH APPLE SNOW TOPPING

1 pkg. butterscotch pieces
1 small can evaporated milk
1 can pumpkin
½ c. sugar
1 T. flour
½ t. salt
1 t. ginger
1 t. cinnamon
½ t. nutmeg
¼ t. ground cloves
3 eggs, slightly beaten
1 unbaked 9" pie shell
APPLE SNOW:
1 egg white
⅓ c. sugar
1 t. grated lemon peel
1 medium apple, freshly grated
Few grains of salt

Combine butterscotch pieces and evaporated milk in top of double boiler; heat over hot water until pieces are melted. Remove from heat. Blend in pumpkin. Combine sugar, flour, salt, ginger, cinnamon, nutmeg, and cloves. Blend sugar mixture and eggs into butterscotch-pumpkin mixture. Pour into unbaked pie shell. Bake at 400° for 50 minutes or until knife inserted near edge comes out clean. Cool.
Top with Apple Snow: Beat egg white until foamy; beat in sugar gradually. Beat in lemon peel and salt. Add grated apples; beat at least 10 minutes longer.

Mrs. Elvis Mason

PECAN CUPLETS

PASTRY:
2 c. flour
1 t. salt
¾ c. shortening
5 T. cold water
PECAN FILLING:
1 c. sugar
1 c. light corn syrup
3 eggs
1 t. vanilla
3 T. butter, melted
1 c. pecans, chopped

Cut together shortening, flour and salt. Sprinkle water over mixture. Mix with fork. Form into ball. Roll pastry out, cut with 6-oz. juice can. Place circles in small muffin tins. Fill each with 1 t. pecan filling. Bake 10 minutes at 400°, reduce heat to 350°, bake an additional 15 minutes.

Filling: combine ingredients except pecans and beat lightly. Add pecans last. Makes about 4 dozen.

Mrs. David Grafe

SHERRY WINE CHIFFON PIE

1 c. milk
½ c. sugar
3 eggs, separated
1 c. sherry wine
½ t. nutmeg
½ t. salt
1 c. heavy cream, whipped
1 T. gelatin, soaked in 4 T. cold
  milk

Combine milk and sugar; heat to boiling point. Put in top of double boiler, add well-beaten yolks, nutmeg and salt. Stir constantly; add wine slowly and soaked gelatin. Cook until it coats the spoon. Cool slightly; fold in stiffly beaten whites. Cool until firm; blend with whipped cream. Place mixture in cooked pastry shell, cover with sweetened whipped cream. Chill before serving.

Mrs. K. N. Hapgood

FRESH STRAWBERRY PIE

2 pints fresh strawberries
  washed and stemmed)
1 c. sugar
3 T. corn starch
1 8-oz. pkg. cream cheese,
  softened with 1 T. cream
1 half pint whipping cream
1 9 or 10″ rich pie crust, cooked

Mash 1½ pints berries (reserve ¼ pint to top pie) in sauce pan; add sugar and corn starch. Cook over low heat, stirring constantly, for 10 minutes or until thickened. Cool. Spread cream cheese over bottom of pie shell, top with cooled strawberry mixture. Whip cream, cover pie, and top with whole strawberries. Pie may be prepared the day before serving, but must be covered well with saran wrap. It may be prepared without whipping cream the day before, then whip cream and top 2 hours before serving.

Serves 8 or 9.

Mrs. Ralph D. Gibson, Jr.

DESSERTS

AMBROSIA

Fresh oranges
Coconut, freshly grated
Canned crushed pineapple, or
   fresh
Sugar
Kirsch or brandy (optional)

Peel oranges (4 large ones should be enough for 4 people.) Retain any juice. Combine sections with an 8½-oz. can crushed pineapple with juice. Add desired amount of coconut and sugar. When the flavor is adjusted to suit you, pour in a little of the liqueur. Chill well. Serve in berry bowls or sherbert cups with fruit cake or cookies.

Mrs. L. G. Pondrom

CARAMELIZED APPLE TART

PASTRY:
1 c. flour
⅛ t. salt
3 T. sugar
¼ lb. butter
3 T. ice water
FILLING:
6 T. butter
½ c. sugar
3 c. apples, peeled and sliced
2 T. brown sugar

For pastry sift flour, salt, and sugar into a bowl. Cut in the butter with a pastry blender. Add water and toss lightly until a ball of dough is formed. Chill 1 hour.

For filling use a deep 9″ pie plate and spread 3 tablespoons of butter on the bottom. Sprinkle 3 tablespoons of sugar over it. Arrange the apples in layers. On each layer sprinkle some of the remaining sugar and dot with butter. Roll out the pastry and cover the apples with it. Bake at 375° for 30 minutes. Cool 5 minutes then invert to ovenproof serving dish, so that apples are now on top. Sprinkle with brown sugar and place under broiler until sugar melts and top browns. Serve warm.
Serves 6-8.

Mrs. Clint M. Josey, Jr.

CHEESE BLINTZES

16 crêpes
FILLING:
1 lb. cottage cheese
3 T. butter, softened
2 3-oz. pkgs. cream cheese,
  softened
½ c. sugar
1 egg
1 grated lemon rind
1 t. vanilla
½ c. sour cream
GLAZE:
1 16-oz. can sour cherries (drain
  and reserve juice)
½ c. sugar
2 T. cornstarch

For filling, cream butter and sugar. Add the remaining ingredients. Place about 2 T. filling in each of 16 crepes and roll up. Place seam side down in a pan and warm in oven (350° for 10-15 minutes) before serving. Top with fresh strawberries or cherry glaze.

For glaze, mix sugar and cornstarch. Add to juice and heat to boiling. Cook until thickened and add cherries.

Serves 8.

Mrs. Virgil Pate

ALMOND CREAM FILLING FOR CREPES

Basic dessert crêpes
1 c. sugar
¼ c. flour
1 c. milk
2 eggs
2 egg yolks
3 T. butter
2 t. vanilla
½ t. almond extract
½ c. crushed almonds, toasted

Mix sugar, flour, and milk together; cook over medium heat until thick and stir 1 or 2 minutes longer. Beat eggs with the egg yolks; remove pan from fire and *slowly* add eggs, always stirring. Blend in butter, vanilla, almond extract, and crushed almonds. Place on low heat and stir until mixture thickens. Grease pan or serving dish with butter; add crêpes which have been individually filled with almond cream filling and cover with foil. May be refrigerated until ready to bake. Refrigerate any remaining filling. While having dinner, bake crêpes in 300-350° oven for 20-25 minutes. Serve with fresh whipped cream topping or grated, unsweetened chocolate on top or both for color.

Serves 8-10.

Mrs. Bedford Shelmire, Jr.

DEEP APPLE DISH WITH RUM SAUCE

8-10 large tart apples, peeled,
    cored, and sliced
1 c. sugar
1 t. cinnamon
Juice and grated rind of 1
    orange
4 T. butter
½ c. brown sugar
½ c. flour
½ c. butter
RUM SAUCE:
1 c. sugar
½ c. butter
4 egg yolks, well beaten
4 T. brandy
½ c. rum
Sweetened whipped cream

In a large bowl toss apples, sugar, cinnamon, rind and orange juice. Dot with 4 T. butter. Mix brown sugar, flour, and ½ c. butter and spread over top of apples. Bake at 350° for 1 hour or until golden brown in color. Serve warm and pass sweetened whipped cream and rum sauce.

Rum Sauce: Cream sugar and butter. Add egg yolks. Place in double boiler and cook until thick, being careful not to overcook. Add brandy and rum and stir in well. This is very rich, and small portions are adequate after a large meal. Could serve 10-12.

Mrs. William E. Gibbons

BAKED APPLES

Apples
Raisins
Brown sugar
Butter
Vanilla
Brandy or sherry
Whipped cream

Core desired number of apples. Fill with a mixture of raisins, brown sugar, butter and a little vanilla. Bake in a 325° oven for one hour with a very little water in the pan, basting frequently. When removed from oven, pour 1 T. brandy or sherry over each apple. Serve with whipped cream. May be served with brandy burning.

BLENDER CHOCOLATE ORANGE MOUSSE

6-oz. pkg. chocolate chips
2 T. Kahlua
1 T. orange juice
2 whole eggs plus 2 yolks
1 t. vanilla
¼ c. sugar
1 c. whipping cream

Melt chocolate over boiling water in the top of a double boiler. Add Kahlua and orange juice and allow to cool. Using high speed, blend eggs, vanilla, and sugar for 2 minutes. Add cream and blend for 30 seconds. Add chocolate mixture and blend until smooth. Spoon into pôt-de-crèmes. Chill 2 hours. Serve with extra whipped cream.
Serves 4.

Cookbook Committee

BISCUIT TORTONI

30 small macaroon cookies
2 egg yolks, slightly beaten
½ c. granulated sugar
¼ t. salt
1 c. milk, scalded
1 envelope gelatine
¼ c. cold water
½ pt. cream, whipped
1 t. vanilla
2 egg whites

Place macaroon cookies, 10 at a time, between two pieces of waxed paper and crush into fine crumbs with a rolling pin. Slide crumbs into the bottom of an ungreased, flat, rectangular (2-quart) Pyrex dish. After all the crumbs are in, distribute evenly over the bottom and pat with fingers. In the top of a double boiler combine the egg yolks, sugar, salt, and scalded milk. Cook over hot water, stirring constantly, and being careful not to curdle the mixture. When it reaches a custard-like consistency, remove from the heat. Have the cold water already measured into a cereal bowl. Sprinkle the gelatin over the top of the water. After the gelatin is completely softened, add it to the hot custard, stirring it in thoroughly. Cool the custard in the refrigerator. When the custard mixture begins to congeal, whip the cream, add the vanilla, and fold into the mixture. In a separate bowl with clean beaters, beat the egg whites until stiff and dry. Fold this also into the mixture. Pour this mixture over the crumbs in the Pyrex. Chill overnight.
Serves 8.

Mrs. John H. Bissell

CANTALOUPE SUPREME

1 cantaloupe, seeds removed
Fresh fruits in season
Powdered sugar
¼ c. kirsch
1 T. slivered, blanched
   almonds

Cut a round from the top of a large cantaloupe, leaving it cup-shaped. Scoop out meat with a round-bowled spoon into small balls. Make a mixture of fruits in season such as pineapple, strawberries or raspberries, and the melon balls. Sprinkle with sugar and almonds, and pour the kirsch over it. Fill melon with mixture, chill and serve.

Mrs. W. W. Overton, Jr.

CHOCOLATE CREAM IN CHOCOLATE SHELLS

SHELLS:
8-oz. Cadbury milk chocolate bar
CHOCOLATE-ALMOND FILLING:
6-oz. Cadbury milk chocolate almond bar
15 regular marshmallows or 1½ c. miniature marshmallows
⅓ c. milk
1 c. whipping cream
CHOCOLATE LEAVES:
Semi-sweet chocolate

For shells, melt bar in the top of a double boiler and stir until melted. Remove from heat and cool slightly. Place 10 foil-lined paper cups (2¾" each) in a muffin pan. Evenly coat the insides, starting with the bottoms. A silver teaspoon may be used to do the bottoms and part way up the sides. Finish by using a table knife to smooth the sides up to the tops. Any thin spots may be touched up after chilling for 10 minutes in the refrigerator. Chill the shells in a covered container in the refrigerator overnight. Gently peel the paper cups from the chocolate and replace in the refrigerator. These will keep for several weeks if stored in the refrigerator in an air-tight container. About an hour before serving, fill with filling.

For filling, chop candy into small pieces and place in the top of a double boiler. Melt with marshmallows and milk over hot but not boiling water. Cool. Whip cream and fold into the chocolate mixture. The shells may be garnished with either chocolate curls or leaves. Return to refrigerator before serving. Also may be frozen.

For leaves, pour melted semi-sweet chocolate over small ivy leaves or other small leaves. After the chocolate sets, pull the leaves by their stems from the back, leaving chocolate leaves. The leaves packed in small candy boxes make wonderful Christmas gifts.

Makes 10 servings.

Cook Book Committee

OLD FASHIONED BUTTERMILK GINGERBREAD

2 c. flour
1 c. sugar
4 t. cinnamon
2 t. ginger
1 t. nutmeg
1 t. soda
1 t. salt
1 c. salad oil
1 c. cane syrup
1 c. buttermilk
2 eggs
1 t. vanilla

Sift dry ingredients. Add to liquid mixture. Pour into 9"x13" greased pan. Bake at 325° for 45 minutes to 1 hour. Serve with a warm custard sauce.
Serves 12-16.

Mrs. Jack Houston Davis

KULICH
Russian Easter Dessert

1 c. milk
1 c. water
2 pkgs. yeast
7 egg yolks
1 whole egg
1 vanilla bean or 1 T. vanilla
1 c. powdered sugar
¾ lb. sweet butter
¼ c. currants and candied fruit, chopped
¼ c. citron, chopped
1 jigger brandy
Enough flour to make hard dough (about 8 cups)
2 T. cardamom seeds, crushed (optional)
4 T. almonds, chopped

Crumble yeast in a large bowl. Add water and lukewarm milk and stir until smooth. Add 1 cup flour and mix with wooden spoon. Add yolks and 1 T. sugar and mix. Cover bowl with cloth and set aside in a warm place to rise until doubled in volume. Cream butter and remaining sugar and add brandy, whole egg, rest of flour, vanilla, currants, candied fruit, almonds, and cardamon. Combine this with the yeast mixture and knead until dough is smooth and elastic (about 20 minutes.) Set aside to rise again until dough is doubled in volume. Punch down and fill tall cylindrical cans about ⅓ full (can use 6 1-lb. coffee cans.) Cans should be brushed with melted butter. Let rise in pans for 30 minutes and bake at 400° for 10 minutes. Reduce heat to 350° and bake 50 minutes to 1 hour or until bread is browned and done. Let cool in the pans for 15 minutes before tipping it gently onto a cake rack. Slice in rounds across the cake. Serve with paskha.
Serves 12-16.

Mrs. Edward W. Rose III

HOLIDAY PUDDING

1 c. prunes, cooked and mashed
½ c. sugar
1. c. nuts, chopped
½ c. milk
Dash of salt
1 T. water
⅓ c. flour
1 t. baking powder
½ t. cinnamon

Mix all ingredients well and pour into a buttered baking dish. Place in a pan of hot water and bake at 350° for 30 minutes or until firm. Serve with sweetened whipped cream. Can be mixed early in the day and baked as dinner is being served.

HOT FUDGE SAUCE

1 can Eagle Brand milk
3 squares unsweetened
  chocolate
1 c. sugar
½ stick butter
1 t. vanilla

Mix milk, chocolate, and sugar in the top of a double boiler until smooth. Add butter and vanilla. Heat until smooth. Keep in the refrigerator and reheat for servings.

Mrs. Mickey Hudnall

CLAFOUTI aux POMMES

2½ lbs. cooking apples, peeled,
  cored and sliced ¼" thick
  (about 6 cups)
6 T. butter
⅔ c. sugar
½ c. brandy
Milk
4 eggs
2 t. vanilla
¼ t. salt
1 c. sifted flour

Sauté the apples lightly in 5 T. of the butter until they are golden but still firm, not mushy. Sprinkle them with the sugar and pour the brandy over them. Leave for ½ hour, then drain off and measure the liquid. Add enough milk to make 2½ cups liquid. Preheat the oven to 400°. Combine the 2½ cups liquid, eggs, vanilla, salt and flour in a blender and blend for 1 minute (may have to be done in two batches, depending on size of blender.) Butter 2 baking dishes or deep Pyrex pie plates with the remaining butter. Pour a thin layer of batter from the blender into each one and put on an asbestos pad over low heat until set. Divide the apples between the two plates, spreading them over the set batter and pour the remaining batter over them. Bake for 35-40 minutes or until the batter is set and cooked through but still moist and custardy. Reduce heat to 350° for the last 10 minutes if batter is getting too brown on top. Serves 12.

Mrs. Mark Lemmon, Jr.

PASKHA
(Russian Easter Dessert)

4 c. sugar
4 lbs. pot cheese or farmers cheese
1½ lb. sweet butter room temp.
12 hard-boiled egg yolks
1 pt. heavy cream
1 pt. sour cream
4 oz. slivered almonds, chopped
1 t. lemon rind, grated
1 vanilla bean, finely chopped or 2 T. vanilla
½ c. candied orange peel, chopped
½ c. lemon peel, chopped
½ c. citron, chopped

Three hours before preparation wrap cheese in a wet cloth napkin and put in a colander under a weight to drain. Put through a meat grinder or mash together well the drained cheese and hard-boiled egg yolks. Put the vanilla bean through the grinder or cut into tiny pieces into cheese mixture. Blend butter and sugar with a wooden spoon or electric beater until smooth. Mix together cheese and egg mixture with the butter and sugar mixture until smooth. Add the almonds, already mixed candied fruit, and lemon rind. Whip heavy cream until stiff and gently fold into the cheese mixture. Fold in the sour cream. Line a paskha form or clean flower pot with 2 layers of wet cheese cloth. Fill mold with paskha and bring edges of cheese cloth over top. Place mold or pot in a shallow dish to catch liquid that runs off. Set a weight on top of the cheesecloth, perhaps a dish filled with 2 or 3 heavy cans of food. Press for 2 days in the refrigerator. When ready to serve unwrap cheesecloth from top and invert paskha onto a platter. You may decorate paskha with additional almonds and candied fruit. Serve with kulich. (Once unmolded, the paskha can be safely kept in the refrigerator for at least a week.
Serves 12 to 16.

Mrs. Edward W. Rose III

PINEAPPLE FRITTERS

1 fresh pineapple
Sugar
Kirsch
BATTER:
½ c. flour
¼ t. salt
1 egg
1 T. melted butter
½ c. flat beer
1 egg white

Peel and core pineapple and cut it into slices ¼″ thick. Cut each ring in half. Sprinkle with sugar and kirsch and let stand for 30 minutes. Make batter by sifting flour and salt. Beat egg, add butter and combine with flour. Add beer and stir mixture until it is smooth. Let batter stand at room temperature for 1-2 hours until it is light and fluffy. Fold in stiffly beaten egg white just before using. Drain pineapple slices well and dip them into fritter batter. Drop them, a few at a time, into deep hot fat (370°) and fry them until they are delicately brown. Drain fritters well on absorbent paper, sprinkle with sugar and glaze under the broiler.

Mrs. Jack Vaughn

PRUNE WHIP

⅔ c. stewed prunes, pureed in
    food mill
5 egg whites
½ c. sugar
½ T. lemon juice

Add the sugar to the prunes and cook about five minutes. The mixture should be the consistency of marmalade. Cool. Beat the egg whites until stiff. When the prune mixture has cooled, add the lemon juice and then fold the mixture into the beaten egg whites. Pile lightly into a pudding dish or souffle dish and bake 25 minutes at 300°. Serve warm with whipped cream.
Serves 6 to 8.

Mrs. Dan C. Williams

LANCERS CLUB'S
STRAWBERRIES ROMANOFF

8 oz. seedless raisins
2 oz. brandy
8 oz. light brown sugar
1 t. cinnamon
Pinch of nutmeg
2 pts. sour cream.
Strawberries

In blender, pureé raisins with the brandy. Add sugar, cinnamon, nutmeg, and sour cream. Blend well. Serve over fresh strawberries.
Serves 10-12.

ORANGE-POACHED PEARS

24 medium Bosc pears
2 lemons
3 c. water
1½ c. sugar
2 c. white wine
1 c. orange-flavored liqueur
10 cloves
3 wide strips orange peel
½ c. brandy

Carefully peel pears, leaving the stems intact. Drop the pears as they are peeled into a bowl of cold water, acidulated with juice of 2 lemons. In a saucepan, bring water and sugar to a boil over moderate heat and simmer the syrup for 5 minutes. Arrange the pears on their sides in one layer in a 14x10″ baking dish and pour white wine mixture with liqueur, the syrup and cloves over them. Add orange rind to liquid and bring to a simmer on top of the stove. Cover with aluminum foil and bake pears in a 375° oven for 30 minutes. Remove foil and turn pears onto other sides, lifting them carefully by the stems. Replace the foil and bake the pears 20-30 more minutes or until they are tender. Carefully transfer the pears by the stems to a deep dish, add brandy to juices and ladle the juices over the pears. Let pears cool and chill overnight. Serve with the juices and pass a bowl of slightly sweetened whipped cream flavored with orange liqueur, or serve with chocolate sauce.

Mrs. Searcy Ferguson, Jr.

CHOCOLATE MOUSSE

2 1-oz. squares unsweetened
  chocolate, melted
½ c. confectioners sugar
1 c. milk, heated
1 envelope unflavored gelatin,
  softened in 3 T. cold water
¾ c. sugar
1 t. vanilla
¼ t. salt
2 c. heavy cream, whipped

Combine chocolate and confectioners sugar in saucepan. Gradually add hot milk, stirring constantly. Place over low heat and stir until mixture reaches boiling point but do not boil. Remove from heat; stir in softened gelatin, sugar, vanilla, and salt. Chill until slightly thickened. Beat until light and fluffy. Fold in whipped cream — chill 3 to 4 hours.
For decoration: whipped cream and almonds. Definitely make the day before. Serves 8.

Mrs. Arthur C. White

KAHLUA MOUSSE

1 c. sugar
1 c. water
12 oz. semi-sweet chocolate
  chips
4 eggs
Dash of salt
⅓ c. Kahlua
¼ c. Cognac
3 c. whipped cream

Combine sugar and water in a saucepan and heat slowly until sugar is completely melted — about 5 minutes. Place the chocolate pieces in a blender with the eggs and salt. Turn blender to slowest speed and add the syrup in a steady, slow stream. Blend until smooth. Add Kahlua and Cognac and mix. Fold in whipped cream. Put in individual serving dishes or quart mold or casserole. Chill several hours. Freezes beautifully. At serving time, top with a dollop of whipped cream.
Serves about 12.

Mrs. Lawrence H. Wilson, Jr.

MAPLE MOUSSE

4 egg yolks
¾ c. maple syrup
1 pt. heavy cream
Whipped cream
Toasted almonds

In the top of a double boiler, combine beaten egg yolks and maple syrup. Stir over boiling water until mixture thickens and coats spoon. Remove from fire and cool. Fold whipped cream into cooled mixture and turn into mold. Cover tightly and freeze without stirring for 4 or 5 hours. Serve in parfait glasses with spoonful of whipped cream and almonds.
Serves 6.

Mrs. Mark Lemmon, Jr.

FROZEN PUMPKIN MOUSSE

1½ c. canned pumpkin
1 c. sugar
1 t. cinnamon
1 t. nutmeg
½ t. cloves
3 T. grated preserved ginger
¼ t. salt
1 c. milk
½ c. Cognac
1 t. vanilla
2 c. heavy cream

Combine pumpkin, sugar, spices, salt and milk. Blend, then add Cognac and vanilla. Fold in whipped cream and place in 2-qt. mold and freeze 3 hours. Serve with rich cookies.
Serves 8.

Cookbook Committee

HOT CHOCOLATE PUDDING

3 1-oz. squares chocolate
1 c. sugar
4 eggs, separated
¼ t. salt
2 t. vanilla
½ pt. whipping cream

Melt chocolate in the top of a double boiler and add ⅓ c. sugar. Stir until sugar is dissolved. Whip egg yolks until lemon-colored; then add ⅓ c. sugar. Beat egg whites with salt until soft peaks are formed; then beat in remaining ⅓ c. sugar. Combine yolks and whites. Fold in chocolate mixture and add vanilla. Turn into a well-buttered 1½-qt. casserole; set casserole in a pan of hot water and bake 30-40 minutes at 375°. Top with whipped cream and serve immediately.
Serves 6.

JUDY'S POT-DE-CREME

½ lb. sweet chocolate
½ c. light cream or half and half
3 egg yolks, slightly beaten
1 c. heavy cream, whipped
¼ c. pistachio nuts, chopped
¼ c. rum

Melt chocolate in cream on top of double boiler over boiling water. Stir until smooth. Beat egg yolks in a bowl and pour a small amount of hot chocolate mixture over them, stirring constantly. Keep adding chocolate to yolks until most of it is in the mixture, stirring vigorously. Return the mixture to top of double boiler for 3 minutes. Stir constantly. Remove from heat, stir in rum and cool. Fold in the whipped cream and pour into cups. Chill several hours or overnight. At serving time, garnish with more whipped cream and a few pistachio nuts.
Serves 6-8.

Mrs. John Bagwell

FLOATING ISLAND

4 egg yolks
2 T. flour
½ c. sugar
Pinch of salt
1 pint heavy cream
Vanilla or almond flavoring
MERINGUES:
1 egg white
¼ c. sugar
½ t. flavoring used in above

Beat yolks well. Sift flour, sugar and salt. Beat flour mixture into the yolks. Heat the cream almost to the boiling point and pour it over the yolks. Stir well and return to pan. Cook slowly, stirring constantly with a wooden spoon, until custard is thick enough to coat the the spoon. This will take about 10 minutes. If custard becomes too thick, a little cream will thin it. If the eggs curdle, beat the custard with a rotary beater until smooth. Flavor to suit yourself, either almond or vanilla or both. Chill. Serve in berry bowls with meringues on top, putting them on at the last minute. For meringues, beat egg white until very stiff. Add sugar gradually, beating all the time. Add flavoring. Spray Pam on cookie sheet, but do not grease. Drop meringue mixture from a teaspoon and bake at 200° until meringues are dry but not too brown. Cool and store in a tin. If they become limp, a few minutes in a warm oven should restore their crispness.
Makes 20 meringues.
Custard will serve 4.

Mrs. L. G. Pondrom

BLENDER EGG CUSTARD — CARAMEL

1 c. hot milk
1 c. light cream
⅓ c. sugar
¼ t. salt
2 eggs
Brown sugar

Put eggs into bottom of glass container of blender. Cover and blend at low for 2 minutes. Add sugar and salt and blend at low for 1 minute. With blender on low, remove filler cap and slowly add the cream, blending well. Then add hot milk in same manner. Blend well. Place t. of brown sugar in bottom of individual custard cups; then fill with mixture. Place molds in a pan of hot water and bake at 325° until custard is set and knife comes out clean — approximately 45 minutes. Chill. Very quick and easy.
Serves 4.

Mrs. A. C. Black

ENGLISH BOILED CUSTARD

2 quarts milk
12 eggs
2 coffee cups sugar (or to taste)
1½ T. vanilla
½ pint whipping cream
   whipped with 2 T. sugar

Heat milk in a large double boiler until quite hot but not boiling. Beat eggs until light and fluffy in mixer. Add sugar and vanilla and beat again. Add slowly to hot milk, stirring constantly with wooden spoon or rubber spatula. Cook until mixture becomes fairly thick, stirring (approx. 12 minutes). It will become thicker when cold. When thoroughly cold, fold in the whipped cream. Top with nutmeg. Other flavorings may be added if desired.
Serves 8-10.

Mrs. James B. Hudnall III

CREME BRULE

1 qt. heavy cream
2″ piece of vanilla bean
4 T. sugar
8 egg yolks, AT ROOM
   TEMPERATURE
Pinch of salt
Brown sugar

Scald cream with vanilla bean. Add sugar and stir until dissolved. Beat egg yolks until lemon colored (most important that eggs be at room temperature.) Stir hot cream mixture into egg yolks with salt. Strain into quiche pan or individual soufflé dishes, set in hot water, and cook 55-60 minutes at 350° or until custard is set. Cool, then refrigerate. Push brown sugar through a sieve onto the custard. Smooth, then run under broiler 3-6 minutes. WATCH VERY CAREFULLY! Cool, then refrigerate. Cannot be put in the broiler more than one day ahead.
Serves 4-6.

Mrs. M. Weatherby Carr

CREME CARAMEL

4 eggs
⅓ c. sugar
Pinch salt
½ pint whipping cream
1 t. vanilla

Beat eggs, sugar and salt until thickened. Heat cream until it begins to steam, but do not let it boil. Pour hot cream over eggs, add vanilla, stir well. Ladle into custard cups, from 4-6 depending on size of cups. Set filled cups in a pan of cold water, with water coming up to within an inch of the tops of the cups. Bake this in 350° oven until centers feel firm to touch. Cool, then refrigerate. Run a small knife around the outside of the cup and unmold to serve.
Top with Caramel Sauce.
Serves 4-6.

Mrs. L. G. Pondrom

LEMON CREAM AND BERRIES

4 egg yolks
1 c. sugar
4 T. lemon juice
1 T. cornstarch
½ c. water
1 t. vanilla
2 t. grated lemon rind
Dash of salt
1 c. heavy cream, whipped
3 pts. fresh raspberries or 2 pts.
    fresh strawberries mixed
    with 1 pint fresh or frozen
    blueberries.

In a mixing bowl, beat egg yolks, ½ c. sugar and lemon juice until light. In heavy saucepan, combine remaining ½ c. sugar, salt and cornstarch dissolved in ½ c. cold water. Cook until thick and clear over high heat. Remove from heat and beat in egg yolk mixture. Place over very low heat and stir constantly until thickens slightly. Remove from heat, add vanilla and lemon rind, and cool completely. Whip cream and fold into cooled sauce. Chill. Serve the berries in a crystal bowl with the lemon sauce on the side.
Serves 6-8.

Mrs. Edward W. Rose III

LEMON CHIFFON PUDDING

1 c. sugar
4 T. flour
¼ t. salt
2 egg yolks, beaten
¼ c. lemon juice
Grated rind of lemons
1 c. milk
1 T. melted butter
2 egg whites, stiffly beaten

Mix sugar, flour, and salt. Add alternately to yolks with lemon juice, rind, milk and butter. Fold in egg whites. Pour into individual custard cups, place in pan of hot water. Bake 30-40 minutes at 350°. Turn upside down to serve. (Sauce has now formed.)
Serves 4.

Mrs. Virgil Pate

MANDARIN ORANGE CHEESE CREAM

8 oz. cream cheese
⅔ c. powdered sugar
1 egg yolk
1 t. grated orange peel
1 T. orange flavored liqueur or
    frozen orange juice
¾ c. whipping cream
Mandarin oranges

Soften cream cheese and beat in powdered sugar. Beat in egg yolk, peel, and liqueur or juice. Pour in whipping cream and beat until soft peaks form. Spoon into 6 oz. wine glasses and chill. Top with mandarin oranges, if desired.
Serves 4-6.

Mrs. L. Franklin Beard

MANGO SLICES

2 or 3 canned mango slices
1 t. frozen orange juice
Shredded coconut

For each serving, place 2 or 3 mango slices in ramekins. Add 1 teaspoon of frozen orange to each and sprinkle with shredded coconut. Place in a 400° oven long enough to brown the coconut. Serve with a cookie.

Mrs. J. Murray Smith

PERSIMMON PUDDING

1 c. persimmon pulp
1 egg
⅝ c. sugar
¾ c. flour
½ t. baking powder
½ t. soda
¼ t. salt
¼ c. melted butter
1 c. milk
1 t. cinnamon
½ t. ginger
¼ t. nutmeg

Combine all ingredients and put into a 2-qt. soufflé dish. Bake in a water bath for 1 hour at 350°. Serve with a hard sauce. Serves 8.

Mrs. Searcy Ferguson, Jr.

STRAWBERRIES IN SWEDISH CREAM

2 pints fresh strawberries, hulled
2 c. heavy cream
1 c. sugar
1 envelope gelatin
1 pt. sour cream
1 t. vanilla

Mix together cream and sugar in a saucepan. Heat gently. When sugar dissolves, add gelatin. Stir over very low heat until gelatin dissolves. Do not allow to boil. Cool slightly until it begins to thicken. When cool, fold in sour cream. Flavor with vanilla. Chill in refrigerator until firm. Before serving, stir in berries. Serves 8-10.

Mrs. Judy Weatherford

APRICOT SOUFFLE

1 8-oz. pkg. dried apricots
1 T. lemon juice
2 c. boiling water
¾ c. sugar
Juice from cooking apricots
8 egg whites

Cook apricots with lemon juice and boiling water until very soft. Add sugar and stir until sugar is dissolved. Put into blender and pureé until smooth. Cool completely. Beat egg whites until stiff. Stir about one fourth of the egg whites into apricot mixture and then fold remaining egg whites in rapidly and thoroughly. Attach buttered foil collar to sugared soufflé dish (use heavy duty foil, folded over lengthwise — attached at top with straight pin.) Place dish in pan with 2" of boiling water. Bake 25-30 minutes at 400°. Remove collar gently and serve immediately with sweetened whipped cream (do not whip it stiff — just gently). Serves 8.

Note: You can cook the apricots hours before dinner, whip the egg whites and fold in just before baking.

Mrs. George Spencer, Jr.

BRANDY ALEXANDER SOUFFLE

2 envelopes unflavored gelatin
2 c. cold water
1 c. sugar
4 eggs, separated
8 oz. cream cheese
3 T. crème de cocoa
3 T. brandy
½ pt. heavy cream, whipped

Soften gelatin in 1 c. water. Stir over low heat to dissolve. Add remaining water. Remove from heat and blend in ¾ c. sugar and beaten egg yolks. Return to heat and cook 2-3 minutes, until thickened. Gradually add to softened cream cheese, mixing until well blended. Stir in crème de cocoa and brandy. Chill until slightly thickened. Beat egg whites until soft peaks form. Gradually add remaining sugar, beating until meringues are stiff. Fold in egg whites and whipped cream. Wrap a 3 inch collar of foil around top of 1½ quart soufflé dish. Secure with tape. Pour mixture into dish and chill until firm.

Serves 14.

Mrs. John J. Kendrick, Jr.

SURPRISE CHOCOLATE SOUFFLE

1 16-oz. can bing cherries
¼ stick butter
1 c. toasted pecans, chopped
½ stick butter
¼ c. flour
1 c. milk
1 c. sugar
¼ c. cocoa
Pinch of salt
4 eggs, separated
1 t. vanilla

Drain cherries and cut in half, removing stones if there are any. Spread ¼ stick melted butter on bottom and sides of a shallow soufflé dish. Spread cherry halves on the bottom of the dish and sprinkle with pecans. Melt ½ stick butter and blend in flour. Add milk, sugar, cocoa, and salt and cook slowly, stirring constantly until the milk is hot. Pour this over the well-beaten egg yolks and return to pan. Cook, stirring constantly, until the custard thickens and coats the spoon. Remove from heat and let cool. Add vanilla. Beat egg whites until very stiff and fold into the chocolate sauce. Pour on top of the cherries. Set the bowl in a pan of cold water and bake at 350° for about 45-50 minutes or until the top is firm.
Serves 6.

Mrs. L. G. Pondrom

COLD COFFEE SOUFFLE

1½ envelopes unflavored
   gelatin
1½ c. water
1 c. milk
¾ c. sugar
¼ t. salt
2 T. instant or freeze-dried
   coffee (or expresso if
   desired)
3 eggs, separated
1 t. vanilla

Mix gelatin with water; add milk, sugar, salt, and coffee. Place mixture in a double boiler and heat until it is scalded and gelatin is dissolved. Beat egg yolks and add to the coffee mixture; cook until custard coats spoon. Remove from heat and add vanilla. Mix well. Place in refrigerator to chill until consistency thickens and becomes syrupy. Remove from refrigerator at that point, and beat well with a rotary beater (or in a blender) until mixture is very smooth. Beat egg whites until stiff. Fold into the coffee mixture. Pour into individual sherbet glasses or ramekins and chill until firm. Garnish with chocolate curls at serving.
Serves 6.

Mrs. John W. McDonough

GINGERBREAD SOUFFLE

3 T. flour
3 T. butter
1 c. milk
3 eggs, separated
1 heaping T. ginger
½ t. each of allspice, cloves and
   cinnamon
SAUCE:
1 c. sugar
⅔ c. water
1 T. flour
1 T. butter
1 t. vanilla

Melt butter in the top of a double boiler, add flour and milk. Cook until thick and add egg yolks, then spices, and beaten whites. Cook on top of stove in a pan of hot water for 40 minutes. For the sauce cook sugar, flour, and water until flour is well done. Remove from fire and add butter and vanilla. Serve on top of soufflé.

Miss Alma Walne

GRAND MARNIER SOUFFLE

8 egg yolks
⅔ c. sugar
½ c. Grand Marnier
10 egg whites
Pinch of cream of tartar

Beat egg yolks with sugar over hot water in a double boiler until mixture makes a ribbon when held up and allowed to pour back into a saucepan. Add Grand Marnier and beat over a bowl of ice until cool. Beat egg whites until firm, not dry, and add cream of tartar. Fold into and blend thoroughly, but lightly, with yolk mixture. Pour into a buttered and sugared soufflé dish, and bake at 400° 12-15 minutes, or until risen and delicately browned. Serve at once.
Serves 4.

Mrs. Edward H. Tenison, Jr.

COLD LEMON SOUFFLE

5 eggs, separated
1 c. sugar
1¼ t. finely grated lemon rind
½ c. lemon juice
2 envelopes unflavored gelatin
⅓ c. cold water
1 c. heavy cream

Fasten a collar of waxed paper or foil around a 5-cup soufflé dish extending 2 inches above the top. With an electric beater, mix egg yolks with sugar, beating 4 minutes at medium speed. Soak gelatin in water, warming to dissolve. Cool slightly. Stiffly whip egg whites and half whip heavy cream. With rubber scraper, stir gelatin into lemon mixture, then fold in cream and lastly egg whites. Pour into prepared soufflé dish. Chill at least 2 hours. Just before serving, carefully peel off paper collar.
Serves 6 to 8.

Mrs. Walter N. Kuntz III

COLD ORANGE SOUFFLE

1 c. cold water
2 envelopes unflavored gelatin
2 6-oz. cans frozen orange
   concentrate
Grated rind of 1 large orange
8 eggs, separated
½ t. salt
1 c. sugar
1 c. heavy cream

Place water in top of a double boiler and sprinkle the gelatin over the surface to soften. Beat the egg yolks lightly and add salt. Combine egg and gelatin mixture and beat well. Place over boiling water and cook, stirring constantly until gelatin dissolves and mixture thickens a bit — about 4 minutes. Remove from double boiler and add orange concentrate. Chill over ice until mixture drops from a spoon into soft mounds. Beat egg whites a little, then gradually beat in the sugar and continue beating until the egg whites are stiff. Whip the cream. Fold the whites into the orange mixture and then fold in the cream.

Arrange a collar of double wax paper — which has been buttered around the 1½ qt. soufflé dish. The collar should come two inches above the top of the dish. Fasten with string and paper clip. Pour mixture into dish and chill firm. Remove collar and press praline powder, macarooon crumbs, or toasted powdered almonds around the exposed sides of the soufflé Decorate top with orange or mandarin sections (optional) and whipped cream forced through a pastry tube. Serves 10-12.

Mrs. Julian A. Wells

COLD PEACH SOUFFLE

2 envelopes unflavored gelatin
½ c. cold water
2 eggs, separated
1 T. lemon juice
¼ t. salt
½ c. sugar
2 10-oz. pkgs. frozen peaches,
   thawed, retaining juice
¼ c. apricot liqueur
1 c. whipping cream, whipped
MELBA SAUCE:
1 pkg. frozen raspberries,
   thawed and drained
½ c. currant jelly
1½ t. cornstarch
1 T. cold water

Sprinkle gelatin over cold water to soften; then dissolve over hot water. Combine egg yolks, lemon juice, salt, sugar, and a little of the peach juice in the top of a double boiler; cook over boiling water while stirring until thick and sugar is dissolved. Add dissolved gelatin and blend well. Pureé the thawed peaches in the blender and add egg mixture to blender along with apricot liqueur; blend briefly but thoroughly. Transfer into large bowl. Beat egg whites until they stand in precise peaks and fold into peach mixture. Whip cream until thick and fold into mixture carefully. Tie a 6″ collar of wax paper around a 2 quart soufflé dish. Brush dish and collar with melted unsalted butter. Pour mixture into soufflé dish, sprinkle with white granulated sugar and chill until firm. Serve with or without Melba Sauce.
Melba Sauce: In a saucepan, mash raspberries. Add jelly; bring to a boil. Add cornstarch mixed with water. Cook, stirring, until clear and thickened. Strain if desired and cool.
Serves 6-8.

Mrs. John W. McDonough

RICOTTA TORTE

1½ lb. ricotta, well drained
3 T. flour
5 T. sugar
4 egg yolks
Grated rind of ½ orange
Grated rind of 1 lemon
1 T. rum or Cognac *or* 1½ t.
   vanilla
2 T. currants
4 T. pine nuts, lightly toasted
3 egg whites, stiffly beaten
3 T. confectioners sugar
1½ t. cinnamon

Mix ricotta, flour, sugar and egg yolks. Beat for 7 or 8 minutes. Then add other ingredients except egg white. Mix well. Fold in beaten egg whites. Bake in buttered 9 inch cake pan at 375° for 45 minutes. Do not open oven door. Cool and sprinkle with the confectioners sugar and cinnamon which have been mixed together.

Mrs. James Lambert

PRALINE SOUFFLE

½ stick butter
¼ c. flour
1 c. milk
¼ c. sugar
6 eggs, separated
2 T. dark rum
⅛ t. salt
¼ t. cream of tartar
¼ c. sugar
1 c. praline powder
1 c. heavy cream, whipped
Sugar to taste

Fit 2½-qt. soufflé dish, buttered, with band of wax paper, doubled and buttered, to form standing collar extending 3″ above rim. In saucepan, melt butter over moderate heat. Add flour. Cook roux, stirring constantly, for 2 minutes. Add milk, ¼ c. sugar and cook until thickened. Remove pan from heat. Add egg yolks, one at a time, beating well after each addition. Add rum. Beat egg whites with salt and cream of tartar until they hold soft peaks. Add ¼ cup sugar, gradually. Beat until stiff. Add ⅔ cup praline powder to yolk mixture and fold in ¼ of whites gently but thoroughly. Pour mixture onto remaining whites and fold together until there are no traces of white. Pour into soufflé dish and smooth top. Sprinkle ⅓ cup praline powder over soufflé and bake in 375° oven for 35 minutes or until set. Remove paper collar and serve with sweetened whipped cream. Les Fréres Troigros pours 2 tablespoons rum, heated and ignited, over cooked soufflé.
Serves 8.

Brook Hollow Golf Club

FROZEN MOCHA TOFFEE DESSERT

8 lady fingers, split
2 T. instant coffee crystals
1 T. boiling water
1 qt. coffee ice cream, softened
4 chocolate-covered toffee bars, frozen and crushed, about 1 cup
½ c. whipping cream
2 T. (or more) crème de cacao or Kahlua

Line bottom and 2″ up sides of an 8″ spring form pan with split lady fingers. Dissolve coffee crystals in water and cool. Stir together ice cream, coffee, and crushed candy. Spoon into pan, cover, and freeze. Before serving, combine cream and liqueur. Whip to soft peaks. Spread over top of ice cream; layer and garnish with candy pieces.
Makes 8-10 servings.

Mrs. Hobby H. McCall

CAKE:
6 egg yolks
1 c. sugar
2 T. orange juice
2 c. grated pecans
2 T. flour
¼ t. salt
½ t. baking powder
6 egg whites, beaten
FILLING:
1 c. whipping cream, whipped
Zest of 1 orange
2 T. Curacao
1 T. powdered sugar
FROSTING:
6 oz. melted semi-sweet
    chocolate
½ c. sour cream
½ c. powdered sugar
1 egg yolk
TOPPING:
1 c. brown sugar
½ c. melted butter
¼ c. whipped cream
2 c. powdered sugar

AUTUMN NUT TORTE

Beat egg yolks and sugar until light. Add remaining cake ingredients and pour into a well-buttered and floured pan (or one lined with waxed paper). Bake at 350° 25-30 minutes. Let cool, split, and fill with filling. Chill cake. Then frost with frosting and top with praline mixture. Use spatula to lightly pull chocolate through praline. Add whipped cream only after carmelization has occurred. Refrigerate 2 hours.
Serves 8-10.

Cook Book Committee

1 pt. sour cream
1½ c. dark brown sugar
2 T. rum
1 t. cinnamon
½ t. nutmeg

RUM AND SOUR CREAM SAUCE FOR FRUIT

Mix all ingredients together. Serve over strawberries, blueberries, or green grapes.

½ c. sugar
¼ c. water
1 c. boiling water
1 t. vanilla

CARAMEL SAUCE

Put sugar and ¼ c. water in a heavy pan deeper than a skillet. Cook quickly, stirring often. As water cooks away the sugar will return to a granular state. Scrape off spoon often with a knife. When grains begin to melt, turn heat to low so that sugar will brown slowly. Stir continually. When all lumps are gone add the boiling water. Some of the sugar will harden, but boiling will melt it again. When sauce is smooth remove from heat and add vanilla. Do not refrigerate. Sauce will keep in a tightly closed jar at room temperature for a long time. If too thick when ready to serve, add a couple of tablespoons hot water and stir well. Use on top of Creme Caramel or ice cream. Chopped toasted pecans or almond slivers are attractive on top of the caramel sauce.

Mrs. L. G. Pondrom

BUNUELOS (BUN-WAY-LOWS)

12 flour tortillas
1 jar coconut oil
½ lb. butter, melted
Cinnamon
Sugar
Allspice
12 scoops vanilla ice cream
Kahlua (optional)

Deep fry tortillas one by one in coconut oil on both sides until light brown and crisp. Place on paper towel; pour on melted butter and drain each. Sprinkle with cinnamon, sugar, and allspice. Top each hot tortilla with one scoop vanilla ice cream and Kahlua, if desired. These are best made individually and are a good item for teamwork — one person frying while the other finishes the preparation.
Serves 12.

Mrs. H. Leslie Moore II

HOT LEMON SPONGE

1 large lemon
2 eggs
1 c. sugar
3 T. flour
1 c. Half and Half

Grate rind of lemon and then extract the juice. Beat eggs well. Add sugar, flour, Half and Half, lemon juice and rind. Mix well. Grease a 1 quart soufflé dish or casserole with soft butter. Pour the lemon mixture into it. Put it in a pan of water deep enough so that the water comes to within an inch of the top of the dish. Bake at 350° for about an hour. Serve the sponge hot. The top will be firm while underneath there is a lovely sauce.
Serves 3-4.

Mrs. L. G. Pondrom

SNOW SQUARES

1 stick butter
1 c. sugar
2 eggs, separated
1 15-oz. can crushed pineapple, drained
1 c. chopped nuts
1 12-oz. box vanilla wafers, crushed
1 c. coconut
1 c. whipping cream, whipped

Cream butter and sugar. Add beaten egg yolks, crushed pineapple and nuts. Fold in well-beaten egg whites. In a 9-inch square Pyrex pan, layer ⅓ of crushed vanilla wafers, then ⅓ of the creamy mixture until you have 3 layers with creamed mixture on top. Let stand at room temperature 12 hours, then in the refrigerator for at least 12 hours. Before serving top with whipped cream and coconut. Can be frozen without the whipped cream and coconut.
Serves 8 to 10.

Mrs. Larry M. Nobles

ENGLISH TRIFLE

1 qt. milk, scalded
3 eggs, lightly beaten
½ c. sugar
1 Sarah Lee frozen pound cake
   (or 20 macaroons)
1 c. dry sherry
Red raspberry or black currant
   jam
Whipped cream for topping

Pour scalded milk over combined eggs and sugar. Cook and stir constantly in double boiler until mixture coats silver spoon. Set aside to cool. Slice cake into thin slices and sprinkle cake with sherry. Spread cake slices with thin layer of raspberry jam. Cover bottom of 11x7 serving bowl with slices of cake. Pour some of the custard over layer of cake slices. Repeat layers, making last layer custard. When ready to serve, trim with whipped cream and touches of jam. Best one day old.

Layers of whipped cream may be inserted if a richer trifle is desired.

Mrs. Nelson Phillips, Jr.

VALENTINE BOMBE

1 envelope unflavored gelatin
¼ c. sugar, divided
⅛ t. salt
½ c. milk
10-oz. pkg. frozen raspberries,
   thawed and drained
½ t. vanilla
2 egg whites
1 c. heavy cream, whipped
3-4 c. angel food cake, broken
   into bitesize pieces

Mix gelatin, 2 T. sugar and salt in a pan. Stir in milk and dissolve over low flame. Remove from heat and add raspberries and vanilla. Beat egg whites until stiff and slowly add remaining 2 T. sugar. Fold into gelatin mixture. Fold in whipped cream and angel food cake pieces. Turn into a 2-qt. mold or parfait glasses. Chill

Serves 6-8.

Mrs. George W. Bramblett, Jr.

FRESH APRICOT ICE CREAM

2 lbs. fresh apricots (or same
   amount of canned)
1¼ c. sugar
2 c. light cream
2 c. heavy cream
1 c. milk
⅛ t. salt
1 t. vanilla

Dip apricots, a few at a time, into boiling water for about 30 seconds until skins will slip off easily when peeled. Plunge into cold water and remove skin. Cut apricots in half and remove pits; place halves in electric blender container. Blend apricots until smooth. Combine puréed apricots and remaining ingredients in a container of 4-qt. electric or handchurn ice cream maker.

Mrs. Mark Lemmon, Jr.

CARAMEL ICE CREAM

4 c. milk
½ c. sugar
3 whole eggs
1¾ c. sugar, caramelized
1 qt. cream
¼ t. salt
1 T. vanilla
¾ c. boiling water

Scald milk in a double boiler. Beat sugar and eggs together until light and add to the scalded milk. Stir until it thickens. Add ¾ cup boiling water and the salt to the caramelized sugar, stirring over a low flame until smooth and mix with the custard while still warm. When cool, stir in cream and freeze.
Serves 10.

Home Economics Club, 1948 Junior League
Cookbook

MACADAMIA NUT ICE CREAM

3 egg yolks
¾ c. sugar
2½ c. hot milk
1 t. vanilla
2 c. heavy cream, whipped
¾ c. rum, or less, to taste
¾ c. macadamia nuts, chopped

In the top of a double boiler, beat egg yolks with sugar until the mixture is light. Gradually stir in hot milk. Put the pan over hot water or low heat and cook mixture, stirring constantly, until it is a little thicker and coats spoon (never gets very thick). Remove pan from heat. Strain custard, stir in vanilla, and let it cool. Fold in whipped cream. Freeze the ice cream in a churn freezer, if possible. Or freeze it in coldest part of refrigerator. When cream is almost frozen, beat in rum and nuts. Freeze the ice cream until it is firm.

Mrs. Mark Lemmon, Jr.

MARVELOUS LIME ICE CREAM

1⅓ c. fresh lime juice
5 c. sugar
3 quarts milk

Mix lime juice with sugar. Add milk. Freeze in electric freezer.

Mrs. Charles M. Best II

RUM COCONUT ICE CREAM

1 qt. vanilla ice cream, softened
1 7-oz. pkg. frozen coconut
  flakes
½ c. rum
SAUCE:
1 6-oz. pkg. semi-sweet
  chocolate bits
1 T. butter
¼ c. light cream
2 T. powdered sugar
⅓ c. rum

Pour rum over thawed coconut and mix well with ice cream. Pack this into a mold or in a freezer container which can be well-covered. Return to freezer. This is at its best when not too hard. Let it sit out at least 15 minutes before serving.

For sauce, put chocolate, butter, cream and sugar in the top of a double boiler. Heat over warm but not boiling water until chocolate is melted. Add rum and serve hot. The sauce will keep indefinitely in a closed jar in the refrigerator, heating over hot water just before serving. Can be thinned with a little rum if necessary.

Serves 8.

Mrs. L. G. Pondrom

GINGER ICE CREAM

3 c. granulated sugar
2 qts. whipping cream
½ lb. jar preserved ginger (not
  crystalized — imported
  Chinese is best)

Add sugar to cream and freeze. When frozen, remove dasher and add ginger, which has been cut into very small pieces, and its syrup. Mix in thoroughly with a long-handled spoon. Pack in ice and salt and leave about 3 hours.

*Miss Ela Hockaday, 1948 Junior League
Cookbook*

LEMON ICE CREAM

1 qt. milk
½ pt. whipping cream
1½ c. sugar
Juice of 3 lemons
One lemon sliced very thin

Stand sugar and lemon 1-2 hours. Chill all ingredients and freeze.

Makes ½ gallon.

Mrs. Evelyn Taylor

HEAVENLY PEACH ICE CREAM

1 qt. heavy cream
1 pt. half-and-half
4 eggs
½ c. Eagle Brand milk
2 c. sugar
¼ t. salt
1 t. vanilla
1 qt. crushed fresh peaches

Heat 1 cup each of cream and half-and-half in the top of a double boiler. Slightly beat eggs. Add Eagle Brand, salt, and 1½ cups sugar (mix remainder of sugar with peaches.) Add a little of the hot cream to egg mixture and gradually add egg mixture to cream in double boiler. Cook until mixture coats spoon, stirring constantly. Remove from heat. Cool. Add remaining cream and peaches. Freeze as usual in a 1-gallon freezer.
Makes 16 1-cup servings.

Mrs. Joe M. Bashara, Jr.

BLENDER RASPBERRY ICE CREAM

1 T. orange juice
4 strips orange rind
1 10-oz. pkg. frozen raspberries, partially thawed
⅔ c. sweetened condensed milk
1 c. heavy cream, whipped

Into blender, put orange juice, orange rind and raspberries. Cover and blend on high speed for 20 seconds or until smooth. Remove cover and with motor on, gradually add in a steady stream the condensed milk. Fold raspberry mixture into whipped cream and turn into a refrigerator tray. Freeze (covered with wax paper or foil) 2-3 hours or until frozen. Makes about 1 quart and can be molded with vanilla ice cream in the center of a melon mold.

Mrs. Julian Wells

STRAWBERRY ICE CREAM

3 pints fresh strawberries or
3 16-oz. pkgs. frozen strawberries, thawed and drained
2½ c. sugar
Juice of 3 lemons
½ pint whipping cream
1 12-oz. can Carnation Whole milk

Put strawberries in blender and add remaining ingredients. Fill ice cream freezer and freeze.

Mrs. Robert P. Lancaster

AVOCADO SHERBET

Avocado
Juice of ½ lemon
1 t. gelatin
2 T. cold water
¾ c. grapefruit juice
¼ c. sugar
¼ t. salt
1 egg white, stiffly beaten
Grated rind of 1 lemon
Pickled onions

Scoop out the pulp of a very ripe avocado and mash with a silver fork. Add
lemon juice and mix thoroughly. Soften
gelatin in cold water. Add this along
with grapefruit juice, sugar, salt and egg
white to pulp. Freeze the mixture to a
mush and add lemon rind. Beat until
fluffy and return to a tray and freeze,
stirring down from sides twice during
freezing. Serve in ice-cold melon halves
surrounded by tiny pickled onions.
Serves 6.

PINK "CHAMPAGNE SORBET" WITH ASSORTED COOKIES

1 qt. lemon sherbet
½ pt. raspberry sherbet
1 c. pink champagne
2 boxes assorted cookies

In a large bowl, soften lemon and raspberry sherbet. Beat together to blend
well. Stir in ½ c. of the pink champagne,
reserving ½ c. Pack back into the sherbet
containers. Freeze until very firm — at
least 2 hours, longer if possible. To serve:
scoop into six 6-oz. parfait glasses. Serve
immediately with some of reserved ½ c.
champagne poured over, or store in
freezer until serving time and pour
champagne over at last minute.

Mrs. Mark Lemmon, Jr.

MIXED FRUIT MILK SHERBET

1 quart sugar
2 quarts milk
1 20-oz. can crushed pineapple
3 bananas, mashed
Juice of 4 lemons
½ 6-oz. can frozen orange juice
  (concentrate)

Add half the sugar to the milk, stir to dissolve. Add remainder of sugar to the
fruit mixture. Combine all ingredients
and freeze in 1 gallon ice cream freezer.
Makes 16 1-cup servings.

Mrs. Joe M. Bashara, Jr.

GRAPE SHERBET

1 pt. grape juice
1 qt. half-and-half or milk
Juice of one lemon
1 c. sugar
Candied violet

Dissolve sugar in grape juice over low heat. Cool. Add half-and-half and lemon juice. When cool, freeze in ice cream freezer. Decorate with candied violets. Serves 10.

Mrs. Searcy Ferguson, Jr.

ORANGE SHERBET EXCELSIOR

4 c. fresh orange juice
3 c. sugar
2 c. water
Juice of 2 lemons
2 t. grated orange rind

Boil all ingredients for 5 minutes or until sugar is dissolved. Cool. Place in ice cream freezer and freeze. Serve in orange shells. Tangerines may be substituted for the oranges.
Serves 6-8.

Mrs. Searcy Ferguson, Jr.

MRS. FLYNN'S LEMON ICE

4 c. water
2 c. sugar
1 T. grated lemon rind
1 c. lemon juice
Dash of salt

Combine water and sugar. Bring to boil and boil 5 minutes. Chill. Add lemon rind, juice and salt. Pour into pan and place in freezer. Stir every 30 minutes. When ice begins to form on bottom and sides of pan, take a fork and mash it or break it up. Freezing process takes several hours, so watch it closely. This can be made the day before using.
Serves 6.

Mrs. Mark Lemmon

STRAWBERRY SHERBET

4 pts. hulled fresh strawberries
2 c. granulated sugar
1½ c. orange juice
½ c. lemon juice
¼ c. Cointreau or Grand
　Marnier

Do several days ahead of serving. Put half of berries, sugar, and juices in blender. Blend on high speed until smooth. Pour into 12x8x2" dish. Repeat with other half. Stir in Cointreau. Freeze until partly frozen. Turn into mixer bowl and beat at medium speed until smooth. Return to dish, cover with foil and freeze. Let it stand at room temperature 10-15 minutes before serving. Serve in sherbet dishes.
Serves 8-10.

Mrs. George Spencer, Jr.

WATERMELON ICE

2 round watermelons
1 c. sugar per quart of pulp
3 lemons per quart of pulp
Bitter chocolate

Carefully cut a circle from the stem end of one melon to make a lid. Carefully remove the pulp. This melon will be used later to serve the ice in. It acts as an insulator also to keep the ice from melting while being served. Remove the seeds from the pulp of both melons and pureé pulp in a blender. Add 1 cup sugar, the juice of 3 lemons and a little grated lemon peel to each quart of pulp. Freeze in an ice-cream freezer, or freeze in a refrigerator tray, stirring occasionally; when mushy, whip and return to tray. To make watermelon seeds, melt chocolate over hot water. Pour into a paper cone and squeeze out drops onto waxed paper or onto a marble surface. Cool. When ready to serve, place melon ice and chocolate "seeds" in melon shell in layers. Cover with stem lid.
One quart serves 8.

ICE CREAM VARIATIONS

Lime Ice Cream
> Mix with peeled fresh lime wedges, top with a dollop of heated Bacardi rum.

Coffee Ice Cream
> Stir in chopped rind of orange and chocolate kisses or chocolate chips.

Pineapple Ice
> Jolt it with pieces of candied ginger, chopped fine.

Chocolate Ice Cream
> Stick it with skewers of candied or fresh orange peel, splash it with Cointreau or Triple Sec.

Lemon Ice
> Frame it with sections of canned tangerines or mandarin oranges, douse it with the can's syrup reduced with a glug of bourbon.

Peach Ice Cream
> Gravel it with ground almonds dampened with apricot brandy.

Mrs. Mark Lemmon, Jr.

TABLES OF WEIGHTS AND MEASURES

STANDARD

Pinch = that which can be held between the thumb and forefinger (less than ⅛ teaspoon)

Dash = less than ⅛ teaspoon

1 teaspoon = ⅓ tablespoon

1 tablespoon = 3 teaspoons

5⅓ tablespoons = ⅓ cup

16 tablespoons = 1 cup

2 tablespoons = 1 fluid ounce

2 cups = 16 fluid ounces = 1 pint

4 cups = 32 fluid ounces = 1 quart

4 quarts = 1 gallon

8 quarts = 1 peck (dry)

4 pecks = 1 bushel

16 ounces = 1 pound

METRIC

Volume

1 teaspoon = 5 milliliters

1 tablespoon = 15 milliliters

1 fluid ounce = 30 milliliters

8 fluid ounces = 236 milliliters (approximately)

1 pint = 473 milliliters (approximately)

1 quart = .946 liter

Weight

1.1 ounces = 30 grams

3.6 ounces = 100 grams

9.0 ounces = 250 grams

1.1 pounds = 500 grams

2.2 pounds = 1 kilogram

AVERAGE CAN SIZES

CAN SIZE	WEIGHT	CUPFULS
8 oz.	8 oz.	1
#1	11 oz.	1⅓
#1½ or #303	16 oz.	2
#2	20 oz.	2½
#3	3 lb. 3 oz.	5¾
#10	6½ lb.	13

EMERGENCY SUBSTITUTES

1 t. baking powder = ¼ t. baking soda + ½ t. cream of tartar

1 square chocolate = 3 T. cocoa + 1½ t. butter

1 T. cornstarch = 2 T. flour when used for thickening purposes

1 c. sour cream = 3 T. butter + ¾ c. milk used in any sour-milk recipe

1 average egg = 2 oz.

    Yolks: 12-14 = 1 cup

    Whites: 8-10 = 1 cup

1 c. all-purpose flour = 1 c. + 2 T. sifted cake flour

1 c. biscuit mix = 1 c. flour, 1½ t. baking powder, and 2 T. shortening

1 c. milk = ½ c. evaporated milk + ½ c. water

    OR 4 T. dry milk + 1 c. water

1 c. sour milk = 1⅓ T. vinegar + 1 c. sweet milk

1 c. sugar = 1 c. molasses + ½ t. soda*

    OR 1 c. honey + ½ t. soda*

    OR 1 c. maple syrup + ¼ c. corn syrup*

    *Reduce liquid in recipe by ¼ cup

Wines

THE FOUR TYPES OF WINE

Still table wines: most commonly used, almost never over 14% alcohol, can be red or white, sweet or dry and are served with food.

Sparkling table wines: these also are never over 14% alcohol and include champagnes which incidentally can be served all through a meal.

Fortified wines: reds or whites to which brandy has been added increasing natural alcohol content to 20%-22%. These include Sherry, Port, Madeira, Marsala etc.

Aromatics: red or white wine fortified with brandy or neutral spirits. Known as the "aperitif", it is taken before lunch or dinner. Vermouth is the most famous aperitif and Dubonnet, Byrrh and St. Raphael are other examples.

LETTING A WINE "BREATHE"

Many wines need to have their corks removed so they can "breathe" the oxygen in the air. Open all red wines ahead of time before serving and leave cork out; younger reds need one to two hours, older reds need less time, and the closer to the end of its life cycle a wine is, open and drink immediately because it can even deteriorate in the glass. Young red wines without sediment will oxidize faster if decanted. Generally Burgundies need less time than Bordeaux; and great Bordeaux will need more time than lesser Bordeaux. White wines and roses generally do not improve after uncorking. Non-corked pasteurized wines with screw-top closings are unaffected by "breathing" for in truth nothing could make them either much worse or any better.

THE "HOW" OF DECANTING

The purpose of decanting is to get rid of the harmless but necessary sediment and frankly, to show off a beautiful decanter. Before decanting, stand bottle for a day or two at an angle so sediment will move down to corner or punt of bottle. Pull cork without shaking or moving bottle, wipe lip of bottle, hold bottle, label up, in front of a light (the little Tensor lights are ideal), hold decanter at angle up to lip of bottle and pour gently. The light will enable you to see the point at which sediment begins. Stop there and remainder of wine can be filtered through paper coffee filter. Decanting is not difficult — it takes a steady hand and practice makes perfect.

THE IDEAL WINE RACK

Since a case of wine weighs 30 to 32 pounds, it should be sturdy; have safety back stop, hold both full and half-bottles at a slight angle so the cork is higher than the base of the bottle yet angled so the wine covers the cork. And since one of the pleasures of wine is its infinite variety, a good wine rack should be stackable with good, dependable safety so additional wine racks can be added at your pleasure.

INDEX

The Dallas Junior League Cookbook

5500 Greenville
Suite 803
Dallas, Texas   75206

Please send me _____ copies of your cookbook at $8.95 per copy, plus 75¢ to cover postage and handling, plus 45¢ sales tax for Texas residents. Enclosed is my check for $_____ .

☐   ($10.15 per copy for Texas residents)
☐   ($9.70 per copy for out-of-state)

(Make checks payable to Dallas Junior League Cookbook.)

Name _____

Street _____

City _____ State _____ Zip _____

The Dallas Junior League Cookbook

5500 Greenville
Suite 803
Dallas, Texas   75206

Please send me _____ copies of your cookbook at $8.95 per copy, plus 75¢ to cover postage and handling, plus 45¢ sales tax for Texas residents. Enclosed is my check for $_____ .

☐   ($10.15 per copy for Texas residents)
☐   ($9.70 per copy for out-of-state)

(Make checks payable to Dallas Junior League Cookbook.)

Name _____

Street _____

City _____ State _____ Zip _____

The Dallas Junior League Cookbook

5500 Greenville
Suite 803
Dallas, Texas   75206

Please send me _____ copies of your cookbook at $8.95 per copy, plus 75¢ to cover postage and handling, plus 45¢ sales tax for Texas residents. Enclosed is my check for $_____ .

☐   ($10.15 per copy for Texas residents)
☐   ($9.70 per copy for out-of-state)

(Make checks payable to Dallas Junior League Cookbook.)

Name _____

Street _____

City _____ State _____ Zip _____

The Dallas Junior League Cookbook

5500 Greenville
Suite 803
Dallas, Texas   75206

Please send me _____ copies of your cookbook at $8.95 per copy, plus
75¢ to cover postage and handling, plus 45¢ sales tax for Texas residents.
Enclosed is my check for $ _____ .

☐ ($10.15 per copy for Texas residents)
☐ ($9.70 per copy for out-of-state)

(Make checks payable to Dallas Junior League Cookbook.*)*

Name _____

Street _____

City _____ State _____ Zip _____